WITHDRAWN

THE STORY OF GERMAN METHODISM

"I believe that God makes use of instruments."
—John Zwahlen to Wilhelm Nast, in a letter from
Wheeling, West Virginia, December 26, 1838.

WILHELM NAST

The Story of German Methodism

Biography of an Immigrant Soul

By PAUL F. DOUGLASS, Ph.D.

With an Introduction

By BISHOP JOHN L. NUELSEN

ILLUSTRATED

MCMXXXIX

THE METHODIST BOOK CONCERN

NEW YORK   CINCINNATI   CHICAGO

Printed in the United States of America

PREFACE

The history of the mission of the Methodist Episcopal Church to the Germans should have come from the pen of Bishop Nuelsen. His career, together with that of his father, spanned the epoch of the movement. Until very recently Bishop Nuelsen himself expected to write the volume which only he was eminently fitted to prepare. When it became increasingly apparent that the record would never come from his hand, it seemed imperative that the book should be written immediately while Bishop Nuelsen could act as critic and counsellor. He was anxious to have the work begun. John A. Diekmann, whose determination to preserve the unity and institutions of German Methodism had kept *The Christian Apologist* robust and active, took the necessary initiative, made plans for the publication, and the financing of the research and editorial work necessary for the project, and with Bishop Nuelsen selected the person to undertake the task.

This history of German-speaking Methodism is offered to the friends of the movement with no misgivings. The feeling of universal disappointment that the great scholar of the Church and the Christian statesman of two continents is not the author of the present work is shared by no one more strongly than by the humble servant who has been called upon to do what he knows, had it been so ordained, would have been the crowning achievement of Bishop Nuelsen's career of scholarship.

When the urgent invitation to substitute came, the present writer had been engaged for three years constructing the first English biography of the astronomer, Nicholas Copernicus. He had lived in Frauenburg and in Heilsberg and was concerned with the great revolution by which man had discovered his own insignificance as the inhabitant of a globe which was a mere celestial speck flying around the sun. Drafted into the service of the Church by the insistence of Doctor Diekmann, he reluctantly laid aside his own beloved project and devoted himself, not without misgivings, sacrifices, and regrets, to the research necessary for the preparation of this history. As the months went by and the project began to take form, the writer made his own discovery. He was writing the story of another revolution quite as important, perhaps more so, than the immortal statement of the heliocentric theory set forth by the humble monk of Frauenburg in *De Revolutionibus Orbium Caelestium*. This revolution concerned the heart and not the skies. As man had become aware of his own unimportance by the discovery that the earth on which he lived was not the "center of the universe," so in the human revolution brought about by man's discovery that he has a divine significance if he but

v

wills it, the author found a continuity to his own researches. When man begins to think of himself as a creation of God, for whom God cares so much that he became incarnate in the flesh and experienced supreme suffering in his demonstration that God takes the initiative in seeking moral unity and fellowship with man, a new kind of human being emerges. Man's conviction that "God's grace is more abundant than his needs" is a conception which cannot be subordinated among the monuments in the history of human thought.

The writer has become convinced that the present volume is a needed one. The ignorance concerning the German work is unbelievable. After a lecture before a forum in New York State, the writer asked the leading Methodist clergyman in the city about the program and condition of the German Methodist Church across the square. "I don't know the pastor's name," he said. To an inquiry about the condition of the property, he replied: "I think the congregation must be prosperous. The church is in good repair."

"What is the German Methodist Church?" he was asked.

"Oh," he said with a shrug of his shoulders, "it's something like another denomination."

Such a gulf exists and has always existed because of the language barrier. If this work can do something to make the Methodist Episcopal Church aware of the rich contribution which the Germans have made to its life, then one of the purposes of the undertaking will have been realized.

The ministry of the Germans has been experienced on both sides of the ocean in many cases when the organic connection of the mission was not fully appreciated. As the manuscript for this book was partially completed, the writer's mother fractured her arm. As an angel of mercy, Sister Luise Krumm, in stiff white hood and apron, came to care for her. Sister Luise was born in Westphalia, had been trained in the Methodist hospital in Frankfurt-am-Main, and in 1935 came back to America to serve as Ludwig Jacoby had once done in Germany. The mission to the Germans after ninety years was bringing to an American home a healing touch of Christian service in a wholly unexpected way.

"Have you thanked God that your arm is broken?" the Sister inquired. "In God's plan everything has its purpose," she said. Sister Luise had started a woman's heart thinking. It was as the Moravians once had awakened John Wesley's soul to spiritual curiosity by their serenity in an ocean tempest.

It is needless to mention the linguistic difficulties involved in the preparation of the volume. Constantly working with the German documents, the writer is forced to read in the script and to think and write in English. The result is a tendency to fall into awkward grammatical constructions.

The illustrations need a word of explanation. They have been

selected, as far as possible, to represent the individuals at the period
in their lives when they were in the midst of their creative work.   In
some cases, too many to be satisfactory to the writer, this criterion of
selection has not been realized.   Some persons who eminently deserve
pictorial recognition are absent from the gallery because their photographs were not available.   It is always the case that many names
are missing from the record, names of men and women who have
formed the substance of the Church.   To those unmentioned thousands apology is hereby made as a tribute is paid to them.

The research work was made easier by the untiring effort of
Sister Julia Gross, curator of the Museum of German Methodism
housed in the Bethesda Institutions in Cincinnati, Ohio, and of Frau
Amanda Heitmeyer, who for so many years has served as the
efficiently intelligent secretary in the offices of *The Christian Apologist.*
The research librarians of the New York Public Library have rendered a service in tracing documents far beyond the fondest expec-
tations.   To his father, who through a long and active ministry has
loved the Church of Jesus Christ with a singular devotion, the writer
owes a debt of many gratitudes which can never be expressed in words.

To John A. Diekmann, may it be said in conclusion: But for your
insistence this volume would have been a biography of Nicholas
Copernicus.   But for you the history of the mission to the Germans
might never have been written.   If this narrative, this biography of
an immigrant soul, is successful in showing how a revolution in the
human heart can join homes across the sea in the brotherhood of
Jesus Christ, then it is also a guidebook in a way of international
understanding more potent and enduring than treaties and diplomatic
missions and armament rivalries.   But for you this summary of the
spiritual traditions of the German-speaking constituency of the Methodist Episcopal Church would not have appeared to welcome *The
Christian Apologist,* robust in its centennial year.   But for your
initiative, that voice of German Methodism itself would not still be
heard.

To Bishop F. H. Otto Melle he wishes to say: You have spared
yourself no effort in your co-operation in the preparation of this volume which is evidence of how once hands were joined across the
sea because hearts first had found their common home at the Cross
of Jesus Christ.

Your Methodists and our Methodists must be one as never before.
We must never forget that but for Spangenberg and Peter Böhler
and *Herrnhut* the British soul of John Wesley would never have been
fired by the passion which spread as the flame of Methodism.   We
must never forget that but for the earnest preaching of circuit riders
on the American frontier the scholarly and rationalistic German mind
of Wilhelm Nast would never have created an international unity
through hearts redeemed by the grace of our common Lord.

On two continents Methodism speaking two languages must be the conscience of two states, proclaiming that contrite hearts, which have known the grace of God, always find a citizenship in a Kingdom which has no boundaries. May this biography of an immigrant soul be but the record of a great beginning of an enduring peace of the lands of our Methodism.

For one who for many months has lived with the records of German-speaking Methodism, who has worked in his own quiet Vermont library, peopled by scores of photographs of a century of disciples become as familiar as the Yankees on the broad Main Street, it is difficult to write with the complete detachment and objectivity necessary for the historian. The writer has tried to confine his own emotions to this foreword. If to some the pages which follow seem blind to sentiment, he can only say that he has tried to remain faithful to the codes of historical research. If to others, critical historical scholars, he seems at times to display an enthusiasm, he must confess that his heart has perhaps on some few occasions run ahead of his pen.

May he close his own introduction to the reader's intimate confidence by a reminder of something which our world needs very much to concern itself about? Those who were tutored in German Methodist homes recall the first proposition in Nast's catechism. Those who are making their acquaintance with the mission to the Germans for the first time should make the words a part of their mental furniture:

1. Was soll deine vornehmste Sorge sein?
(What should be your chief concern in this life?)

Das Heil meiner Seele.
(To save my soul.)

Matthew 16. 26. Was hülfe es dem Menschen, wenn er die ganze Welt gewönne und nähme Schaden an seiner Seele?
(Matthew 16. 26. What is a man profited, if he shall gain the whole world, and lose his own soul? or what shall a man give in exchange for his soul?)

PAUL F. DOUGLASS.

House of Representatives
Montpelier, Vermont
April, 1939

CONTENTS

CONTENTS

PART II

INTRODUCTION

BY BISHOP JOHN L. NUELSEN

Many strands have been woven into the pattern which is presented today by the American nation and by American Christianity. American civilization is not homogeneous. Neither are the creedal nor the sociological forms in which the religion of Jesus Christ finds expression in America of a uniform design. Nearly every nation and race on this globe have made some contribution. The American nation is a composite. And so is American Christianity.

This situation is not accidental. It is not the result of the senseless play of blind forces. The story of America is the unfolding of a purpose of the Divine Creator and Ruler of mankind. It cannot be a mere accident, that this great continent of North America, the physical and geographical and climatic conditions of which are very favorable for human habitation, while its natural resources afford abundant opportunities for the sustenance in comfort of millions of men, women, and children, should have remained unknown to the nations of the world until the time when millions in Europe and later in Asia were forced by religious persecution, political oppression, or economic misery to search for other countries to live in, and when the peoples of the Old World had reached a degree of development that they were equipped for discovering and making habitable a distant new world.

The vast virgin continent of North America for the first time in human history offered the possibility of an outlet for the multitudes of war-torn, misery-stricken Europe, a vast area, where the nations and races could live side by side, not forced into one empire by subjugation under a hated foreign rule, but where they met and mingled as independent, self-determining, self-respecting fellow beings bound together by one common urge, namely, to build a commonwealth in which civil and religious liberty and equality before the law as the foundation of a free country should prevail; a civilization that should not be enslaved to inherited prejudices nor cramped by historic precedents. To be sure the pattern was not clear before their eyes in all its details. But vague as the ideas of the early settlers may have been, one thing is very clear in the light of history: *America was a new world.* The immigrants and their descendants were the builders of a new civilization; the outcome was a new race and culture. *The American nation is an evidence of the fallacy of the modern theory proclaiming racial purity, consanguinity, and a common soil as the cornerstone and prime condition of national achievement.* The American nation is far from being racially pure. It does not want to be so. Its greatness lies in fusing the best elements of different races into one new race, assimilating the most valuable traits that have been developed in the course of centuries in each race in all parts of the world; eliminating the inferior or deteriorating features by either atrophying or sublimating them. Thus America is to fulfill its divine mission of being the melting pot of the historic nation out of which crucible a new world is to emerge.

The most important contributions in that historic development were made by the Latin, the English, and the Germanic races. It has been well said that among the early settlers the Latins furnished officers without an army, the Germans an army without officers, the English furnished officers and army. There were approximately 600,000 Germans and their descendants in America in 1790. They were not in leading positions as were the English and the Scotch-Irish and in the South the French, but they formed the army of intrepid pioneers, of patient plodders of the soil, of industrious thrifty farmers, of reliable religious citizens, infusing these valuable traits into the character of the nascent nation.

As the story of the Germanic element forms a distinctive chapter in the "Epic of America," so the story of *German-speaking Methodism in America* is worthy of a distinctive place in the glorious history of American Methodism and American civilization. It is a chapter in the "Epic of American Methodism," permeated by the same spirit, the compelling power of a new affection, of the joyous abandonment to the claims of the Master, of overwhelming zeal to win souls for Christ, and also of pioneer daring that gave its distinctive note to early Methodism.

Prof. J. Alfred Faulkner calls the progress of Methodism among the Germans in the United States "almost a miracle in religious history." [1]   Bishop Thomas Nicholson writes: "The story of the origin, growth, and development of our German Methodism is an epic. It is a fascinating story. I regard it as one of the most inspiring, informing, and significant chapters in our Methodist history, if not in the history of Protestantism itself. The account of the education, development, religious struggles, final conquest and achievement of Dr. William Nast is to me one of the great stories in Church history. Not even the members of the present-day German Conferences, to say nothing of the rank and file of our general Methodism, have much idea of the very great contribution which this branch of our Church has made to Christianity in general, and to Methodism in particular." [2]

The story of German-speaking Methodism began a century after the conversion of John Wesley at the time when the second wave of German immigration overflowed into the Middle West; it grew

---

[1] W. J. Townsend, *A New History of Methodism*, Vol. II, p. 139.

[2] Souvenir of the Ninetieth Anniversary of German Methodism.

steadily in strength, reaching its peak at the beginning of this century; it subsided when the World War came to an end.

Numerically, German-speaking Methodism was never very strong. At its height in 1915, it numbered ten Annual Conferences with 644 preachers and 63,260 Church members. Including its overflow into the German-speaking countries of Europe, viz., Germany, Switzerland, Austria, Hungary, and Jugoslavia, it never reached more than about 1,200 preachers and 120,000 Church members. However, its significance cannot be measured by statistics. In his classic work on the *History of England* after giving a brilliant account of Methodism, Thomas H. Lecky states that the Methodists themselves are the least result of the Methodist movement. This is eminently true with reference to the German Methodists. The number of German Methodists are the very least result of German Methodism. Not only that a careful computation shows that in addition to the sixty odd thousand members at a given time, approximately half a million souls were reached by the gospel preached by German Methodist preachers and joined the Methodist Church. There is a wider aspect and a deeper significance of German Methodism than can be expressed by statistical tables or charts or pictures. Its real and lasting historic significance is to be seen in the fact that it is a chapter in the century-long history of the mutual relation of the two great types of Protestant Christianity in America, the Anglo-American and the Teutonic types. The strength of evangelical Christianity is rooted in the peoples of the English and of the German tongues. The world-wide reformatory movements, aggressive and sweeping, aiming to apply the ethical and spiritual principles of Jesus Christ to the inner life of man as well as to the social relations of the human family have been carried mostly by these nations, while on the whole the Romanic and Slavic nations have been the stronghold of Roman and Greek Catholicism. Whatever helps these two interpretations of the gospel of Jesus Christ to come in closer touch, to understand each other better, to learn one from the other, to supplement their own deficiencies by the strength of the other, will be an enrichment of the common faith and a quickening of the common Christian life. The progress of Christianity as well as the progress of civilization is hindered by national or religious isolation, is promoted by the exchange of spiritual values, of modes of their interpretation and methods of their application to the ever-changing conditions of human society.

Methodism has not been a mere incident in the religious history of the world. It has been the beginning of a new epoch. The farther away we are carried by the streams of history from the life and time of the founders of Methodism, the more clearly we discern that direction of currents and cross-currents was changed by these mighty forces liberated by the Methodist movement.

German Methodism is not a mere incident. It is not the begin-

ning of a new epoch, but it is one if not the most potent factor in
bringing into contact and linking together German and American types
of religious life. No other Church has done so much *to unite and
interpret the best traits of German inwardness and American activism.*
The German Lutherans were in America in large numbers a generation or two before German Methodism was organized. They had
scholarly pastors, strong churches, synods, and institutions. But
they remained a distinctively German organization. German in their
emphasis upon intellectualism in religion, upon fine theological dis-
tinctions, German in their reliance upon ecclesiastical order in their
adherence to an individual gospel dealing mostly with the life to come,
and German also in their exclusiveness. They did not mingle with
American Church life. They scrupulously avoided all contacts. They
remained parochial, a part of the old country in the new world. The
German and Dutch Reformed Churches did not long retain their original characteristics. They soon amalgamated with the prevailing American type, making their contribution to be sure but losing their identity.
The Baptist Churches have done a valuable work, but they were never
considered and do not claim to be an exponent either of the universal
traits of the common evangelism or of the distinctively German Protestantism. Their insistence upon one and only one mode of baptism
gives to them an isolated place in the religious life of the Germanic
countries. The Evangelical Association and the United Brethren, originally called German Methodists, remained comparatively small as
long as they limited their sphere of activity to the German immigrants;
when they became English-speaking Churches they lost their German
type.

While all the Churches of German tongue had their mission and
their tasks, it was the distinctive mission of German Methodism to
realize the best traits of the two dominant types of Protestantism in a
glorious combination of personal, individual gospel faith and collective
social work.

The historic mission of German Methodism in America was to represent in American Methodism and thus in American Protestantism
the best parts of German religious life, the power of intense spirituality,
the cultivation of the inner life, in the forms of a sane mysticism, the
value of systematic, thoroughgoing religious instruction of the children, the steadying influence of loyalty to the revealed Word of God,
while German Methodism in Europe, the offspring of German Methodism in America, has demonstrated in the midst of the static, state-
bound and state-governed Churches of Europe the vitality and dynamics
of the American ideal of a self-governing, self-supporting Free Church
the membership of which is not compulsory, regulated by state law but
voluntary, constrained by the love of Jesus Christ, under compulsion
of experiential, evangelistic, and social passion. Thus German Methodism in America has conserved the best traits of German spirituality.

German Methodism in Europe has instilled into European Church life the best traits of American Christianity. The pioneers of German Methodists in America were men of broad German culture, who had enjoyed careful religious training. They were men and women who knew their Bible, their catechism, their hymnal. All these treasures were hidden in the recesses of their subconsciousness; treasures, yes, but hidden. Methodism brought to them the spark of vital Christian experience and all that dead memory matter was transformed into living impulses and volitions. They learned to know Christ as their personal Saviour and Master and his magic touch changed those hymns and Bible verses and definitions of the catechism into the pure gold of the Kingdom. And what they had received from German religious training, from German intellectual discipline, from German theology, they freely bestowed on others and built these traits into their Church organization. Wilhelm Nast was the founder of German Methodism. But Wilhelm Nast was also one of the very first who made America acquainted with the wealth and depth of German evangelical theology.

The story of young Wesley's spiritual development and the story of that young German immigrant, who came to America a century later, offers a striking parallel. John Wesley, the founder of Methodism, and Wilhelm Nast, the founder of German Methodism, in their own lives and in their work fused into one the two currents in Protestantism. An impartial appraisal of American Protestantism must accord a leading influence to these two men. John Wesley was a typical Englishman, Wilhelm Nast a typical German. Wesley was what psychologists call an extrovert. He was a clear, logical thinker, to be sure, who did not undertake anything without thorough premeditation. But his thinking, his meditation, was merely the necessary preparation for his action. He did not stop with reaching a logical conclusion nor was he satisfied with gaining a vision of some blessed truth. He was constantly driven by an irresistible urge to translate his convictions into active service. This extrovert tendency gave to him a note of sternness. His tremendous will power which subjected every mood and inner impression to the control of strict self-discipline and forced every sentiment to expression in practical service, even at the cost of constant self-sacrifice, made him harsh in his demands, not only upon himself, but likewise upon his fellow men. His own life and his ministry were the exponents of the demands of the law of God. His religion was formal, legal, servile, repellent in its effects. His contact with German piety during his voyage to America, in his intercourse with the Germans in Georgia and later in Germany, gave to his religious life the trust, love, tenderness, that warming of the heart, which changed his character and made possible a ministry radiating sympathy and love, attracting the souls of men to the Author and Source of Christian love.

Nast was by nature an intróvert, a scholar, a mystic. His ideal was the quiet study where he was immersed in books; far from the tumult of the world. His sphere of self-expression was the writing of theological treatises. The contact with the aggressive spirit of the Methodists in America, with their consuming zeal for the salvation of their fellows, their missionary fervor, their resourcefulness in bringing to bear the message of the gospel to conditions in the New World as a practical, creative force influencing and transforming the social and cultural life of the coming nation, gave him a new outlook of life and impressed upon his character the extrovert traits he needed to do his real lifework.

Without German Pietism John Wesley would not have had a warming of the heart. He would have remained a devoted, strict churchman, somewhat bigoted, fulfilling his ecclesiastical duties unflinchingly, but he would never have gained access to the hearts of the multitudes, he would not have kindled a fire that enlightened and warmed the hearts and lives of millions in all parts of the globe and changed the spiritual atmosphere of the world.

Without American activism Wilhelm Nast would have led a useful life as a scholar and professor, hidden in his classroom and study, the author of learned books, which accumulated distinction and dust in the libraries of theological seminaries, but he would never have become the founder and leader of the hosts of German Methodists, who made valuable and permanent contributions to the religious life of America and of continental Europe.

The German Methodists did not remain aloof from American Methodism or American Christianity. They did not build their own little Germany, isolated, parochial, narrow, self-sufficient; they built, in course of time, their own organization to be sure; but that was done in order to increase their efficiency. They remained an organic part of the great Church and of the greater nation, not heedlessly and foolishly flinging away the inheritance of centuries of providential dealings with their nation, but preserving the best traits, accommodating them to the new conditions, opening their minds and hearts and lives to the new currents of power transmitted by American Methodism and thus enriching their own lives and the life of the great Church. The future Church historian analyzing the various elements in the complex picture of American Protestantism will recognize in German Methodism a force that has done a twofold work. First, *it has introduced into American Church life some of the finest traits of German Christianity, and secondly it has been one of the most efficient agencies for Americanization that America has produced.* It has become one of the most valuable training schools for Christian citizenship. The German Methodists have never been an isolated block in the life of the nation. They have never been a reactionary group hankering back to Old World social customs and political loyalties. In every move for civic righteousness and Kingdom ideals they were on the side of advance. Hence it has never been difficult for individual German Methodists to feel at home in our English-speaking churches, when the time came for them to join English-speaking churches. And our English-speaking churches were never afraid to receive our German members into their fold, apprehensive lest some reactionary foreign element would disturb the harmony of the Church and block its program. On the contrary, they have been very eager, only too eager at times, to receive German Methodist lay members and ministers knowing that they could absolutely count on them. Men trained in German Methodism have rendered distinguished service in the wider fields of church activities. And when the acid proof came and the fiery trial was precipitated in the dark days of the World War, the German Methodists were loyal to the last man. They could not be expected to be jubilant. Shame on them, if they had been! But their loyalty to the country of their adoption rang true and was demonstrated by their willingness to suffer, to bleed, to die.

It is not a vain boasting but stating a historic fact when I maintain that no other German-speaking Church has in the last hundred years done so much to introduce immigrants from the Old World into the spirit of American evangelical Christianity and make them staunch supporters of promoters of the ideals of Protestant Americanism as did the German-speaking Methodists.

Turn now, if you will, to Methodism in Germany; Methodism in Germany and in Switzerland is no incident. It is not the result of planning and scheming for the spread of the Methodist Church. It is not the outcome of denominational imperialism or of selfish denominational aggrandizement. It is, historically speaking, the result of the retroactive influence of German immigration to America. German Methodism in Europe is the child of German Methodism in America. The child in whose life and growth the best elements of the enriched life of the parents come into fruition. The child who in its own sphere and environment does the same kind of work, which the parent has been called by God to do, namely, to mediate between the German and the American types of evangelical Christianity, to establish contacts to infuse into secluded and exclusive German Lutheranism the currents of life that pulsate in American Christianity. Not to Americanize Germany. It is no more the mission of German Methodism in Europe to Americanize Germany than it was the mission of German Methodism in America to Germanize America. But it is its mission to be in Germany and the other German-speaking countries of Europe the exponent of the power of a religious life that combines the inwardness of the German type with the activism, the vitality, the evangelistic fervor, the missionary impulse, the social passion, the civic implications of American Christianity, and thus to be a link between the two types upon whose co-operation the future of Christian civilization depends.

German Methodism in America has done a great thing, much greater than we can understand at this time, in what she has accomplished in America and for America. But it has done a still greater thing by giving to the Church and to the world Methodism in the German-speaking sections of Europe. With the exception of one Conference, the East German Conference in the large cities along the Atlantic Coast, German Methodism in America has ceased to exist as a separate organization. This is not a sign of any loss of spiritual power. The merging with the English-speaking Conferences is not due to any weakness inherent in German Methodism, nor is it an evidence of senile debility. German Methodism has not given up its independent existence because it had lost its vision and become unfaithful to its mission. German Methodism has fulfilled its mission. The giving up of its separate organized existence and merging the creeks and small rivers of its life with the mighty stream of the life of our great Methodist Church was in obedience to a higher vision. It demonstrated a clear discernment of the currents that are giving direction to historical development, to sociological organizations, and that are molding the shape and structure of the Church of Jesus Christ within the nation. German Methodism is not now a mere memory. It is a living, spiritual force.

The thought that with the merging of the German Conferences in America, German Methodism should pass out of the thought of the Church has been weighing heavily on the heart of the leaders of the German branch, especially on the mind of Dr. John A. Diekmann, the present editor of *Der Christliche Apologete,* which was founded one hundred years ago by Dr. Wilhelm Nast, the founder of German Methodism. He succeeded in enlisting the interest and the support of some sons of German Methodism, notably of Judge Alfred K. Nippert, of Cincinnati, the son of a prominent German Methodist pioneer, and he secured the services of Dr. Paul F. Douglass, who at great personal sacrifice undertook the work of writing the story. Dr. Douglass, who has made a name for himself as a painstaking scholar and a brilliant writer by his previous publication, *God Among the Germans* and other volumes, has accomplished this task in a marvelous way. With true historic instinct, coupled with indefatigable zeal and sincere sympathy, he made himself thoroughly familiar with the sources, the files of *Der Christliche Apologete,* the printed Minutes of the Conferences, as well as a mass of written reports and letters, preserved in the historical library of the Bethesda Institution at Cincinnati, supplemented by the archives of the Methodist Book Concern at Cincinnati. The result of his labors is this fascinating and authoritative account and fine interpretation of the *Story of German Methodism.*

JOHN L. NUELSEN.

Geneva, Switzerland
February, 1939

PART I

CHAPTER I

THE GERMAN IMMIGRANT IN AMERICAN CULTURE

When Europe became psychologically and biologically dynamic at the beginning of the seventeenth century, the human structure of the earth was profoundly disturbed. For twelve hundred years the population of the Old World had scarcely exceeded one hundred and eighty million inhabitants. Between the Congress of Vienna and the World War it swelled to nearly half a billion human beings. In 1630 the population of the whole earth had been hardly that.[1]

This growth of population was contemporaneous with equally important events. New worlds were being discovered and new homes for people opened up. A new technique of production known as Capitalism was dominating the industrial activities of men. A new authority in religion based on the biblically informed conscience was asserted against the venerable system of the Roman Catholic Church. It was called Protestantism. A new political theory known as Constitutionalism was making the justification of government the consent of the people governed. A new arrangement of international society was developing. Nationalism was corroding the universal community of the Church of Rome.

Such a dynamic combination of events had to produce profound transformations in every condition of human living, external as well as spiritual. Hopes, hatreds, convictions, intolerance, adventure, ambition, opportunism, exploitation, persecution, avarice, and altruism found expression in national and civil wars, commercial and class rivalries, free and coerced migrations. A new culture of earth was in process of development.

One of the profoundly important and novel consequences of this dynamic culture of Europe as the conqueror of an unknown world was migration. For the first time in human history human beings began to migrate in vast numbers from one continent to another over the seas. The little trickle of emigrants from Europe in the seventeenth and eighteenth centuries swelled into a mighty stream in the nineteenth. Between 1841 and 1930 more than thirty-seven million immigrants entered the United States. Because of its temperate climate, its rich resources, its vast unsettled lands, and its political and cultural freedom North America, and the United States in particular, was the magnet which pulled upon Europe across the stormy waters of the Atlantic.

Economic and political conditions in Germany, adding pressure to the natural Teutonic *Wanderlust* (passion for wandering), drove

1

swarms of Germans to America in a vast *Völkerwanderung* (migration of peoples) until in the 1890's the improvement in industrial conditions in the Reich, which was flooding the earth with goods "Made in
Germany," broke the human floodtide. When the census of 1900
was taken, it showed that the population of the United States included
7,310,604 persons of German blood and German parentage. America,
at the turn of the century, was a people of English, German, Irish, and
Scotch stock, the Germans standing in numbers only slightly behind
the British.[2]

Thirteen families, fifty persons in all, mostly Mennonites and
Quakers, left their homes in Crefeld, Germany, in 1683 to settle in
what was to become Germantown, near Philadelphia. These Germans
were the advance guard of a wave of Teutonic migration from Switzerland, Württemberg, the Lower Rhine, and especially the Palatinate.
Protestant difficulties in living under the political rulership of Roman
Catholics in the region set in motion a stream of emigration vital to
the development of America. The Roman Catholic line of Neuburg
had come to power in 1685 with the extinction of the Reformed line
of electors. Louis XIV, of France, claiming several parts of the
Palatinate, and waging war to assert his claim, overthrew Protestantism
in many places and turned over the churches to Roman Catholic priests.
Violating the provisions of the peace of Westphalia, Louis had a clause
inserted in the peace of Ryswick (1697) to the effect that in those
portions of the country then occupied by the French the Roman
Catholic religion should not be disturbed. The Roman Catholic rulers
gave ear to the Jesuits and by appealing to the provisions of Ryswick
began a systematic oppression of the Protestants. Elector Johann
Wilhelm forcibly undertook to administer Protestant church property,
and required the Lutherans and Reformed to give the Romanists equal
rights to the use of the churches. Children of mixed marriages were
required to be instructed as Roman Catholics. Even in the Reformed
University of Heidelberg several professorships were filled by Jesuits
who made themselves most obnoxious by their constant charges of
heresy against the Reformed professors. Not until the beginning of
the reign of Maximilian Joseph (1799), who refused to follow the
path pursued by his bigoted predecessors, did the persecuted Protestants receive any recognition of their rights. To the Germans who
fled from the Palatinate, religion meant a reality which had been
tested by fire and sword.

By the time the Revolutionary War broke out, the German population of America was somewhere in the neighborhood of a quarter of a
million. The Teutons had settled mostly along the frontier line from
the Mohawk in New York south to Georgia. Spreading along the
Piedmont plateau lying east of the Appalachian ranges, they had also
grouped into little colonies in the great valley lying between the Blue
Ridge and Allegheny Mountains.

In the nineteenth century another and greater *Völkerwanderung* began. It continued nearly a century, bringing more than five million souls to the New World. The natural restlessness of the European peoples was stimulated by the commercial ventures of transportation companies. Agents of ship lines began to advertise in Middle Germany. Affected by economic uncertainty at home, peasants and village artisans were only too anxious to listen to steamship ticket salesmen. Religious differences among Catholics, Lutherans, and Reformed, together with misunderstanding between state churches and the Mennonite, Quaker, Baptist, Mystic, and Pietist sects prompted other serious-minded Germans to seek the tolerance of the New World. Others came frankly with selfish and materialistic motives, while still others, impoverished by the continual warfare among German chieftains, wanted relief from the plundering of their flocks and cattle and the confiscation of the fruit of their labor. Some fled to Russia and Ireland, but most of them finally reached American shores.

Migration, sweet though its hope, was a difficult step. Unsanitary sailing boats spread disease. It is estimated that a sixth of the passengers died aboard and were buried on the high seas. Such conditions did not deter the Continentals. They considered the risk worth the end and an indentured service of two years to repay the cost of transportation cheap. Of the opening decades of the nineteenth century Beard appropriately says that the

> gates of the land were flung open to the peoples of the earth and it seemed highly moral to write over the portals the fine humane phrase, "Asylum for the Oppressed of Every Land." [3]

Emma Lazarus's appropriate words were well inscribed on the Statue of Liberty:

> Give me your tired, your poor,
>   Your huddled masses yearning to breathe free,
> The wretched refuse of your teeming shore.
>   Send these, the homeless, tempest-tost to me,
> I lift my lamp beside the golden door!

That such an asylum existed was fortunate in the middle of the last century. The artisans of England were sinking into hopeless poverty. Engels did not overstate the case in his descriptions of the time. The distress of the peasants of Ireland, groaning beneath the burden of absentee landowners, was intensified by the potato famine to such an extent that within two decades more than half of Ireland's laboring population was carried across the Atlantic to be incorporated into the political and cultural life of the United States. Similar conditions prevailing in Germany sent forth another flood of German emigrants to seek their fortunes in the New World. The blight that blasted the potato crops of Ireland struck the Rhine Valley and sections of southern Germany. Political discontent was added to economic affliction. German radicals, encouraged by the furore unchained by the revolution of 1848, made heroic efforts to cast off the despotic rule of kings and princes by agitations and uprisings. Temporary revolutionary successes were followed by fierce reaction and invidious recriminations upon the defeated champions of liberty. America was indeed an asylum to these victims of poverty and politics. By 1830 the German movement to the United States swelled into a mighty human stream. In the third decade of the century one hundred fifty thousand entered the ports of America; in the fourth decade, nearly a half million; in the fifth decade upwards toward a million, reaching the high tide in 1881 and 1882, in which two years alone nearly a half million came as settlers.[4]

It was not long until it was discovered that the German immigrant was making distinctive contributions to American culture. The cultural idealism of the Teuton met the moral idealism of the Puritan half way. The resultant combination produced some of the grandest of American institutions as well as some of the sharpest cultural cleavages. The German heritage of idealism was transmitted through literature, philosophy, and religion. The Puritan principles were standards of conduct for escaping from the sin of worldliness. Each needed something more to complete a balanced way of life. Diverting men's minds from the materialistic aims of American society, the Germans emphasized the more beautiful aspects of living. It has been well said that

> German culture shook the young American giant out of his stupor and awakened him to thinking thoughts and emotions of all humanity.[5]

The humbler virtues of these immigrants were well adapted to make the German a substantial element in the community and to make the Germans as a class prosperous. Wherever they settled in large numbers, the community received a peculiar stamp. The Germans had respect for law, a fine sense of honesty and promptness in the discharge of business obligations, dogged persistence, a devotion to industry, and an ethic of economy as rigorous as the traditional New England thrift. The German paid his debts, loved his work—*Arbeit macht das Leben süss*[6]—had an inborn sense of duty, exemplified simple home life, agitated for personal liberty, and expressed everywhere a strong trait to individualism, conspicuous as independence in politics and particularism in religion.

The Germans, too, were a gregarious people. They were never quite as happy and their social organization was never complete until they had associated themselves into *Vereine*.[7] The Anchorites of Euphrata chanted in mixed choruses. The Moravians of Bethlehem cultivated vocal and instrumental music. The settlers in Cincinnati organized themselves into *Turnvereine*.[8] In southern Ohio they developed *Sängerfeste*,[9] and in 1849 held the first meeting of the United Singing Societies of the West in the Queen City with two hundred thousand people on the grounds at noon. Wherever he went the German founded societies for social, philanthropic, religious, and cultural purposes.

If the German was fond of his food and took good care of his body, he also bore a religious tradition. The German, if not always an active church attendant, was generally a thinker on the subject of ultimate values. The Teutonic love of life made German faith so wholesome and buoyant that even when it expressed itself in Pietism it was not pessimistic. The Pietist was content with the rulings of Providence. His tranquil optimism (*Zufriedenheit*) beamed from his face and impressed itself on the smiling landscapes his labors produced. Paul Gerhardt,[10] Germany's greatest hymn writer, expressed the spirit of Pietism in these words:

> *Die Welt ist mir ein Lachen*
> *Mit ihrem grossen Zorn.*[11]

The tide of German immigration, bearing all these traits of cultural tradition, met the stream of westward migration from the East at the junction point of Ohio. Men were seeking new lands in the great movement toward the Pacific. Their search for cheap land in the vast unsettled prairies being opened up to settlement was motivated by economic hope. This was made more insistent partly by dissatisfaction of young men with the conventional social order in the East, and partly by reaction against organized religion. Ohio, where the migrants went, was a rough country. In Cleveland Jesus was carried in a ribald procession in effigy and a mock celebration of a communion service was performed with the curb as an altar.[12] Religious infidelity was more prevalent than in the more settled communities of the East. It was a fact worthy of special mention that Governor Thomas Worthington (1814-1818) and Governor Jeremiah Morrow (1822-1826) both said grace at meals. The stabilizing influence of religious organizations in the new communities, however, was recognized by even the coarsest elements of the population, as is shown by the fact that at the time of the establishment of the first church in Cleveland practically all adult males in the village signed the subscription list.

The coarseness of the morals of the westward migrants was joined in Ohio with the strangeness of the Germans in language. In 1830 hardly five per cent of the population of Cincinnati was of German origin. By 1840 Germans comprised a quarter of the population. In 1848 and after, as a result of the economic competition created by a new flood of immigrants, racial prejudice against these "Forty-eighters" sprang up, although the democratic philosophy, critical intelligence, and artistic sensibilities of the Germans soon made the Queen City one of the first cultural centers of the nation.

The older elements in the population were already talking of the necessity of limiting

> the swarms of indigent foreigners whom the selfish policy of sundry European governments is vomiting upon our shores, and who, from their ignorance, vicious habits, and former associations, are better calculated to swell the numbers or increase the violence of a mob, or to assist an ambitious and unprincipled demagogue in overturning the liberties of the country than to discharge with soberness and discretion the duties of American citizens.[13]

One of the numerous German characteristics not completely understandable to the more staid elements of the community was their different, fun-loving approach to living which was not in the tradition of the settlers from the East. At the end of the day's work the Germans relaxed in pleasure. Their behaviour furnished a contrast to the busy American who took his pleasure seriously. They sang; they drank. Typical of the German theory of life was the German student song, so often attributed to Luther:

> *Wer nicht liebst Wein, Weib und Gesang,*
> *Der bleibt ein Narr sein Lebenlang.*[14]

It was this conspicuous attitude toward life which worried the Methodists. By coincidence, the Methodists, always concerned with conventional morality, were the strongest and most influential religious group in the Ohio valley. Morality to the Methodist was a first step to patriotism, and the Methodists have always made patriotism and religion companion virtues.

The Methodists had reason for their anxiety over the spiritual welfare of the settlers. The flood of immigration into the Ohio valley threw social organization into confusion. Religious activity was generally considered by the newcomers a performance which would be attended to later or not at all. The energies of life were expressed in other and secular channels. The German *mores* added glamour and style to the life of young settlements, for the Germans who came to Ohio were not the same group of pious, religious people who had found Penn's Pennsylvania so congenial in decades before. Their enthusiasm for life broke forth in song in beer gardens. Sunday was more a day for *Ausflüge*[15] than for worship. If the German immigrants had religious motives, their leadership was in the hands of pastors in name, who were too often irresponsible religious adventurers, the associates of brewers and saloonkeepers, who constituted for the most part the official boards of the churches they served. Cincinnati at the time was a liquor center. Eight German breweries and three distilleries operated there. A German infidel and Catholic press of five or six papers were all bitter and scornful in their mention of the Methodists. The Methodist was stereotyped into the pattern of a joy killer, a temperance worker, and a tightlaced fanatic. He was a symbol of what the brewers, the adventurers, and the libertines hated. The honor was properly conferred, for Methodism on all its fronts was a "spreading flame" of revivals which burned with determination to escape the sins of worldliness. Methodists were concerned with one paramount objective—the conversion of sinners. They attacked the problem with a pick-and-shovel technique. And Methodists were doing business in the Ohio valley. The pages of *The Western Christian Advocate* of these courageous years were filled with the reports of changed lives. Methodists were describing their work in a vocabulary all their own. A typical letter to the editor of the *Western* will illustrate the point:

> *Marietta Circuit, Ohio Conference, March 3, 1835.*
> Brother Morris:
> It affords me no small gratification to say to the friends of Zion that "God is with us." About the 1st of January we had intimations of good in the conviction and conversion of three or four. But it was not until about the 10th of January that we were able to say: "Of a truth, God hath visited his people." His convicting spirit rested upon the congregation; and they who came to mock, remained to pray, and the cry: "What must I do to be saved?" was extorted from many hearts. Night after night for three or four weeks our altar was filled with mourners; and night after night salvation's current flowed, and redeemed souls, happy in the Saviour's love, ascribed salvation unto him. During this period we received ninety-two on probation; and from sixty to seventy, we trust, have found remission of sins. . . . I will only add that the work is still progressing in our church and has extended to the Presbyterian Church in this place, and the cry of both is, "Thy Kingdom come."
> Yours, Edw. D. Roe.[16]

Items like this one were news to Methodists in 1835. The Methodists were having a spiritual experience which made them conspicuous in the life of the time; and they were speaking of those experiences in a vocabulary which could only be understood by men who had shared the experience of conversion.

Population, like morals, was in motion. Methodists were concerned with both. The streams of human migrants were coming and moving on. The Methodist circuit rider, always on the frontier, kept pace with the advancing westward adventure. Writing from Missouri, for example, a correspondent of the *Western,* asserting how the "Macedonian cry" was echoing and re-echoing from the Mississippi, declared:

> The great ocean of population is moving westward, which in a few years will astonish mankind, and nations yet unborn will gaze upon the beauty and splendor of the Western World. We receive our appointments on the frontiers! Next year we are in the rear of the army of pioneers, who have gone by and left us. Before one cry of ministerial destitution has died away, the startling voice is heard again in melting strains: "We are suffering for the means of grace; come and preach to us the way of peace, administer baptism to our children and let us taste

the Holy Eucharist once again in this land of strangers." Certainly no minister of Christ clad with higher and holier responsibilities, in whose soul celestial nature delights to dwell, would be unwilling to forego the ease and happiness of an old country, when souls immortal in a new country were perishing for the means of grace."

Germans, moving on from the Ohio to the Mississippi valley, were in the human procession. The question of a German-speaking missionary, which had been debated in Ohio Methodist circles for more than five years, was raised again to the level of an issue by a letter from St. Louis under date of July 27, 1835. John Glanville, in response to a communication which had previously appeared in the columns of the *Western,* wrote:

Dear Brother Morris:

. . . We have vast numbers of Germans in this and some of the adjoining countries. Many of them are Protestants and all as sheep without a shepherd. They are very industrious but observe not the Sabbath and are in many other respects immoral. They cannot understand our preaching, nor do they like to attend our meetings, but anything in German will call their attention. Could we have some German missionaries here? I am satisfied good would be done among them. . . . I should be sorry to add to your burdens, but if you can help us in this matter you will doubtless serve the cause of God and truth. Yours, etc.

T. A. Morris, editor of the *Western,* published the letter in *The Christian Advocate* on Friday, August 21, 1836, in the middle of the second page with this introduction:

GERMAN MISSIONARIES WANTED

German missionaries are much needed, not only in Missouri, but in Cincinnati and various other parts of the Western country. The Germans desire something done; our people are willing; our general superintendents feel every disposition to act; God is willing to crown the effort with success; and now is the time to strike. We have waited long enough, too long for Providence to do the work without co-operation on the part of the church. The only difficulty is in obtaining men of the peculiar qualifications necessary for the work. But there are doubtless a few ministers of our order, who can speak German with sufficient plainness to be understood; and if the work be only commenced in good earnest, the Lord will raise up young Germans to carry it on with success. Let the question be put directly in the Conference, who can, "who will go for us?" We hope the answer will be heard from more than one, "Here am I, send me."

The letter appeared in the *Advocate* two days before the Ohio Conference met at Springfield. The English-speaking preachers were in a frame of mind to do something about the situation. By providential coincidence Wilhelm Nast, a young man from the Mount Vernon Circuit, was recommended at the same session as a person suitable to be received into the itinerant connection.

CHAPTER II

THE SPIRITUAL EDUCATION OF "W. NAST, GERMAN MISSIONARY"

"You need only to go to Christ."—Willbur Fisk in a letter to Wilhelm Nast.

On August 19, 1835, Bishop Joshua Soule concluded the annual session of the Ohio Conference meeting at Springfield with the reading of the appointments:

> Western Charge—A. Eddy, T. Z. G. Phillips. Fulton County—
> G. Moody. German Missionary—W. Nast.

Behind the making of that last appointment lie two stories. One of them has already been told in the description of the vast intercontinental migration as a part of which Wilhelm Nast came to the United States. The other is the tale of the religious experiences of that same young man who, becoming restless in his Fatherland, had crossed the ocean to the continent of "hope and wealth" at the age of twenty-one.

On March 12, 1833, Willbur Fisk, the president of Wesleyan University, sat down in his office in Middletown, Connecticut, and wrote a letter to a young German scholar sojourning at Benvenu, Dauphin County, Pennsylvania. That he considered the effort well-spent is sufficient testimony to the character of the young man because Fisk, fighting against constant ill-health, had accepted a rule of living that "the way to sell my life to the enemy as dear as possible is to use it *sparingly*, that I may use it longer."[1] Fisk knew young men. His evangelical passion, so sanely tempered by common sense, had made him the confidant of restless men seeking a knowledge of God. "I can assure you, my brother," he declared to a young clergyman, "the devil likes nothing better than to offer up scores of Methodist preachers on the altar of an indiscrete zeal."[2]

President Fisk's letter is so sound in its advice and so descriptive in its implication of the spiritual struggle through which a young man was passing that it is a document of first importance in the history of German Methodism.

My Dear Sir:

Since receiving yours, I have been so occupied as to be scarcely at leisure to write to you; and now I can say but a word. I am deeply afflicted at your sorrow. I sympathize with you, and would fain comfort you. But I am aware, from numerous instances that I have witnessed, that your kind of despondency readily changes every consideration into the same gloomy hue with the other images of the mind, even though such consideration be designed

9

to cheer the heart. Permit me to say, however, if you have not yet obtained relief, I am *confident you will.*

> Can Jesus hear a sinner pray,
> Yet suffer him to die!—
> No, he is full of grace;
> He never will permit
> A soul that fain would see his face,
> To perish at his feet.

You take wrong views of the gospel, my brother. Christ directed "repentance and remission of sins to be preached in his name, beginning at Jerusalem"—sins, not some sins, but all. And that none need despair, he commenced that offer among those whose hands were not yet washed from the blood of him who now, through the same blood, offered them salvation; and who are you, my brother, that claims to have produced a case too hard for an Almighty Saviour? Hell might indeed triumph if this were true, and the blessed Jesus own himself conquered, but thanks to his name, *he* has triumphed; he has led captivity captive, and received gifts from rebellious man. "But it is so just," you think, "to cast you off." Yes, so it would be to cast us all off. But then you "have sinned so much and against so great light." So much the better opportunity for the Saviour to show that "where sin abounds, grace does much more abound."

But let me say again, you take the wrong view of yourself. You think your wretched feelings are in consequence of your being so great a sinner; but it is rather because you do not reject your sins. Christ is willing to save you from your sins; but you cannot trust him, and therefore your sins and wretchedness remain. You say that you need more light and more strength, that you may be able to see Christ and love him; but you mistake. *You only need to go to Christ* that you may have light and strength. Take Christ, then, in the present time for everything. I entreat of you, I command you to receive Christ. The reception of Christ is not merely a privilege which you may possibly attain to by the Divine favor, but it is a duty which you cannot neglect without Divine displeasure. Ask, then, not whether you may receive the atonement, whether God will permit it. You must. God commands it.

You see, then, you have utterly mistaken your own case and the character of the gospel. Do not, then, longer dishonor the Saviour and injure your soul. Remember, "as many as received Christ, to them gave he power to become the sons of God."

Affectionately yours,

W. Fisk.[3]

This letter was read and reread by Wilhelm Nast until it was so tattered that many of its words were entirely obliterated. It ended, however, the correspondence which had been aroused by a sermon preached by Fisk at the annual examination at West Point.

Fisk's letter implied the psychological conditions of human life fumbling for the discovery of God. Sympathetic with possibilities in Nast's melancholy, he wrote with the assurance of a man who had himself discovered God. He spoke of a certain despondency and melancholy, a "wretchedness" which comes from a reluctance to reject sins, of "Christ's directions for the repentance and remission of all sins," of salvation offered through his blood, of the acceptance of Christ and of "grace more abundant than sin which abounds." Fisk was speaking a peculiarly Methodistic vocabulary of experience. The concepts of sinners saved by grace through the acceptance of Jesus Christ belong to the particular universe of discourse of religious experience. Upon that single formula German-speaking Methodism, which Nast was to conceive, became an "instrument of God" changing the lives of men.

Wilhelm Nast was seeking an experience of God. Willbur Fisk could guide him. The principles of this intimate religious experience, which one sought and one was assured he had found, had a homespun simplicity. Sin disqualifies a man for that fellowship with God for which he was created. Guilt results from the commission of sin. Men therefore are in a state of melancholy until they are reconciled with God, which is the mission of Christ—the mission of being the means of bringing God and men into moral unity and practical fellowship. Christ testifies that God takes the initiative in seeking reconciliation because he is the one who has the heart for it. Men need to be made willing. That the willing God seeks to bring unwilling men to his holy fellowship is the uniform teaching of the Scriptures and the heart of the gospel. God sent forth his Son because men were precious to him, and he desired to bring them away from the sin that he hates to his own holy fellowship, which he loves. The work of Christ is to be interpreted as work of a single motive in God, namely, the motive of free grace. When God took the initiative in seeking reconciliation and sent his Son into the world, his motive from which he was acting, and which in Christ he consistently acted out, was grace, or free and undeserved love to men. In the matter of grace the question of deserving does not arise. This motive of free grace to the undeserving was God's motive in sending Christ to the world. The New Testament constantly declares that Christ came to call sinners to repentance. In Christ God and men find genuine reconciliation and live in abiding fellowship: God freely loves and helps men, and men freely love and trust God.

The free gift of grace was a concept which had not yet become comprehensible to Nast. He was seeking it when he first heard Willbur Fisk preach at the United States Military Academy in 1830. He was already groping for something which plagued him because he could not find it. He had been appointed librarian and German teacher at West Point at the age of twenty-two. Along the banks of the Hudson River, which flows past this palisaded fortress, Nast walked with two devout young officers, converted under the preaching of their chaplain, who later became Bishop McIlvaine, of the Protestant Episcopal Church. At their request he began to instruct them in Hebrew because they felt "called" from "military service" into the "service of God." Their request, he said, "so rebuked and deeply humbled" him that he began his spiritual inquiry anew. "The sparks of conviction that still lay dormant" in his heart were stirred. Driven by the thought of his own recreancy, he began to read with great avidity books on spiritual living. Among these was the classic of the day, Bishop Jeremy Taylor's *Rules of Holy Living*. The study of this volume led him into the practice of such a severe asceticism and so abstemious a life that his health was seriously impaired and his theology warped to the harm of his soul.

> My reason [he said] could not comprehend how it could be consistent with divine justice that the sinner should be absolved from the guilt and penalty of his sins without suffering in part himself for his sins.[4]

He wanted to feel the pain and to pay the costs which would be the price of his forgiveness. He could not understand how atonement could come in any other way. To quicken his sense of his own depravity and demerit and to intensify the reality of the necessary "suffering of the lost" he performed a cruel ritual upon himself. Among other rites he held his little finger in the flame of a candle. He carried the scar to the end of his life.

The doctrines of Methodism, in contrast, as so practically preached by Fisk emphasized the grace of God. Nast was, in Fisk's opinion, depending too much upon his own exertions instead of being willing to "be saved by grace." President Fisk had set forth the principle as the "Gospel Charter" in a letter to another young man:

> "Ah, but I am a great sinner," you say; "that is my difficulty, the ground of all my fear!" Say rather, the only ground of your hope in Christ. If you are a great sinner, you are in the better case for Jesus to magnify the riches of his grace toward you. Do you know where it is written, "Where sin *abounded,* grace did *much* more abound?" Has sin abounded in you? Then are these promises for you. O that God would open your eyes to see them, and your heart to feel them! O that you could hear the voice of him who hath said, "Come unto me all ye that are weary and heavy laden, and *I WILL GIVE YOU REST."* Listen to that voice, my weary, sorrowing, burdened brother! O listen and believe! Me thinks I hear that voice come ringing down through the lapse of centuries, sweet and fresh as when first it dropped from his gracious lips. That invitation and promise, my dear brother, is for thee. Does it not fall on thy ear like a powerful charm to break the spell of Satan and set thy spirit free? Does it not meet thy heart and soothe thy soul? Such, I doubt not, is or will be the victory of thy soul.[5]

Despite Fisk's counsel, Wilhelm Nast continued to struggle for five years more before he was convinced that he had experienced a knowledge of God, before he felt "the glad heart" "dancing for joy." A persistent series of contacts with Methodists changed the course of his life, which otherwise might have been just as stereotyped as those of millions of other substantial German immigrants who entered business or industry and just performed their duties faithfully.

Wilhelm Nast was born on June 15, 1807, in Stuttgart, the capital of Württemberg. For three centuries his ancestors had been scholars and clergymen in the Evangelical Lutheran Church of that province. His mother, Ludovicke Böhm, the cultivated daughter of an Austrian army officer, had died when he was seventeen, and his father, Johann Wilhelm Nast, a conscientious public official, a *Finanzrat*,[6] died about the time of his confirmation when he was fourteen. At an early age his upbringing was intrusted to his eldest sister, Wilhelmina, who, like his other two sisters, had married a Lutheran clergyman.[7] He attended the Latin School in Stuttgart and in Baihingen-an-der-Enz. A sensitive boy, bereft of father and mother while small, capable of deep religious experience, living in the pious environment of devout churchmen, he suffered from severe emotional disturbances.

There had never been any doubt about his vocation. It was a family tradition. In early childhood he had been dedicated to the ministry of the State Church. During the few weeks preceding his confirmation day, however, the boy had felt his spiritual inadequacy. He secretly attended the "prayer meetings" of the "despised Pietists." "I humbed myself before God," he says of this period of his life, "and cried often on my knees, 'O Lord Jesus! have mercy upon me!' "[8]

Confirmation day dawned as a gloomy, rainy morning. The fourteen-year-old youth stood trembling and weeping before the altar of the church, answering the questions and taking his vows. As evening came, he went out into the rain, heavy-hearted, in search of "the Lord, whom my soul longed after!"[9]

In a lonely field that wet night the boy had a memorable experience, the reality of which never diminished. Of it he wrote:

> He heard my cries in that hour and sealed the pardon of my sins upon my heart. The next morning, the whole creation appeared to me as it had never done before. Everything looked lovely and glorious. On every spire of grass I saw the imprint of the goodness of God. All about me and all within me praised the Lord. My heart had peace with God and love to all men.[10]

When Nast in the same year took his examinations for entrance to the theological seminary, and actually began his studies in the reformed old Catholic cloister at Blaubeuren, religion was real to him. The reality soon tarnished in a sequence of bitter experiences. The spiritual and mental suffering which began to cloud what he had anticipated as an intellectual experience was no different from that which thousands of boys, reared in the guarded environment of pious homes, have undergone. Since his experience in that lonely field that rainy evening of confirmation day, he had thought of God as an imminent, in-

2

dwelling reality. Now he discovered that when that personal experience became institutionalized into a State Church, worldliness crowded
out the simple piety which brought such courage and comfort to him.

The seminary at Blaubeuren was under the influence of Rationalists
who were dominating German thought. Of this period Nast wrote:

> Instead of being nourished with the sincere milk of the Word,
> that I might grow up thereby to a man of Christ, I was nourished
> with the nectar and the ambrosia of classical paganism.[11]

And again:

> The sole object of my classmates was not to become ambas-
> sadors for Christ, but heroes, poets, and philosophers. Only
> one inquired after the Saviour of sinners.[12]

He had reason for making such a comment. The seminary class
to which Nast belonged contained a remarkable group of young men.
Among his classmates were Wilhelm Waiblinger, the genial Swabian
poet; Eduard Moerike, Germany's most illustrious lyric poet; Friedrich
Theodor von Vischer, the philosopher of aesthetics and poetry; Wilhelm
Hoffmann, the famous court preacher; and David Friedrich Strauss.
Of these classmates, companionship with Strauss was most important.
David Friedrich Strauss entered Blaubeuren when he was thirteen.
His father was a small tradesman who loved literature and thought
more than businessmen usually think. His mother was an intelligent
woman whose piety was practical rather than meditative, although she
had an open eye for the beauties of art and nature. He studied
under the same master as Nast at Blaubeuren. Professor Kern and
Prof. C. F. Bauer, in particular, infused into their pupils a deep love
of the ancient classics.

The friendship between the two young men was a strange affair.
Strauss responded to the interpretation of Christianity in terms of Neo-
Classicism as a duck runs to water. His scholarship was taking a direction which continued throughout his life. The same teachings which
kindled such intellectual enthusiasm in the mind of Strauss increased
the disgust which Nast felt in his heart for all things religious. In
1825 Strauss passed directly from the seminary to the University of
Tübingen; Nast was making up his mind to quit the whole aggravating
academic life. When Nast was wandering through West Point in
search of his soul, Strauss was already an assistant to a rural pastor,
greatly beloved as a preacher and adored by his simple-hearted parish-
ioners. While his roommate was teaching, visiting camp meetings, and
reading literature on holy living, Strauss was industriously engaged in
writing his significant *Life of Jesus,* which immediately after the appearance of the first volume in 1834 and the second volume in 1835
created a sensation and marked out an epoch in the historical treatment of the rise of Christianity. While Strauss *was arguing* with all
the brilliant dialectic of the German Rationalists that the Christ of the

Gospels was the unintentional creation of the early Christians, Nast was determinedly *seeking to know* the Christ which the early Christians *had known*. In 1857 Nast was back in Berlin delivering an address on Methodism to the Evangelical Alliance. His boyhood friend at Blaubeuren, Wilhelm Hoffmann, now a famous court preacher, was present and embraced him with the comment, "God has selected you for a special blessing to the German people." . . . David Strauss had also come to hear his classmate preach. He sat near the rear of the hall and slipped quietly out without greeting Nast, making the comment to a friend, "Nast is not a fluent speaker, but he makes an impression nonetheless." Nast never quite recovered from the stinging apathy which Strauss had apparently shown to his preaching. So great the spiritual and intellectual gulf between the two Blaubeuren roommates had become through the intervening experiences of life. Time widened the chasm between their careers.

In 1870, when Strauss published his lectures on *Voltaire,* written for the Princess Alice in Darmstadt, it was apparent that the truth of Christianity had become still more problematic to him. This spiritual condition was even more obvious in his next and last work, his confession and answer to the four great questions: *Are We Christians? Have We Still Religion? What Is Our Conception of the World? How Are We to Regulate Our Lives?* When Strauss's *Der Alte und der Neue Glaube* [13] appeared as the climax to his intellectual and spiritual career, Nast was the distinguished editor of the foremost German evangelical periodical in America, was the spiritual father of a very significant religious awakening on two continents, and the patron of schools, orphanages, homes, hospitals, and seminaries.

The struggle through which Nast was passing as a student and intimate friend of Strauss had already begun to shape his life for something more than a purely academic service. That, for one thing, was indicated by his refusal to study his lessons on the Sabbath. In correspondence with his sister, Wilhelmina, on the subject, she warned him against "spiritual pride." Like other young college men, his principles did begin to be redefined and his faith altered in bitter inner conflict as the simple piety of his family circle strained under the contact with institutionalized religion and the very different *mores* of the college world. Yet the sight of clergymen on the Sabbath at the card table and in the dancing room and at the tavern bar continued to be offensive to him. The morals of the students were not his morals. The shock of disappointment and the spiritual poverty of his intellectual environment at first caused him to battle with his classmates openly and orally. Then he prayed in secret and held his peace. For a while he bore his ridicule with heroic courage and then gradually began to be assimilated to the type of the group to which he now belonged. He threw off restraint and descended to the lower level of the intellectual, spiritual, and social life about him.

Nast was eighteen when he stood the examination with the rest of his class and was transferred, with Strauss, to the University of Tübingen. In the two years there he felt a growing spiritual bankruptcy which rose as a wall to prevent him from entering the pastoral office. Of these days he wrote:

> During the two years in the University, I got lost in the laby-
> rinth of Pantheism. . . . After I had passed my philosophical ex-
> aminations which is equivalent to graduating in an American
> college, I came to the determination not to enter the three-years'
> course in theology.[14]

In confusion he withdrew from the university and from the service of the Church and paid for the instruction which he had gratuitously received from it out of his own means. He was not unmindful of the consequences of the choice he was making. He wrote:

> My remaining in the service of the Church would have secured
> me wealth, honor, and ease; but my conscience did not permit me
> to profess and teach a doctrine which I did not believe from the
> heart, or at best which I interpreted in an entirely different sense
> from the Church. I was not willing, for the sake of a living, or to
> please friends, to make a solemn promise of preaching according
> to the articles of religion in the Lutheran Church, which rational-
> ism had taught me to reject, and which I saw was rejected by
> most of the doctors of divinity and their scholars. I was con-
> scious, too, that according to the Holy Scriptures, I was no Chris-
> tian, and nothing appeared more absurd to me than that a man
> who is himself unreconciled to God and resists his Holy Spirit
> should dare to preach the word of reconciliation.[15]

Disillusioned with both God and man, he went back to Stuttgart, where he found comfort in the preaching of Ludwig Hofacker [16] and an anchor once again in the pious family circle of his sisters and their clergymen husbands. There the story might have ended. A young man, from a pious Christian family circle, doubting his faith after contact in the field of higher learning, disillusioned by the spiritual poverty, place-hunting, and easy satisfaction of ecclesiastical circles, became dissatisfied with himself. His spiritual roots had been cut. Planless, like a ship without a rudder or compass, he wandered—first to Vienna, then to Munich, and suddenly, under another inspiration, to Dresden with the idea of becoming a philosopher of art and to visit his beloved poet, Ludwig Tieck. Like a father, Tieck advised him to return to Tübingen and complete his theological studies. But Nast's mind was already distracted by another thought. A tender, hopeful word was on the lips of all Europe. *AMERICA!* The New World! How many thousand hearts were longing for its freedom!

He wrote:

> I heard much of the liberty of the United States, and was in-
> formed that there was a scarcity of classical teachers.[17]

In the company of his old roommate, Strauss, he went to Weinsberg to consult the Prophetess von Prevorst, a clairvoyant who enjoyed a wide popularity at the time. When he was presented to her by a friend, she said:

> Your young friend has great anxiety, not only for himself but for his intimates as well. He will soon take a trip . . . to a distant land and there he will find peace in his heart.

Nast's mind was made up. On September 28, 1828, at the age of twenty-one, he arrived in New York. From the moment of his arrival, he seemed destined to be unable to escape the Methodists.

Nast's supposition that in America there was a dearth of educated men capable of teaching languages and literature was correct. He promptly found a position as a tutor in Millersburg, Pennsylvania, and in his twenty-second year took a similar position in an English family living at Duncan's Island, not far from Harrisburg, Pennsylvania. Here during the summer of 1829 he tutored the two sons of a widowed lady of wealth and culture. More significant than the position, however, was the fact that the mother was herself a devout member of the Methodist Episcopal Church. Her home on Duncan's Island was a regular preaching place for the itinerant ministers of the Baltimore Conference. Nast became acquainted with the Methodists and with numerous clergymen and circuit riders who visited the family. The contacts with them were congenial to him. They were all the more so because of less fortunate experiences which he had had in New York. Before he had left Germany he had "resolved solemnly to be a better man" and for that purpose he had brought with him a letter of introduction to a prominent Lutheran minister in Manhattan. He had been repelled, however, by the cool reception which he received and his subsequent early associations were not favorable to the inner purposes of his heart. The contact with the Methodists, on the other hand, the whole bearing of the circuit riders and converted men, their personal kindness to him, impressed him deeply. He wrote, "What I there heard and saw, stirred up at once the sparks of conviction that still lay dormant in my heart."

In the fall of 1829 he left this home to accept a call as librarian and teacher of German in the United States Military Academy at West Point. It was here that the preaching of a Methodist educator, Willbur Fisk, stirred him so deeply.

The scarcity of trained teachers in the field of higher learning, and in the field of languages and literature in particular, made Nast's services in demand. At the end of the school year of 1830 he left West Point for a visit to his Methodist friends at Duncan's Island. While he was stopping at Gettysburg, Pennsylvania, on his journey he received and accepted a call to a professorship of languages in the Lutheran college there. He was to begin his duties with the opening of the institution in the fall. But circumstances led him to another course.

When he arrived at Duncan's Island he was greeted by a group of Methodist preachers of the Baltimore Conference, who were on their way to a camp meeting on the banks of the Juanita River. Upon their invitation, he accompanied them. This was the first camp meeting he ever attended, but the camp meeting as an "instrument of God" was to play a vital part in the building of German Methodism. Of this experience, the young scholar wrote:

> It pleased God to awaken me thoroughly at a Methodist camp meeting, in Tuscarawas Valley, Pennsylvania, the second time. The scales fell from my eyes. I saw and felt that I had despised the atoning blood of Jesus Christ—that I had been blinded by Satan and had heaped wrath upon wrath. I did not harden myself against this call of God, which I considered the last, but wrestled, and with many tears, supplicated God to forgive my sins and renew my heart. *I had now found a city of refuge in the Methodist Church.*[18]

Nast could not seem to avoid the Methodists. Methodists seemed to cross his path at every turn. He wrote:

> One Methodist preacher after another raised my spirits, from time to time, and kept me from sinking into despair, by pointing me to the Lamb of God that taketh away the sins of the world. When I was on the point of giving up the struggle, I was again encouraged by the members of the Church who prayed fervently with me and for me. And often did I hear in class meetings and love feasts, this people of God testify, from blessed experience, that Jesus casts out none that come to him. Never can I forget the gratitude which I owe to my Methodist brethren. They will receive their reward in heaven. Through their faith and love, the smoking flax was kept from being quenched. I did not let the Lord go until he blessed me.[19]

Nast was so touched at the time and felt such enormous guilt for his apostasy from his early piety and the sinfulness of his subsequent life that he returned to Gettysburg, relinquished the position the Lutherans had offered him, and immediately sought out a Methodist class leader. At the close of a prayer meeting held at the time in this town, he tremblingly asked if he might join the class. His name was entered and he was recognized as a probationer of the Methodist Episcopal Church. He had found now among the Methodists something which revived and re-enforced the conviction he had felt that first confirmation day when he said that "on every spire of grass I saw the imprint of the goodness of God. My heart had peace with God and love to all men."

While he was in this state of emotional disturbance and spiritual discovery, Bishop McIlvaine again addressed him with the invitation to become teacher of German and Hebrew in Kenyon College, a Protestant Episcopal school located in Gambier, Ohio. He consented, but his deep mental anguish and frequently self-imposed penances had so impaired his health that he was advised first to seek restoration of mind and body. He therefore spent the winter of 1833-34 on a farm of a Methodist in Gallia County, Ohio. Here he was found by Adam Miller, who was later to play such an important part in the building of German Methodism.

Miller had become interested in missionary work among the Germans in the Ohio Valley through an advertisement in *The Western Christian Advocate,* which he read while riding his horse around his circuit. In it Bishop Emory pleaded for a missionary who could speak German and French and who was willing to go South. Miller, who spoke "Pennsylvania German," at once devoted himself to the mastery of the "European German" tongue but was completely lost in acquiring the native pronunciation for the want of a tutor in the pure continental language. He found the tutor quite accidentally. To obtain a German New Testament and some other language books, Miller had set out from his circuit in the hills of Virginia to visit his father in northern Ohio. In passing through Zanesville he heard reports of a young German named Wilhelm Nast, who was said to be a fine scholar and to have had some religious experience. Although Nast at the moment had started down the Muskingum River on a flatboat, Miller followed him to Galliopolis, Ohio, where he landed, and finally made his acquaintance in a small farmhouse where he was employed in giving instruction to a few young children. The result of the meeting was unexpected. Miller prevailed upon Nast to accompany him to his circuit in Virginia. Despite the young scholar's protest, Miller found a horse for him in the neighborhood. On a cold February day in 1834 they galloped off for Guyandotte, Virginia, preaching, exhorting, and praying on the way. Nast seemed incapable of escaping the Methodists even in a secluded farmhouse off the Muskingum River! Once settled in the Virginian mountains Miller prevailed upon Nast to translate the *Articles of Religion,* the *General Rules of the Discipline,* and to write them in English characters so that he could read them. Nast in addition during the winter translated the sacramental services. Then, taking the opportunity made by Miller's absence at a quarterly meeting, Nast quietly stole his way back to Ohio alone, leaving Miller behind, but more than ever determined to fit himself for the German work.

In the fall of 1834 Miller was appointed to Point Pleasant Circuit, Virginia, where he began to preach to a large German settlement. Here he had opportunity to use the work which he had encouraged Nast to do for him before he so unceremoniously took his departure northward earlier in the year. He read to his classes Nast's translations of the *General Rules.* The receptiveness of the people led him to make this entry in his journal:

> Seeing their earnestness and great desire for religious instruction, I could but think of the many Germans scattered all over

our country like sheep without a shepherd. I believed that the Lord would yet convert Brother Nast and send him forth among the thousands of Germans to gather them to the fold of Christ.[20]

It was at this point in his experience that Miller wrote his letter to *The Western Christian Advocate* appealing for missionaries to work among the Germans. When he returned to Ohio at the close of the Conference year, he found Nast happily engaged on the faculty of Kenyon College. Nast shared his dormitory room with Miller and during the night confided to him that he "must and would preach," that if the Church would not receive him and give him work, he would teach in some college and devote the proceeds of his labors to supporting a preacher. It was a happy night for Adam Miller. With the appointment of Nast as German missionary to Cincinnati, Miller shouted his approval with "Hallelujahs."

In the spring of 1834 Nast had gone to Kenyon College, where he was warmly received by the faculty and students alike. Although his mind now had become more tranquil, he was still dissatisfied with himself. During these days he frequently visited and was greatly influenced by intercourse with a Methodist cobbler named John Smith, who himself later became a member of the Southern Illinois Conference.

Despite his academic duties, Nast found time to attend the Methodist meetings in the region. On Sunday evening, January 18, 1835, he attended a powerful revival in the Methodist Church in Danville, Knox County, Ohio, where Adam Poe was preaching. He knelt at the altar with other penitent souls, but did not feel the comfort of faith which so many others about him seemed to be sharing. As he left the church, he looked back at the "happy converts," still at the altar, shouting praises to God. He went back, knelt, opened his mouth to pray, and at that moment felt the "witness of the spirit."

The experience through which Nast was going was a turning point in his life. Of its consequences he wrote:

> It was on the 18th day of January, 1835, that I was born again, unto a lively hope, with joy unspeakable and full of glory to an inheritance incorruptible and undefiled, and that fadeth not away, renewed in heaven for those who are kept by the power of God through faith unto salvation. I gave myself to the Lord without reserve. I could not refrain from confessing publicly what great things the Lord had done for me and how merciful he was to me. I also warned and exhorted my fellow men. I became convinced that now was the time to perform the service in the gospel, which my parents promised to the Lord in my stead, and to become a witness of long-continued patience of our great Shepherd, in seeking that which was lost.[21]

Wilhelm Nast had experienced the great crisis in his life. It was his Aldersgate. From that point his career took a new direction. Next morning he told his students and fellow professors what the Lord had done for him. Calling them together in his room, he prayed with them and courageously before his associates gave thanks to God for his wonderful salvation. The preparation of Wilhelm Nast had been completed. Within two weeks he had received an exhorter's license and in July he was granted the license of a local preacher. On September 15, 1835, he was admitted on trial into the Ohio Annual Conference in session at Springfield. At twenty-eight years of age, Nast was ready for service. He wrote:

> It pleased the Spirit of grace to make the Methodists the instrument of my conversion. I freely confess that a deliberate and prayerful comparison of what I have seen with my own eyes, heard with my own ears, and felt with my own heart, with what is contained in the Holy Scriptures, has induced me to prefer the Methodist Episcopal Church to the Church of my fathers, and I have as yet found no reason to regret my separation from it, but am, every day, more thankful for the high privilege which I enjoy as a Methodist.[22]

CHAPTER III

THE BEGINNING OF THE MISSION TO THE GERMANS IN OHIO

Nast arrived in Cincinnati soon after the adjournment of Conference with his appointment, the promise of an annual income of $100 voted by the Conference as the salary of the German missionary, and his religious experience. That was his entire equipment. For many long months it did not seem enough.

Cincinnati in the fall of 1835 was a dynamic Ohio River town, the "Queen City of the West." If it was the industrial and merchandizing center of the expanding Western territory, it was also the Western center of Methodism which had organized itself around the publishing interests of the Western Methodist Book Concern. Whatever may have been the influence of the English-speaking Methodism in the region, however, it certainly was not brought to bear in the interests of the missionary activity of the young German scholar who had come to the city. The English-speaking Methodists were indifferent to the arrival of the German in their midst, except for occasional and polite comments in *The Western Christian Advocate*. If they were indifferent, the Germans, as far as they were aware of Nast's appearance, were openly hostile. They did not relish the idea of a "Methodist missionary" among them. Their hostility broke forth openly and frequently into persecution of the solitary Nast and but for the intervention of the law would sometimes have flared into mob violence. Jesters in beer gardens raised their glasses in toasts of insult and ridicule. The Catholic and infidel press did not give much space to his arrival or to his activities, but took occasion to mention his presence and purpose often enough and with sufficient irony to make his name a familiar symbol.

Where was Wilhelm Nast to begin his work? He had had no experience as a missionary. He had had no training in a parish. Fresh from the classroom, he was versed in dealing with students, but untutored in the approach to sinners on the streets of dynamic Cincinnati. *How* was he to begin? There was only one answer to the question—begin at the beginning where Christ began; where Peter began. He did; and then bent his effort toward organizing the converts into classes in the proper Methodist fashion. As far as he could gain access, he visited from house to house. He passed out tracts in a meager volume which he could afford. He made personal contacts when he found an individual even indifferently sympathetic to his passion. He preached in private. He preached in the open. He

22

preached in the home of a converted Catholic to a few Catholic families who had been searching the Scriptures; and he usually preached in the evening, partly for want of a meeting place at other times of the day and partly because he could not expect a congregation during the hours when other churches were in service. The continued and contemptuous attacks of the press he used as publicity for drawing out a hearing. Although his first sermon had been preached in the vestry of Wesley Chapel to the congregation of about twenty-four Germans and twelve English who represented the Methodists interested in supporting his first effort, he later preached in a schoolhouse on Elm Street and in good weather every Sunday afternoon in the open. Soon he was also preaching on Main Street in Asbury Chapel.

The work was frankly discouraging. It could not have evoked more unsatisfactory response. At the end of the second quarter he himself admitted, "Though little has been done, none but the Lord could do it." [1]

Although he did not know it, he was, however, making contacts which later were to be of vital importance to German Methodism. One of these was with James Gamble, an Irish soap maker and active Methodist layman. Although Gamble understood no German, he opened his home to the missionary for preaching and class meetings and invited in some of his German friends. Impressed by the fervor of Nast's prayers, Gamble became a firm friend of the language mission. That one of Nast's daughters should later marry into the Gamble family and consecrate so large a part of the vast fortune to the development of the German Methodist work was a consequence which neither the elder Nast nor the elder Gamble could foresee.

Whatever the ultimate results of his efforts, he did not feel optimistic at the time. He was just as discouraged with the size of his classes as he was with the number of his converts. At the end of the second quarter he had nine class members. At the end of the third quarter the number had increased by three to twelve. At the end of the fourth quarter, Nast's year of work and the $100 appropriated by the Ohio Conference had produced but three actual converts. Neither Nast nor the Ohio Conference was satisfied. It is difficult to decide whether missionary or Conference was the more discouraged.

One of the converts was a woman, Caroline Müller, of whom little else is known other than that she was the first German Methodist to enter heaven, triumphant in the faith. The second convert was Edward Hoch, a man of powerful physique who became Nast's personal bodyguard, protecting him from violence on the streets. Hoch was the father of the later noted temperance governor of Kansas. The third convert was *John Zwahlen*. He had been converted by the second sermon which Nast preached in Cincinnati. If Nast had made no other convert in the first year of his missionary activity, neither the

Conference nor the missionary could have had reason for complaint, for this same John Zwahlen in 1840 led the building of the first German Methodist Episcopal Church in the world at Wheeling, West Virginia.

Zwahlen's life history was representative of the experience of the first German Methodists. He was born in Winterthur, Switzerland, on Christmas Day, 1808, one year after the birth of Wilhelm Nast. Baptized on New Year's Day, 1809, he lost his mother in his sixth year and was brought up by his paternal aunt. At the age of fourteen he had been confirmed in the Reformed Church and had shown a considerable spiritual insight. In the company of his oldest brother, he had landed in New Orleans on December 12, 1832, and went shortly by river boat to Cincinnati. Like other newcomers, he was interested first of all in earning a living. At this time John's early religious training began to reassert itself in a longing to make the acquaintance of pious individuals. He went to church, was sometimes affected by the sermon, and had heard of the "Methodists"—which fact he hastened to qualify by saying that he had heard of the Methodists "but never anything good of them." [2]

> I became [he wrote] desirous to hear them for myself. I thought perhaps they were persecuted for righteousness' sake. How to hear them I did not know. English I could not understand and of German Methodist preachers there were none.[3]

His inbred interest in religion led him to concern about the faith and souls of other German-speaking settlers. He was concerned because of the experience of his own spiritual loneliness. Concerning this state of mind he wrote:

> While thinking of the great number of Germans in Cincinnati going astray like myself, I concluded that if the Methodists were the people of God, they would also be induced to send preachers to the Germans.[4]

Zwahlen was therefore in a spiritually receptive mood when he heard that the Ohio Conference had sent Nast to Cincinnati as a German missionary. He went to hear him the first time he preached in the Wesley Chapel of the Fourth Street Methodist Episcopal Church. The sermon "cut" him "to the heart." He went back a second time to hear Nast preach on the text "Thou art the Man." Obviously affected, he went to the altar in decision when the invitation was given. Of his conversion he wrote:

> Finally, I thought that the whole world cannot help me when I come to die, and so I arose and went to the altar but did not obtain an evidence of the pardon of my sins. About three weeks after this, as I was going home from a meeting, with my heart all melted and broken up, I went to my chamber; several times falling on my knees, while praying to God, I for the first time felt the love of God powerfully shed abroad in my heart.[5]

He promptly joined with Nast in sharing the difficulties of forming a class among his fellow countrymen. In the fall of 1837 he was recommended by the official board of Wesley Chapel for a license to exhort, and received his credentials in 1838. In the fall of the same year he was sent to Wheeling to see if anything could be done for the Germans there.

Yet Nast was discouraged with his results, but not with the necessity for the work. "If I should not succeed in winning my countrymen to Christ," he declared with honesty, "I would beseech my brethren not to give up the German cause." During the third quarter of his first year, General Conference was in session in Cincinnati. Nathan Bangs, the corresponding secretary of the Missionary Society, receiving Nast's report that he had now twelve members in his class, wrote the following preface to his missionary summary recording the work of the quadrennium:

> The tide of immigration which is settling so strongly from Germany to this country makes it desirable that we should adopt some efficient means for their enlightenment and salvation. That there should be seven thousand Roman Catholics in the city of Cincinnati and three thousand Protestants, is a fact which should awaken the serious inquiry in every pious mind. "What shall I do for their spiritual benefit?" [6]

Nathan Bangs did not offer any suggestions as to what should be done. Nast's report following this introduction commented on the disinclination of the Germans to attend his public appointments and showed how as a result he was forced to visit almost wholly from house to house.

He concluded:

> Such a work requires a combination of strong faith, lively hope, and ardent love, with talent and experience, in each of which I feel myself very deficient. [7]

He reported to Bangs that since his arrival three-quarters of a year before about twenty-three Germans had been brought under awakening influence. Eight of them were Roman Catholics. About a dozen, he said, expressed "the hope of heaven" and twelve allowed their names to be inscribed on the class rolls. Some Germans, he continued, attended his meetings once, and when the sermon was half over would get up and walk out, never to return again. He was distributing tracts at the entrance to beer gardens, he wrote, preaching in several places outside the city, visiting from house to house, extending personal invitations, dealing with rowdies as well as educated Germans who attended his meetings for the sole purpose of breaking them up, and being attacked by the German press, which ridiculed him at every opportunity.

Nast went to the Annual Conference in September of 1836 with a report as discouraging to himself as it was to his English-speaking brethren. They had never enthusiastically grasped the importance of this mission to the Germans. With a characteristic haste, impatience, and partial information so often exhibited in the deliberations of ecclesiastical bodies, the future of the German work was to be decided. The predominant group in the Conference very foolishly believed in "extensive missions." They were disheartened by the slow progress shown by "intensive missionary work" in the Queen City. The majority had its way. The bishop assigned Nast for the year 1836-1837 to the whole state of Ohio.

His circuit began the first Sunday at Columbus. From that point, the capital and the center of the state, he proceeded on horseback through several German settlements to Basel-on-the-Canal. Leaving Basel, he arrived at Thornville to spend the second Sunday, proceeding during the next week to Newark, to Mount Vernon, to Danville, where he preached the third Sunday. From Danville he rode on through Loudonville, Mansfield, and Galion to Bucyrus, where he preached the fourth Sunday. After the fourth Sunday he went on through the thickly settled German Marion County to the German Settlement near Delaware. He preached there the fifth Sunday, and turned back through Delaware and Worthington to Columbus.

The undertaking was no mean one for Nast. An unskilled horseman riding a balky and erratic horse, he was often thrown from the animal's back into the muddy ditch. With his saddlebags on his arm, he was a familiar sight, pursuing his mount miles on foot before he could recapture him. For one who had spent most of his life up to his thirtieth year in the classroom either as a student or as a teacher, this lack of equestrian skill was to be expected. Nast was, moreover, so absorbed in his work and so disinterested in horses that he could not even recognize his own animal. On one occasion he fed and curried the horse of another man, who walked into the inn and said: "Mr. Nast, why did you go to the trouble of currying and feeding my horse? I could have done it myself." Nast did not know his own mount in the stable. His horse was always his aggravation. On one occasion he became so discouraged with his animal that he dismounted, hitched the beast to a post and kneeled down under a tree earnestly praying the Lord "to control" the "bad disposition" of the horse, "in whose service he was."

Despite his ineptness as an equestrian, he traveled over this three-hundred-mile circuit once a month, preaching in twenty-five places and by the end of the Conference year had traveled about four thousand miles. Although Nast knew from the beginning that the extensive efforts would spell the ruination of the German work, he did his best and laid the foundations for flourishing churches which later developed in Columbus, Galion, Marion, and Bucyrus. How his work produced often unexpected results was shown by the outcome of his acquaintance with "Father" John Schneider, a German who lived on a farm three miles from Galion. Nast would stop at Schneider's place to pick up eleven-year-old Peter, who guided the circuit rider on through the woods which surrounded Galion. Brought to America by his father from Prussia when he was eight, Peter was converted at fourteen. The whole family joined the church and Peter and his brother John both became members of the Central German Conference and effective leaders of the Church.

Although the early Methodist presiding elders had discouraged their circuit riders from matrimony, it had now become an accepted principle that ministers should marry. Upon the advice of a friend, Nast entertained serious matrimonial ambitions. His bride was Margaret Eliza McDowell, eight years his junior. The young woman, of Scotch descent and Presbyterian persuasion, had come under the influence of the Methodists and, at the age of eleven, had been converted in a camp meeting at Duck Creek, near Cincinnati. Nast had made her acquaintance while preaching at an English service in the Queen City. The romance proceeded rapidly and when, toward the end of the year, the presiding elder seemed to feel that the German missionary work should be given up, he married Miss McDowell on August 1, 1836, with the expectation of taking a professorship in a Methodist educational institution. His assignment as missionary to the state of Ohio changed his plans. He soon discovered that two could not live as cheaply as one on $100 a year, especially if one had to roam through all the forests of central and northern Ohio. His bride was therefore compelled to support herself by teaching in Worthington. During the year the young husband was able to return to his wife about every fifth week.

Nast's report on his second missionary year's work was again not encouraging. Only seven had been converted along his three hundred miles of preaching. That figure was four more, to be sure, than in the first year of his more intensive activity in Cincinnati, but still not enough to form a class, to say nothing about the organization of a congregation.

When Nast arrived at the Annual Conference in the fall of 1837, he found sentiment had changed. The champions of "intensive missions" were asserting themselves. Added to the fact that the German population in Cincinnati was experiencing a mushroom growth was the influence of an earnest group of Methodist officials who were concentrated in Cincinnati around the Western Methodist Book Concern. When the bishop read the reappointment of Wilhelm Nast as German missionary to Cincinnati and vicinity, the mission to the Germans in the Ohio Valley actually began. The field was ripe; the number of persons attracted by anything in their own tongue was strengthened by honest seekers to satisfy their own spiritual hunger. Evidences of an awakening consciousness increased from week to week.

During this year services of worship were held chiefly in two places. The most important location was Burke's Chapel on the west side of Vine Street. This was the actual cradle of German Methodism. The preaching services expanded to this chapel from little prayer meeting and class meeting services held in private homes and from preaching services held in schoolhouses. The opening of Burke's Chapel on Vine Street placed a Methodist Church at the very heart of one of the most German sections of the United States. Just above and across the canal, people spoke of the district as "over the Rhine," where beer gardens flourished and orchestras played Sundays as well as week days. Nast was in a strategic location. In the summer of 1838 he was able to organize the first German Methodist society of nineteen members. He was assisted in the work by John Zwahlen, who had been converted by his preaching two years before in Wesley Chapel, and by Franz Nuelsen, an uncle of Bishop John L. Nuelsen.

Franz Nuelsen had joined the Methodist Episcopal Church in Cincinnati through the preaching of Nast. The step was a complete break with the strict Catholic tradition of his family. Soon after his conversion he sat down and wrote a long letter to his mother in Germany, telling her in glowing words the story of his religious experience. Unable to understand the peculiar religious vocabulary in which he wrote, she shook her head and gave the boy's letter to his father. He shook his head and the mother took it to their priest. The priest put on his spectacles and rendered his judgment: "There are only two possibilities. Either your boy has lost his faith or else he has lost his mind." An exchange of letters between mother and son followed, the son assuring his worried mother that for the first time in his life he had "experienced" a wholesome faith. The upshot of the situation was that Frau Nuelsen persuaded her husband to sell his home and business and move the whole Nuelsen family to Cincinnati for the purpose of redeeming the soul of her lost son. The mother little dreamed that her two daughters and two of her four sons in America would be converted, join the Methodist Episcopal Church, and contribute for a century leadership to the mission work.

The second preaching place was Asbury Chapel, a frame house located on Upper Main Street, better known in Cincinnati vernacular as "Brimstone Corner." Here on Sunday afternoons Nast preached, after which from half-past one until three o'clock a sort of Sunday school was held. This developed into the first organized German Methodist Sunday school.

As winter wore away in 1838 Nast and his little group of Methodists began to think of the observance of the holy sacrament. On March 18 the morning sermon was preached in Asbury Chapel in German by Adam Miller. Nast followed with exhortation, and Miller administered the sacrament. In the afternoon a love feast was held. In the evening Miller preached again in German, this time with

ADAM MILLER

He was instrumental in the conversion of Wilhelm Nast

*"The Methodist Church was my home. Christ was my Saviour,
and Heaven my aim"*

greater freedom in the use of the language. The editor of *The Western Christian Advocate,* L. L. Hamline, was present to tell of his religious experience, the story of which Nast translated.

That Adam Miller should have administered the first holy sacrament to the German Methodists was an appropriate circumstance. No figure in the history of German Methodism is more appealing in his passion. He called attention to the necessity of the German missionary work in a letter to the editor of *The Western Christian Advocate* in March, 1835, volunteering to learn "European" German to be of use in the program. Miller was born in Maryland two years after Nast had been born in Germany. At the tender age of four months he had been carried by his father to the then western wilds of Ohio in the company of a colony of the stricter sect of the Mennonites called *Omish.* The Omish were a singular people who entertained the ambition of being secluded from intercourse with the society of other people. To this end they purchased as much land as possible in one vicinity and created a distinctive community which increased promptly by immigration from Pennsylvania and Maryland. Here they lived industriously and spoke their own variety of Pennsylvania German.

To understand Adam Miller's passion for Methodism one must first appreciate the strictness of the religious mores of this Omish community. A rigorous morality and a peculiar mode of dress distinguished this sect. Members were not allowed to go to any religious meetings except their own, and no other preachers were allowed to preach among them. Adam's father, however, owned a mill, where he became familiar with the English language and mingled with English neighbors, a heresy which only commercial advantage could justify. The father was guilty of another heresy for which there was no legitimate Omish justification. He sometimes stole away to attend Methodist meetings!

On a Sabbath when Adam was sixteen, his father fell into conversation with a Methodist local preacher who taught school in a neighboring village. The result of the visit was that Adam was sent to this Methodist to learn the English language while he was recovering from a dislocated ankle joint and could not work on the farm. A fond friendship developed between Adam and the teacher, who on one occasion invited the boy to attend a quarterly meeting.

"Now," said the teacher, "when we get to the meeting on Saturday night, they will have a bench out in front of the pulpit, to which they will invite all seekers of religion." Adam continues the story:

> As soon as the Saturday-night sermon was over, the bench was put in front of the pulpit. At once, upon the invitation, I went forward and kneeled down. All alone at first—my heart all broken up, willing to do anything to obtain the religion that my kind teacher had talked so much to me about—but now my troubles

thickened around me. I had never been at such a meeting. In the moment of excitement I had forgotten many things that had been told me, and what to say I did not know; but in an instant it occurred to me I would listen with attention and what I heard others say, that I would say. Just as I had formed this purpose, a pious sister commenced clapping her hands and shouting "Glory to God!" at the top of her voice, and with that I commenced, in broken accents of half German and half English, to cry "Glory to God!" and to follow up the whole commenced to clap my hands. My teacher soon came to me, asking whether I had found peace, to which I replied: "No!! I feel very bad. I am a lost sinner," and continued to repeat the words I had caught from the pious sister. He said to me, "You must not say 'glory,' but say 'Lord,' have mercy on me, a sinner." I soon did according to his instruction; but at the same time commenced to claim religion on the ground of my past moral life. Instead of trusting in the Saviour, I trusted in my own good works.[8]

From that point the religious experience of Adam Miller was directed toward that religious discovery which was always the strength of German Methodism—the discovery of free grace. Against the protest of relatives, but with the tacit approval of his father, he joined the Methodist Episcopal Church on trial. His grandfather protested this action. Calling him to his deathbed, he entreated the boy to return to the religious community from which he had torn himself loose. Miller describes that scene in these words:

The Lord gave me great liberty and power to talk to him and to explain to him the nature of repentance and conversion. He wept profusely and seemed anxious to hear me talk about this new way. He said to me he had never fully given me up for lost, to which I replied: "No, I am not lost, but saved through God's mercy." I finally asked the privilege of praying with him, to which he readily consented. The power of the Lord came down, and I believe the venerable old man of eighty looked to Jesus and found peace in the believing. Many of the members of his own church stood around and looked with astonishment on the scene. I was strengthened in the faith. The old man was comforted, and when I left the room, his aged wife followed me into the yard and wished me to make to her some further explanations about this religion, which I cheerfully did. She was much affected and I went on my way rejoicing. I could now bear the persecution to which I was subject with a glad heart. The Methodist Church was my home. The members of the church all treated my kindly. Christ was my Saviour and heaven my aim.

Jesus, all the day long,
Was my joy and my song.[9]

The experience is worth recording in a history of German Methodism because it describes the conviction with which individuals accepted the gift of grace which was the chief doctrine of the Methodists. From the deathbed of his grandfather, Adam Miller went forth with the serious purpose of preparing himself for leadership. "My want of earlier opportunities was my misfortune," he declared. "My neglect to improve the future would be my fault."

His missionary work began at home. Inviting his sister to go with him to a quarterly meeting, she was "happily converted to God." Their younger brother, reluctantly following Adam and his sister to a camp meeting seven miles away, was also convicted and the three joined in prayer for the family. In a few years the father, the mother, and all the members of the family had experienced the grace of God.

In 1830 Adam, throwing a small bundle of clothes over his shoulder, left home for Knox County, Ohio, to learn a trade and study with his old teacher. It seemed inevitable that he should be licensed to preach and be received into the traveling connection. His schoolteacher, encouraging him in his ambition, endorsed a note so that he could buy a horse. A brother Methodist sold him a saddle for four dollars a month with twelve months' credit, and another brother fitted him out with a pair of saddlebags on the same terms. A neighboring woman took her husband's old plaid cloak, ripped it out, turned it inside out, and fixed it for him. Another "good sister" gave him a few pairs of socks. His outfit was completed with an old rain-soaked white hat, his own; a pair of shoes made for him by still another Methodist brother, and a pair of leggings he had made from the skirts of an old frock coat. With this outfit and fifty cents in money, he started for Mansfield, twenty-five miles away, where Conference was being held. He spent his fifty cents for pasturing his horse during the Conference session, and arrived at his field, four hundred miles away, the Nicholas Circuit, Virginia, without money. His circuit covered three hundred and fifty miles, which he was able to cover every four weeks, preaching at thirty-one appointments.

Circuit life agreed with him. Under a constant diet of bear meat, venison, cornbread, and an occasionally good mess of pork and beans, his health, which had never been too robust, improved. At the close of the year the brethren paid each circuit rider fifty-one dollars as the salary for the preceding twelvemonth. With close economy Miller had saved thirty dollars of that sum to pay on his horse and other small debts which he had contracted. During the four years he remained in the hills of Virginia he paid all his debts, which made him, as he said, "free to go where God would open the way," but at the same time he nearly forgot the German language.

In the meantime Miller was brought back from his appointments in Virginia to the Greenville Circuit on the Indiana line. The privations which he suffered in this place were severe indeed. Despite the inadequacy of the salary and refusing the offer of a good teaching job with the comment, "I am an itinerate in the Methodist Church and not for sale to any higher bidder," he remained at his difficult job.

Adversity in the "work of the Lord" did not dampen his passion nor injure his pride. He appeared at a camp meeting near Troy, Ohio, in the summer of 1836 so poorly dressed that a minister gave him five dollars, with which he bought stuff for pantaloons and vest. His wife traded a fine watch which she had been given when they were married for a good piece of broadcloth and when he went to Conference in the fall he was dressed as well as most of the others. "We had," he wrote in his *Journal*, "to endure many privations and hardships for the gospel's sake and never thought of giving up the ministry on account of the embarrassments." In the fall of 1838 he was appointed to the Milford Circuit, near Cincinnati, from which time he became a life-long associate of Nast and a leading figure in the building of the German work.

No honor could have been more deserving or more deeply appreciated than that given to Miller in calling upon him to administer the communion to the German congregation assembled in Asbury Chapel on that winter Sabbath of 1839. In 1840 Miller was made superintendent of the German Mission of the Ohio Conference. Appointed to Cincinnati in 1841, he succeeded in 1842 in leading in the construction of a $4,000 brick church edifice on Race Street, which has ever since been as *die Muttergemeinde* [10] of German-speaking Methodism.

The romance of the movement never diminished for Miller and his love of converted Germans never died. In 1843 he published a valuable little source volume under the title of *Origin and Progress of The German Missions in the Methodist Episcopal Church, including an Account of the Christian Experiences of Some of the Converts from Popery and Infidelity, as Furnished by Themselves.* In 1859 he expanded his biographical studies of the leaders of the German work with a more extended volume entitled *Experience of German Methodist Preachers.* These two volumes constitute the most valuable documented source materials on the human beginnings of the German work. Miller's strenuous activities finally told upon his health, whereupon he studied medicine, took the M.D. degree, and became a successful homeopathic physician in Chicago. He died in Chicago, in July, 1901, like Nast, at the age of ninety-two.

The Annual Conference of 1838 was at hand. Though more progress had been made during the year than in previous years and although the foundations of a Germon work seemed to be fairly well established, the Annual Conference was not at all unanimous in its opinion about its continuation. True, Nast reported to the Conference the founding of a congregation of thirty members, yet important groups held the attitude that little of permanent value could be accomplished among "the infidel foreigners who seemed to have Roman Catholic leanings." The issue was sharply drawn at the point of Nast's suggestion of the necessity of a German language press. Nast had made his position clear at previous sessions. At the end of his first year as missionary to Cincinnati he had declared:

> It is as difficult to preserve as to raise up a German branch of the Methodist Episcopal Church, as none of our doctrinal and devotional books, not even our *Discipline,* are to be found in the German language.[11]

At the end of his next year as missionary to Columbus and the state of Ohio, he had pleaded before the Conference:

> In short, the German Church and nation needs as great a work of reformation as the Church of England did in the time of John Wesley. And unless his doctrine bursts in floods upon the German immigrants, enlightening, alarming, and converting them by hundreds and thousands and exerting such a reaction upon Germany that the pulpits and colleges and universities and common schools will all feel it, there is reason to fear that the importation of German literature and German people will exercise as demoralizing an influence upon the Americans as the French once exercised upon the Germans. These are not imaginary apprehensions, brethren. For the German immigrant, among whom there have been of late many well-educated and wealthy men, are about to hold yearly conventions, in order to perpetuate the German language and literature, German sentiments, manners, and customs; and if headed by some infidels, they will form themselves into a party strongly opposed to the religious observance of the Sabbath and the benevolent institutions of this gospel-favored country.
>
> We might exercise a saving influence upon the Germans through the press, by publishing in the German language some of our doctrinal tracts, the Wesleyan Catechism, Fletcher's Appeal, some of Wesley's sermons, and, as soon as possible, a German Methodist periodical.[12]

The crisis in the Conference session was faced by L. L. Hamline, editor of *The Western Christian Advocate,* then forty-two years old. He was convinced of the value of the language mission and said so with telling effect. He not only led the movement for the vote which defeated the faction in the Conference which wished to abandon the German work; he led the Conference to a vote to authorize the organization of a German language paper. When the appointments were read, Nast was made the editor of a publication, yet to be named, and Peter Schmucker was appointed missionary to Cincinnati to continue the work Nast had begun.

The work among the German Methodists began in earnest in the fall of 1838. Promotion of *The Christian Apologist,* as the journal was named, went side by side with the development of the mission. Rarely if ever has the history of a publication been so closely related to the development of a movement. The next two years were "glorious years."

CHAPTER IV

"GLORIOUS YEARS" OF EXPANSION

The elevation of Nast to the editorial chair of the *Apologist* opened a new period in the history of German-speaking Methodism. Nast did not cease being a missionary. His field of effort was merely widened. He became a kind of "bishop-at-large" of the German work. His appointment left vacant the appointment of German missionary to Cincinnati. The leadership of that young congregation was now doubly important because the Queen City was the hub of the work, the seat of "Brother Nast."

Nast's successor was *Peter Schmucker,* an experienced preacher who had left the Lutheran Church in Newark, Ohio, to join the English-speaking Methodist Episcopal Church there. He had two techniques in the expression of this passion. The first was the distribution of tracts. The other was the revival service. On the streets, at the doorsteps of homes, on the wharves as river boats docked at Cincinnati, he distributed his Christian polemic literature. For three months he devoted himself to the spiritual development of his little congregation, and then proceeded to lead a revival which had the result that in his first year of ministry in Cincinnati he added eighty new members to his Church.

Schmucker was fifty-four years old when he came to the Cincinnati Mission. He was in the full height of his power. Born in Michelstadt, in the Grand Duchy of Hessia-Warmstadt, he had been brought to America by his father, who settled on a farm in Shenandoah County, Virginia. His religious experience had begun at the age of eighteen when he visited a camp meeting being held by the United Brethren. He "fell under conviction," and entered the Lutheran ministry because his parents were of that faith and two of his brothers already were Lutheran pastors. His success in the pastorate in revivals and in making conversions was so unusual that he was decried as a "Methodist." Although he was one of the five pastors who signed the articles of the constitution of the General Synod of the Evangelical Church of the United States at Hagerstown, Maryland, in 1820, he moved in 1822 from Virginia to Newark, Ohio, where he had no parish. He worked during the week and preached voluntarily on Sundays when the opportunity to do so offered itself. Nearly ten years later he and his wife joined the Methodist Episcopal Church. After he had worked a few years as a local preacher, Nast visited him in 1838 and prevailed upon him to take up work in the Ohio Conference. Schmucker spent two years in Cincinnati, and in 1840 went on to Louisville, Ken-

tucky, to found another mission. In March of 1842 he moved on
South from Kentucky to found still another mission in New Orleans.
In October of the same year he was gratified to be appointed superintendent of the American Tract Society. In the fall of 1843 he was
appointed superintendent of the German mission in the Ohio Valley,
where his organizing ability found free field. Traveling from mission station to mission station in stage coaches, on canal boats, and on
horseback, he suffered a breakdown and had to give up the work in
1848. A poet, lover of music, and a good singer, he had given a necessary trained leadership at a time when the German missions were
expanding rapidly and an adequate pastoral leadership was difficult to
find. Nast paid a merited tribute to him when he said, "Peter
Schmucker glorified his office."

During Schmucker's Cincinnati pastorate a life was changed, which
made a rich contribution to the Church. On November 6, 1838, a
twenty-six-year-old German landed at New Orleans, secured employment through the good offices of a friend from his own German village, and became a part of the "pagan" immigrant life of New Orleans.
While he was conversing with his friend one day, he was told of a
curious sort of people in Cincinnati.

> They pray much [said the friend] but they do not drink, nor
> dance, nor gamble, nor swear; they are all fools.

To which description Heinrich Wilhelm Ahrens exclaimed, "That is
the people I have longed to see for years."

Early on the morning of May 2, 1839, a young man disembarked
from a river boat at the wharf in Cincinnati and set out to find an
acquaintance from his native town, who had settled there. After
breakfast the husband went to work and the wife visited with the
young man about the "wonderful dealings of God with them in this
country." Let Ahrens tell the story:

> After awhile she said they had left the Lutheran Church and
> joined a church called the Methodist. A thunderclap from a
> clear sky could not have astonished me more than hearing these
> words. What a few moments ago I believed to be an answer to
> my prayer, I now believed to be a punishment of God, who, for
> my breaking all my most solemn vows, had led me into the hands
> of the most dangerous enemies of Christ, in order to deliver
> me the more surely into the hands of the devil. In great anxiety
> I hastened out of the house, taking my friend, who had come from
> New Orleans, with me. When we got into the open air, I said
> to him:
> "Henry, we have fallen into evil hands; what shall we do?"
> "What do you mean?" said he.
> "Why," responded Heinrich, "can't you see? These people have
> denied the faith and gone over to anti-Christ; they belong to that
> strange sort of people which the Bible designates as the harlot
> of Babylon, with her mysterious cup of sorceries, possessing a
> supernatural power to fascinate men and deliver them over to

the devil; and how shall we escape such a power except we leave them immediately?"[1]

The friend was unconcerned. Unable to find another boarding place, Ahrens was compelled to remain in the home of the Methodists.

The next day a man entered the house, whom my suspicious mind set down as *one of them*.

Ahrens listened to every word the visitor spoke, watched every movement, but could not detect anything wrong. As the stranger was leaving, he stepped up to Ahrens, spoke a few kind words, then stated simply

that the sinner was saved by grace, that the greatest sinner could be saved and that it was possible for every one to know that *God had forgiven his sins* and that he was an heir of heaven.[2]

That summary of religion found a responsive chord in Ahrens's being. The stranger then told him how to read the Bible, how to pray, and said good-by. The gentleman was none other than Peter Schmucker, German missionary of the Methodist Episcopal Church.

For three months Ahrens accepted every invitation to the altar and awaited the opening of camp meeting. After a few days there he felt a change in life:

My heart seemed to be emptied of all its wickedness; a stream of life and power and glory was flowing into it—the love of God was shed abroad in the heart by the Holy Ghost—the Spirit of God bearing witness with my spirit that I was a child of God. With wondering and delight I beheld a real change in everything that surrounded me. There was glory above me and glory beneath me and glory around me and glory in my soul. This was the 17th day of August, 1839.[3]

Ahrens was soon convinced that his resolution "never to join the Methodist Church" had been folly. He united with it, was granted an exhorter's license by Peter Schmucker on October 20, 1841, given a local preacher's license a few months later, received on probation in the Kentucky Conference, and appointed to Maysville, Kentucky.

Wherever men thought of work among the German immigrants, they wrote to Nast. Thus it happened that in the fall of 1838 some of the stationed preachers invited Nast to visit Pittsburgh. He did and left an organized society of thirty members as the result of his work. On October 23, 1838, Nast wrote to the editor of *The Western Christian Advocate:*

I found them about ten in number, mostly males—husbands without their wives. Their number has increased to thirty-five so that we could form two classes. Several of the wives have been baptized into one spirit with their husbands; about fifteen in all have experienced religion during my stay. The people are truly craving the sincere milk of the gospel; nowhere have I found it so easy to preach. I labored a whole year at Cincinnati for twenty-four members. Several of the members immediately entered upon the right spirit of the work—they went home not only to pray for themselves but to pray with and for their friends and neighbors. To give you some instances—

I stayed all night with a family where the husband was a member but had not a clear witness of his acceptance with God. The Lord met us at the family altar in the morning. The brother then went to his work, but returned in a short time, sighing and heavy laden—he said he could not work—he wanted to pray more; we called in his wife. The Lord visited us in power; and whilst he was blessed, his wife began to cry for mercy, and has also, since that time, experienced religion. I visited another family, of which only the father was a member of the German class. He was seeking religion. He prayed with the family; the mother became affected first, then her son, then her son-in-law, then his wife, and even a Roman Catholic girl who lived in the family fell under conviction. The whole family joined the church.

Let me relate one more:

A brother who was very zealous, although opposed by his wife, had a meeting appointed in his house. I preached on the third and fourth verses of the fifth chapter of Matthew and opened the door of the church. His wife was the first that literally rushed forward, seized my hand, confessed herself a great sinner and told the congregation, with a flood of tears, how wickedly she had opposed her husband and how patiently he took it; he would not cease to pray for her. She experienced religion that following morning and will, no doubt, be a helpmate to her precious husband. They are an excellent couple, living by faith in the Son of God, who has given himself for them. In love feast she sat in the middle of the congregation, and when she rose to give her testimony, she would not content herself to stay where she was, but came out, walked up the aisle to the pulpit, and then turning and facing the congregation she told, in language that would have melted the hardest heart, what the Lord had done for her poor soul:

My dear brethren, the Germans whilst unconverted, turn an entirely deaf ear to religion, but when they hear the voice of the Son of God, and find him to be the good Shepherd, they become, generally, dead to the world, and make religion their all-absorbing theme. Thanks be to the good Lord, the Friend of sinners.

The experience in Pittsburgh was gratifying to Nast for a particular reason. He wrote:

Five years ago [1833], I left Pittsburgh with nothing but blackness and darkness before me. I went away weeping and said, on the point of despair: "Though he slay me, yet will I trust in him." Blessed by God, the Son of righteousness rest upon my hopeless soul with healing in his wings. I returned to preach that Jesus will not pass by any, else he would have passed me by. Truly, those that go weeping, bearing precious seed, shall surely return with joy, bringing their sheaves with them. The Lord keep us faithful to the end.[4]

Among the converts at Pittsburgh was twenty-three-year-old *Engelhardt Riemenschneider*. He had been born in Kurhessen and brought up according to the strict form of the Reformed Church. He was singularly unmoved by religious experience until his twentieth year. He wrote of this experience while still in Germany:

> The first time my heart was affected was under a sermon from these words: "If these should hold their peace the stones would cry out."
> At the conclusion I felt that I must amend my ways or be eternally lost. I made this known afterward to one of my friends who, in a rationalistic manner said, "The priests always make it worse than it is"; and he and other of my friends succeeded in quieting my fears again, and I continued for some time longer to live undisturbed in sin. The second time I was awakened to see my condition was in a tavern, where I and several young friends, on a Sabbath evening, were together drinking wine. As I stood at the bar and reflected upon our conduct, I came to a clear conviction that we were on our way to ruin and the more I thought of it, the more dreadful the place appeared to me. If in that night a religious man had been with me who could have directed me to the Law of God, I might have been converted immediately.[5]

Riemenschneider, uneasy at American restraints, where he had come for a visit, and especially rebellious against strict Sabbath observances, decided to return to Germany where he had "something of an inheritance coming to him." His presence in Pittsburgh was explained by his visit to his uncle there before sailing for Europe. Nast was preaching in a schoolhouse in the neighborhood. "Although I thought nothing of the Methodists," he wrote, "yet as the preaching was in German, I concluded to go and hear him."

The missionary technique of Nast is nowhere better described than in Riemenschneider's explanation of what followed:

> The first sermon that I heard went like a two-edged sword through my soul and I again felt myself a great sinner. In this call, I received a strong impression that this might be the last, and I went home with a determination to give myself to God. I now, for the first time, commenced praying upon my knees. Sleep departed from my eyes, and I spent whole nights in wrestling with God in prayer. When I went to the table to take food the impression came to me, "You are not worthy of it," and so I often retired from the table without my meal. With these feelings I continued to visit the church. Brother Nast circulated the "Articles of Faith and General Rules of the Methodist Church," of which I took a copy and was thankful for it. I read the General Rules with great attention, and concluded if the Church kept these rules it must be a pious one.
> Upon the following evening, after the General Rules were distributed, Brother Nast said: "All those who have read our General Rules and think they can get along better by uniting with us in our work, can give us their names." I was convinced that this was the place for me; but I was anxious that someone should lead the way, as there was then no German Methodist society formed there; however, as no one went, I resolved to

follow my convictions, and went forward and gave my name to the church, with the determination fully to consecrate myself to the service of God, whereupon about twenty followed, and this was the commencement of the Pittsburgh mission.[6]

His conversion followed his joining of the Church. On a Saturday evening Nast was preaching on the subject of Naaman's leprosy. Riemenschneider was so affected that he fell from the bench and began to cry aloud for mercy. His restlessness continued for three weeks. Of this period he wrote:

> Some of my former friends said that the Methodists had put a bad spirit into me; others thought I was crazy; and, as I was daily growing thinner and paler, it was generally thought that I would not live long. Until one evening at prayer meeting I gave myself as a poor, lost, condemned sinner to Christ, trusting alone in his merits. It was then that the day of grace dawned in my heart. The joy that I felt I could not describe, and the evidence of my acceptance was so clear that no enemy could make me drop it.[7]

In December, 1838, John Zwahlen, who had been one of the three converts of Nast's first missionary year in Cincinnati, was sent to Wheeling, West Virginia, to solicit subscriptions for the *Apologist* and to look around to see if anything could be done for the Germans in that growing center in a religious way. His dual commission was not at the time unusual. It was the way Nast was looking at things. Nast's editorial position had not handicapped his missionary activity. It actually made it more advantageous, because Nast had become a traveling salesman in the interests of his *Apologist,* and his converts became the same. It was hard to tell whether he was more anxious to take subscriptions or to make conversions. The two things were so closely related that he was coming to the point where he could not distinguish between the two. To be a subscriber was to him almost the same thing as being an ardent German Methodist. His faith in his publication was so great that he never doubted that a reader would become a convert and that no convert would feel complete without being a regular reader of the periodical. The two went together and the two passions were carried with Nast wherever he went. Zwahlen had caught the "disease," for it was contagious.

He arrived in Wheeling on Saturday, December 23, and was warmly welcomed. On the next day he held worship in the afternoon and evening. The interest was so wholesome that within two weeks he was holding meetings every day. On December 26, 1838, three days after his arrival, he wrote to Nast:

> For Monday I appointed a class meeting and invited all that were in earnest to save their souls. After class meeting I read the General Rules and gave an invitation to join the Church. Twelve came forward and gave me their hands. Christmas morning, at six o'clock, I held a prayer meeting—at ten and three o'clock, I tried to exhort them from the Word of God. The Lord

was with me—four joined and a woman cried aloud for mercy. In the afternoon, God worked again, to my astonishment. Several were converted and cried aloud. Some professors were stirred up to seek for more of the love of God. One was brought into the liberty of the children of God. Pray for us! It is the work of the Lord. The brethren think I should stay here till the river opens. I do not feel as if I could do anything myself; yet, I believe that God makes use of instruments.[8]

He remained two weeks, exhorting the seekers and praying with them. During the fortnight he formed a class of twenty-four. After what he describes as a "glorious two weeks' meeting," he returned to Cincinnati and "reported what the Lord had done for us." During Zwahlen's absence Riemenschneider preached. When he returned, he asked the young man to go twenty miles into the country where a number of Germans had no preacher. He went.

My first visit [he wrote] was crowned with the conversion of five or six souls. This encouraged me, and I afterward visited these people and each time remained eight days with them. The effect was that in four months about forty souls were converted.[9]

The Quarterly Conference at Wesley Chapel shortly granted Zwahlen a license to preach, and Bishop Morris, who as editor of *The Western Christian Advocate,* had shown such concern for the German work, sent him back to Wheeling to take care of the little flock. In July, 1839, he was received on trial into the Pittsburgh Conference and was returned as missionary to Wheeling. Of his experience Zwahlen wrote:

God was with us in this new mission, sinners were awakened and converted, and we soon found ourselves under the necessity of building a house of worship. Although the times were hard, we went to work in good earnest, our German brethren took a deep interest in this work, and gave very liberally to help it forward. I laid the matter before our English brethren, and they helped us liberally. We commenced the work in faith and the Lord helped us. By the next conference (1840) our house was finished and we had eighty-three members. This was the *first German Methodist Episcopal Church* built in this country. It was dedicated by Brother Nast. His heart was filled with gratitude to God for that which he had done for us. But if we now look over our German missionary work, we have abundant reason to bow in gratitude before God. May he continue to bless us![10]

Such was but the beginning of the work of Zwahlen. He lived to the age of 90, and was one of the most successful evangelists produced by German Methodism.

The work was pushed out in all directions from the center of Cincinnati. In 1839 the Monroe Mission was established by the Pittsburgh Conference. After a series of conversions through the instrumentality of Zwahlen and Riemenschneider, C. C. Best, a local preacher from the Erie Conference, was appointed to lead the work. Adam

Miller, having been appointed at the Ohio Conference of 1839, missionary within the bounds of the Cincinnati and Lebanon District, rode through the Scioto country and recommended to the next Annual Conference the establishment of several new missions and the establishment of a German mission district. In 1839 a society was also organized in Lawrenceburg, Indiana, twenty-two miles from Cincinnati. Nast preached here repeatedly. On the occasion of his second visit to the group, ten joined the Church. German missionaries by this time were not only preachers but circulation agents for language literature. Bishop Soule, writing to Adam Miller, said:

> In all your missionary visitations, you will take a deep interest in obtaining patronage for the *Apologist* and in circulating the German hymnbook and such tracts as are published in the German literature.[11]

By the end of 1840 nine regular missionaries were in the field, in addition to Nast. The morale of the work was strong. Schmucker's leadership in Cincinnati had brought the Queen City society to encouraging gains. He had become a familiar figure, preaching in the market house, peddling tracts and invitations from doorstep to doorstep, distributing Bibles and Testaments, greeting the steamboats at the river wharves and presenting the boatmen with literature. In the year he took in forty-eight new members. The rising tide of unemployment, however, seriously crippled his work. In April, 1840, he wrote that only seventy of the one hundred forty members he had taken in remained. The others had found it necessary to leave the city for want of work.

Schmucker's enthusiasm for the tract as a means of Christian influence was expressed in his notes in *The Western Christian Advocate*. On one occasion he described his work as follows:

> I have distributed about one thousand or twelve hundred tracts in the city of Cincinnati, on the streets, in houses, and on steamboats. Nearly all the tracts were thankfully received, and I had interesting religious conversation with many. On steamboats, too, I have met with most kind receptions even by some of the boat captains. On one boat, the captain of which could speak the German language, nearly all the hands were Germans, and could read. I gave them all tracts of religious periodicals. They took their hats and caps off and thanked me, and asked me not to forget them; but on their return from New Orleans to visit them again—and said they had not heard a sermon in their language in three years.[12]

Later he added:

> Brethren, I need not tell you why I have written the above. Our object is to save souls—we leave no means untried—different means may be applied under different circumstances, when we go out in the highways, lanes, and hedges, or visit sinners in their houses, tracts may be distributed to great advantage. They should be accompanied with remarks, when necessary prayer

and exhortation, as the opportunity may offer. To the American Tract Society, I would beg leave to say, we have hundreds and thousands in this Western valley. They have a claim on your charity. I have distributed not less than thirty thousand pages of German tracts among them within eighteen months and could have done much more, but for the want of means.[13]

German Methodism was being led by men who were convinced they had "experienced Christ." Their enthusiastic "conviction" was producing results. Between August 12 and 20, 1840, German Methodists, in association with their English-speaking brethren, held a camp meeting six miles north of Cincinnati. The Germans held their own worship service in one of their own assembly tents. Fourteen or sixteen Germans were converted. The open-air meeting was a great success, thousands of people being on the grounds on Sunday. The revival in the Monroe Mission, meanwhile, had been followed by wholesome action so that at the close of the first year the missionary could report a hundred and fifteen members. *George Danker*, leaving the Lutheran Church with forty-two of its members because his congregations were "offended at his preaching so much like the Methodists," added a hundred and three members to the Marietta Mission, which had been created by a division of the work of the Monroe Mission. Zwahlen was completing an exciting year in Wheeling, with Riemenschneider and *Heinrich Köneke* at his side. Köneke tells the story of his conversion in his native town of Zeven in the kingdom of Hanover in this way:

From such a miserable life God delivered me in 1834. In the night between the 26th and 27th of December, I had been playing cards from two o'clock P. M., till twelve o'clock at night, and lost considerable money. On the way home the thought came into my mind, 'How wrong have I done!' All my money is spent, and in the morning I shall much need it. I have an industrious wife and five children at home, and yet I spend everything in a wrong way." With this thought, it appeared as if God from heaven spoke to my heart, saying, "Also against me hast thou sinned." While these thoughts were passing in my mind, I could not move a step. Many of my past sins were brought to remembrance and my heart was so affected, that in the midnight hour under the open canopy I was constrained to cry aloud, while tears flowed from my eyes in greater quantities than they had ever done before. How long this continued I cannot tell. I finally went home with a heavy heart and with a firm resolution to forsake my ungodly companions and to regulate my life according to the Word of God. I had also received so much light, as led me not to depend upon my own strength, but to pray to God that he might aid me to put my good resolutions into practice.

I now believed in the honesty of my heart, that I ought not to express my feelings to anyone in our village, notwithstanding I would gladly have done it had I believed that I could find one among them that was likeminded like myself. This brought me to think that perhaps the people—of whose religion and piety so much was said—might be of the same mind as myself, and, consequently, a desire was awakened within me to have some conversation with them. I had often heard that they severely condemned dancing, playing cards, drunkenness, and such like things. This induced me to believe that I should agree with them. They lived twenty miles from my place of residence, and had been converted through the instrumentality of Moravian missionaries—I now, for the first time, made known to my wife that I wished to visit the people. She, however, was not satisfied with my purpose and besides this, she had noticed that in the few weeks past I had been industriously reading the Bible, and she was afraid that I should bring as great a reproach upon her and myself as lay upon these people themselves. This threw me into a state of painful anxiety, and I secretly prayed to God that he would teach me the right way; and he so ordered it, that in the course of two or three weeks, a man met me on the street whom, from his dress, I judged to have come from that place. I spoke to him, and asked him whether he came from T———— or B————? "From B————," was the answer. I then said: "Please tell me what kind of people those are in your neighborhood, who have all kinds of nicknames and hold meetings out of the church?"

"I am one of them," was the reply, upon which he looked very friendly at me. I was now, with an anxious heart, much interested in him.

He commenced with an account of conversion and the new birth, and of the lost condition of the natural man, etc. I then related to him how it had lately been with me; and upon which he said that God had awakened me, and that I should seek, through Jesus, for the pardon of my sins. He explained to me, as well as he could, the way of salvation, and exhorted me not to be ashamed of being a follower of Christ, but willingly to take up and bear the cross, and seek out others, and meet with them to read the Bible and engage in prayer. He then left me, and I followed his advice. I often prayed with deep penitential feelings, but always in secret places. I wished to pray publicly in my family, yet a false shame kept me back.

At this period of my repentance, my wife noticed that I was really in earnest, and the people soon began to scoff at me. My wife then laid every hindrance in my way; and when she found she could not accomplish her object, she commenced weeping and lamenting that I had exposed her to so much reproach. She had eleven brothers, and a large number of relatives. For two evenings in succession she was very much enraged. The third evening I had some fearful forebodings, but I continued in prayer to God. On this evening I was indeed put upon the severest trial that I had ever experienced. She urged me more earnestly to give up my religious course entirely, and told me that if I continued to live in this way she would leave me. After various threatenings, which I cannot describe, I finally asked myself, "What shall I do?" The peace of my family will certainly be destroyed. I sprang up, not being able any longer to endure it. I got my Bible in order to read in it and as I opened it read in the superscription to the 116th Psalm: "Comfort for the afflicted." Then, thought I, with a sorrowful heart, and tears in mine eyes, this may be something for me. As I read the first verses I felt as though the Psalm had been written expressly for me. When I had read it through, I had such comfort and such a strengthening of my faith, that I resolved with renewed courage to take up my cross, and concluded that the hand of the Almighty could change my situation. I therefore once more prayed to God with a stammering voice. I read the Psalm again, and then retired to rest quietly, my wife having by this time gone to sleep. But I could not sleep the whole night long, being filled with hope and confidence in the Almighty power of God; and then, with watching and prayer I waited anxiously for the day.

The next morning she would not speak to me. I, however, addressed her as follows:

"Beloved wife, I have nothing to say to you. If I had seven wives opposing me, and if each of them were seven times worse than you are, it would not be in their power to turn me from my purpose for in my temptation God has strengthened me. Come and see this Psalm."

She would not, however, read herself, so I commenced, and she listened with patience. And from that hour I had by the grace of God the victory. My wife was changed and never persecuted me again."

Through Köneke's influence a group of kindred spirits began to meet together to sing and pray. In two years the little society increased to thirty members. About this time, like so many hundreds of thousands of his countrymen, Köneke had heard much of America and its religious liberty. He and his wife agreed to emigrate and landed at Baltimore on January 11, 1836. Moving on to Wheeling they began to hold family meetings together, which grew to a group of about three dozen. After attending the English-speaking Methodist Church, and finding its atmosphere congenial, Köneke wrote to Nast asking him to use his influence in having a missionary sent to Wheeling. When John Zwahlen arrived in December, 1838, he was welcomed by Köneke and his wife. No family rejoiced more in the progress which the mission was making in 1840. Köneke himself now began to preach in the Marietta Mission. He had the satisfaction of reporting a hundred and seventy members at the end of his first year. The Marietta Circuit, covering an area of twenty-eight hundred square miles largely in Belmont County, Ohio, where Swiss and Alsatians had settled, was important if for no other reason than that *Ludwig Nippert* came from Captina, which was in the territory.

The Pittsburgh Conference had by this time become interested in the German work and appropriated funds for a missionary to the Allegheny Mission in the vicinity of Pittsburgh. The work was pushed out from Cincinnati to the Allen and Scioto Missions; but the important landmarks of the first year of the decade were in other directions. In the fall of 1840 the Ohio Conference appointed Peter Schmucker to the task of establishing a mission in Louisville, Kentucky. The next spring Schmucker described his work in this fashion:

I commenced my labor in Louisville in the streets; after awhile I got the use of a little private schoolhouse and now I have the use of the Presbyterian Church. I have more hearers, on an average, than I ever had in Cincinnati. For four weeks past we have been much disturbed by the German rabble, during which time the church has been stoned every night, excepting the last. I have now seventy-three probationers in the society, all received in about two months. We receive from five to ten every Sabbath. Some have found the pearl of great price, and others are seeking day and night. Few days pass in which we have not to read, sing, and pray with seekers of religion, and sometimes from morning till night. Here are more awakened Germans than I ever saw in any one place. . . .

This mission now embraces some who were Lutherans, German Reformed, and Romanists; others grog sellers and grog drinkers; and others, again, musicians, publicans, and sinners. We have both rich and poor and high and low. Some are converted and others unconverted. May the Lord bless and help us! . . .

We have powerful enemies: A German press, a host of Romanists, several hundred grog sellers, and two or three times as many grog drinkers. All these are out in battle against us, talking against Schmucker and the Methodists every Sabbath, printing against us every week and slandering us, in short, at all times and places.[15]

Two months later Schmucker wrote to Adam Miller:

The intolerable persecutions we have here, doubtless, prevents many from joining me, and will probably cause some of my young recruits to break the ranks. I am frequently compelled to defend my doctrine on the streets. All the German priests and preachers in the city have held forth against me, and Mr. ———— is slandering me and the Methodists in his paper nearly every week; but still the people come to hear, several going away convicted, and others coming back again to seek salvation; and blessed be God, they find it too.[16]

The Sunday school had by this time sixty scholars and eight teachers. The missionary collection was especially important.

How shall we speak of our missionary collection? (wrote Schmucker to Adam Miller on April 28, 1841). Truly the days of old seemed to have returned when Israel's daughters so freely gave forth their ornaments for the beautifying of the Lord's tabernacle. In addition to $46.87½ in money, various articles of jewelry were brought into the treasury of God. The donors testifying both by word and deed, that since they had found through grace that priceless jewel of their souls, they had no longer any use or desire for the tinsel adorning of such outward show.[17]

One member gave three gold finger rings; his wife three gold breast pins. Another brother, in addition to a gold breast pin and finger ring, gave a *trombone* worth $25.

On August 23, 1841, Schmucker reported forty-five full members; forty-eight on probation; "laid aside for neglect of duty," ten; removed, six; and "two died happy in the Lord." Under his guidance a tract

3

society was formed and received of the American Tract Society forty thousand pages of tract, toward the payment for which the Church contributed generously.

Despite the fact that economic conditions were playing havoc with missionary collections, making them only a third of what they had been in the previous year, the English brethren did not let the mission work among the Germans suffer. On the contrary they expanded work. In 1841 six new missions were established which carried the work south, west, and east.

In 1840 three brothers, converted Methodists, moved from Cincinnati to New Orleans. From the Southern city they wrote entreating letters to Peter Schmucker, their former pastor, to come and help them found a society. In the spring of 1842 Schmucker, at the direction of Bishop Roberts, made the trip south to see what could be done in the field. He organized a class, appointed a class leader, and when the work rapidly expanded entrusted the work to Karl Bremer, who had been converted in Germany and licensed as a local preacher in America. Schmucker himself returned north because the division over slavery was becoming intense and he would not remain in a Church which tolerated slavery.

> Since the departure of Brother Schmucker [Bremer wrote to Nast under date of October 9, 1842] we have kept our meetings up—for some time past. I have generally exhorted the people from the Word of God, four times a week, as far as the Divine Being gave me grace and ability.[18]

Nast, in the meantime, had been to the Atlantic seaboard. On March 12, 1841, the *Apologist* printed this item of news:

> With this number the editor takes leave of absence from his readers to make a trip East.

He was taking one of his combination tours as circulation agent and mission builder. A group of New York Germans had been converted while attending an English-speaking Methodist meeting and were concerned to do something for their fellow countrymen. Among the group was *Anton Tiemann,* whose son Daniel later became mayor of New York. When Nast heard that this little group was meeting in a part of the English-speaking Church on Elizabeth Street, he decided to make the trip to the metropolis to see if something could be done for the "countless Germans" settling in the great cities of the Atlantic Coast. Ludwig Jacoby, who substituted for Nast in the editorial chair of the *Apologist,* published the item on May 14, 1841, to the effect that Nast

> is so very busy it has not yet been possible for him to make a report of his trip in the *Apologist.* He has many subscribers for the *Apologist* and is now busy with everything for the preparation for a German mission. The field is ripe for harvest and the Lord will also send workers here into his field.

Nast was indeed very busy. Addressing the New York Conference on the need for a German work among the immigrants, so in need of spiritual ministry, he brought the body to the point where it voted to found a German mission in New York. He preached to well-attended congregations during the spring days and persistently solicited subscriptions. Taking the occasion of Bishop Soule's endorsement of the mission work before the annual session, he proceeded to sell to the members and friends of the Conference the *Apologist,* to be paid for by them and distributed gratis to the Germans.

The Philadelphia Conference was being held at the time and Nast hastened to go before it, reporting on the mission work and peddling his wares. His effectiveness was matched by his resourcefulness. Atheists as well as the faithful turned out to hear this heavy-tongued and curious Methodist from the West. On one occasion a "Rationalist" announced at the close of a sermon that he would refute what Nast had said. The congregation listened quietly and then joined with Nast in prayers for the conversion of the gentleman; after which Nast announced that on the next Sunday he would "defend the works of God." Scarcely had Nast begun to preach a week later when a bellowing broke out from a group of intoxicated men. Nast was not discomfited. He merely commented that all "Rationalists" were not always witnesses for "reason."

With a considerable interest developed, Nast looked around for a leader for the work. He called to New York a preacher from the West named Nathanael Callender, who understood some German, but was serving an English-speaking congregation. Callender's command of German quickly proved too scanty and he was succeeded by *Charles H. Döring.* Döring, born in a small town near the city of Hanover, had received the customary religious instruction of the State Church. Though he seemed inclined toward the ministry, he drifted into business and during ten years in Bremen and Göttingen dropped his religious observances entirely. The reports of the New World which were in circulation in Bremen encouraged him to study English. Though his mother would not give her consent for his emigration, he bought his ship ticket and in 1836 arrived in Baltimore after a fifty-one day voyage. He was fortunate in obtaining employment in a dry goods store operated by a Methodist. He boarded with the family and was invited to take part in the family devotions. Of his first impression of family worship, he wrote:

> He read, sang, and then kneeled down for prayer. This was all new to me. I never before had witnessed a family worship. Their kneeling down was against my feelings. I hesitated a few moments, not knowing what to do, whether to kneel down with them or not, but reflecting it could do no harm, I kneeled down and continued to do so afterward.[19]

Döring began to visit English-speaking Methodist Churches for the purpose of improving his command of English. "He caught the spirit" and wrote to Nast his intention of entering work in the "vineyard of the Lord." He went on to Allegheny College, where he was repeatedly begged by Nast to enter active work to fill the posts opening so rapidly by the spread of the mission work. He refused and finished his course, during the last year of which he preached to a large and attentive German congregation in Meadville, was licensed an exhorter in 1840, and received on trial by the Pittsburg Conference in 1841. He was immediately transferred to the work in New York. Within six months he had a mission group of fifty-seven. After sixteen months in the metropolis, he was transferred to the Pittsburgh mission. *Johann Christian Lyon,* who had been sent to New York as his assistant, succeeded him. Lyon was an experienced pastor. A tireless missionary, he was a magnetic preacher. In English or German he could hold congregations in his evangelical spell. His leadership brought about the building of the first German Methodist Episcopal Church in New York.

The work in the East developed rapidly from this point. Adam Miller came on to develop the work in Baltimore and to explore the field in Philadelphia. Other leaders began to work in New Jersey at Rahway and Newark. They pressed up the Hudson to Poughkeepsie, Albany, and Schenectady and spread west to Buffalo. By 1849 the work in the East had to be organized into a German District of the New York Conference. Lyon was appointed the first presiding elder. He went to Boston in 1852 to appeal for the establishment of the work in the New England metropolis. A congregation was founded at Roxbury and another at Caneadea. In the meantime *J. W. Freund,* entering on his work in 1854, was preaching through New Haven, Meriden, and Hartford, Connecticut, and proving himself to be a capable evangelist.

What was taking place in the East as a result of Nast's visit to New York was taking place in the West with the arrival of *Ludwig Sigismund Jacoby* in St. Louis. Jacoby had been born in *Alt-Strelitz,* Mecklenburg, in 1813 as the fifth of six children of a pious Jewish family. He had regularly attended the synagogue in Germany with his grandfather and repeated regularly the Jewish evening prayer, "Into thy hand, O God, I commit my spirit, whether I wake or sleep." At the age of fifteen he began a six-year apprenticeship with a Hamburg merchant. He then became a traveling salesman, with headquarters in Leipzig, where he was converted to Christianity and baptized in the Lutheran Church. In 1838 he visited relatives on business in England and continued on to America. In 1839 he was in Cincinnati teaching German and industriously at work on a brief German grammar which was successfully published. It was at this time he became acquainted with the German Methodists. He wrote:

> Of a German Methodist Church I had never heard. One evening, however, a young man, to whom I gave instruction in Eng-

lish, asked me if I would not go with him to the German Methodist Church Sabbath evening, as it was a real theater—a place
of much amusement.[20]

He went and went again for the purpose of making fun of Nast's
preaching—

Satan [he said] suggested to me that I should look right
earnestly at him to see if I could not make him laugh. I did so
and instead of making him laugh, became myself an attentive
hearer.[21]

During the course of his sermon, Nast said: "There may be a
Saul among us, whom God will convert into a Paul." Jacoby attended
prayer meeting the next Thursday evening, but, he wrote, "my knees
refused to bend until one of the brethren prayed that God would grant
that sinners might bend their stubborn knees before it should be too
late." On the next day he was invited to Nast's home where they
prayed together, and Nast loaned him *Fletcher's Appeal*. On the Monday night before Christmas, 1839, he joined the Church. At watch-
night service he experienced his "transformation," was licensed to
exhort, and began to preach along the canal in Cincinnati—without
results.

Ten days after his conversion Jacoby wrote in the *Apologist:*

My German Brothers:

To those who look down with such disdain upon the Methodists,
I should like to give a short explanation of what the Methodists
believe and want.

Methodists are the kind of Christians who have come to such
an insight through the grace of God that they make no demands
upon God through their own righteousness, but are so created
that in their natural condition they are able to do only evil and
nothing good. They believe, therefore, that no one but Jesus
Christ can bring them to the Heavenly Father; but they see at
the same time that if they want to receive the forgiveness of their
sins through Jesus Christ, they must take their cross upon themselves and follow him. How does this begin? They search God's
Word and there it is written: "No man can serve two masters."
If one will therefore remain a man of the world and follow the
lusts of the flesh, he cannot follow Christ. He must avoid the
evil world and his whole searching must be to become like Christ.

To keep him in the way, God has ordained means of grace to
be used. In the prayer and class hours he hears from his brothers
and sisters, how God has been so gracious to them, and how
otherwise it goes with their spiritual life. He listens to the
exhortations of the class leaders, and tells himself how far his
salvation has been revealed to him. Further, at the beginning
and close of the meeting earnest prayer for the strengthening
of the faith is made. All this can only serve to teach the seeker
of salvation how great God's goodness is and what Jesus can do
in the hearts of men.

My only wish is that all my German fellow countrymen could

see the joy which prevails in such meetings and if their hearts are not of stone, they certainly could not resist the spirit of God.

Now is such a man to be despised? If you are reasonable men, you will say: "No, he is worthy of our attention." And such a man is a true Methodist. I am often asked why the Methodists try to hold aloof from all worldly society. To that I can only answer with the first Psalm of David.[22]

A common faith and religious experience brought Jacoby into association in Cincinnati with Amalie Theresa Nuelsen, who had come to America in 1839 with two of her brothers. The story of her conversion can best be told in her own words:

> On my first Sunday morning in Cincinnati my brother introduced me to a neighbor who was to take me to the Catholic Church. In the evening I accompanied him to the Methodist Church. Brother Schmucker was preaching· on a text from John 3. 5—I had never heard such a sermon before. I was deeply moved and a fear came over me that I might die without being ready for death. The effect of the sermon was lost in subsequent days as I went around with my friends. From them I heard many special stories of the Methodists and how they were misleading people. I developed a fear of their classes and prayer meetings. A little while later I visited a camp meeting where my unconverted heart was laid bare. Such anxiety and sorrow overcame me that I should fall from the faith in which I was brought up.
>
> Before I left the Fatherland our priest had told me when I was uneasy to go to a priest in whom I had confidence. . . . So I decided one Sunday morning to go to confession. . . . Scarcely had I completed the customary introduction, when the priest asked me a shameless question.[23]

After some debate over the justification for the impertinence, the priest inquired whether Miss Nuelsen had eaten meat on Friday. When she admitted that she had, he asked if she was not conscious of the sin she had committed. She replied, in a vocabulary which she had acquired from her brother, that the Holy Scriptures taught that "God's grace should be enjoyed with thanksgiving." The priest's answer was that such abstinence was a commandment of the Church. To this observation, the young woman insisted that the Church commanded many things and offered to do many things which were not in harmony with the Holy Scriptures.

The continuation of the confessional conversation between the Father Confessor and the immigrant girl was astonishingly frank. The priest was skeptical as to whether Miss Nuelsen was actually a Catholic. The outcome of their "discussion" was his refusal to grant her "absolution." She replied that she intended to take the Lord's Supper when she wished, and that if he would not give her absolution she would go to another German Church. The threat was successful and she was granted the privilege of going to the sacrament upon the condition of coming to confession on three successive Sundays. She hesitated and replied that she was in the habit of going to confession only when she felt the need of doing so. The priest, despite her own impertinence, gave her the sacrament. In an excited condition and with an unwilling heart she partook.

But that was not the end of the story. She went to her room and cried the whole afternoon, because she had gone to the Lord's table with an unchristian attitude of humility. She prayed that God would forgive her great sin. From that time her appreciation of the Catholic Church grew less and less and she attended more and more only out of respect for the wishes of her parents.

At this time she went to live in the Nast family, where she found a "peace for which she had been seeking." The serenity of the family circle, the sincerity of the family prayers, which she did not fully appreciate, the Nast children—all these things combined to give her thoughts a new direction. Though she was considered a member of a Protestant household, she observed all the Catholic holidays. For a year she rebelled against becoming a Protestant. Her heart was torn by inner conflict between two allegiances. The conflict was resolved while she was listening to Peter Schmucker preach at a camp meeting. Tears of joy streamed down her cheeks as she experienced the "grace of God" and looked toward "Golgotha." On the same evening she joined the Methodist Church, and soon after, in September, 1840, was married to Jacoby by Schmucker.

By the ceremony a Jewish family was joined with a Catholic family through the free grace of God and their common faith was given expression through the instrumentality of the Methodist Episcopal Church. Protestantism meant something to both Jacoby and his wife. They had embraced it of their own discovery and against their family traditions. Christ's sacrifice had given them both a confidence in the dignity, the freedom, and the responsibilities of Christian life. The experience of God's free grace had given them both a religious certainty which neither could ever doubt.

Their first appointment was West, to Missouri. On August 1, 1841, Jacoby, his wife and five-weeks'-old daughter arrived by steamboat in St. Louis. The conventional morals of the large and active German population were as repugnant to the Methodist ideals as they had been in the Ohio Valley. The immigrants spent Sunday "in dancing and card playing" and had little to do with what meager religious programs were in the Mississippi Valley. The Jacobys, however, rented two humble rooms. Within two days after he disembarked from the river boat, Jacoby was on the street distributing tracts with the assistance of a sexton of an English-speaking church. He promptly rented the use of a part of a Presbyterian Church, located at Seventh and Biddle Streets. On Sunday morning Preacher and Mrs. Jacoby went to their "church." The wife was not particularly encouraging.

"You can preach today, my dear man," she said to him, "to me and the empty pews." Her husband replied laconically, "We'll see."

Going to the belfry, he pulled the rope so long and so violently that the church was soon filled. Among the curious members of the congregation was a devout Catholic and his wife, who exclaimed after the service: "This man is no atheist, but a converted preacher. To men of this type alone can the Church be trusted."

His preaching place was filled the next Sunday by the recommendations which this Catholic and his wife spread abroad to the inhabitants of St. Louis. But the congregation was not substantially composed of religiously inclined individuals. Many came to laugh, mock, and break up the meeting. When they were unsuccessful in so doing inside the edifice, they went outside and hurled stones through the front and back doors. They shot off pistols outside the windows. On one occasion they smeared the whole stair landing with cow manure, and on another evening covered all the stairs with tar and pitch which stuck to the soles of the shoes of the congregation so that when they came from the church their feet made a sticking, cracking noise which caused the gangs of hoodlums, congregated for the sight, to laugh.

And still Jacoby was not visibly discouraged. He extended his preaching to the market house, to assorted congregations. The German press warned him in no uncertain language against the continuation of this program. His reply was to climb back on the butcher's block, give a short prayer, and preach.

Hardly had he begun his sermon on the Sunday after the press had promulgated the one-man warning, than a storm of abuse from the ruffians broke loose. The mob swore, mocked, and hollered: "Beat the fellow dead! Break his bones!" They rushed him from the block, knocked off his glasses, and were threatening to kill him when a "Yankee" braved the mob, raised the question of Jacoby's personal liberty, and drove back the gang bully with a punch in the nose. He then wrapped the frail preacher in his coat and took him to the home of an English Methodist. Jacoby's companion, a preacher named Christopher Bonn, a young lathe-turner who had come to America from Kurhessia in 1842 and been converted in St. Louis, was meanwhile pulled into the hands of the mob and was being carried off to the city prison when an acquaintance recognized him and exclaimed:

"Hello, Doctor, what in the world is going on?"

Bonn announced quietly, "These people want to take me to jail."

"What crime has this man committed that he is being imprisoned?" the friend asked the mob.

"He has been holding Methodist meetings in the market, and such a man needs to be complained of," the crowd roared.

Bonn assured them that no court process could be executed on Sunday. He went surety to the mob for the preacher's appearance at court on Monday. The tables, in the meantime, were turned. Bonn was released, the leaders were arrested and fined from $50 to $200. The disturbances ended with this incident, as far as mob violence was concerned, but continued in the form of individual attacks and ridicule. On another occasion the Jacobys were attending prayer meeting. When they returned and went to the nursery room where their daughter was sleeping, they found the cradle room stoned, the window broken, and a rock actually in the cradle.

Despite such evidence of hostility, Jacoby's efforts in St. Louis were producing a society. A year after his arrival, on August 7, 1842, he dedicated the church which had been produced by his missionary activity. At the close of the second Conference year his society had a hundred members. When the church was dedicated, the hoodlums burned brandy on the cornerstone and placed a jug full of liquor on the spot. Jacoby answered the next winter by leading one of the men who had participated in the insult to Christ.

Jacoby's fertile mind and restless ambition drove him to push out the work. He founded the first day school in St. Louis and installed Heinrich Nuelsen as its first teacher. He began to work in South St. Louis, and to preach in the home of Philip Barth, who had come to St. Louis as colporteur of the American Tract Society.

Work among the Germans in Missouri and Illinois expanded rapidly. By 1845, eleven German circuit riders were covering the territory now included in the states of Missouri, Illinois, and Iowa, which regions in the same year were organized into a German-speaking district. Jacoby was made the first presiding elder of the district. As an example of his work, Jacoby wrote in his journal:

> We got up at five. I took Brother Haas's horse, because mine was still lame. At quarter before seven we were on our way. I rode through a burning prairie. . . . Also I came through a forest which a few days before had been burnt over by fire. About five, I came to Iowa City. The Iowa River is so low I forded it without difficulty. At the first cabin I inquired how to get to Br. Pl. He was not home. I went to Br. Dr. C., where I will remain overnight. I have a terrible headache and fever.[24]

The influence of such missionary circuit riders in actually "bringing religion" West to the German settlers can only be appreciated by seeing what happened to family life when the "grace of God" became a reality through the instrumentality of the Methodists. What took place in the case of the family of *August Fallgatter* happened again and again, multiplying the effectiveness of the work. August Fallgatter had left his native Saxony as a young college student in the 1840's. Philosophically congenial to the atheistic attitude which was the fashion of the time in Germany, he settled at Watertown, Wisconsin, and soon married a young Catholic whose people had migrated to the United States from Alsace at the close of the Napoleonic wars. About 1860 Fallgatter, his wife, and six children joined the westward procession to northeastern Iowa, where he purchased land for $1.25 an acre, which in the late 1890's sold for $100 an acre. He immediately began to improve the land and built log barns. The house was made of lumber hauled eighty miles overland by ox team from North McGregor on the Mississippi River.

The Fallgatters were the advance guard of a little community which developed. Threatened by an Indian uprising, the settlers appointed Fallgatter to direct the defense because he had had military training in Germany. The industry and commonsense of the family was evidenced by the way in which the human as well as the physical environment was brought under control. The farm, employing mostly German labor, produced with encouraging abundance. Beer was brewed upon the place, and the farmers drank it as freely as water. Three of Fallgatter's sons married into Protestant families and became leaders in Christian activities. One son became a minister. A daughter, educated in a Catholic convent, was later converted in a Methodist Church in Iowa. How the Methodist moral standards affected family life is indicated by the agreement which Miss Fallgatter made with her fiance that no alcoholic beverages should ever be in their home. She became one of the first White Ribboners in the section, and the older children of the family became active members of the Independent Order of Good Templars.

When August Fallgatter was an old man he boasted that he owned more land than anyone else in Howard County and had twenty-five grandchildren. Two of his sons were operators of a chain of grain elevators through the northwest Iowa and South Dakota areas. The grandchildren made a splendid showing in the fields of education, religion, business, agriculture, and home life. A granddaughter, Clella, whose mother had died when she was thirteen, went to the mission field in China in 1912 under the auspices of The Woman's Foreign Missionary Society, married a Methodist minister, Fred R. Brown, and together they served many happy years in the Orient.

The Fallgatter tradition of enterprising, hard-working, independent, and thrifty character softened by the Methodist influence into the solid foundations of the American way, was repeated thousands of times in the history of German Methodism.

The missionary work had now become so extensive that its history can only be recorded by instances of how the work was carried West. Schmucker had led Philip and Sebastian Barth to conversion in Louisville. They had gone West to St. Louis as representatives of the American Tract Society. As already mentioned, Philip Barth had built up a little group to which Jacoby preached in the Barth home. Sebastian Barth had taken out an exhorter's license and was preaching through Missouri and Illinois, and selling German Bibles and tracts. In the course of his travels he had visited several times the German settlements on the Herman Circuit and had pushed as far West as

Jefferson City. Jacoby singled him out as a promising traveling preacher, and in 1843 succeeded in persuading him to ride the Versailles Mission Circuit, which included seven counties and stretched from Lexington to the mouth of the Osage River. During the first year he stopped at fifteen preaching places on his rounds, which covered three hundred miles, over a period of three weeks. "Often," he wrote in his journal, "I mount my horse in the evening and ride the whole night, because the huge prairie fires do not plague the animal as much as by day."

In 1844 Nuelsen was assigned to Barth as an assistant. He borrowed $100 from his widowed mother at ten per cent interest, bought a horse, saddle, and necessary clothing, and on a salary of $75 a year went off into the forests to preach. By 1845 a second German district had to be organized. It was called the "Quincy District," and Jacoby was assigned to it as presiding elder. Köneke took his place as presiding elder of the St. Louis District.

The German-speaking work was developing as effectively in other directions. The two-year pastoral time limit necessitated constant shifting of preachers, but the brief periods of leadership were sometimes beneficial. Men, like the times, were restless. Upon each new appointment the missionaries attacked their fields with new zeal.

In 1843, John Lyon could write of the New York Mission:

> In the midst of a population of from fifty to sixty thousand native Germans, composed of the most heterogeneous mass of depravity, we have raised the standard of the cross, and nearly two hundred souls have fled for refuge to the hope set before them.[25]

Riemenschneider, sent to the mission established by the North Ohio Conference in 1841, was rejoicing:

> I have twelve regular appointments, and am about taking up several more. I travel around in my circuit every three weeks, which is upward of three hundred miles in circumference. I have now in this mission thirty-eight members and the most flattering prospects for the future. I also feel more encouraged to labor in the vineyard of the Lord than ever.[56]

By 1843 the Church could no longer doubt the future of the German missionary program. A line of missionaries from the shores of Lake Erie to New Orleans, including most of the principal cities along the Western water courses, from New York and Baltimore west to Iowa and Jefferson Cities, had been developed. Twelve houses of worship had been built. About twenty-five missionaries were employed. The society at Louisville had already been erased from the mission list, as the Germans there had begun to support their own pastor. Jacoby wrote in this year:

> The prejudices of our German countrymen are giving way more and more; they begin to discover that we only intend to

explain to them the words of life, and to point them to the
Saviour. It is true, many are pained at our prosperity; however, the greater part of them are only such as lose their tem-
poral gain through the conversion of their fellow men. In the
front ranks of these, are the Catholic priest and whisky seller,
and, notwithstanding their effort in every possible way, by
slander and mockings to impede the progress of this work, they
cannot retard it. Four of our societies are now engaged in building meetinghouses. *The Christian Apologist* is daily getting
new subscribers, and the editor is now sent by our English
brethren here, to the principal cities in the East, in order to ac-
quaint the Germans there with our paper, and to enter into closer
communion with Germany. German books for religious instruction and encouragement are being published and everything possible is done to extend the work.[21]

Methodism was achieving its advances among the Germans because
of the determined devotion of its preachers and their wives. When in
1849 H. C. Dreyer was sent from Versailles, Missouri, to Chicago,
his wife made this entry in her journal:

After our few belongings were packed at Versailles, we began
our difficult journey. Part of the way our goods were trans-
ported on ox wagon. We sailed on the river to St. Louis; from
there on the Mississippi and then further, it began to get dark.
My husband walked into the city to find lodging while I sat with
the sick child on the trunk. My husband did not return. The
howling wind penetrated my whole body, while my heart was
almost discouraged. He, however, could not find any rooms in
the big city. A brother gave us one of his two rooms until my
husband could build a parsonage. Lake Street was covered with
planks. We could have neither wells nor cisterns. We bought
water for six cents a barrel. Drinking water was very bad;
cholera claimed many victims. Our oldest boy died also. Yet
we are not discouraged if only souls can be saved.

The part which was played in American history by the Methodist
circuit rider was an important one. Keeping pace, as he did, with
the westward movement of the frontiers, he shared all the hardships
of the life of the frontiersman with the single purpose of giving a
moral balance to the hectic social moves of new and migrating communities. Theodore Roosevelt, calling attention to the debt of gratitude
America owes to the Methodist circuit rider and pioneer preacher,
wrote that the Methodist purpose was to see that the pioneer's "pressing material cares and the hard and grinding poverty of his life did
not wholly extinguish the divine fire within his soul." Reminding
men of their responsibility to God and the necessity of "God's grace"
for the forgiveness of their sins, the Methodists did their part in
leavening the unsettled and often demoralizing life on the westward-
moving frontiers of American development.

CHAPTER V

THE CHRISTIAN APOLOGIST GIVES GERMAN METHODISM A VOICE

The proposal for a German language press was openly propagandistic. Exactly three years after Nast went to Cincinnati as missionary he returned in 1839 as editor. The membership of German-speaking Methodism neither justified nor necessitated such a journalistic venture. It was scarcely fifty at the time. Methodism was willing, however, to attempt the publication of a printed agent of evangelical Protestantism among the immigrants. If on the one hand it was an advertising medium for the propagation of Methodist theology, on the other it became polemic and defended the fundamental principles of evangelical Protestantism and Puritan morals with a conviction which did not weaken for an entire century.

"As reasons for publishing a German Methodist periodical," Nast said at the close of the Conference year, 1837:

> I would only mention, that the Roman Catholics publish at present a German religious paper at Cincinnati, and that nearly all the political papers in the German language are filled with invectives against Christianity.[1]

Pointing out that a few religious books were appearing in "miserable" translations, Nast argued:

> If private individuals undertake it for the sake of making money, how could the church run any risk in doing it with an eye single to the glory of God, assisted by the patronage of perhaps a thousand German members within her pale, and by the agency of her itinerant preachers throughout the Union? The spirited support of the traveling connection, in spreading either the paper or the other publications, would of course be indispensable to our success. And I hope that if we would only attempt the work, we would meet with more support than we imagine.[2]

Nast was right. That there was a growing demand for such publications and a periodical in particular to represent the interests of the Protestants became increasingly evident. Hardly had Nast returned from Conference when he received a letter from J. B. Anthony, a clergyman living in South Carolina. Anthony wrote:

> When I saw your report in the *Advocate* last summer, respecting your wish to publish some of our works in the German language or to publish a German Methodist paper, I determined (though a poor Methodist traveling preacher) to give something for that purpose, if the work went on. I immediately made in-

quiry of two other brethren of this Conference who speak the German language, and we agreed to give *ten dollars each,* to be disposed of as the publishers might think best. If, therefore, you, as another brother, should undertake to publish a German Methodist paper, we will give $30. If all our traveling brethren that speak the German language would volunteer to be German missionaries, we would, with the blessing of God, soon form German circuits.[3]

The 1837 session of the Ohio Conference, already impressed with the suggestion of Nast concerning language publications, appointed a committee of three to take the matter under consideration and to make a report. The committee recommended that it was not expedient to enter extensively into German publication at the time. As a compromise it recommended the publication of the three numbers of the *Wesleyan Catchism,* the *Articles of Faith,* and the *General Rules.* These publications soon came from the press, but their appearance did not stifle the agitation for the language periodical. Sentiment for the journal grew. The compromise of the committee report only served to encourage the demand. In February a letter was printed in *The Western Christian Advocate* from Thomas Dunn, a member of the North Ohio Conference, setting forth a proposition for the support of the paper.

Waynesburg, Ohio, February 15, 1838.

I wish to remark, that there are a number of German families within the bounds of this circuit. Some individuals among them have embraced religion and joined our church. While looking over the fields already ripe for harvest among this numerous and interesting people, and reading some things in the *Advocate* on the subject, I have most ardently desired that some plan might be adopted to instruct them in the doctrines and *Discipline* of the Methodist Episcopal Church. The commencement of this work, I believe, should be by publishing a *German Christian Advocate,* in connection with our establishment at Cincinnati. It is well known that the Germans are scattered throughout our work in every direction. Such a paper, freighted with gospel truth—could be thrown among them—and the simple fact of its coming to them in their own language, would induce them to read. Their minds would thereby be enlightened, their prejudices removed, and as many of them as cannot read English, would learn to understand it so as to be edified under our ministry. They would come out to hear us preach, and would gather into the church. Further, I am confident I could get a number of subscribers to such a paper in the bounds of this circuit. I will not lengthen out my broken remarks on this subject, but propose to be one of three hundred who will donate $10 each, to aid in commencing such an enterprise. Who will respond, or rather, who will not?

T. Dunn.[4]

The awakening to the need for the paper spread. That its cost had to be underwritten by the English-speaking Church was a fact accepted on all sides. The aid was promptly volunteered. It was quite as much accepted that the paper should be a propaganda sheet for the Methodists and that it should be the Christianizing agent among the language group.

The proposal of Dunn found a warm response from Adam Miller, who hastened to volunteer his contribution and take the opportunity to give his reasons for such enthusiastic support. He wrote:

> First, it is a thing much to be desired by us, as a church, that all who live among us and mingle in our society, should have a knowledge of our doctrines and disciplinary usages, and of these, by far the greater part of the German population of this country are entirely ignorant; for what information they have about us is principally from those who are our opposers, and who most shamefully misrepresent us; consequently the thousands of our German neighbors know as little about the doctrines of the Methodist Episcopal Church as many of the untaught tribes of the forest. And when we consider the great number of Germans now filling up our cities and country (if the tide of German immigration should continue in regular ratio, for a few years to come as it has for a few years past in many places, one third, if not more of the population will be Germans; if I am correctly informed, it is about that now in the city of Cincinnati) it will, from this view, be doubly important to introduce some plan of operation, in which we shall most likely succeed, to diffuse among our neighbors that knowledge which we believe so highly important to man's happiness here, and his welfare hereafter. I would not, however, be understood to say, that the Germans who came to this country are all unenlightened with regard to the all-important doctrines of religion; for many of them are taught to read the Bible from childhood and are taken through a regular course of religious instruction: but I do say, that a great majority of those even who have the name Protestants, are in the dark with regard to the doctrine of salvation from sin, regeneration, the witness of the Spirit, etc., as taught and believed by us. Now, while they, through the German papers circulating through the country, hear us misrepresented, they will stand aloof from us, and our way to do them good will be closed up, in a great degree, while those prejudices are retained against us. . . . Much has been done to enlighten the Indians, the Africans, and indeed almost all heathens in every land. This is as it should be, and much more should be done than has been done. But are not souls in our own vicinity perishing for the lack of knowledge, equally as precious as those at a distance—and does not the future prosperity of our country much depend upon the course we pursue, in reference to the thousands immigrating from other countries? Will not, then, my brethren wake up to this subject? Will the proposition to raise three thousand dollars be met by those who love the prosperity of Zion? While we plead for this, we feel that we are pleading the cause of precious and immortal souls. I can assure you that three thousand dollars are to me an insignificant consideration, when held in competition with a blessed hope of immorality and eternal life. . . .
>
> Yours, in the vineyard of the Lord,
>
> Adam Miller.[5]

The editor of *The Western Christian Advocate* now threw the whole weight of his editorial columns into the cause of German language publications, which by this time had centered on the issuing of a periodical. He opened his columns to Nast who, with a fiery pen, declared that the publication of a *German Christian Advocate* was a project "which will furnish the only antidote against the efforts of wicked and unreasonable men, to quench the last strivings of the Holy Spirit in the hearts of the misguided German immigrants." [6]

The Methodist Mission to the Germans was at a decisive point. Nast knew it. He described the situation in stinging phrases:

> There has been felt a great deal of apprehension and sympathy with regard to the increasing influx of Roman Catholic immigrants; but how much blacker appears the cloud, when we see the majority of *Protestant* German immigrants, miserably captured by clerical pirates, who under the flag of an orthodox Christian church, lay in wait for unwary souls to make them scoffers of salvation, and opposers to God! Who can be more like sheep without a shepherd than the German immigrants? The one part held in the iron grasp of superstition, the other receiving the deadly drought of infidelity, from the hand of those who should administer to them the pure Word of God: both parties operated upon by the unremitting influence of a weekly press, the more fatal, as there is none to contradict—no herald of salvation, no advocate of Bible religion, "no voice of wisdom crying in the streets, in the chief places of concourse," in the opening of the gates: "How long, ye simple ones, will ye love simplicity? and the scorners delight in their scorning, and fools hate knowledge?" Shall then, error alone open its wide mouth, and truth be dumb? If we desire them to be partakers of our holy religion, what means more adapted to the nature of the case and the spirit of the age; what more powerful instrument against false doctrines; what speedier pioneer, to prepare the way of the Lord for traveling preachers, could we use, than the contemplated paper, exhibiting the doctrines and *Discipline* of the Methodist Episcopal Church, by extracts from our standard works? It would make its way through all opposition, to every region of country, and every class of society. The effects which it might have upon the Roman Catholics as well as Protestants, in this country and even upon Germany, are indeed incalculable. I am happy to say that within a few days two German and two English brethren gave me their names, to make part of the three hundred.[7]

Nast took the occasion to cite the progress already made in the German work. Congregations were growing larger each Sabbath. Eighteen had been received into the Church since Conference. The *Articles of Religion,* the *General Rules,* and the *Catechisms* were already being printed in German and their appearance was being awaited with excitement. The Tract Society had authorized him to translate such tracts as he thought best in their appeal to the Germans. The Lord's Supper had been administered to Methodists for the first time in the

German language in Cincinnati. But the moment was serious, he said, unless the Methodists took action. He warned:

> He shall then shortly see these nominal Protestants, who are filled with heathenish frenzy; Presbyterians, Methodists, and Baptists, united with Roman Catholics and Jews, into one great flock in order to build again the great Tower of Babel, if the undertaking does not fail on account of the builder's madness.

As a demonstration of how the publication could be of value in religious polemics, Nast wrote the dialogue between a captain and a parson, respecting the other world:

C. What a pity it is, Mr. Parson, that we know nothing of our state after death. Of what avail is all our knowledge if we remain in the dark upon this point?

P. It must not be dark, though we should not know the certainty of it. But do you think such knowledge would be a benefit to us?

C. How do you mean?

P. You, sir, are now captain.

C. Yes. sir.

P. If I now should tell you, as soon as you open this room and go you will be major, what would you do?

C. The answer is plain—I would go in.

P. And if the man knew that he would pass, immediately after death, into a better state of existence, what do you think would he do if he met with any trouble or vexation?

C. Um! In all probability, he would blow out his brains.

P. I think so, too; by far the greater part of mankind would leave their stations before their time. Judge then, what dangerous gift God would have bestowed, if he had given us a certain knowledge upon this subject. He would have destroyed his own work.

C. This is true. I will therefore not be major before the time.

That was a demonstration of the kind of argument which Nast would like to disseminate.

The editor of *The Pittsburgh Conference Journal* joined the growing chorus of approval of the project and proposed Nast, "a man of more than ordinary literary acquirements, and withal a native German," as the right man for the editorship and Cincinnati as the "very place for a German paper." *The Pittsburgh Journal* volunteered itself as a clearing house for contributions at $10 a subscription in raising the $3,000 necessary for the venture.

The movement for the raising of the $3,000 by the $10 contributions from three hundred individuals began as an enthusiastic demonstration of support. The columns of *The Western Christian Advocate* were effective. "I wish I could contribute three hundred times $10; you should have my name for the whole amount called for," wrote J. K. Miller, from the Pittsburgh Conference. "I am ready with my $10 as soon as you say 'Send it on,' &c." J. B. Finley added his voice with a contribution, declaring: "There ought to be no neutrals. . . . It is our duty to send help. Let me say, through you to the Western world, that we have, in the providence of God, foreigners thrown among us—many German foreigners—who are to be our future neighbors, and to marry with our children, and to take hold on the helm of government, and to bear a part in the steering of our political ship."

Letters from Germans began to come into the *Western* office. These were translated by Nast and duly published. "I have resided about eighteen months in the United States," wrote one immigrant.

> My native country is the kingdom of Hanover. Why I was induced to leave my Fatherland, a loving mother and affectionate friends, and go to a strange land, I begin now to understand. I see in it the finger of God. It was his inscrutable providence which inspired me. . . . The infinite grace of our Lord opened my eyes, under the preaching of the Methodist ministers, to see the bottomless abyss, at the edge of which I unconsciously stood; and this mercy pointed out the way and the means by which I should escape the wrath to come—faith in the Lamb. To the intended *German Christian Advocate,* I wish all success, and I will cheerfully contribute to it—according to my ability.

The letter was signed by the name subsequently to become well-known, C. H. Doering. "I make haste to send you my name, and $10 subscription," wrote A. W. Elliott. "I feel an indescribable joy at this movement." "It was a happy thought," proclaimed *The Christian Advocate and Journal.* "Germany MUST have the advantage of the Methodist doctrine, and she WILL have them before long, God favoring the attempt," wrote the editor of the *Western.* From Washington, Mississippi, B. M. Drake wrote:

> I have only seen a few brethren since the proposition came under my notice, and with a very little effort, I send you nine names, subscribers of ten dollars each, to meet the proposition of Brother Dunn. I am at a loss to know how to send you the money, as our currency would be of little use to you. So as soon as the paper is commenced, you may consider me as responsible for the whole, and call on me by draft or otherwise. . . . To the Germans we owe much. But for the zeal and intrepidity of Luther, and his associates, we might all have been the slaves of Rome to this day. The idea of having our standard theology circulated in the heart of Germany is a bright vision to me. What may not God work by its means?[8]

Despite the enthusiasm the first six months of the campaign resulted in the pledging of only $1,500. The slowness of the drive prompted William Simmons, from Zanesville, to scold in the columns of the *Western:*

> Brethren, I call on you in the name of God, whose stewards you are, not to close your eyes this night until you bow before your Maker, and pray for the Germans, and about this paper, for twenty-five minutes; then I shall know what you will do. God

knows, and you know that you have been making money rapidly for a few years. Just think of it for one minute—from four to six dollars per hundred for pork and beef, and everything in proportion. You have built houses and barns, and bought more farms at from ten to forty dollars per acre, and will you not pay ten dollars? Your Heavenly Father can take it off your doctor's bill, or add it to the price of a horse; but you are not actuated by motives so sordid. You willingly pay five or six dollars for a bushel of clover seed. Why? Because you expect thirty, sixty, or a hundredfold. Give, O give your ten dollars to start the *German Christian Advocate,* in Cincinnati; then look at the increase, through time; then cross over the Jordan and behold the golden harvest.[9]

"Can we do unto others as we would they should do unto us, and not solicit our German neighbors to take the *Apologist?*" wrote James Boyd Austin, from Pickaway County, Ohio. "I have presented the prospectus to a number of Germans, and have succeeded in obtaining four subscribers. . . . May heaven bless and help the enterprise, and save the Germans of North America and of the world."

As the fund grew and the dream of a *German Advocate* came within reach, the question began to be raised as to whether the publishing agent at Cincinnati had the right to commence publication without the authority of the General Conference. To decide the issue the Book Committee at Cincinnati sent J. F. Wright to New York to attend the meeting of the Board of Bishops. The board unanimously recommended the commencement of the publication, provided that it could be brought out without loss to the Methodist Book Concern. Although the underwriting of the printing costs had not been completed, a prospectus was promptly prepared and active solicitation for subscribers began. At the same time a committee was appointed to prepare an address to the members and ministers of the Methodist Episcopal Church. This was a lengthy document, designed to complete the solicitation of funds. "No human mind," it began, "can invent weightier or purer motives to benevolent action, than those which have pressed a number of Christian philanthropists into the service of this *Christian Apologist.*" Referring to the proposed journal as our German "missionary bishop," the address declared:

It is to travel over the whole land, to teach and warn, and by the blessing of God, to convert and build up. It is to visit several thousand families weekly, and discourse to men, women, and children—to good and bad, pious and profane, on the subjects of sin—death—and the judgment; and above all, to tell about Jesus, the new birth, sanctification, and the felicity and glory of the saved.[10]

The address described the influx of Germans in bold terms:

You may say of them as the Romans said of the early Christians, "Every place is full of them." We deem it safe to assume, that there are more Germans in the Mississippi Valley than there are Indians beyond the Rocky Mountains. . . . Now, bethink you with what zeal the Church is commissioning the messengers to pass over the deserts and scale the mountains of the remote West, to reach some eighty thousand Indians who know not God. . . . Immigration from Europe, and especially from Germany, ceases not, but increases constantly. Floods of life, and mind and moral energy, are setting in upon us. . . . We can scarcely expect, judging from past and present, that the Indians in successive generations are to form a part of the militant Church. Not so with the Germans. Their conversion may be desired not only for themselves, but for Zion's sake in all climes and ages. There is strength in German character, which must inevitably give it influence. Their mental aptitudes—their habits of secular diligence and carefulness, should enlist concern as well as partial admiration. . . . Let them become a leaven of malice, and unless saved by Omnipotence, the Church and nation are undone. Let them become a leaven of holiness, then liberty, and science, and heaven-born religion, may concert their holy and everlasting jubilee. Germany is sparing us more elements of moral good or evil, than any other nation of any continent can furnish us, whether it be for peace or war. What shall we render for such kindness?

The address was designed to raise the $600 still necessary to complete the underwriting fund. In the meantime, at the fall Conference in 1838, Nast had been appointed editor of the new publication and the publishing agent at Cincinnati was at work on the plans for printing and distributing it. While the first number of *Der Christliche Apologete* is dated January 4, 1839, it was actually prepublished for circulation purposes. At the time of the first issue, *there were only fifty German Methodists,* yet the first issue was assured of a hundred subscribers.

During the century which has gone since the *Apologist* was founded, it has never changed its editorial formula. If the first issue was designed as "a defender of evangelical truth, a courageous representative of church interests, and a guide to conversion," the same purpose continued to dominate its program for a hundred years. Throughout its long existence, it has first of all been the *instrument of conversion.* It has secondly been the *proclaimer of the truth of Protestantism,* the herald of theological truth as set forth in Methodist doctrine. In the third place, it has been *the defender* of public and private morals. From the first issue it was outspoken, not against the Roman Catholics as people, but against the theological system of bondage promoted by the Church. It has been untiring in its work for temperance, human freedom, and missions. Consistently written in the purest literary German, second to no other language periodical, it has always been edited with a scholarly skill which never dampened its evangelical passion and has been a medium of "information, education, and entertainment."

Der Christliche Apologete and *Evangelische Zeitung* and *Die Deutschen von Nord Amerika* appeared at Cincinnati on Friday, January 4, 1839. It was a four-page sheet, 17x11 inches, edited by Nast and published by the Methodist Book Concern. It explained that the name *"Apologist"* was really a more pleasing word for the German *"Verteidiger,"* thanked the English-speaking brethren for the $2,400 which they had so generously contributed for the promotion of the periodical, discussed the nature of "Neighborly Love," quoted John Wesley on "Tolerance," discussed the Sunday school, essayed on the "Wrath of God," and then stated in no uncertain language the religious orientation of the journal as follows:

1. The incarnation of Christ as the manifestation of God in the flesh.

2. The satisfaction of the divine law through the death of Christ, who united in his person divinity and humanity, and whose vicarious suffering atones for the guilt of man.

3. The original and wholly depraved nature of the human race and the magnitude of sin in the eyes of God.

If salvation by faith was the theological direction of the *Apologist,* Protestantism was its passion. German Methodists were in principle and practice violently opposed to the religious system represented by the Roman Catholic Church. The position was graphically represented in a typical editorial in the issue of April 26, 1844, under the caption, "Protestantism and Popery."

> Question: What do you call yourself?
> Answer: A Protestant.
>
> Question: What is a Protestant?
> Answer: A person who protests against Popery.
>
> Question: What is Popery?
> Answer: The religion of the Church of Rome, whose members are Roman Catholics or Papists.

The elaboration of the meaning of Protestantism was followed by the statement of nine points of difference from the Roman Catholics, the so-called "nine chief arguments." The editor proceeded with a lengthy polemic to substantiate his position: (1) because the Church of Rome considered the Pope "the sovereign of the Christian Church on earth," calling him "Papa, Pope, Father" while Protestants believed "that Christ alone is the head of his body, the Church, in heaven and on earth"; (2) because the Church of Rome considered it proper in prayer to call upon the Virgin Mary and the saints, "even to bow the knee before crucifixes, paintings, and relics," while the Protestants held the Bible to teach that God commands man "to worship alone God the Father, the Son, and the Holy Ghost," three persons in one God, threatening the "sternest judgments against genuflections or any degree of adoration, of any kind or likeness of him"; (3) because the Church of Rome taught "that its members should have no judgment of their own in religious things" while the Protestant follower of Jesus Christ was "called upon to have his own judgments in the matters of religion and carefully to test whether they shall serve the salvation of the soul, whether that which he believes is founded upon the Word of God, the so-called Bible," which should be in the hands of everybody, and which the Protestants alone hold as the certain guide of faith; (4) because the Church of Rome believed that "poor sinners such as we can perform worthy works in the eyes of the Lord, which can have influence in our justification as also through doing acts of merit for saints" while the Protestants believe that faith in the fact that Jesus Christ died upon the Cross can alone justify man, "good works being the necessary and unpreventable fruit of such belief"; (5) because the Church of Rome had added the sacraments of confirmation, penance, last unction, ordination of priests, and marriage to the only two rites of baptism and the Lord's Supper "established by Christ"; (6) because the Church of Rome taught transubstantiation, which the Protestant held a false theory and the worship of the Hostie a sacrilege; (7) because the Church of Rome believed in the repetition of prayers as a penitence and held public prayers in Latin, a tongue unknown to most of the members of the parish, while the Protestant believed prayer a privilege to be enjoyed in the vernacular; (8) because the Church of Rome believed that the forgiveness of sins, "past, present, and future," lay with the priests, it residing "unconditionally in their power to dispense such forgiveness for money," while the Protestant believed that "God alone in Christ can forgive sins," that a preacher may offer this forgiveness to every sinner who is "truly repentant, has a living faith in Christ and a firm determination to lead a new life"; and (9) because the Church of Rome believed in a "place between heaven and hell, called purgatory, where a cleansing from sin takes place after the soul has left the body through prayer and the reading of masses by a priest paid for the purpose, contrary to the Protestant belief that "after death the departed soul awaits the resurrection of the body in the condition of sin in which it left the world until the day of judgment."

The *Apologist's* position was amply fortified by generous citation of the scriptures. The German Methodist manifesto was strong because the conviction of the subject was so earnest. Theological correctness was a vital issue in the hearts of men who had experienced catastrophic conversion. Any teaching that diluted the power of God's mercy for repentant men and any system that interfered with the manifestation of divine grace "more abundant than man's needs" were unnecessary spiritual hazards thrown in the path of man. The position, in various forms, was repeated and emphasized throughout the whole history of the *Apologist* and German-speaking Methodist Church. The emphasis never reached the level of acrimonious insistence; it was always affirmative of the Methodist theological methodology.

The *Apologist,* like the German Methodists in general, insisted with conviction, if not always with humility, that the "Methodist Church possesses *all* the characteristics of the true Church of Christ." For this position the Germans had a strong theoretical support. It was a Church, to them, strictly founded upon the letter of Holy Scriptures, access to which in his own vernacular was the right and duty of every Christian. Salvation through faith and works issuing from grace, rather than grace from works, was the mechanism of Christianity. And the Christian conscience, fortified by the knowledge of the Bible, was the ultimate guide of the Christian. The *Apologist's* editorial position in relation to the Roman Catholic system was therefore taken on theological grounds. The crusade against the Catholic system by constant criticism and affirmation of the Protestant position gave a doctrinaire position to the paper. This was proudly acknowledged. The fact that the *Apologist* was openly propagandistic and polemic was admitted with enthusiasm by the publishers.

If the genius of the *Apologist* theologically was evangelical Protestantism, its moral standards were strictly Methodist when Methodism meant opposition to worldly pleasures. The intensity of the editorial program against Catholicism was matched in intensity only by the crusade against alcohol. For example, the issue of May 31, 1844, contained a "Contradiction of Grounds for the Defense of the Enjoyment of Brandy." It began by asserting that:

> Many loquacious men who do much for Christianity are of the opinion that they can drink a *"Schnapps"* every day to increase their energy without injuring their religion.

They say:

> I do not believe that the Lord forbids the moderate enjoyment of brandy.

We answer:

> A man cannot use brandy every day without playing traitor to Church and the Word; brandy has ruined many in body and soul. . . . A drinking man shows by his example that he does not consider brandy poison. . . .

> Moderate drinker: In conclusion, I demand of you in the name of the Lord: Put on the yoke of God. Be strong in the Lord and the power of his strength. . . . See yourself as a drunken man. . . . Then go to him and say, Brother, you have drunk too much poison.

The *Apologist* was equally stern in its insistence upon the observance of the Sabbath. From reading the columns of the paper the historian is convinced that the answer to the question so often raised in the

Apologist, "Warum bin ich ein Methodist?" (Why am I a Methodist?), was as much one of practical morals as theological dogma.

German Methodism had hardly begun to grow than it was faced with the acute moral and political problem which was decided only by the Civil War. If the German preachers left no doubt of their position, the *Apologist* in its editorial policy was more circumspect. After the General Conference of 1844, it maintained a significant silence over the division of the Methodist Episcopal Church on the Andrews question. It printed a full factual account of the Andrews incident and then in sportsmanlike fashion printed the protest of the Southern delegates to the ruling on Andrews. Later it gave fully the reply of the Northern delegates to the protest. But by July 6, 1845, it was outspoken on the subject:

> It is impossible to take up the defense of slavery without making the work of God in the true Christian sense a mockery.

The position of the Germans themselves on the slavery question was never in doubt. The first session of the Central German Conference, held in Cincinnati in August, 1864, with Bishop Morris presiding, had communicated officially to President Lincoln not only its sympathy and prayers, but also assured him of the support of the whole German Methodist Church. The resolutions concluded with these words:

> That, although we are not native born in this land, although in the divine providence our cradle was rocked on the other shore of the Atlantic Ocean, we rejoice in the precious right of being called American citizens; and in thankfulness to the Union, and its symbol, the glorious stars and stripes, we do not want ourselves to be surpassed as the truest and most devoted sons of the Republic, and that we rejoice over the fact which is confirmed by the enlistment rolls of the army, that the German branch of our Zion has delivered its full contingent; . . .
>
> That we, as preachers of the gospel, consider it as our privilege and our duty to intensify the loyalty of our congregations to the Government and to speak openly against the evil of slavery and the danger threatening our land.[ii]

The President replied to this demonstration of confidence in longhand to Nast as follows:

> Reverend and Dear Sir:
>
> It is with feelings of cordial gratification, that I acknowledge the reception of your communication of the 20th of October covering the Resolutions of the Central German Conference of the Methodist Episcopal Church adopted at their recent session.
>
> I have not been unprepared for this definite and unequivocal statement of the continued loyalty and devotion of the Church you represent to the free institutions of the country of your adoption. The conduct of your people since the outbreak of this

desolating rebellion has been the best proof of the sincerity of your present professions.

I trust it is not too early for us to rejoice together over the promise of the speedy removal of that blot upon our civilization, always heretofore, a standing menace to our peace and liberties, whose destruction so long desired by all friends of impartial freedom, has at last been rendered possible by the crimes of its own reckless freedom.

I am very truly,
Your obedient servant,
A. Lincoln.

The Northwest German Conference, meeting at Galena, Illinois, in September, 1864, took action similar to that of the Central. It resolved:

1. That we love our adopted Fatherland and take part in its difficult tribulations with all our hearts.

2. That we revere our present Government, honor it and feel obliged to support it with our strength.

3. That the war for freedom be continued with all strength and power until the last rebel either is taken prisoner or conquered and the whole Union re-established.

4. That to this end we come to the assistance of our Government. Our sympathy, our prayers, our goods, and our blood shall be dedicated to our Government and our country.

5. That we treat all those who seek to lay any hindrance in the way or to use their influence under the cloak of loyalty to the prejudice of the welfare of our land, no better than rebels with weapons in their hands.

6. That finally we pray God to give our President wisdom that our arms may triumph and our land soon be blessed with an honorable peace.[12]

On January 30, 1865, the *Apologist* was willing to credit the Germans with contributing to the abolitionist cause. "Missouri," it declared:

is a free state 60-4. And who is to be thanked for this shift in opinion? . . . Only the Germans have brought it about. As the moloch of secession, so Missouri has now been torn from the slavery interests. Without despair, without wavering, without rest they have worked thirty years for this glorious day. . . . Never has the German genius celebrated a more glorious, consequential triumph.

The Civil War was a cause for which the German love of liberty beat loud; yet the *Apologist* dealt with the problem with restraint. The editor was more concerned with the need of unity and co-operation of the evangelical churches than with the war itself. It was, however, not anxious to have the Church reunited without repentant Southern hearts. It declared in the issue of July 31, 1865, that there could be no intention of "throwing out bait of a premium for rejoining the Church from which they have separated in 1844." Such union had to come about "through an inner conviction" of what the Church meant.

The editorial policy was equally farsighted in its recognition of the fact that the problems of the nation were not solved by the winning of the war. "No one can deny," the *Apologist* pointed out,

> that the abolition of slavery is not completed with the extension of the right to vote. . . . The abolition of slavery means giving the right to vote to those to whom it heretofore had been denied. It also means the right to the free disposition of person by his own free will, the protection of his family life, the unqualified right to work and to full equality before the law.

When after two decades German Methodism had "become of age" with the organization of German-speaking Conferences, the *Apologist* was already an influential American publication, unsurpassed in the vigor of its editorial program and the intelligent Christian conviction of its purpose by any other religious journal. The *Apologist* had become, and deserved to be, the instrument for making German-speaking Methodism articulate. It gave the language mission a voice.

CHAPTER VI

METHODISM ORGANIZES ITS ADVANCES:
THE CONFERENCES

One of the strengths of the Methodist system has always been that it organizes its advances. The system becomes more enduring than the strengths or weaknesses of individual preachers. If the "organization" had not joined the often sporadic efforts of the itinerants, Methodism would not have grown to the powerful Protestant denomination that it is. When enough individuals had "experienced religion" to make a class, the group was established by the appointment of a leader to it. When enough classes had grown up to warrant the founding of a society, a church was organized. When enough churches existed to demand the supervision of a presiding elder, a district was built. When districts grew too numerous, they were co-ordinated by episcopal supervision into a Conference.

Within a decade after Nast was appointed missionary to the Germans in Cincinnati, the work had grown to such proportions that questions of proper administrative supervision were being raised and the problem of how the German-speaking work was to be integrated with the work of the English-speaking Conferences was forced to the level of deliberate discussion. The issue became a sensitive one as the Germans developed a class consciousness on their language basis. German preachers began to talk and write about the need for a central organization to promote the work of the mission. Nast himself proposed through the columns of *The Western Christian Advocate* a "German Conference." Peter Schmucker, though favoring the proposal, feared the step was too radical for the English brethren. As a more practical solution, he proposed that the German work be consolidated into two districts, one of which would be connected with the Ohio Conference, the other with the Missouri Conference. Despite a heated controversy over the slavery question, the General Conference of 1844 found time to organize three German-speaking districts following in substance Schmucker's plan: the Pittsburgh District, consisting of Karl H. Doering as presiding elder and six preachers; the Cincinnati District, with Peter Schmucker, presiding elder, and ten preachers; and the St. Louis District with L. S. Jacoby, presiding elder, and thirteen preachers—a total of thirty-two effective German workers if the presiding elders be counted in.[1]

The session of the Ohio Conference which followed in September of 1844 at Marietta was an important one. German preachers were present from the Pittsburgh, Indiana, and Kentucky Conferences.

Of this meeting at Marietta, the first general conclave of the German missionaries, Ahrens wrote that they felt themselves as a "family of likeminded workers in the great vineyard of the Lord." The Germans from this time on were "organization conscious." They were just as militant in their missionary crusade—perhaps more so—but they wanted administrative units of their own.

The Ohio Conference in 1844, moreover, authorized Nast to make a trip to Germany to prepare a report on the possibilities of the extension of the missionary work to the Continent. Ahrens was to substitute for Nast in the *Apologist* office. New societies, in the meantime, were being organized to an extent which necessitated in the Conference year of 1845-46 the addition of the Indiana District, with Nast as presiding elder, and in the year of 1846-47 of still another district known as the North Ohio.

On September 3, 1845, the Ohio Conference met in Cincinnati with twenty-seven German preachers present. Only four were absent for causes of health or distance. The Germans held services every evening in the Race Street Church, filled the altar, had communion, and rejoiced in love feasts. Afternoons the preachers met in the schoolroom of the same church to discuss the needs of their German work. The conclusions of the discussions were productive. They resolved to set aside a prayer meeting hour every second Thursday evening for an "instructive discourse" on the "duty, necessity, and blessedness of the spreading of the gospel," to be followed by a public offering for the promotion of the work. Because the Sunday School Union of the Methodist Episcopal Church was publishing no Sunday-school literature in the German language, the group requested the board of the Union to make an appropriation for the publication of German-language Sunday-school literature at the plant of the Western Methodist Book Concern. To support this proposal with money as well as petitions, the group bound itself to "endeavor to pay" a quarterly assessment of one cent for every pupil and teacher toward the support of the Sunday School Union, and "at all events" to take such annual collections as the Ohio and Illinois Conferences might order. This 1845 session of the Ohio Conference, which found the little group of Germans discussing even more intimately their own peculiar problems in their own Race Street Church, was a landmark in the history of German-speaking Methodism. Here German Methodism became articulate.

When reports read at the Conference in 1846 showed a gain of four hundred and sixteen members, the session became outspoken in its demand for the prompt publication in the German language of Wesley's sermons. It requested more tracts about the beliefs and constitution of the Methodist Episcopal Church and proposed Nast as the author. The Germans repeated their requests to the Sunday School Union to supply their Sunday schools with reading materials in the German language and asked the Book Concern, as soon as the publication could be underwritten by subscription, to print Doering's *Commentary on the Discipline* and Schmucker's *Notebook.*

The prestige which the German work and the German leaders were gaining was apparent when the Ohio Conference met in Columbus in 1847. It elected Nast as one of the ten delegates from the Conference to the General Conference.

In 1848, when the Ohio Conference met in Newark, the German preachers founded their own tract society. By 1850, when the Ohio Conference met in Chillicothe, the Germans were taking their own problems in their own hands. As evidence of the fact they memorialized the book agents to make payment in advance unconditional in subscriptions for the *Apologist.* They further repeated their request for the publication of German Sunday-school papers. They were even promoting their own work with profits from their own enterprises. At Nippert's request they contributed $200 out of the treasury of their tract society for the distribution of tracts in Germany. The Ohio Conference followed by underwriting between $400 and $500 for the same purpose. Jacoby had gone to Germany the previous October to carry the mission work to the Continent.

In 1851 the Ohio Conference, meeting in Springfield where sixteen years before Nast had been appointed the first German missionary, created another district, known as the North Indiana. At a meeting of the German members, Nast proposed anew the formation of a German Conference. The question arose in the course of a discussion as to the wisdom of dividing the German work between the Ohio and Indiana Conferences. Nast's idea caught fire and resolutions were adopted petitioning the Conference for the appointment of a committee to study the question and report. On Monday morning the report was made in detail and published in the *Apologist* on October 2, 1851:

> *Resolved,* That in the opinion of this Conference, the time has come to form the German work, which at present is related to the Ohio Conference, into a German Annual Conference.

> *Resolved,* That this proposal be recommended to the consideration of the next General Conference to place the German preachers at present in the Ohio Conference in an independent German Conference.

These proposals were unanimously adopted by the annual session. When the General Conference met in Boston in May, 1852, it named a committee on German work. In the New England metropolis it became evident, however, that a number of German preachers had changed their opinion about a German Conference. One district presented a petition in opposition to such an arrangement and another district, though silent, was known to be hostile to the idea. A group

from the Illinois Conference sought successfully to have the General
Conference release them from the Illinois and join them with the
Rock River Conference.   Such divisions among the Germans them-
selves caused the English-speaking brethren to be wary of too hasty
action on the subject.   They delayed and for the time being joined
the Indiana District and the North Indiana District with the South-
East Indiana Conference, and the Cincinnati, North-Ohio, and Pitts-
burgh Districts, with the Cincinnati Conference.   The same General
Conference divided the Ohio Conference by organizing the Cincinnati
Conference and the Ohio Conference.

When the Cincinnati Conference met in Urbana, Ohio, in 1855 and
elected Nast to the General Conference, the German-speaking members were convinced of the absurdity of associating a single German
District with a whole English-speaking Conference.   Resolutions were
again passed petitioning the General Conference to integrate all the
German work in the Cincinnati Conference and organize a German
Conference.   When Nast brought the matter before the Conference
it was, after hot debate, laid on the table for reasons of "policy" and
"want of time."

The Germans, however, did not forget their need of literature,
even though they were concerned with problems of organization.   They
asked the General Conference for a monthly Sunday-school journal.
The Germans of the South Indiana Conference meanwhile resolved
to petition the book agents to bring out German baptismal certificates,
German membership certificates, a German edition of Bishop Baker's
Explanation of the Church Order, printed exhorter's and local preacher's licenses, and to allow rebates for new subscribers to the *Apologist*
to cover cost and postage and loss, and the inclusion of a German
course of study in the next edition of the *Discipline.*   The requests
were granted.

The General Conference assembled on May 1, 1856, in the chamber
of the House of Representatives in Indianapolis.   Jacoby was back
from Germany, successfully seeking the organization of a mission
Conference for Germany and Switzerland, but his effort to have the
General Conference found a Book Concern in Bremen was futile.   He
was successful in getting $1,000 annually to support the publication
in Germany and Switzerland of materials in demand.   At once Nast
asked the Committee on Book Concern to arrange for a German Sunday-school paper.   In May, 1856, at Indianapolis, the *Sonntagschule
Glocke* (Sunday School Bell) was born, and made its first appearance
the following October.

The question of the proper organization was raised again by the
demands of the Pittsburgh and Indiana Conferences that the German
districts, included within or adjacent to their boundaries, be associated
with their Conferences.   The Committee on Conference Boundaries
deliberated the request, refused, and set up the principle that not less

than two language districts should be related to a Conference. Nast now thought it the right time to work for the organization of a German Conference, but Bishop Scott counseled that in a quadrennium a better plan could be worked out to divide the work into three or four German Conferences. Nast consented to wait his time.

The result was that the Cincinnati and the Ohio (formerly Pittsburgh) Districts remained in the Cincinnati Conference while the North-Ohio and Michigan Districts were incorporated into the North-Ohio Conference. The North-Indiana and the South-Indiana Districts remained in the Southeast Indiana Conference. These six districts remained thus located until the German Conference was formed in the year 1864.

The situation as it existed in 1860, however, was increasingly unsatisfactory. The German work was organized as parts of nine Conferences in the United States.

Conference	District	Number of Appointments
New York	New York	23
Upper Iowa	Galena	9
	Minnesota	13
Cincinnati	Cincinnati	12
	Ohio	10
North Ohio	North Ohio	11
	Michigan	12
South Illinois	St. Louis	12
	Belleville	11
Illinois	Quincy	10
	Beardstown	10
	Missouri	15
South Indiana	South Indiana	13
	North Indiana	12
Rock River	Chicago	12
	Wisconsin	11
	Burlington	11
	California	4
Work in Germany[2]	Bremen	4
	Oldenburg	7
	South Germany	4
	Switzerland	2

The impossibility of long continuing German-language districts within English-speaking Conferences had for years been increasingly evident. The German Mission had all kinds of peculiar problems which did not concern the English-speaking brethren and which they did not understand. Many of the German itinerants had such a meager command of English that they could not even follow the proceedings of the Annual Conferences. Despite these facts, the Germans had been so warmly received by the English brethren, presiding elders, and bishops in the Annual Conferences that many of them were reluctant to sever the bonds of brotherhood which united them. They feared a religious isolation behind a language barrier. The wisdom of the course was a moot question in the decade preceding the organization of the German-language Conferences. Although the subject died out as an issue after 1864, it was always a source of dispute. If, on the one hand, their establishment led to a unity of the German missionary work so that it enjoyed a growth which perhaps it never could have attained attached to English-speaking Conferences, on the other a gulf widened between the German and English-speaking Church. The Germans, who were forced to master English, were genuine Methodists, devout, supremely loyal and constructive. The English, who knew very little German indeed, soon forgot the German Mission. As far as English-speaking Methodism was concerned, German Methodism was often almost another denomination. The tragedy of the situation culminated in the indefensible attitude taken by many toward the German Methodists during the World War. Their isolation had become too complete.

German Methodism fortunately had grown to such a strength that a continuation of its ineffectual organization was impossible. A map of the expansion of the work would have shown that the German missionaries had followed the streams of German settlers from Cincinnati west, south, east, and north with the moving frontiers. By 1864, a reference points in the history of German-speaking Methodism, the German work, divided up into the eighteen districts included 306 German preachers and 26,145 members.

In all the proposals for a German Conference it was evident, nevertheless, that no unity existed among the Germans themselves as to what form the organization of their work should take. In the fall of 1862 Bishop Ames decided to administer a strong medicine for this disease of disagreement. He dissolved the Cincinnati District and divided it among the three English-speaking districts. He did the same with the South Indiana District of the Southeast Indiana Conference by dividing the German appointments among the four English-speaking districts. The situation which resulted was so unsatisfactory that practically every German preacher was convinced, if not of the wisdom, certainly of the practical necessity of the German-language Conference. The seven German-speaking delegates elected to the General Conference in 1864 went to Philadelphia as a unit to petition for the organization of independent German-speaking Conferences. On October 18, 1863, the editor of the *Apologist* was able to report in his columns that the German-speaking preachers in the various Conferences with which their work was associated were unanimously in favor of a full-fledged German Conference.

The Committee on German Work of the Cincinnati Conference, meeting in Xenia, Ohio, in September, 1863, summarized the status of the language mission and declared itself in favor of the organization of German-speaking Conferences. The memorandum read:

Your Committee to whom this subject was referred, have had the same under consideration, and beg leave to present the following as their report:

The work of grace among this portion of our European immigration has been to us, and still remains, a source of great denominational gratification and a cause of devout gratitude to God.

Nor is its reflex influence upon the German Churches and people of Europe less interesting and hopeful. An effete ecclesiasticism, with strong rationalistic tendencies, needs the vitalizing influences of a spiritual Christianity, and we believe that God, in his providence, has designed Methodism for the accomplishment of this work.

We have been intensely interested in the inception and carefully guarded the early development, of this German revival in this vigorous young Republic, and now, as it approaches its majority, we feel very much as the affectionate parent does when the dew of his youth is departing from a fondly-nurtured son, and he begins to feel the pressure of manly responsibilities and a burning desire to carve out a destiny of his own. It is not because he ceases to love the paternal domicile and cherish the hallowed endearments of home, nor that he is impatient of proper restraint, but a sense of *personal* responsibility to God and the world urges him on at the expense of every necessary sacrifice, and he cannot stay. Deep is the paternal solicitude which follows his steps, but the intelligent parent would not reproach him for his course or recall him from it. Restraint at such a time would but paralyze his energies and leave him in the arms of his doting mother a *monster baby*.

Methodism has been from the beginning the birth and ward of special and unfolding providence, and it will be well if it continues in the future, as in the past, to follow the leadings thereof. As Mr. Wesley did not see whereunto his class meetings were leading, little more could the future of German Methodism be seen from the first successes of Dr. Nast and his coadjutors. While we renew the exclamation, "What hath God wrought!" and feel impressed with the importance of this work, we should carefully study its wants and use our best endeavors promptly to supply them.

To the minds of those best acquainted with it, separate Conference organizations appear to be a necessity for the further successful prosecution of the work. It is candidly admitted that some difficulties will attend such a change, but they are by no means insuperable. We will submit a few reasons why this measure should in our judgment be adopted.

Let us survey the field which is now ripe for the harvest, and is inviting our German reapers to gather it. The German immigration to this country has scarcely slackened at all, and there are now indications that a very large increase will soon set in; and for the benefit and salvation of those, Methodism needs the most efficient organization, and should put forth her most vigorous efforts. Surely this is no time for us to diminish our missionary appropriations to it, and so contract the work and force many of our missionaries to abandon it altogether. The face of German Methodism has also been turned to the East, and the conversion of every German soul in this country produces responsive throbs of religious emotion in the hearts of relatives and friends in the Fatherland. Its fruits have been seen there, and we have as a consequence in Germany an Annual Conference, with its pastoral charges, literary institute, and publishing house. And even the densely-populated region of Southern Russia, where our brother Flocken is now laboring, is open to our German missionaries. What a vast and interesting field is this, and what tremendous responsibilities press upon us! The homogeneousness of this work would seem to require, in this country as well as Germany, Conferences entirely German, which, instead of embarrassing our work, would, in our opinion, relieve it of many of its present embarrassments, which we see no other way to remove.

Although in most places the children of German Methodists rapidly become familiar with our language and identify themselves with us, the continued immigration from the mother country will supply their places, and fresh fields be continually opening to our German ministers. To secure this harvest we should release our German work from its leading-strings, admitting that Germans understand their countrymen better than we, and let it go forth in the vigor of the manhood it has attained, to accomplish its glorious mission, and preserving the unity of Methodism in whatever language it is preached. For we cannot understand the idiosyncrasies of a foreign people as they themselves do, and hence we cannot determine the qualifications of pastors and evangelists for them with any considerable accuracy.

For a considerable period the German immigrants to this country have been of more refined and educated classes than they were formerly. They have now their ecclesiastical and educational institutions in their own language, and not unfrequently disparage our brethren by invidious comparisons, and more than insinuate their incapacity to manage for themselves, and imagine that it is sufficiently demonstrated by a reference to the pupilage in which their English-speaking brethren persist in holding them. It is impossible that this should not be a very serious embarrassment, and in many instances prevent us from gaining access to these more educated and controlling classes of emigrants.

We sometimes hear it objected to the proposition to organize German Conferences, that it would tend to estrangement, and ultimately to division. But in our opinion the opposite result would follow. Certainly the granting of much-needed privilege, where no sacrifice is made by the party granting it, could not lead to estrangement, but, on the other hand, to increased affection on the part of the favored party. Then, our experience from the opposite practice, as in the instances last year of enforcing English-speaking presiding elders over some of the German charges in the Cincinnati and South-Eastern Indiana Conferences, does not exhibit to us strengthened bonds of union, but, on the contrary, a very rapid development of the very estrangement we fear.

The same thing is more fully illustrated by a reference to the history of the "Evangelical Association" in this country, founded by Mr. Albright. He was originally a Methodist, and besought Bishop Asbury to grant the very privilege for which our German brethren, after a pupilage of twenty-five years, are now asking. Upon being refused this favor, he and his German colleagues felt that there was no alternate left for them but to collect their scattered flocks and form a distinct ecclesiastical organization. They have toiled on patiently, and God has graciously blessed their labors, till this body now numbers eight Annual Conferences, above three hundred itinerant ministers, and forty-six thousand members. It supports sixty-five missions, two literary institutions, a publishing house, periodicals, etc. All this might have been saved to Methodism, and doubtless, with our united strength, much more would have been accomplished had the request of Mr. Albright and his co-laborers been granted. And who can doubt that in the event the feeling of Christian fraternity would have been far stronger than it is at present?

Again, there are some who say that it is one of the great trusts of Methodism to Americanize the Germans. If it is meant by this that it is its duty to teach them the use of the English language, we cannot indorse the sentiment at all. We esteem it the duty of the church to adopt the most effectual means to lead the greatest possible number to Christ; and we feel assured that in its very best sense the truly converted Germans are already Americanized, whether they speak the English language or not. They have recently demonstrated this, in the most unquestionable manner, on many a bloody battlefield.

The absolute necessity for a German Conference would be very sensibly felt by us if we could for a short season take the places of the German members of our own Conference. Most of them understand but little of the Conference business, and speak our language too imperfectly to participate in it at all, thus obliging them to feel as if they were ciphers, and helpless for any active enterprise in the Conference. Intricate and important matters appertaining to their work, and the proper character and qualifications of their ministers, elicit but little interest in the Conference, and are hurriedly passed over to their no small grievance and embarrassment. Brethren may plead in palliation a lack of time, but that does not remove the difficulty or relieve the embarrassment under which our German brethren are thus forced to labor. This unpleasant state of affairs does not diminish, but increases from year to year, till our German work is in a very critical condition. Then, the parceling out of the German charges into each of several Annual Conferences frequently interferes with that necessary exchange of ministers, which forces upon them the unpleasant remedy secured by frequent transfers. In this way but little interest is awakened in educational and other Conference enterprises; and if there was, it would be next to impossible to prosecute them successfully. And it is undoubtedly true that a sense of Conference responsibility will give additional vigor and infuse new life and interest in the breasts of our German ministers, and in all parts of our German work, instead of feeling themselves either an incubus or an intangible attachment to the several Conferences with which they are connected.

Let the General Conference, therefore, divide them into about three Annual Conferences in the West and one in the East, if they so desire, and let them hold their sessions at convenient seasons, and go forth infused with new spirit to accomplish their sublime mission and work out a noble ecclesiastical destiny.

Should it be found necessary, as a means of preserving our unity and identity between the German Conferences and the English work, let there be, in addition to our episcopal general superintendency, book and periodical-publishing interests, and our general missionary system, a German assistant corresponding missionary secretary, who could attend to the duties of this, in addition to those of some other position.

These are a few of the many reasons why we propose the organization of German Conferences, and we recommend, as expressive of these views, the following resolutions for adoption:

1. *Resolved,* That in our opinion the interests and proper development of German Methodism will be most successfully promoted by organizing, as far as practicable, the German missions and pastoral charges under our care into separate Annual Conferences.

2. *Resolved,* That we instruct our delegates to use their influence in the next General Conference to effect this arrangement.

3. *Resolved,* That the *Western Christian Advocate* and the *Christian Apologist* be requested to publish this report at their earliest convenience.[3]

Acting upon the requests from the Germans the General Conference in 1864 named a special committee on German-speaking work. The result of its report was the organization of four German-speaking Conferences—the Central German, the Northwest German, the Southwest German, and the East German. German Methodism "came of age" in the Quaker City in 1864.

Central German Conference

That the first German-language Conference should have been organized in Cincinnati was historically appropriate. That the presiding bishop should have been T. A. Morris was equally proper. On August 24, 1864, eighty-two German preachers assembled in the Race Street Church to band themselves together under the authority of the General Conference. Erhardt Wunderlich, Gottlob Nachtrieb, Carl F. Heitmeyer, G. A. Breunig, and John Schneider were appointed superintendents of the Cincinnati, Ohio, Michigan, Indianapolis, and Louisville Districts which were created. The Conference had 8,860 members, 650 Sunday schools, with 8,667 officers, teachers, and pupils, and church property worth a quarter of a million dollars.

Northwest German Conference

The Northwest German Conference was the second to be organized. It met for the first time in Galena, Illinois, on September 7, 1864, with Bishop Scott presiding. Its fifty-seven members were consolidated from the Rock River, Minnesota, Upper Iowa, Illinois, and Ohio Conferences. The total membership of the churches of the Conferences was 5,537. Church and parsonage property was valued at $132,900.

The Conference itself sprawled over a wide area—from Freeport, Illinois, north to LaCrosse and Tomah, Wisconsin, and west to South Dakota and Iowa. Chicago was a rapidly growing commercial city and meat-packing center. Milwaukee was being recognized as a trade and industrial center of the great Northwest. Aside from the societies in and about these urban areas, the Methodist circuits were pioneer outposts. The territory was divided into five districts, the Chicago, Milwaukee, Galena, St. Paul, and Red Wing. To these districts Bishop Scott appointed George L. Mulfinger, Friedrich Kopp, Charles Schuler, Philipp Funk, and John G. Speckmann as presiding elders.

Galena was the oldest district in the Conference, spreading over parts of the states of Illinois, Wisconsin, and Iowa. Mission work had begun in the region when in 1842 and 1843 Jacoby traveled through it from St. Louis. When in 1844 Jacoby was sent from St. Louis to be the presiding elder of the Quincy District, the circuits were expanded north to Milwaukee. In 1845 Wilhelm Schreck developed a series of preaching posts in Galena, then the most important place in the Northwest, and the region around Dubuque and Sherrill. Little colonies of Germans were scattered over the territory where immigrants had been drawn to the wheat fields. Galena was a strategic post and became the first self-supporting post in the Northwest. From Galena, as a kind of Methodist headquarters in the open country, work expanded westward. In 1848 Conrad Eisenmeyer arrived in Milwaukee as the first presiding elder to live in the Northwest. On horseback he rode the states of Illinois, Wisconsin, and Iowa, preaching, converting, and organizing the advance. Eisenmeyer was succeeded in 1850 by John Plank. On his faithful horse "Jo" he rode from Pekin, Illinois, to St. Paul, Minnesota, building a flourishing circuit. Plank was followed by a gifted preacher named Heinrich Fiegenbaum. He was a wise counselor, capable administrator, and constructive evangelist. The work in other sections of the new Conference was built by pioneers of the same type.

The Rock River Conference had been outspoken in its demands for a German-language Conference. In 1863 it had adopted a resolution, forwarded to the General Conference of 1864, declaring that

> it is our conviction that the work among the Germans of this land can best be developed under the circumstances and that the most satisfactory results can be achieved if it were organized into German Conferences.

Southwest German Conference

Before September was over the third language Conference had been organized as the Southwest German Conference. Eighty-seven preachers met with Bishop Janes for the first annual session on September

29, 1864, in the Washington Street Church, St. Louis. Neither the time nor the place was particularly appropriate for a religious rally inasmuch as the Confederate General Price had drawn up his lines in the neighborhood of the city. Conference officers were required to take the oath of allegiance to the Government of the United States. The city itself was under martial law. The territory had been split into bitter groups for years. The passage of the Kansas-Nebraska Bill in 1854, really giving local option on the question of slavery, had only intensified the passions of the population as competition to settle the region developed between the slavery and the anti-slavery parties. "Jayhawkers" and "Guerrillas" disturbed camp meetings.

The Southwest German Conference organized fifteen German districts, spread out in nine English Conferences, into a language unit. The Conference, composed of 87 ministers, reported a membership of 5,308. The church property was valued at nearly $200,000.

Bishop Janes made the appointments of presiding elders to the five districts—the St. Louis, Belleville, Burlington, Quincy, and St. Joseph—by naming Philipp Kuhl, Gerhard Timken, Friedrich Fiegenbaum, Heinrich Lahrmann, and Michael Schnierle.

The position of the German preachers on the slavery issue had never been in doubt. In 1844, when the Missouri Conference was meeting in the Fourth Street Church in St. Louis, the question of "going North" or "South" had been openly raised. Bishop Morris, who was presiding, made his choice for the "North." He was followed by thirteen German preachers, who were promptly transferred to the Illinois Conference. The Southwest German Conference began in this difficult tradition and political environment. When the Civil War was over, however, it thrived.

East German Conference

Nearly two years passed before the fourth language Conference was organized. Twenty-two preachers gathered on April 11, 1866, in the Second Street Church in New York to organize the East German Conference. Although its membership was hardly half that of the three Conferences previously established, its property was valued at $350,000. It was an urban Conference, including the whole region between the Atlantic Ocean and the Allegheny Mountains. Methodism had been carried East by Nast, Callender, Doering, Lyon, and Miller. John I. Graw went north to Schenectady and founded one of the strongest congregations of German Methodism. In 1847 John Sauter started a society in Buffalo, and the next year one in Rochester. Adam Miller had begun the work in Baltimore and John Grimm in Boston.

The type of work done by this urban Conference was somewhat different from that of the more rural Conferences, but it was just as passionately evangelical. That it alone had preserved its German-language identity as late as 1939 instead of merging with the English-speaking Conferences is a testimony to its vitality.

To the two districts of the Conference, the New York and the Philadelphia, Bishop Janes appointed Heinrich Kastendieck and John Zwahlen.

Chicago German Conference

After the organization of the East German Conference no further action was taken until 1872, when the Chicago German Conference was divided from the Northwest German Conference. The first annual session was held in the Maxwell Street Church, Chicago, on September 19, 1872, thirty-six ministers answering the roll call. The Conference included northeastern Illinois, the state of Wisconsin, and parts of Michigan and Indiana, its chief centers being Chicago and Milwaukee, where congregations flourished. The German population in the area had grown so substantially that Methodism had plenty of work to do. Philipp Barth, arriving in Chicago in 1846, was instrumental in building the first German Methodist Church in 1847, a modest frame structure costing $558. By the outbreak of the World War German Methodism in Chicago had grown to 13 societies, 1,800 members, and possessed property worth $172,000.

Bishop Simpson presided at the opening session. Bishop Janes appointed the 48 members of the Conference to their charges on the Chicago, Milwaukee, and Fond du Lac Districts, naming C. F. Loeber, J. J. Keller, and George Haas presiding elders. The membership of the churches of the Conference was 5,149, and 44 local preachers. The church property owned had grown to a quarter million dollars, and 5,232 scholars, teachers, and officers were enrolled in 98 Sunday schools.

South German Conference

The South German Conference, founded two years later, was organized in difficult times. At the invitation of some Methodists who had moved from Cincinnati to New Orleans, Peter Schmucker had gone to the southern city in the winter of 1840-41. He organized a class and appointed M. Tantau class leader. The work developed so encouragingly that in 1843 he appointed Karl Bremer preacher. By 1844 the divisions within the Church over the question of slavery had grown so intense that the congregation was split into factions. Schmucker, disgusted and unwilling to remain in a Church which tolerated slavery, packed up and went by river boat back to Cincinnati. The society which had been founded in New Orleans quite naturally drifted into the system of protest against anti-slavery sentiment represented by the Methodist Episcopal Church, South, and thrived under the leadership of a succession of effective preachers.

Between 1845 and 1850 a new flood of German immigrants was sweeping in through the ports of Texas. They organized into German

societies with the idea of establishing German colonies in the state.
Their industry, thrift, and perseverance made these German settle-
ments prosperous and active. The demand for preachers, especially for
language missionaries, exceeded the meager supply of the Church
South, but it would have none of the men of the Methodist Episcopal
Church.

The Methodist Episcopal Church, however, did not give up. Al-
,though its work was almost smothered by the aversion to the
acknowledged Union patriotism of Methodists, in addition to the
hatred of their stand on slavery, the work struggled along, lingering
at the point of death. Methodists were classed with "niggers." Their
sympathy with the colored race was anathema to the Southerners. A
series of events increased the Southern prejudice.

In 1846 Heinrich Bauer, an elder of the Illinois Conference, came
to Texas in the "biblical fashion" without purse or belongings. He
was fired with the ambition to work among the Negro slaves. The
Texas Conference welcomed him and assigned him as missionary to
the Germans. He served with noteworthy success, administering the
sacrament, but at the end of the year he was dropped by the Conference "because a Northerner could not be trusted in the South."
Thus becoming an independent missionary, he settled in Industry,
Austin County. A group of people of religious sentiments gathered
around him and at their request he began to preach. The result was
the organization of a society, the election of a board of trustees, and
the construction of a church. Bauer continued as preacher until 1854,
when he again took his staff and set out for Nicaragua, where Germans were settling in large numbers. The Church appealed to the
Lutheran Synod for a preacher and was assigned a young Galveston
missionary named Heinrich Jung, who had been converted in the New
Orleans Society in 1844.

Hostility to the Church in general was growing in Texas. Church
members were sometimes subjected to such physical abuse that they
carried scars of the battle the rest of their lives. Churches still give
evidence of bullet holes shot through them by rowdies during services.
The unwholesome situation was made worse by the outbreak of Civil
War. Economic difficulties were added to political animosities. The
monotonous diet of cornbread and beef, as the war progressed, was
the alternative to going hungry. Churches suffered from extreme
poverty. The best men were forced into the army or into hiding.
The Germans, it is true, were not fully cognizant of what was going
on. Many Germans did not know the Church South had separated
from the Methodist Episcopal Church. A number of German societies still were using the hymnals, *Disciplines,* and religious literature
from Cincinnati. As the slavery issue grew more definite, many of
the Germans were reluctant to remain in a Church which defended
slavery. Some outspoken preachers, unable to escape through Southern

ports, stole through Mexico and turned up in Northern cities. The number of German preachers in the South dwindled from fifteen to six.

The situation did not improve when the war was over. The "carpet baggers," who came South to mobilize the strength of the Negro freemen for their political advantage, as well as the Northern clergymen who came South as opportunists to improve their ecclesiastical positions, lowered the opinion of the Northerners in the general mind. Futile gestures from the South looking toward a reunion of the broken Methodist Episcopal Church led eventually to the separation of a congregation of sixty-seven members and their pastor, Karl Biel, from the Church South. When the society at Industry voted in this way to reunite with the Methodist Episcopal Church and communicated the fact through Nast to the *Apologist* readers, other German preachers in the South began to turn back to the mother Church. The society at Industry, by its action of 1866, lost its church property and began to hold services in a schoolhouse. The members and their pastor were received back into the Church by Joseph Welch. At Welch's request, Biel went to Houston on January 3, 1867, where the Texas Conference was being organized. Ninety preachers, mostly colored, from whose shoulders the yoke of slavery had recently been lifted, were assembled. Many of them had preached for years. Although only twenty of the clergymen could read even simple large print, they all knew many Bible verses by heart, could sing psalms from memory, and were well-versed in the Sermon on the Mount. They made up for what they did not know by their emotions. Journalists spoke of the assembly as a "Blackberry picnic."

The importance of this Conference session in the history of German-speaking Methodism was that two German preachers were received as elders. Eduard Schneider, like Karl Biel, had left the Church South to become an active Texas leader of the Methodist Episcopal Church. Karl Urbantke was received on trial. The association of three Germans with so large a group of organized Negro clergymen at once kindled hostility. Public opinion at the time was very irritable anyway. The cost of living was high. The price of cotton dropped precipitously from thirty to seven cents. Meal sold in Houston from $9.50 to $10 a hundred. Railway travel was five cents a mile. The missionary preachers were forced for reasons of economy to travel on the backs of the despised Spanish ponies. Although a part of the congregation in New Orleans came back to the Methodist Episcopal Church and in December, 1870, was transferred to the Central German Conference, the position of the German preacher was not an enviable one. They were hated because they associated with Negroes. They were detested because they apparently were in sympathy with the North. The presence of "carpet baggers" added strength to the hostility and the Southerners lost no opportunity to identify the German preachers with the political opportunists. The prejudice was well established that the German preachers were in league with vicious groups of "abolitionists." Contact with the white Methodists on a plane of equality was even demoralizing for the Negroes themselves. Feelings sometime boiled over into homicide. G. E. Brooks, a preacher of conviction, was shot in the exercise of his pastoral office.

Under these circumstances a division arose among the Germans themselves. Many well-educated and cultured Germans, fleeing from Germany after the revolution of 1848, had settled in Texas. Most of them were hostile to Christianity and pointed with mocking fingers to the sorry condition in the South, for which they held the Church to blame. These organized Germans were given the name *"Lateiners."* They frightened people so they were afraid to go to Church. They warned preachers to keep out of their pulpits if they valued their lives, *"wenn einem seine Haut lieb sei."* The *Lateiners* were remarkably well-informed about the German preachers' co-operation with the Negroes in the English-speaking Conferences. It became actually dangerous for a German to join the Methodist Episcopal Church.

The rapid growth of the Texas Conference was creating new problems. Its Negro membership had increased to 150. *Ernst Stroeter* and J. J. Brunow, coming South from the East German Conference, strengthened the German work. They arrived in Texas at a time when a major part of the congregations of New Braunfels and Fredricksburg had left the Church South and been received into the mother Church by Biel. The innate differences between the Germans and Negroes were so apparent at the seventh annual session of the Texas Conference meeting in Galveston that a commission was appointed to propose a proper division. The result was the organization of the Texas and West Texas Conferences for Negroes, the Austin Conference for English-speaking whites, and the South German Conference for German-speaking Methodists. The organization of a wholly German Conference provoked the *Lateiners* to increased activity, but the mission was now too firmly established to be driven out.

The South German Conference met on January 15, 1874, at Industry, Texas, for purposes of organization, with Bishop Thomas Bowman presiding. Thirteen ministers were charter members. Biel, Schneider, Gustav Elley, Ferdinand Mumme, and Konrad Pluenneke had come from the Methodist Episcopal Church, South. E. F. Stroeter, Wilhelm Pfaeffle, Friedrich Schuler, and Heinrich Dietz were transferred from other German Conferences, and Karl Urbantke, Wilhelm Felsing, Heinrich Homburg, and Anton Ullrich were recruited from the congregations. The names of these men deserve to be preserved in the records of German Methodism because no charter members of a German Conference had more bitter experiences in the Methodist faith.

The first statistics of the South German Conference were modest— 17 preachers, 7 local preachers, 438 full members, 73 members on trial, 9 churches valued at $13,550. Eight hundred and seventy dollars, hardly $1.70 a member, had been contributed for the support of the preachers. Though the ministers were poor, they preferred to go to Conference unpaid rather than to divert funds from church construction and missionary support.

St. Louis German Conference

In the North, changing conditions were forcing adjustments in church organization. Circuit riders had continued Westward as the frontiers of the United States were pressed on toward the Pacific. The General Conference in 1876 recognized the fact by passing an enabling act authorizing the Southwest German Conference by vote and the approval of the presiding bishop to divide itself. When the Conference met on September 13, 1877, in Quincy, Illinois, a committee was appointed to draft the plan. When Conference met in Warsaw, Illinois, the next year the preachers on the Kansas and St. Joseph Districts petitioned for a prompt division. The petition was referred to a committee, which three days later reported as follows:

> Your committee has the petitions of the brethren of the St. Joseph and Kansas Districts and maturely deliberated the grounds specified therein and has noted the boundaries on the map and has been convinced that the following plan would be laid before the Conference:
>
> 1. *Resolved,* That the Southwest Conference be divided.
>
> 2. *Resolved,* That the division be made as follows:
>
> The new Conference shall include the states of Kansas, Nebraska, and Colorado, and as much of Missouri and Iowa as lies west of the following boundary, beginning at the southeast corner of the state of Kansas and then in a straight line to the southeast corner of Morgan County, Missouri, thence north to the northeast corner of Chariton County, Missouri, from thence in a straight line to the northeast corner of Worth County, Missouri, and from thence north through Iowa to the southern border line of the Northwest German Conference.
>
> 3. *Resolved,* That the eastern part of the divided Conference be called the "St. Louis German Conference" and the western part the "Western German Conference."[4]

The divisions remained substantially as originally made. The region in western Iowa, which fell in the West German Conference, was later given back to the St. Louis Conference.

The St. Louis German Conference opened its first session on September 3, 1879, in St. Louis with Bishop Bowman presiding. The 81 members of the Conference were appointed to charges on the St. Louis, Belleville, Quincy, and Burlington Districts. J. M. Dewein, Charles Rodenberg, H. Naumann, and Philipp Kuhl were made presiding elders. The membership of the churches of the Conference totaled 8,244, and 112 local preachers. Property was valued at $399,-160. Sunday-school enrollment exceeded 10,000 teachers, officers, and scholars.

West German Conference

Nine days after the St. Louis Conference held its first session, 37 preachers, pastors of 2,811 members, met in St. Joseph, Missouri, to organize the West German Conference, Bishop Harris presiding. Its territory seemed unbounded. Vast areas of fertile plains were being opened up to settlers. A constant stream of migrating human beings moved into the territory, pressing the frontier farther and farther west. Many of these people, however, most of them, probably, were motivated by purely materialistic reasons. Becoming restless in more established communities, they had "gone West" to better their circumstances. Religious interests, if present at all, were usually secondary. Rainfall sometimes made these agricultural settlements prosperous, and drought sometimes drove the people on in search of better locations. On the then far Western prairies the social organization of cattle ranchers was not favorable for intimate contact or serious spiritual expression.

Mission work, encouragingly begun, too often ended in work discouragingly given up. In 1884 Rudolph Fiegenbaum opened a mission in Atchison, Kansas. He was succeeded by *Friedrich Hauser,* under whose able and self-sacrificing leadership a thriving society developed, a beautiful church was built and parsonage erected, only to be sold on the ebbtide. The same sad sequence was repeated in Salina, Kansas, in Nebraska City, Fremont, York, Pittsburgh, Fairmont, Parsons, Weston, Missouri, Kansas, Brunswick, Carrolton and Waverly, Missouri.

North German Conference

The process of the division of Conferences necessitated by the Westward expansion of the United States reached the Northwest German Conference nearly a decade later. The German immigrants since 1850 had settled to a large extent along the fertile plains of the Mississippi and the Minnesota Rivers. Societies were established by the circuit riders and from 1851 to 1861 all the German congregations in Minnesota were included on the St. Paul District. *Heinrich Fiegenbaum* had to travel as presiding elder 400 miles by steamboat from Galena, Illinois, to visit the churches in Minnesota. The area over which the churches were spread had become so vast that Methodism, still organizing its advances, saw the wisdom of establishing the North German Conference. Divided from the Northwest German Conference, it included the territory covered by the states of Minnesota, North Dakota, and the northern part of Wisconsin. The Conference organized itself at Minneapolis on October 12, 1887, with Bishop Fowler presiding.

California German Conference

Hardly had the Church dealt with organizational problems in the great Northwest than it was forced to think of Methodism beyond the Rocky Mountains. America was organizing its advance to the Pacific

Ocean. It was not that German Methodism was a novelty on the Coast. August Kellner had begun to preach to the Germans in San Francisco in 1855. In 1856 Karl Dierking had opened a mission in Stockton, and G. Bollinger had begun to preach in Sacramento. They were re-enforced in 1864 by the arrival of C. H. Afflerbach and F. Bonn.

The sociological situation was not favorable to religion. The gold rush had brought a mass of money-hungry men to the Coast and left the worst there. The Spaniards, Mexicans, and Orientals gave a Catholic or pagan complexion to the Pacific culture. The population was predominantly male. While mission work was difficult and progress exceedingly slow, those who did "experience religion" were stalwart figures, their benevolence contributions establishing records of generosity.

Until 1889 the German mission was organized in a German district as a part of the California Conference. On September 18, 1891, it was organized as a Conference, the first session being held in San Jose, California. It founded its own Conference paper, *Am Stillen Meer,* (On the Pacific Ocean) and developed a valuable deaconess and welfare work.

Pacific German Conference

The work west of the Rocky Mountains expanded up the Coast so that early in the new century administrative reorganization was necessary. The Pacific German Conference was the last of the ten German-speaking Conferences to be organized. The first session was held in Portland, Oregon, on September 7, 1905, with Bishop McDowell presiding. The German appointments in the Oregon Conference had been organized into the North Pacific German Mission in 1892, the work having spread northward from California. As early as 1882, a little society of twenty-nine members was thriving in Portland. It had been organized by F. Bonn, who arrived in the city in 1880. Oregon was a good field for Methodism because many German Methodists from other parts of the United States had migrated there. Led by such seasoned pastors as F. W. Buchholz, J. Braüer, W. Esslinger, Adam Bühler, A. L. Koeneke, A. Klippel, H. Hansen, and G. Hartung, the stations were substantially established.

Pacific German Methodism, separated from the educational institutions of its own denomination by thousands of miles of mountains, prairies, rivers, and lakes, felt the need of a school on the Coast. The Pacific German Conference promptly proceeded to support a German department in Willamette University, located in Salem, Oregon.

With the organization of the Pacific German Conference, the language mission had completed its organization with that of the nation. German-speaking Methodism and the United States of America had grown up together.

CHAPTER VII

CAMP MEETING EVANGELISM

The Methodists were not afraid of emotion in religion. If anything characterized their meetings, it was that they "felt" their faith. From John Wesley on down through the whole line of leaders and into the masses of the Church a wholesome respect for the intellect was expressed, but the Methodist emphasis was always first upon "the heart." When the class leader inquired, "How goes it with your heart today, brother?" he was inquiring about the subject that concerned him most. It is wrong to believe, however, that the Methodists desired to work the people up to a state of religious frenzy at every meeting. Although the preachers did not object to hearty shouts of "Amen," "Praise the Lord," and "Hallelujah" during sermons, prayers, and testimonies, they did their best to repress wild emotional extravagances. Yet the technique of the revival and its peculiar annual reunion known as the camp meeting were used by the Methodists more perhaps than by any other denomination. It is quite probable that the revival method is one of the uniquely outstanding features in the history of American Protestantism and through the revival the impact of the gospel upon the problems of American society has been brought to bear more earnestly than through any other channel.

The camp meeting was a product of the wave of revivalism which began in the hills of southern Kentucky when a Presbyterian minister moved there from North Carolina in 1796. The Cumberland revival reached its climax in 1800. In June of that year thousands of people attended an outdoor meeting held on the Red River. The very fact that such meetings were being held attracted other people, sometimes from great distances. They came prepared to spend several days on the ground, bringing their provisions and their families with them.

During the first two decades of the nineteenth century the camp meetings became a particular Methodist affair and for three or four generations played an important part in the spread of Methodism. It was not long before every presiding elder's district held such a meeting. It has been estimated that by 1812 at least four hundred Methodist camp meetings were being held. The Methodists even brought the institution from the Western frontiers to the conservative East. Even in staid old New England the camp meeting took root and flourished.

Although emotional disorders were customary, the camp meeting was the means of creating an environment in which a vital religious experience took place. Such a result was to be expected. Many came earnestly in a state of high spiritual expectancy. They were ready and willing for something to "happen" to them. They looked forward for weeks and months to this great annual event. Because frontier life offered such an extremely limited range of interests, the camp meeting was appreciated as a place to go, an incident which broke up the otherwise monotonous year. Frontier life gave opportunity for few social contacts and provided meager opportunities for coming in touch with the current happenings of the world. The result was that the settler's mind was apt to be completely dominated by whatever ideas he chanced to meet. Any idea in circulation was a welcome relief to the muscular routine of felling trees, pulling stumps, breaking virgin soil into cultivation, and doing chores. In the environment of the camp grounds, the individual, no matter for what reason he had come, was brought face to face with the compelling interest of the day—personal religion.

The Methodist preachers may not have been trained in psychology. At that time there were not even yet the rudiments of a science of psychology. But the preachers knew how to practice it. They kept a single subject before the crowd, thundering forth the terrors of hell with hortatory rather than expository sermons. The camp meeting was well adapted to the itinerant Methodist system, not only because it could mass the members of the scattered little societies in a single place, giving the strength of numbers, not only because it relieved earnest but untrained preachers from the exacting demands of serving a single congregation, but also because through it a few preachers could extend their influence over a whole region.

The German took to the camp meeting with enthusiasm. Its gregarious outdoor organization made a natural appeal to his nature. It was to him an *Ausflug* (outing) with a religious purpose. It is doubtful if any group in Methodism was more conscious of the value of the camp meeting as an instrument of religious experience. From their scanty incomes the Germans set aside week by week, month by month, little savings to take them to the grounds. They did more than that. They prayed for specific souls to be saved and they pooled their little treasures to send those for whom they prayed to the camp meetings. That German camp meetings should not have developed to any considerable extent until after the Civil War was due to the belated development of German Methodism. In all, there were probably thirty or thirty-five. Some became established institutions, others were discontinued after a decade or two or merged. The German camp meetings, as a rule, began on Monday evenings and lasted through until Sunday night. Families and their relatives and individual congregations pitched their own tents and covered the floor with straw. They gathered their fuel from the forests and cooked outside their canvas homes on old-fashioned stoves.

The camp meeting was an event in the lives of the German preachers. Up to the time of the World War few of them ever took a vacation. Some preached for forty years without taking a week for rest, but when camp meeting time came, they would go with their entire families.

The first really German camp meeting was held seven miles outside of Cincinnati in the Mill Creek Valley in August, 1839. By 1845 another was flourishing at Laughery, Indiana, under the leadership of Christian Wittenbach.

The camp meeting which grew up around the country church at Santa Claus, a parish of some one hundred and seventy members, was typical of the others which developed. In the fall of 1852 L. H. Lukemeyer instituted the camp meeting. By 1857 more commodious grounds were developed and a little temporary village of tents sprang up around the central preacher's tent. This was pitched in the rear of the grounds and connected with a platform and a pulpit. The boys of the church would almost daily cut down mulberry trees and dig them into the ground for shade. A lard-oil lamp supplied the light for the platform of the preachers, and two large camp fires upon a kind of altar provided the light for the congregation in the night. The seats consisted of logs laid lengthwise toward the preacher's platform with loose twelve-inch side boards laid across these logs. The seats had no backs. The altar for communion services, and at which men, women, and children kneeled to pray for salvation, was constructed of rough boards nailed on stakes driven into the ground.

Despite the religious enthusiasm, it was necessary for the camp meeting directors to have watchmen on duty not only to keep the fires burning but also to preserve order as groups were always present with the intention of disturbing the assembly. Even the prayer circle which brought the meetings to a close was often abused by dozens of young men who wanted the privilege of shaking hands with "God-fearing girls." They would squeeze the feminine hands so hard that the girls to some extent refused to take part in the ceremony. Even Sunday meetings finally had to be abandoned because as many as five hundred or a thousand people would drive over the grounds for a Sunday pastime and eat the free meals which were served.

By 1887 the Santa Claus grounds had become almost a wilderness from the trampling of thousands of feet. The trees were dead like the grass. Upon the proposal of J. G. Schaal, farmers who still owned forest land donated trees for a tabernacle. The next year witnessed what the Santa Claus people spoke of as a "Pentecostal" meeting. The season had passed with apparently lifeless sessions, despite excellent preaching. At about nine o'clock on the evening of closing, the preacher arose to say that in his opinion the time had come for bringing the meetings to a close. While he was speaking a man came forward for prayers. He was followed by another and still another. Instead of closing, the congregation began to pray with these men and women. Schaal notes in his record that

> the cry for salvation became so general and so great, that we were unable to close before eleven o'clock, when more than thirty souls professed to have found the Lord in the pardon of their sins and the regeneration of their souls.

Before the dining hall was erected the sacrifice of the people of the Santa Claus Church in feeding free of charge both guests and animals was great. One tent holder served fifty at one meal.

The lard lamps gave way to gasoline light and torches. The gasoline improvements were followed by a Delco electric plant. The external changes were evidences of an equally important internal transformation in the spirit of the meetings. By 1913 many evidences pointed to the necessity of giving up the program of the annual camp meeting. In 1917 a change in management was made and a camp meeting association was organized. The physical equipment of the grounds was improved.

While the camp meeting by the middle twentieth century was something of an anachronism, the record of its influence upon the Methodist society in Santa Claus is witness to the spiritual vitality of the former years—22 men given to the ministry, 5 women given to the deaconess work, and 5 others to miscellaneous church activities. In all 32 Christian leaders were nurtured in Santa Claus.

Similar to the Santa Claus camp meeting was Berger Camp Grounds, the center of the former Chicago German Conference. Located twenty miles southeast of Chicago in a rural neighborhood, Berger grounds were started in the woods owned by the father of John A. Diekmann, one of the most faithful and capable leaders of German Methodism during the period of the merger of the German and English Conferences. The preachers lived in a shelter shed, from which the platform was built. At the evening services a dozen torches were fastened to the trees and gave hypnotic atmosphere to the forest scene, which added much to the setting. The preachers delivered their sermons without notes and the congregation knew all the songs by heart. The people sat on planks erected under the trees. The ground was covered with straw. While the women and children lived and slept in tents, most of the men slept in the barn, perhaps eighty to a hundred of them on the hay, never bothering to take off their clothes. Although a good deal of food was brought by the campers, the neighboring farmers furnished milk, butter, eggs, and potatoes, and fodder for the horses.

The meetings as a rule lasted from six o'clock in the morning to eleven o'clock at night. The schedule included prayer meetings, testimonials, song services, four or five sermons, and exhortations. After every sermon during the day, as well as in the evening, people were invited to the mourner's bench. The meetings usually closed on Sundays about midnight. The campers formed a great circle, each person holding a lighted candle. Songs were sung, concluding with the customary "God be with you, till we meet again." Prayers became fervent; the preachers made a last urgent appeal to sinners. It was not unusual for a dozen or more persons to be converted at this closing "ring service."

The Berger Camp Meeting Grounds followed the same lines of evolution of other associations. The tents gradually disappeared. The organization bought more woodland. Individual families began to build substantial cottages. A tabernacle seating twelve to fifteen hundred was erected and dignified with a wooden floor, comfortable benches, a large platform, electric lights, and even screens which protected the worshipers from mosquitoes and flies. The camp meeting gradually died away and with it the appeal for conversions. With the growth of the Epworth League Institute, the old-fashioned meeting nearly vanished. Its memory has been kept alive by well-attended meetings on Saturdays and Sundays with preaching and rousing song services on Sunday afternoon.

The German Methodist Camp Meeting at Lakeside, Ohio, was heralded in 1873 when a German wandered to the grounds of the flourishing English-speaking meetings, and went to the altar when the invitation was given. Unable to discuss the condition of his soul, the English brethren sent out an emergency call for the nearest German preacher four miles away across the bay. This incident at once gave birth to the thought that a German camp meeting ought to be held at Lakeside, especially since large colonies of German and Swiss people were located in various counties of Ohio, Pennsylvania, and Indiana. It was the direct occasion of Nast's visit to Lakeside during the meeting of 1874. From that visit arose the invitation to the Central German Conference to join with their English-speaking brethren at Lakeside. In the fall of 1874 invitations came from the Central Ohio and North Ohio Conferences to the Germans to become joint patrons with them in the conduct of the camp meeting.

The first German meeting was held on the grounds in 1875. Twenty conversions were reported. During the first year the English and German-speaking groups held several joint meetings. Russell Pope lined the hymns, first in English, then in German, following which all sang the same tune but each in his own language.

Lake Park soon proved too noisy for the meetings, especially on Sundays when excursions landed on the dock. About 1877, therefore, the Germans moved to South Park. For several years the meetings were held in the open or under a large tent, but in 1883, an auditorium was built at a cost of $2,400. Of this sum the Lakeside Association paid $1,600 and the Germans $800. On the morning of the dedication, Heinrich Liebhart preached the sermon. A collection was taken and in twenty-five minutes $1,200 was raised.

In the early years German Lakesiders depended but little upon the accommodations provided by local enterprise. Many brought all their supplies with them—tents, blankets, food, pans, and kettles. At night some of the men moved the plank seats together under the big tent, and with plenty of straw for bedding, slept comfortably.

After returning home the Germans did not forget Lakeside. They organized "Lakeside Societies," the members of which paid into the treasuries a fixed weekly amount on a sort of Christmas club plan. The Germans added to their scanty budgets by arranging for excursion rates. In 1902, for example, they had a round-trip rate of $5 from Cincinnati, Pittsburgh, and Indianapolis.

Camp meetings were also developing in the East. In the year 1850, one had been held in a little forest in East New York, and later in Bay Ridge, Long Island. In the year 1860 many Germans developed the habit of visiting the English camp meeting held at Sing Sing on the Hudson. Finally they began to congregate in a tent of their own.

In 1872 a flourishing meeting began at Sea Cliff, twenty-five miles from New York on Hempstead Bay. So many Germans attended that they were offered the site. On August 5, 1873, the first German camp meeting was held in the tabernacle placed at the disposal of the Germans by the Sea Cliff Association. On September 30, 1873, the East German Camp Meeting Association was formed. The property developed to a value of about $30,000. In 1902 a summer school for youth was inaugurated.

The same story could be told of the camp meetings at Watertown and Brillion, Wisconsin, formerly on the Milwaukee District of the Chicago German Conference; at Epworth Heights, twenty-one miles northeast of Cincinnati, where German meetings were discontinued shortly before the World War, when the tabernacle burned down; at Hollywood, formerly the center for the California German Conference; at Clitonia, Nebraska; Lake Creek, Missouri; and Redfields, South Dakota.

The camp meeting was an event, or better, an institution of vital importance. It was the dynamo of conversion. It was something more; it was the occasion which the leaders of German Methodist institutions took to promote their causes. It is doubtful whether the educational ventures of the Church could have been maintained without the camp meeting. The presidents and leading professors of the colleges came to preach and lecture. The boys and girls saw the great men of the Church. Students were enrolled for the opening of the fall term. Then, too, under the spirit of the assembly, the people were more willing to make donations and gifts, many of them small, but in the aggregate a vital source of revenue. The directors of hospitals and homes found the camp meeting as advantageous as the educators. If the camp meeting was the instrument of conversion, it was also the focal center of institutional support.

CHAPTER VIII

METHODISM REPAYS ITS DEBT TO GERMANY

Because the human and spiritual history of America was so closely interwoven with that of Germany, it was inevitable that Methodism should some day extend its life and organization to the Continent. Although Methodism was British in its geographical origin, its spiritual traditions were the product of German religious influence upon the life of John Wesley. A spiritual understanding among "hearts" bound American Methodism with German piety from the very first when Wesley made the acquaintance of the Moravians on his voyage to Georgia.

Englishmen who spoke German in the year 1740 could be counted on the fingers of one hand. When Wesley boarded his ship and discovered twenty-six fellow passengers traveling in the company of their Bishop Nitschmann from Herrnhut likewise to Georgia, his interest was immediately awakened. Because these Moravians understood neither English nor Latin, John Wesley determined to master their language—German. Their singing impressed him in particular [1] and the German Church song was the means by which Wesley learned the German language. Between February 6, 1736, and December 2, 1737, while he was in Georgia, Wesley translated thirty-three hymns from German into English. Translating Paul Gerhardt's *Befiehl du deine Wege*, Wesley wrote:

> Through waves and clouds and storms
> He gently clears the way;
> Wait thou His time so shall this night
> Soon end in joyous day. [2]

His daily contact with the Moravians and his subsequent contact with other Germans developed in him a deep appreciation of their childlike, joyful faith, of their earnest prayers, of their sharing of their religious experiences, of their conviction of the religious method of justification through faith. His industrious work upon the German songs made a profound impression upon his soul. The young churchman in Georgia could not work over the words of Dessler's *Mein Jesu, dem die Seraphinen* without profound emotion and then translate:

> Into Thy gracious hands I fall
> And with the arms of faith embrace:
> O King of Glory, hear my call!
> O raise me, heal me by Thy grace!

96

> Now righteous through Thy wounds I am;
>   No condemnation now I dread;
> I taste salvation in Thy name,
>   Alive in Thee my living Head![3]

He could not return to England the same after translating Gerhardt's *O Jesu Christ, mein schönstes Licht* in these words:

> In suffering be Thy love my peace,
>   In weakness be Thy love my power;
> And when the storms of life shall cease,
>   Jesus, in that important hour,
> In death as life be Thou my guide,
> And save me, who for me hast died.[4]

The German sentiments echoed his own spiritual strivings. When Wesley had sailed for America in October, 1735, as a missionary to the Indians, he declared:

> My chief purpose is to save my own soul. I hope to learn to understand the true gospel of Christ so that I can preach it to the heathen.

The religious impression which the behavior of the Moravians had made upon him by their calmness in the storm on his passage he never forgot. When he became acquainted in Savannah, Georgia, with a group of sixteen other Herrnhuters who had settled there with Bishop Spangenberg, he felt in a very congenial environment. The experience of his voyage was still in his mind. He remembered the screams of the passengers when the sea broke over the ship, "split the main sail in pieces . . . and poured in between the decks." He remembered, too, how the Moravians, unconcerned with the storm, were singing their evening hymns on deck. He was still searching for the secret of these simple-hearted Moravians when he fell into conversation with Bishop Spangenberg. The young man had inquired of the Herrnhuter about his future effectiveness. Spangenberg replied that he could not answer until he had asked two or three questions:

"Do you know yourself?" he began. "Have you the witness in yourself? Does the spirit of God bear witness with your spirit that you are a child of God?"

Wesley was confounded; when he hesitated in answering, Spangenberg increased his embarrassment by asking:

"Do you know Jesus Christ?"

"I know," replied Wesley, "that he is the Saviour of the world."

"That is well," continued the bishop, "but do you know that he has redeemed you?"

Such spiritual frankness had to make an impression on Wesley. When Wesley organized a class hour, the forerunner of the class meeting, in Savannah in the Easter season of 1736, its members were exclusively German and its climate was spiritual frankness.

If Wesley had come to America to "save his own soul," he had made some progress. When he was ready to return to England he could say that

> the faith which is necessary is a certain, firm confidence in God that through the merit of Jesus Christ my sins are forgiven and I can share again the favor of God.

That Germans should again play a vital part in his religious quest upon his return to London was an unusual coincidence. He left America with a letter of introduction to Count Zinzendorf, who was in England at the time. This letter brought him into contact with Peter Böhler, a young man of twenty-six, fresh from the University of Jena where he had come under the influence of the Pietists. On February 17, 1738, Wesley and Böhler started out to visit Oxford together. During the course of their conversation Böhler exclaimed: "My brother, my brother, this philosophy of yours must be exterminated."

Wesley said nothing, but later asked Böhler if he should give up preaching. "Certainly not," the German replied; "preach the faith *until* you have it and then you will preach the faith *because* you have it."

Subsequent companionship with Böhler developed in Wesley such a sensitive religious consciousness that he was "ripe" for the Aldersgate experience on the evening of Wednesday, May 24, 1738. The reading was certainly in German. Tired and distressed as he was and still only a beginner in the German language, it was the spiritual environment rather than the German words that precipitated his "awakening." Following that event, in company with four Englishmen and three Germans, he sailed for Rotterdam. Traveling down the Rhine to Cologne, he spent Sunday with Peter Böhler's father, Konrad Böhler, and on July 1, 1738, arrived in Marienborn, where a community of brethren lived. Here, as a guest of Count Zinzendorf, he discussed religion and especially justification through faith. He took comprehensive notes and asked questions freely. After a fortnight in Marienborn, he traveled on by way of Gelnhausen, Eisenach, Erfurt, Weimar, Jena, Halle, Leipzig, and Dresden to Herrnhut, where he spent another two weeks.

Wesley's personal contact with the German Christians had awakened and deepened his faith. The experience in Germany completed his spiritual education at the hands of his continental friends. He had been taught the necessity of conversion by the simple Germans while he was trying to save his own soul in America. Spangenberg and Peter Böhler had pointed him in the direction of the discovery of salvation by faith. While an unknown German layman was reading Luther's preface to the Epistles to the Romans in the little Moravian church on Aldersgate Street, he had felt his heart "strangely warmed" as he experienced the reality of justification through faith in the sequence of the "blessedness of the forgiveness of sins" and the "certainty of salvation." By his journey through Germany, he had made the personal acquaintance of "Christians in earnest" and had seen at first hand the community of fellowship which a common experience of God could produce. That Germans and Methodism should have been separated for nearly a century was unfortunate. It was particularly so because the first Methodist service in America had been conducted by Germans.

On August 18, 1760, a New York news sheet published this item:

> The ship *Perry*, Captain Hagan, arrived last Monday, after a nine-weeks' voyage from Limerick, Ireland. It brought a number of Germans, whose fathers had left them there in 1710. Because there was not room enough there, they decided to try their fortune in America.

Here the story of German Methodism might have begun. But it did not. Among the German-Irish in the group of immigrants were Philipp and Margaret, David and Peter Embury (Imburg), Paul and Barbara Heck, Nicholaus and Peter Shouldness (Schultheiss), Valentin Debtler, and Elias Hoffman. They all sought land, land to cultivate hemp and flax for linen manufacture. But first they found it necessary to remain in New York to make their living by hand work. Some of the group had come to a living faith in Christ through contact with Wesley and his assistants in Ireland and had associated themselves with the Methodists. As far as is known, these were the first Wesleyan Methodists of German blood to arrive in America. Despite the fact that Philipp Embury was a local preacher, these Germans did not seem to hold any meetings. They were strangers in a strange environment. Embury joined the Lutheran Church in New York, and his children were baptized by a Lutheran pastor. But when Barbara Heck found her brother playing cards with friends, the religious conviction fell heavily upon his shoulders. She ordered him to preach. His congregation comprised four Germans and a Negress slave. In the summer of 1766 this German-Irish immigrant preached the first Methodist sermon in America.

The Methodists lost a great opportunity at the time because their imagination was not yet capable of conceiving of a language mission. True, the Methodist circuit riders influenced such men as Simon Müller, Heinrich Böhm, and Jacob Gruber, and they experienced salvation. Böhm recounts occasions on which in his father's barn or in the open, Strawbridge, Asbury, Abbott, and the other pioneers preached in English, after which one of the German preachers proceeded in the mother tongue. Despite Asbury's travels through German settlements in Pennsylvania, Maryland, and Virginia, and the circulation of his assistants through German colonies on the Hudson and Mohawk Rivers, no German congregation was formed. On Asbury's missionary tours, his traveling companion and principal helper was this same Heinrich Böhm who, because he preached mainly in German, had in some places in the Ohio Valley larger congregations than Asbury. Whatever spiritual experience was created by contact with the Methodists only deepened the loyalty of the people to other churches. If Asbury and the other leaders had had a better understanding of the needs and the future of the Germans in America, movements which sprang from the roots of Methodism, the *Vereinigten Brüder in Christ* and the *Evangelische Gemeninschaft* might both have developed as organic parts of the Methodist Episcopal Church. Asbury belatedly recognized the fact and later preached a memorial sermon for Philip William Otterbein, from the pulpit where the co-founder of the *Vereinigten Brüder* had been elected bishop in 1784. If John Wesley seemed unable to escape from the influence of the Germans, if William Nast was constantly thrown together with the Methodists, so it seemed inevitable that Methodism should be bound up closely, if belatedly, with the German people.

The influence of the German experience of John Wesley was not absent from the Section III of the first *Discipline* approved by the Conference which met at Baltimore on Monday, December 27, 1784. It read:

> We are thoroughly convinced that the Church of England, to which we have been united, is deficient in several of the most important parts of Christian discipline; and that (a few ministers and members expected) it has lost the *Life and Power of Religion.* We are not ignorant of the spirit and designs it has ever discovered in Europe, of rising to pre-eminence and worldly dignities by virtue of a national establishment and by the most servile devotion to the will of temporal governors; and we fear the same spirit will lead the same Church in these United States (tho' altered in its name) to similar design and attempts, if the number and strength of its members will even afford a probability of success; and particularly to obtain a national establishment which we cordially abhor as the great bane of truth and holiness, the greatest impediment in the world to the progress of vital Christianity.

Certainly natural bonds of religious appreciation existed between the Methodists and the Germans. German influence had ripened John Wesley's heart for service to England. Methodist influence had converted Wilhelm Nast for service to the Germans.

The extension of the German mission to the Continent was in the natural direction of growth. The demand came from the Fatherland itself. German immigrants wrote of their religious experiences in America to their families who had remained in the old country. The strangeness of the reports in some instances turned to curiosity and curiosity in others became understanding. Letters began to come back to America from Germany, asking for the kind of preachers the reports described. "Why, then, doesn't a preacher like that come to Germany sometime?" they inquired.

In an effort to discover whether sufficient strength existed in Germany behind the entreaties to warrant a continental work, the Missionary Committee sent Nast to Germany in 1844 to make a study of the possibilities and report. He visited Christoph Gottlieb Müller in Winnenden, rejoiced in the great work being carried on there, but was convinced that religious freedom was so curtailed and that life was so dependent upon the State Church and the favor of the prince that it would be unwise to undertake a missionary work in the Fatherland. If conditions changed, he said, the project should be reconsidered in the light of the altered circumstance.

Such a change of circumstances did take place when a wave of revolutions swept the Continent in 1848. Nast and Jacoby, delegates to the General Conference of 1848 meeting in Pittsburgh, took advantage of the situation to send their petition to the bishops, asking for a missionary to Germany. After long deliberation, the request was acceded to. In 1849 the May meeting of the Board of Bishops and the subsequent session of the General Missionary Committee decided to begin the work on the Continent. The bishops entrusted the leadership of the work to Bishop Morris. The choice was well made, for Morris in his days as editor of *The Western Christian Advocate* had shown an intelligent enthusiasm for the language work. In June of the same year Bishop Morris appointed Jacoby, then presiding elder of the Quincy District of the Illinois Conference, as missionary to the land of his birth.

The appointment could not have come at a more unsatisfactory time as far as Jacoby was concerned. Worn and weary from the heavy duties of superintending the German work on the hundreds-of-miles circuits of the open spaces of the West, he was ill and in the process of arranging his affairs so that he could take a year of rest. Health was only one of the reasons why the invitation to go to Germany as missionary was not joyfully received. Frau Jacoby had an aversion to returning to the Fatherland under any conditions. Her husband proposed another preacher as a substitute for the work, but upon the insistence of German friends, he considered his duty. Bishop Morris was so uncertain about how he would receive the offer that he communicated the news to Jacoby officially through Nast:

> May 24, 1849
> New York

Rev. L. S. Jacoby
Dear Brother:

    The General Missions Committee and the Board of Managers of the Missionary Society recommend that a mission be begun in Germany. The provision has also been made for two missionaries. The bishops have commissioned me first to send only one and if the report of the first is favorably received, then to let the others follow later. We wish that you might go to found a mission in the old Fatherland, provided, however, that your

health will permit, and that you are willing to undertake the
work. Please give me your answer soon so that we can come to
a decision in this matter.

May the Lord lead you and me in this affair.

Your associate,

Th. A. Morris.[5]

Nast was considerate of his friend when he transmitted the communication to him with these words:

Dear Brother:

I have just received the enclosed lines to be forwarded to
you. Bishop Morris informs me of your nomination with the
note that the final decision depends upon your own conclusion.
May the Lord lead you in this important matter.[6]

Preacher and Frau Jacoby finally capitulated to the pressure groups.
They sailed from New York on the S. S. *Hermann* on October 20,
1849, which date was the occasion of his thirty-sixth birthday. He
was equipped with five dollars' worth of literature, which he had purchased from the tract society, and a few New Testaments given him
by the Bible Society with the promise of more. The diary which
he kept during the voyage indicates that he was troubled about how
his work was to be begun and equally troubled as to the value of the
whole missionary project. Ten days out of New York he wrote in
his journal:

Tuesday, October 30: It seems as though I see more and more
light. The Lord will lead it all. I heard from an English brother,
the ship's engineer, that there is no church in Bremerhaven and
that there are also enough English sailors always in port to hear
English preaching. The Lord will open doors and ways. . . .
I must pray more and be willing to surrender everything for
the Lord. . . . Now they are beginning to play cards and the
little Filipinos are so curious. How much grace it is going to
take to be able to educate the children in Germany to piety!
Here, too, the Lord helps. He hears prayers.[7]

At noon on Wednesday, November 7, he made notes in his journal
which showed relief and yet anxiety that he was finally at the des-
tination where his work was to begin. As the boat plied its way
slowly up the Weser, he saw the outlines of the port. It was up to
him to decide where his first work should commence. Bishop Morris
had directed him to begin either in Bremen or Hamburg, two of the
four free cities in Germany.

He wrote:

Here is the place where I must and can work. But am I
the man for the job? That is the question. I have neither the
health nor the strength for that. Yet the Lord will help. I go
in the morning, the Lord willing, to Bremen, and there I will
soon experience what I have to do. The Lord will bless me in
Germany. . . . O Lord, help; O Lord, let the work succeed.[8]

On November 10, 1849, he was in Bremen. He wrote in his journal:

So I will work in God's name and hope for his blessing.

The sensibilities of the missionary were shocked with the moral conditions on the Continent—especially by the utter disregard of the Sabbath that prevailed everywhere. He longed for America. Methodist morality was in conflict with what the Methodists called the paganism of the worldliness of society. It was the same conflict which had aroused the Methodists to missionary action among the Germans a little more than a decade before in the Ohio Valley.

That there was need for a militantly evangelical church in Germany there can be no doubt. That America should have the effrontery to send missionaries to an old Protestant people with glorious spiritual traditions was a question which had worried the Methodist leaders from the beginning of the deliberation of the wisdom of opening a mission on the Continent. That was the reason why Nast had been sent to Germany in 1844 to conduct a survey. Jacoby was very humble about his work when he thought of his position.

The external secularism was only the first evidence of a series of circumstances which pained Jacoby and his wife, who had so unwillingly accompanied him. The religious condition of the German people was a sorry one. In one village of 1,800 inhabitants, a correspondent reported, only two men came to morning worship. A vicar, in telling of his congregation, said that he had only four men and no women or children and that he often had no one in the church at all. In the parsonage on Sunday morning, he said, the washing was industriously wrung out! Parishes in the State Churches were large and the clergy had of necessity little close spiritual contact with the people. In Berlin, at the time suffering from a poverty of churches, 80,000 souls on the average belonged to a single parish. A church district comprised 120,000 human beings in its area with but one church with 1,500 seats and 3 pastors. No one could say that the field of religion in Germany was overcrowded. Surely a place for the Methodist activity was there.

That there was a place for the Methodist doctrine soon became evident to Jacoby. Secular thought dominated philosophy and science. Rationalism dominated theology. Worldliness had influenced the codes of conduct of the clergy. Of the preaching of God's grace "more abundant than man's sins" there was little.

In such an environment Missionary Jacoby was ready to begin his work—to begin just where he had begun in St. Louis more than eight years before. His experience in the West had taught him that planless preaching did not lead to any permanent results. The foundation of the work, he felt, must be laid by multiplying the influence of actual conversions into the co-operation of the faithful in common action. But where should he begin to preach? While he was looking for a hall he made the acquaintance of a *Herrnhuter,* who invited Jacoby to meet a little company of friends on Sunday evening in his home and talk about Methodism. Accepting, he preached his first sermon in Germany in December, 1849, in the little dwelling twenty miles distant from Bremen. The tiny gathering was a spiritual event.

While Jacoby was absent from the city of Bremen a gentleman called upon his wife, expressed his desire to meet her husband, and suggested that they obtain the *Krameramthaus* in which to hold services. After the first refusal of the hall, Jacoby was in a Bremen store buying furnishings when the proprietor, the chairman of the trustees of the *Amthaus,* after visiting with him and discovering that he was the same individual who had applied for the use of the hall, assured him that he should have it. The rent was three Reich thaler a Sabbath. Jacoby thought the coincidence providential and on December 23, 1849, preached his first sermon in the hall to a congregation of about four hundred, on the text from 1 Timothy 2. 4, "Who will have all men to be saved, and to come unto the knowledge of the truth."

He sat down in the first flush of his apparent success and wrote to Nast:

> Since I have found no hindrance in a political respect, I have announced quite openly the purpose which brought me here. The Lord opened the way to me in a wonderful manner. I was acquainted with vital Christians who rejoiced over my arrival and were helpful in every way. I have had at once a greater part of our tracts and our general rules printed. . . . Since the Sabbath here is so secularized, I have had the tract of The American Tract Society about the secularization of the Sabbath printed. . . . Unable physically to preach twice a Sunday, I announced the service at 7.15 in the evening of December 23. . . . You can believe that I went with pounding heart. . . . Here I was, a poor preacher, about to appear before a meeting accustomed to hear pious and scholarly preachers such as Mallett. . . . I prayed to God to support me. As I came, I saw the whole room and lobby filled with people and many who came late had to be turned away.'

The hall was soon too small. Jacoby preached every Sunday evening, rented a private house for social meetings because the *Amthaus* hall was not available on weekdays, and opened his own flat as a center for the interested for prayer meetings. The growth of the congregation was so rapid that the larger hall in the *Amthaus,* seating eight hundred, was engaged. Jacoby rented this for Sundays and midweek services. Conversions began, among which were two young men who proved to be leaders in the Methodist work—Ernst Mann and Adolf Lüring.

On January 17, 1850, he extended his work to a dance hall which he had rented on *Buntentorsteinweg,* a Bremen suburb inhabited by the lower classes.   Here his sermons were often interrupted by the unruly conduct of the congregation.   But he was not discouraged. He pressed on to Baden, fifteen miles away, and preached to large congregations in a schoolhouse.   In feeble health, Jacoby was assisted by E. C. Poppe, a helper and colporteur.   Jacoby begged the Missionary Society for reinforcements.

The response to his appeals came in a letter from the Mission Board:

February 18, 1850
New York

Dear Brother:

Your valued communication of January 1 has been received and has been considered at the first opportunity of the Mission Board.   The communication was received with obvious interest and the following resolutions were thereupon adopted:

1. *Resolved,* That Brother Jacoby be empowered to rent a suitable place for holding worship services in Bremen, for not more than $150 a year.   Likewise he shall be authorized to rent suitable rooms for a dwelling.

2. *Resolved,* That he be empowered to spend not more than $250 for furnishing his dwelling, the same to be carefully inventoried and kept as the property of the Mission Board.

3. *Resolved,* That Brother Jacoby be allowed to spend a sum of not more than $100 for furnishing the room for worship.

4. *Resolved,* That he be given permission to spend a sum not to exceed $50 for the printing and distribution of tracts.

5. *Resolved,* That the opinion of the Mission Board is that the mission in Germany should be strengthened by the sending of another missionary.

6. *Resolved,* That it is the opinion of the Board that a fortnightly periodical be published and that for that purpose Brother Jacoby be empowered to bring out such a publication as soon as $500 can be collected for the purpose.

The letter concluded with these words:

And now, my dear brother, permit me to say that we are very much encouraged by your letter in which you express the hope of finding entrance to the hearts of the German people for the purpose of bringing them Methodism.   *We as a denomination are very much indebted to Germany and hope now to be able to pay the debt.*   You know that John Wesley received much light from pious German preachers and what a blessing it will be, when some of their sons can let again the light in the gospel be turned back on Germany.   If the General Conference which meets in May approves the sending of a second missionary to Germany it probably will be Brother Doering.[10]

May God bless you and your family and let your mission flourish.

Awaiting assistance and despite his failing health, Jacoby was working tirelessly.   In April, 1850, he formed a class of twenty-one, received them on trial on Easter Sunday, held the first Lord's Supper on the same day, and on Easter Monday had a love feast.

The spring of 1850 was virtually spring for Methodism in Germany. The first Quarterly Conference, considered by Jacoby as the "birthday" of Methodism in Germany, was held. On May 25 the first issue of the *Evangelist,* Germany's own *Christian Advocate,* appeared with a printing order of two hundred copies. The circulation of the *Evangelist* increased to the point where it nearly rivaled the circulation of the *Apologist* itself. The paper, which had so cautiously been suggested by the Mission Board, had been subsidized for the first year by the gifts of two brothers, Charles and Henry Baker, of Baltimore, Maryland. At the same time the publishing firm of J. G. Heyse, of Bremen, brought out a Methodist songbook in an edition of a thousand copies. This was sold out within two years and had to be reprinted. Friends in America were generous in subscribing for the *Evangelist* with the request that it be sent to interested families in Germany. By the end of May, Christian Feltman, assisted by the Tract Society, had opened a free library, loaning books without charge in the hope of spreading evangelical Christianity.

The first issue of *Der Evangelist* appeared at Bremen on Saturday, May 25, 1850, as a fortnightly publication. The masthead was dignified with the pragmatic exhortation of 1 Thessalonians 5. 21, "Prove all things; hold fast to that which is good." It proclaimed the "glorious wish"

> *die Gnade unseres Herrn Jesus Christus sei mit dir!* [11]

This was the theme song of the first and subsequent issues:

> And what wish could be more precious [asked the editor]. Through grace . . . you will be led to self-recognition, through it it will become clear that you are burdened with the wrath of God because of your sins, that the divine sorrow over your sins is at work within you, driving you to the Cross of Christ where alone you can find rest.

The editor felt it necessary to introduce himself quite impersonally.

> "Perhaps you ask: Where do you come from? What do you want here? . . . I will try to allay your curiosity as satisfactorily as possible.
> "I came from the other side of the great ocean, from the United States of America as a respresentative of my elder brother, the *Christian Apologist.* My desire is to help build the kingdom of my Saviour.
> "My brother declared war on 'fire water' from the beginning and I hate this poison [*Gift*], which disturbs the health of many, ruins the happiness of families, and has ruined so many souls. . . . With politics I have nothing to do."

This introduction, written in the first person, was a remarkably frank and pointed explanation.

The contents of the issue included a poem, an article on the "Mission of Methodism," an "Exhortation to Children Blessed of God," and a temperance discussion. Items reprinted from *The Christian Apologist* were labeled "A."

The article on "Fire Water" as the opening gun of Methodism's courageous stand on alcohol deserves to be recorded:

> The poor pagan Indians understand the effects of alcohol better than the great physicians of the sixteenth century. The latter believed that its use would prolong life and called it *"Lebenswasser"* [Life water.] The Indians called it *"Feuerwasser"* [Fire water]. It burns not only when ignited, no, it burns also when drunk. It disturbs not only the bodily strength, understanding, and reason of man, but it disturbs the soul, leads it farther and farther from God and hurls it finally into the eternal fire.[14]

The first issue of the *Evangelist* took the full stand on the grounds of Methodist morals. On page 6 is published an outspoken article of the "Purpose of Sunday," quoting a text,

> "Remember the sabbath day, to keep it holy."—Exodus 20. 8.
> The purpose for which this day was established was to fix a time when man shall raise his eyes from worldly and secular affairs and cares and pleasures of men to Him, the Creator and Preserver of all things, to him, the Saviour, to him the Judge of all men—that the knowledge of the one true and living God may be preserved in consciousness and be used in developing different life relationships to the end that all shall be led to adore and worship him and to experience for themselves, the blessings of his wise guidance.

A news summary dealt with cholera in Texas, census figures in the United States, and included items of moral implication.[15]

The issue also announced the Methodist services and advertised literature available in German.[16] It was published by the press of Johann Georg Heyse.

Jacoby's duties were made heavy indeed by his supervision over the new periodical. His own schedule in addition was so strenuous in proportion to his health that he had no time to answer the many calls which were coming from a distance for Methodist preaching. Sunday afternoon at three o'clock a class met in his own apartment. Sunday evening he preached at the *Krameramthaus*. Monday evening he held prayer meeting in his own home. Wednesday evening he preached again in the *Amthaus*. Thursday evening he held prayer meeting at *Doventor*. Friday evening he preached in the dance hall at *Buntentorsteinweg*. Saturday evening he held prayer meeting at *Stephantor*. His health finally kept him from attending the Thursday and Saturday meetings but he was unfailing in his attendance at the others. Urgent demands for his services were coming from Hanover, Oldenburg, and the suburbs of Bremen, but he was too feeble to respond in any large way. Help came when, on June 7, 1850, *Karl H. Doering* and

Ludwig Nippert arrived in Bremen. They were received with open arms.

Nippert began his work at once. Blessed with good health, a strong physique, and an unquenchable passion, he started with characteristic energy to preach in the suburbs of Bremen the evening after his arrival. He proved to be one of the most tireless, bravest, truest, and successful missionary workers of the Church. Born in Goersdorf, Alsace, on March 23, 1825, Nippert had migrated with his parents to America and settled at Captina, a German colony on the borders of Belmont and Monroe Counties, Ohio. The family was orthodox Lutheran. Nippert described their religious life in this way:

> On the Sabbath, in the forenoon, they went to the Lutheran Church, to which they belonged; and the afternoon was spent in visiting, hunting, or going to the tavern. In these pastimes the minister not unfrequently took part and with the members of his church emptied the glass and often went staggering home. Of true experimental religion there was nothing said, much less possessed. I knew none among those Germans who lived there that was acquainted with the power of religion. It was a "valley of dry bones." [17]

The Methodist circuit riders were working up and down through Belmont County and making such an impression upon the community that the local Lutheran pastor felt it necessary to warn the Nipperts often "with all earnestness against the Methodists, as deceivers and enthusiasts," and advise them that to befriend these peculiar fanatics would be nothing less than to renounce the faith of their fathers.

Not heeding his warnings, many in the community, and the Nipperts in particular, continued to discuss the Methodists. Nippert's mother one evening walked a mile to attend a meeting at which Riemenschneider was preaching.

Of this event Nippert wrote:

> After midnight we all went to bed, though she had not yet returned. About two o'clock she came and having awakened us, told us that the Lord had pardoned her sins, that she felt an inexpressible joy in her soul and that now she firmly believed the Methodists to be the people of God. My father (a Lutheran elder) now fell into a deep godly sorrow and could not rest day or night. He often went five miles over bad roads to attend the Methodist meeting and seek the prayers of the Church. Finally, after three months seeking in this way, the Lord had mercy on him and blessed him also. [18]

Ludwig Nippert was hurt. "The preacher who trained us in catechism," he wrote:

> endeavored to fill our minds with prejudice against the Methodists. I hated them from my heart, because I believed they were bad people. I was displeased when my parents were converted and could not bear to be called a Methodist, and, if any of my schoolmates called me by this name, I was immediately ready

to fight. I continued to visit the Lutheran preacher and was confirmed in a short time; but God ordered it otherwise. In 1840, the fifteenth year of my age, I, too, was awakened under the preaching of Brother Riemenschneider.[19]

Nippert deliberately joined the Methodist Episcopal Church, "which step," he wrote, "I have never regretted."

A few months after his conversion he went to Cincinnati, learned the art of printing on the *Apologist,* attended scrupulously to his religious duties, went regularly to Sunday school, and profited much by his association with Nast, Adam Miller, and Wilhelm Ahrens. When he was seventeen he took charge of a class. When his four years of apprenticeship as a printer were up, Nast faced him with the issue of preaching, and, after a struggle he was licensed by the Monroe Mission in 1846. At the age of twenty-one he was received into the Ohio Conference.

First sent as assistant pastor to Louisville, he moved to Indianapolis and founded the society there. In 1847 he moved to Pittsburgh, and in 1848 to Columbus, where he rode the Delaware Circuit. He was now anxious to go to California but, instead, he arrived on June 7, 1850, in Bremen, Germany.

With characteristic energy he preached his first sermon, as already mentioned, without delay. The day after his arrival in Germany he was two miles out in the open country beyond the city of Bremen. The congregation was assembled on the open floor of a farmhouse. The crowd, anxious to see and hear a "Methodist," pressed into all the available space. It was a strange location for worship—"horses and pigs to the right of the congregation, bellowing cows to the left, with hens cackling and flapping their wings." The animal background did not disturb the spiritual appreciation of the people. They listened with rapt attention as the congregations always did when Nippert preached. He was a *Volksredner* [20] in the highest sense of the word. Gifted with a keen sense of humor, a pictorial style, a persuasive voice, and the most devout and contagious evangelical passion, he was able to make an impression upon his hearers to an extent enjoyed by few preachers.

> I sought to preach [wrote Nippert of his first sermon in Germany] as if I were in the presence of God; there seemed to be a great hunger for the Word of God among the people.

John McClintock, an English-speaking preacher who had accompanied Doering and Nippert to Germany and who, like the others, had been seasick on the voyage, preached in the parlor of the American consul the first English Methodist sermon ever delivered in Bremen the Sunday after their arrival. In the afternoon the "Methodists" met for a general class meeting in Jacoby's home. Testimony followed testimony. Tears of gratitude and joy ran down the cheeks of the brothers and sisters. In the evening they adjourned to the *Kramer-*

amthaus to hear Doering preach to a congregation of approximately eight hundred. The people sang magnificently. During the meeting, as Nippert recorded in his journal, a man came from a village four hours' away to contribute $6 of missionary money with the request that the "Methodists" visit him and preach. On Monday evening a missionary meeting was held. Jacoby told of the Methodist missionary work in Africa. When the meeting broke up a brother stood at the door receiving contributions, totaling $5, for the work. No demonstration could have been more typical of the German Methodist loyalty to all the activities of the Methodist Episcopal Church.

On Sunday, June 16, 1850, an event took place which marked a date into the religious history of Germany. On that day the first Sunday school was opened in Germany in the city of Bremen by the Methodist missionaries. The Sabbath school, as it existed in the United States, was practically unknown on the Continent. The response to the work was unexpected. The little group of eighty children enrolled at the first session soon grew to three hundred. Wherever the Methodist work spread, the Sunday school went with it. A second school was promptly established at the mission center on *Buntentorsteinweg,* a third in Vegesack. Wherever a preaching station was established, a Sunday school was opened. Everywhere the youth work was hailed with delight. Lutherans, alarmed that Methodism should be gathering the children so successfully under its influence, was forced to adopt the Church school and under the direction of the State Church the movement spread over Germany.

On July 14, 1850, Nippert was able to report in the *Apologist* that preaching services were being held in (1) the Krameramthaus; (2) on Buntentorsteinweg; (3) in Walle, a village an hour's ride from Bremen; (4) Bremenhaven; (5) Vegesack, a little village of three thousand inhabitants; (6) in the two towns of Thedinghausen and Baden; (7) in Tarnstedt and Hebstedt; (8) in Hastedt, a suburb of Bremen; and (9) Sunday school in the Krameramthaus, Bremen.

The expansion of the work took place fearlessly without modification of any of the peculiar Methodist techniques—earnest extempore preaching, hearty and lively singing, prayer with bold responses of approval and "Amens," class meetings, and outdoor meetings. The methods were novel in Germany. Letters describing religious experiences of converts in the United States, sometimes read in public assemblies, and occasionally even from the pulpits of State Churches, fanned the flame. The converts of the mission in Germany were precipitated by their experience into action.

The second Quarterly Conference was held on August 19, 1850. The reports of the work were encouraging. Two hundred pupils and seventeen teachers were reported in Sunday schools. Wessel Fiege, a colporteur, was granted the first exhorter's license in the country. In the evening sixteen members were received into full connection, the first class to be taken into the Methodist Episcopal Church in Germany. Jacoby remarked, as he handed Fiege his credentials, that at no distant day capable preachers would be sent from Germany to America, a prophecy which was abundantly fulfilled.

Jacoby was conscious of the importance which the first class of full members had for the future of the work. He wrote:

> In large measure it depends upon them how the work shall be built. If they show themselves to be true Christians in their homes, in the world, and in the work of the Lord, then there will be no doubt not only that we shall become a flourishing society, but also that Methodism in its purity shall be spread and make its contribution to the spiritual life of Germany.[21]

The work had grown so rapidly and so unexpectedly that the bishop was forced to appoint Jacoby superintendent of the mission. At the end of the year 1850 the field had to be divided into two districts, Bremen-city and Bremen-district. Jacoby presided over the former, Doering and Nippert over the latter, although the work in both regions was directed by the same Quarterly Conference.

What the missionaries were doing in Germany cannot be appreciated without reference to the first Watch Night held on December 31, 1850. The Methodists assembled in the smaller hall of the *Krameramthaus* while a *Silvesterabend* ball was going on above them in the larger hall generally used by the Methodists. At the opening of the service Doering preached, Nippert exhorted. Plans for administering the Lord's Supper after the first preaching were interrupted by the increasing size of the congregation, resulting from a movement from the ballroom above to the service below. Jacoby preached again. Nippert exhorted again in the now crowded room. The earnestness of the preaching was making its impression.

On March 1, 1851, Jacoby reported on the state of the work as follows: L. S. Jacoby, superintendent; C. H. Doering, L. Nippert, missionaries; C. Poppe and C. Nahrmann, colporteurs; W. Fiege, Ropke, and E. Wunderlich, assistants.

The assistance now available enabled Jacoby to travel about Germany in response to demands for Methodist preaching. He traveled into southern Germany, visited Württemberg, and in February of 1851 visited Saxony.

The work in Saxony found leaders in two brothers, Erhard and Friedrich Wunderlich. Erhard migrated from Russdorf in Saxony-Weimar to America in 1849. Settling in Dayton, Ohio, he came under the influence of the Methodists and was converted. Of his emigration from Germany and subsequent conversion he wrote:

> As I could not find a good situation, in the fall of 1849, I came to America. This was a source of grief to my aged mother, as she believed that by going from under her care I would finally sink into infidelity and be lost. . . . I came to America careless and

thoughtless, when God through his good providence had brought me among his people in Dayton, Ohio. I was so far gone astray as to oppose religion and persecute those who professed it. Yet, it was not long till I was convinced of the error of my ways. Now, although I had become willing to repent of my sins, I was not willing to become a Methodist. . . . But—as I now had the name of Methodist, I at once determined to seek till I found what they professed to enjoy. I sought earnestly, and after two weeks I found on the 24th day of December, 1849, at the altar of prayer, the pardon of my sins in the blood of Christ. As much as I had previously despised this people of God, so much the more I loved them now; and as much as I had felt lonely in this country, so much the more I felt myself at home, especially among God's people. I wrote to my mother and told her what the Lord had done for my soul.[22]

Despite his report to his mother that he intended to remain in America, he was persuaded by her to return. On September 1, 1850, he arrived in his home town to perform his military obligations. His bold witness attracted a number of spiritually anxious individuals who constantly sought his counsel and help. It was not long before crowds came out to hear his exhortation. In the old home on the manor, he held family worship. The servant girl was caught by his passion and converted. Some of his former comrades, interested in the letters which he had written from America, joined the prayer group. Yielding to constant requests to tell the story of his religious experience, he began to preach in such fashion that a revival broke out. He told his story day after day. His aged mother was converted, then his brothers. His success was bound to arouse the jealousy of the pastors of the State Church. A year after he arrived home, for example, he was telling his story privately in a weaver's home to a group of twenty-five when a howl broke loose outside A procession of about fifty excited and drunken men filed in the home, cursing and shouting "we want to hear the Methodist!" The apprentice lighted the candle. When Wunderlich said he was not holding a public meeting, the ruffians seized him, pulled him over the table behind which he was standing, and told him to "get out quick!" Hardly had he begun to run when he resolved to face the crowd. He went back through the black night, was beaten by the mob, and "forced" to flee. A devil's cap was put of his head to make him look ridiculous. Mob action was only one form of abuse. He was brought before magistrates, banished from some places, and imprisoned in others. In *Dittersdorf* he was holding family worship one morning. The police raided the house, found a Bible and hymnal on the table, and accused him of holding public meetings. The Lord Judge before whom he was finally brought declared:

We do not need you as a missionary in our principality and we do not want you; if you hold meetings again you will be turned over to your provincial sovereign. If you come back, you will get a quarter year in the workhouse. If that does not help, a half year. We will be done with you.[23]

In Zeulenroda he was arrested again and put in jail, first for two days, and then for eight, for the crime of preaching to public assemblies. The following summer he was sitting one moonlight evening in the garden of a friend in his sleeping garments. Recognized, he was thrown into jail. Three fellow prisoners, arrested for other causes, recognized him. "When did you get back?" asked one. "As far as I can see, it's Mr. Wunderlich from Russdorf!" commented the second prisoner. "What, is the Methodist back again?" said the third.[24]

On another occasion, when he was sentenced to a week in prison, he was brought to the jail about ten o'clock at night and put in with three fellow prisoners who proved to be infidels. They had been circulating revolutionary books. When the men were locked in their four cells and the keeper had retired, this conversation took place:
"Who in the world have they brought in now?" asked one.
"I believe it is the Holy Father from Rome," responded a second.

> "What!" exclaimed the first, "Holy Father here, again! Now do tell me what is yet to become of Germany! We were put in because we did not pray; and if we get out and go to praying we will be put back here again, for the Holy Father is here because he prayed too much. It is better for us to go to AMERICA, for there we will not be imprisoned for praying." [25]

Harassed by arrests, prohibitions, and fines, he found one field after another closed to him. Upon Jacoby's advice he packed his bag and left for America, that "Holy Land of Freedom," in 1853, where he was received into the Ohio Conference and continued effective work in the ministry. Groups of his friends followed him to the United States, most of them settling near Wheeling, where they strengthened the Methodist work.

Erhard Wunderlich left his work in Saxony in the hands of his brother Friedrich. The latter promptly rented his estate and effectively devoted himself to Methodist leadership. In Russdorf he transformed a barn into a chapel. Although crowds joined in his services, he was harassed as his brother had been before him. Yet he consistently paid the $10 fine assessed for violation of the order prohibiting his services. On occasions when he refused to pay his cows were seized and sold at public auction. He continued to defy the authorities, shaming them as he could, until a kind of religious freedom was granted in the Grand Duchy in 1864.

When Jacoby visited Russdorf in February, 1851, he found 130 members organized into nine classes. On June 11, 1865, Friedrich

Wunderlich was ordained as a preacher. He was summoned to Waida by the superintendent of the State Church, who explained to him that as a member of the State Church he did not have any right to give communion. "Also," said the superintendent, "either get in the Church or get out."

"In that case," replied Wunderlich, "I will go over to the Methodist Church." Fifteen immediately followed his example. Wunderlich was ably assisted in the work in Saxony by Carl Dietrich, who, like Friedrich, had been converted through the efforts of Erhard Wunderlich.

The beginning of Methodism in Germany was difficult. A picture of the problems faced can be given by examining the troubles of the preachers in Saxony. Saxony seems to have had a deep-seated aversion to the Methodists. John Wesley himself complained against the turmoil which was excited by his presence in 1738. As he traveled through the land, he was forced to wait an hour and a half at the gate of Leipzig before he was allowed to enter the city. Before he was permitted to spend the night in Dresden, he was dragged from one magistrate to another for more than two hours "with the usual impertinent solemnity."

> I wonder very much [wrote Wesley] that healthy human understanding and universal humanity do not make an end of this inhuman procedure against foreigners, since in nearly every German city, in Frankfurt, Weimar, Halle, Leipzig, and Dresden we were exposed to this treatment. I do not know what can be said in defense of the custom. In a time of solid peace, it is an injury to everyone, even to the heathen code of guest friendship.[26]

In Neustadt he could not even find a lodging. Finally, after hours of search, he came to a little *Gasthaus* (lodging house)

> but they told us plainly, we should have no lodging with them, for they did not like our looks.[27]

If John Wesley had made his journey a century and a half later, he would have been even more astonished. Methodists were allowed in Saxony to hold divine service only in certain so-called "free places." In other villages, permission was granted only for worship in homes.

Bishop Nuelsen, examining hundreds of magistrate records in Saxony, performed a service to the history of Methodism by making the documents available. A few of these need only be cited.

To Frau C., in S.:

> If the cessation of these house devotions for Methodists is not have been held in your home, to which members, and especially children, of the Evangelical Lutheran Church have been admitted. If the cessation of these house devotions for Methodists is not

guaranteed, you will be charged for admitting non-Methodists the sum of thirty marks or a corresponding imprisonment for each individual case expressly forbidden.[28]

To Herr C. B., in Schneeberg:

Pursuant to a report of the gendarmes, it has come to our attention that on November 15 of this year you took part in the Methodist meeting house in Witzschdorf in a Methodist meeting in which a sermon was preached from the altar and hymns sung and which had the character of a divine assembly and that you yourself participated in such discourse. Inasmuch as by special supplementary order to the decree of the Royal Ministry of Culture and Public Instruction dated August 13, 1881, the holding of Methodist devotions is allowed only in specially defined "free places" to which group Witzschdorf does not belong, so under threat of a fine of a hundred marks and fourteen days in prison you are to abstain from organizating and taking part in such divine assemblies and holding such devotions in Witzschdorf as well in all other localities of the district in which the Methodists are not expressly permitted to hold divine assemblies through High Ministerial Decree.

Royal Prefect Flocha, December 20, 1886.

The Methodists were allowed to give "lectures" in connection with their worship in homes, but they were required to have police approval for each talk, after submitting the title of the lecture to the police.

To Herr E. S., in P.:

Be advised that you will limit the leadership of your "religious meetings" in this district according to the interpretation of the Culture Act in which song and prayer with or without participation of those assembled, is to be wholly stopped and is limited to the performance for each time for which a permit is given according to Paragraph 4. If you do not comply with this—you will be fined 200 marks for every violation or given a corresponding jail sentence for every meeting held unpermitted.[29]

To Herr H. B., in Ch.:

Your proposed assembly, at which according to your notice of the second of this month you are to speak on "The Christian Church" is hereby forbidden because the Royal High Prefect has seen pressing danger to the public peace and order according to past experience. The interdiction of your devotions in Wildenau continues. . . .

In response to your request of the 29th of this month, we are forced to say that such permission for holding a religious lecture in the castle cellar cannot be granted, since within three weeks you have already given three lectures of the same type in the same place.

The Police Board.

The limits to which the public authority was willing to go can be seen from the following notice:

To Herr C. S., in P.:

> It has come to the knowledge of the undersigned High Prefect that because permission to hold Methodist meetings in Obercrimnitz from time to time has led to disturbances of the peace and misconduct, and that curious individuals in no way connected with the Methodist group, and indeed so great a number that they could not be cared for in the meeting room and since they overflowed into a great crowd before the house and annoyed the neighborhood and interfered with the traffic movement on the public way, so (to avoid further incidents of this kind, which will not be tolerated) it is firmly decreed that entrance of persons who are not Methodists shall not be permitted. *Zwickau,* den 28. Juni 1880.

Official acts such as marriages, baptisms, and funerals could be performed by Methodist preachers only in the so-called "free places." Persons who did not belong to the State Churches even had to be buried before seven o'clock in the morning.

To the Stocking Master Weaver N. zu D.:

> According to information coming to the undersigned Royal High Prefect, you intend to have your newborn child baptized in your home by the Methodist preacher B. in Chemnitz. According to a decree of the Royal Ministry of Culture and Public Instruction B. and every other Methodist preacher have only the right to function in those places and may exercise the rights of a Methodist preacher appertaining to the affairs of the spiritual office in which the confirmation of the Society of the Zwickau District of the Methodist Episcopal Church relates, and since D. does not belong to this classification, the contemplated service by preacher B. is expressly prohibited.

To Methodist Preacher P., in S.:

> According to Section 3 of the regulations for ecclesiastical activity in the parish of Gruenstaedt it is forbidden to the preachers or speakers of the Dissenter's Societies (Methodists) to speak or do any other religious act, that is, liturgical acts, at the casket or the grave of a deceased member of this parish. It has been brought to our attention and has been acknowledged by your action on October 7 that you prayed the Lord's Prayer at the burial of A. T. F. in Pohla at the grave in violation of this interdiction and used a form of benediction, and that in addition to this conduct instead of the funeral being held before seven o'clock as provided by law, it took place in the afternoon. You are advised herewith that future violations of these ordinances will be treated by proceeding against you under penalty of the law.
>
> Schwarzenberg, den 13. Oktober 1886.
Die Königliche Amtshauptmannschaft.

To those who rent the hall in the Restaurant Teichmühle in Thum:

> The undersigned Evangelical Lutheran Pastors' office holds
> it its duty to communicate the following to the persons concerned.
> [Here follows a long complaint over the penetration of sects
> into Germany.]   It is correctly said . . . concerning the Meth-
> odists who are penetrating into Germany that they create the
> spirit of disorder, the soul of rebellion, of arrogance, and of dis-
> integration within Christianity to the confusion of the conscience.
> In short, the Methodist actions are what the Lord cited as the sin
> of the Pharisees (Matthew 23. 15) ; for spiritual arrogance makes
> one into a child of hell.   Herewith the protest is closed.

Thum, den 4, Mai 1887

Das evangelische lutherische Pfarramt.

In concluding his comment on these citations, Bishop Nuelsen wrote:

> State, pulpit, and professor's chair unite to fight the Methodists.
> Are there not in our age, saturated with unholiness at the end of
> the nineteenth century, other powers which one ought to make
> war against other than that little group of order-loving, peaceful
> citizens whose only crime consists in their desire to serve their
> God according to their best knowledge and conscience? "Alas,
> Alas, what a Reformation country this is !" John Wesley cried
> a century and a half ago.[31]

Despite persecution, the Methodist mission had gained a momentum
which had made it a force to be reckoned with.

Jacoby, traveling into South Germany to attend the peace congress
being held in Frankfurt, took advantage of the occasion to visit
Müller. Together these "Methodist brethren" rejoiced in the triumphs of experimental religion through their common efforts. Müller
agreed to adopt the Methodist hymnal and they suggested the continuation of the "informal two-man fraternal conferences."

The meeting established a spirit of co-operation which ultimately led
to the union of the Methodist Episcopal and Wesleyan Methodist
work in Germany. In Frankfurt Jacoby preached to a congregation so
large that the burgomaster was compelled to place a church at his disposal. Typical of how the mission bridged the spiritual distance to
America was shown in the following incident. At the end of one of
the services, a woman came forward to greet him. She had been
interested in the mission through letters written from Poughkeepsie,
New York, where her three children had been converted.

In the middle of April, 1851, the mission staff was re-enforced by
the arrival of Heinrich Nuelsen, who together with his son, Bishop
John L. Nuelsen, was to play such a vital part in continental Methodism for three-quarters of a century. Nuelsen, Jacoby's brother-in-
law, was followed in the beginning of June by Riemenschneider, and
these were joined in 1858 by Wilhelm Schwarz.

This enlargement of the missionary staff enabled Jacoby to travel about in the interest of the extension of the work, especially in northern Germany. He selected first the free city of Hamburg and appointed Doering to have charge of the development of the work. He followed this by the appointment of Riemenschneider to a similar post in the free city of Frankfurt-am-Main. Both missions were opened in July, 1851. Riemenschneider, however, was compelled to wait two months before he could obtain permission to hold meetings. Finally he began to initiate group work in his flat and soon had a congregation of a hundred. The other inhabitants of the apartment house, complaining of the constantly "annoying singing and praying," forced him to stop until he could find another location. In the meantime he had begun work in neighboring Hessia, and was received gladly by French Protestants, who had fled to a little village near *Bad Hamburg* from the persecutions of Ludwig XIV in France. The little community of Friedrichsdorf subsequently gave to the Church useful leaders in the persons of "Father Wallon" and his son Louis, as well as Clément Achard.

Riemenschneider pushed his work out to a hamlet near Giessen in Hessia-Darmstadt, following an invitation to hold meetings in a private home. The burgomaster, schoolmaster, a few deacons of the State Church, and other notables attended. Hardly had the service begun when a gendarme asked for his passport. Unable to produce it, he was thrown into prison for the night. The next day he was brought before a magistrate and ordered forthwith to leave the duchy. At the same time his tracts were confiscated and submitted to the village clergyman for inspection. Prohibitions issued against Methodist meetings soon became so comprehensive that Riemenschneider was forced to confine his labors mostly to Frankfurt and its suburbs.

In Hamburg, Doering, if not experiencing such serious difficulties, was handicapped by the quarters he was forced to use for the work. Although a Sunday school was started and a mission for emigrants begun, the work grew discouragingly slow.

Nuelsen, assisted by Fiege, in the meantime was working in the Bremen district. In Vegesack he remodeled a dance hall into a prayer-meeting room. Following an attack upon him by the village pastor in the local newspaper, a crowd collected in front of the house in which Nuelsen preached and bombarded it so that several persons were injured. The local pastor's petition to the High Senate in Bremen, however, to have the Methodist meetings prohibited was refused and five policemen were detailed to preserve order while Nuelsen preached.

In the Grand Duchy of Oldenburg, in Braunschweig, and in Hanover, Methodism took root and spread in earnest. While in Oldenburg and Bremen the officials protected the Methodists on every occasion, in Hanover and Braunschweig loopholes enough were found in the guarantees of religious freedom to give grounds for harassing the preachers. "Our members who live there," declared Nippert, "are suppressed and tyrannized. . . . If they desire to continue to serve God according to the conviction of their consciences, they have no other choice than to emigrate to America." In the summer of 1851 most of the people who had joined the Methodist Church migrated from Hanover and Braunschweig to America. Among the members of this group was *Hermann zur Jakobsmühlen,* who in 1856 returned to Germany as a preacher, and worked so successfully in Zurich.

While Jacoby was in Winnenden in 1851, visiting Müller, interesting him in the use of the Methodist hymnal and discussing the fraternal relationships between the Wesleyans and the Methodist Episcopalians, he made a survey to find a suitable place to open a mission in Württemberg. He selected Heilbronn, and in the fall of the same year appointed Nippert to develop the work. Nippert wrote in his journal:

> After we arrived, rented a house, and presented our credentials, we began to study how we could and ought to begin our work. My way was soon shown and in the name of the Lord I began to preach and hold meetings. But inasmuch as according to the law no meetings could be held without the permission of the local clergy, and inasmuch as they, with the clerics council had the right to grant or refuse permission to hold the meetings, I had the disappointing experience of finding with the best intentions of doing good, the doors closed. . . . In the beginning nothing was said against my work until our work became so effective that people began to ask what they had to do to be saved.

In the beginning no hindrances were placed in his way. The clergymen of the State Churches were friendly. The spacious room in which he began meetings soon proved too small, and quite unexpectedly the royal barracks were opened to him. In this military headquarters Nippert preached every Tuesday evening to congregations averaging about two hundred. Conversions began and he was able to organize a class of ten, the nucleus of his work in the province.

At Eichelberg, four leagues from Heilbronn, the congregations grew too large for any hall in the village, and meetings were therefore held in the open air. Yet the work in the outlying villages was not easy. Often the meetings were broken up when the local clergy complained of the noise of the Methodist revival which developed. Often Nippert's work was so curtailed that he could only visit from house to house and distribute tracts. Nippert was, nevertheless, equal to the task. He developed a circuit of about a hundred kilometers, which he traveled on foot. By 1852 he had developed the work to the point where "Father" Wallon was appointed to assist him. Wallon experienced such resistance that he was twice imprisoned and finally exiled from the province. He promptly emigrated to America, where he served many effective years in the ministry.

Wallon was succeeded by his son, who founded the congregation in Heilbronn. On January 6, 1864, Riemenschneider and Heinrich Ernst Gebhardt dedicated the chapel and administered the sacrament of the Lord's Supper. As soon as the consistory learned that the Methodist preacher had a congregation of two hundred and had administered the sacrament, Gebhardt was read out of the State Church and was informed that he could administer the sacrament only to those who had withdrawn from the State Church.

The conversion of *Gebhardt* was an event of importance in the history of Methodism. Born in Ludwigsburg on July 12, 1832, he was apprenticed at the age of fifteen to his maternal uncle, a druggist in Stuttgart. Added to the general restlessness of the revolutionary years of 1847 and 1848 when the whispers of "politics, patriotism, and freedom" were on every lip, was the unendurable thought in his mind of being shut up in a laboratory all his life. With the intention of being a farmer, he went off to the country in Bavaria. Bavaria at that time was throbbing with the passion for emigration to South America. After two years at the High School for Agricultural and Forestry Economics at Hohenheim, he sailed in 1852 for South America. The group in which he traveled bought a farm not far from Valdiva, where they landed. After traveling through Chile, he returned to Germany in 1856 and found that his mother had "experienced salvation" through the instrumentality of the Methodists. Ernst Gebhardt often accompanied her to the Methodist meetings. He was converted and joined the Methodist Church, following the example of his mother.

The effect of the conversion in giving up his worldly pleasures, even to the beloved opera, was shown in the following incident. Gebhardt and his son-in-law were walking past the opera house in Frankfurt one day when the latter inquired if he did not want to go into such a "temple of art."

Gebhardt replied:

> Once that was my passion, but from the hour of my conversion I was done with worldly pleasures. What a man has worn out, he will never enjoy again.

At Jacoby's earnest request, Gebhardt gave up the idea of going back to Chile as a missionary and took an appointment to Ludwigsburg and twenty outlying stations. The work at Ludwigsburg had developed from Heilbronn in 1857 in an unusual way. A young man named Gustav Hausser had been so influenced by the reading of Wesley's *Sermons* and a little volume *Wesley and His Collaborators* that he walked to Heilbronn to meet the "Methodists" personally. He was converted under the leadership of "Father" Wallon and soon joined the Church. He began his contribution to the work by distributing tracts, and later joining in a prayer meeting with a soldier and a brickmaker. The group grew and Hausser, consenting to constant demands to preach, formed a group large enough to deserve the appointment of Nuelsen to the society. Nuelsen arrived in the same year of 1857 and found a group of forty members received on trial. He rented a hall and preached to enthusiastic congregations. During the year Gebhardt was converted, together with Johannes Staiger, who later became director of the Book Concern in Bremen, and Friedrich Paulus, who subsequently became one of the scholars of the Church and of great service in the educational work developed in Berea, Ohio. A revival in 1858 promoted the society. In 1861 a part of the *Waldhorn* was purchased and the hall where court balls formerly were held was renovated into a prayer-meeting room, which for a long time served as Methodist headquarters in southern Germany.

Gebhardt, of charming personality and unusual musical talent, served as district superintendent in Bremen, assistant editor of the *Evangelist,* editor of the songbooks *Zionspalter* and *Zions Perlenchoers,* and then went to Switzerland. His dream was to see a close co-operation established between the Methodists and the State Churches. After many disappointments he saw the beginning of the realization of his dream in the *Dissenter's Law* of January 15, 1872, which increased liberty and freedom of conscience allowed in religious affairs.

His contribution to American Methodism began in September, 1881, when he arrived in New York with his daughter, Maria, on a singing tour. During his stay he visited 418 different places, sang in over 1,000 meetings, traveled 3,600 miles by coach, wagon, and sleigh through 32 states and territories. In 1887 he was back in Germany, where his leadership in the total abstinence movement and in the development of the Blue Cross was highly effective. His poems and songs written in the interest of total abstinence were a vital part of the movement. He preached, varied his discourses with singing in his rich baritone and heroic tenor voice of remarkable range, strength, and flexibility, played his harp, and led congregational singing. His influence on his American tour was a lasting one. The musical tradition which he established was continued through the marriage of his daughter Maria to August J. Bucher, the third editor of *The Christian Apologist.*

Switzerland

Methodism had been brought to Switzerland three quarters of a century before the missionaries came to southern Germany. Johannes Fletcher, born along the shores of Lake Geneva, had been converted in England and returned to work in his native country between 1777 and

1781. He held meetings in the forests, and Sunday schools which he conducted were attended by as many as a hundred boys and girls. In 1816 Robert Haldane, an experienced Scotch Methodist, arrived in Geneva, made a contact with the students at the University of Geneva, and attracted such a following that he preached three times a week in the theological auditorium. A number of the students were converted and formed a militantly evangelical group. The Geneva clergy, concerned over the Methodist movement, had a decree made that all pastors must promise never to preach about the manner in which the divine nature is joined with the person of Jesus nor about original sin nor about effective grace nor about predestination. Some of the clergy did not sign the oath, but the effect was to intensify the persecution of the Methodists. The upshot of the decree was the establishment of protest groups, three congregations of which united to form a free church in 1849. Bishop Nuelsen believes that Methodism was a fomenting cause which helped to produce this free church.

Systematic work on the part of the Methodists in Switzerland, however, did not take place until 1855. Ernst Mann, who had come to Bremen from the Bavarian Palatinate, had been converted at Methodist services in the *Krameramthaus*. In 1855 he went back home, where his preaching led to the outbreak of a revival service. Responding to requests which came from relatives in French Alsace, where Nippert had been born, he began to preach in a schoolhouse. At the instigation of the local pastor and schoolmaster a persecution broke out which ended in the arrest of Mann. Between five and six o'clock in the morning two policemen pulled him out of bed, clamped handcuffs on his wrists, and led him away with a chain. Confined in *Weissenburg* for thirty-two days, he learned upon the hearing that he was charged with disorderly conduct. Evidence showed that under his preaching a few people had cried. Sentenced by the court to six days, he used the time profitably in study. At this time he heard of many Germans in French Switzerland who were without religious services because of the difference in language He discussed the idea of a mission to these people with Jacoby. The superintendent approved the program and suggested that he begin work either in Geneva or Lausanne. Geneva was soon eliminated as a possibility, and when the French Wesleyan Church in Lausanne offered its building to him for German services, he accepted it. Mann preached his first sermon in this Swiss city on February 24, 1856. Assisted by the French Wesleyans, his work expanded encouragingly in both French and German Switzerland.

A second missionary effort was begun almost as Jacoby's personal hobby. In June of 1856 Jacoby visited Zurich and was charmed by the city's beauty. He appointed *Hermann zur Jakobsmühlen* preacher to Alpine city in the fall of the same year. Jakobsmühlen rented a hall from a sailmaker on *Thorgasse*. Though the room could have accommodated a hundred, not a single person appeared for the service. Twelve came to the second meeting. From that time on the congregation took over the "Pfauen," a small hotel on the *Zeltweg,* as a church. Here the first Sunday school in Zurich was organized. In 1860 the mission report listed the "Switzerland District" with 112 members, 264 trial members, 3 Sunday schools, and 180 pupils.

The work in Europe had taken root when in February, 1856, Jacoby, at the invitation of the Mission Board, sailed for America to attend the General Conference at Indianapolis. The General Conference authorized the preachers in Germany to organize an Annual Conference. Since March, 1853, the German missionaries had met annually in Bremen. By 1856 ten preachers were in the field and as many helpers. Five hundred and thirty-seven members were reported, and 15 Sunday schools with 1,108 scholars. On September 10, 1856, the leaders met, at Jacoby's call, in Bremen to organize their Conference. Jacoby presided and Doering was elected secretary.

The second Annual Conference was an event. It met in Bremen on September 5, 1857, with Bishop Simpson presiding, and McClintock and Nast present. The Evangelical Alliance was convening in Berlin and Nast took the occasion to give an address on Methodism, which removed much of the prejudices that existed against the movement. Joseph A. Wright, a Methodist layman and minister to Germany, added his influence to Nast's exposition of what Methodism was. As prejudices broke down, new doors were opened up to the work and efforts received a new impulse in both Germany and Switzerland. Persecution in Switzerland was nearly eliminated through the energetic protests of the United States minister at Berne, Theodore Sedwick Fay. Toleration was finally established.

Literature was one of the indispensable instruments of Methodist propaganda. A short time after the Church acquired *Pfauen* in Zürich, Jacoby opened a depository in the parterre as a branch of the publishing house in Bremen. The venture was not successful. On October 15, 1890, a second attempt was made at the direction of an interconference committee and a branch of the Bremen concern was opened under the direction of S. H. Breiter. Two years later a separate Swiss corporation was organized as the Christian Book Concern, with the chartered purpose of "nurturing and promoting religious and moral life and the dissemination of biblical Christianity through the organization of a book and publishing business." E. C. Schmidtmann was appointed publishing agent. From the time of corporate organization the business experienced a continued growth.[32]

The scope of Methodism's mission to the Continent seemed defined when in 1860 the Annual Conference met in Zurich, the first time it was held outside of Bremen. At this session in Switzerland German Methodism in Europe "came of age." Both the *Evangelist* and the *Children's Friend* were self-supporting. The mission was doing its own printing. Membership had increased in the year by 540 accessions. Several new chapels had been built. The chapel in Bremen had to be replaced by a more commodious church.

If Germany had done so much to influence John Wesley's life, now Bishop Morris's wish, expressed to Jacoby, that the Methodists repay the debt in some small measure by influencing the spiritual life of the Fatherland, was being fulfilled. When in 1893 the *Swiss Evangelist* began publication, Methodist machinery for the promotion of the faith was completely organized.

American Methodism's last missionary sent to Germany was *Wilhelm Schwarz*. Born February 14, 1826, in Ober-Achern in the Grand Duchy of Baden, the son of a master mason, he was reared in a Roman Catholic family. Intellectually capable and industrious, he matriculated at the University of Freiburg, where he became the intimate of a group of Catholic priests. The direction of his thinking raised the question in his mind, as the contacts continued, as to whether he was well-advised in preparing himself for the priesthood. The doubt intensified until he decided to give up his studies of Catholic theology and go to that asylum for the distressed, that haven of hope— America. He turned his inheritance from his mother, who had died while he was very young, into money, hired a substitute for his military service, and landed in New York on July 2, 1845.

His welcome in the port city was disheartening. His money was stolen at the dock. To raise funds enough to pay an overnight lodging he was forced to sell a good pair of shoes. Unable to speak English, he finally found work on a New Jersey beet farm. Buffeted from job to job, he apprenticed himself to a blacksmith.

He worked industriously, earned his living, and rejoiced that he had found a congenial home at last. The blacksmith's wife was a pious woman and "God-fearing Christian." She belonged to the Methodist Episcopal Church. Schwarz tutored her children during his idle time, and in return the mother invited the apprentice to attend Sunday school and Church worship. The preacher he first heard was Lyon. The sermon made a deep impression on the Roman Catholic young man. He was even more interested in the Christian communal feeling of the "brethren" and the "sisters." Among his fellow workmen in the blacksmith shop was a young man named Rothweiler, who was concerned with the problem of showing Schwarz the way to God. Schwarz followed Rothweiler's advice and on the Thursday before Easter, 1846, he experienced that "rare peace with God through the Lord Jesus Christ."

Jacob Rothweiler, born on December 3, 1824, in Berghausen, Baden, came to America with his parents in 1839, where he apprenticed himself to a machinist. Converted under the preaching of Lyon, he joined the Second Street German Methodist Church in New York, studying Hebrew. Licensed as a local preacher, he entered the itinerant con-

nection of the Ohio Conference in the fall of 1846. Schwarz followed Rothweiler, was licensed a local preacher on December 6,
1846, and was received into the New York Conference in March,
1848. After preaching in leading churches in Newark, New York, and
Albany, Schwarz was appointed, after earnest solicitation by Bishops
Morris and Janes, to Germany. He arrived in Bremerhaven on Sunday, July 27, 1858. He began his work in Bremen, and two years
later took Nippert's place in Berlin, when Nippert was sent on to
develop the mission at Basel. Serving in Basel also, Schwarz founded
the German mission in Paris. When war broke out between Germany
and France the passions became so intense in Paris that the American
embassy took oversight over the German-Americans in the country.
By August 28 all Germans were notified to leave the city within three
days. Schwarz, in company with his eldest son Karl, took refuge in
Switzerland.

By the time that Schwarz, Methodism's last missionary to Germany,
felt compelled to return home in 1874, German Methodism was firmly
established on the Continent. It was contributing through its theological schools leadership to the Church in America. When the last
decade of the century began, German Methodism could report for
Switzerland 6,342 members in full connection and on trial, 203 preaching places, and 199 Sunday schools with 14,127 scholars and 1,053
teachers and officers. In Germany there were 10,580 members, 11,751
in the Sunday schools. The Book Concern, with a building worth
258,583 marks, had shown a net profit of 33,662 marks during the
year. The circulation figures of the publications in 1890 were important enough to be recorded:

	Circulation
The Evangelist	13,500
Children's Friend	19,800
Mission Collector	13,500
Monthly Messenger	14,000
Friend of Moderation	1,200
Sunday School Magazine	2,300

The theological seminary had educated 208 men. A Preachers' Aid
Society had accumulated funds amounting to 83,051 marks in Germany
and 54,888 francs in Switzerland. A hundred deaconesses were ministering through hospitals and stations. These statistics testify to the
solid foundations which had been laid.

The indirect influence of the Methodist activity was perhaps equally
important. Methodism was actually demonstrating the principle of
voluntary religious activity. It was showing what the "Free Church"
idea meant in actual practice, and it was doing so in the very field
where the State Churches ruled supreme. The importance of Methodism in the German religious scene as the advocate of the Free Church

Movement came to have new emphasis following the National Socialist Revolution in 1933.

The idea of the "Free Church" was stated with clarity by F. H. Otto Melle on October 16, 1928, in a lecture delivered before the Central Committee of the Union of Evangelical Free Churches.[33] "Two concepts are bound together into a unity in the word '*Freikirche,*'" he said. "The terms are '*Kirche*' (Church) and '*Freiheit*' (freedom). Primitive Christianity had two essential characteristics—it was a fellowship (*Gemeinschaft*) and it *was free*. . . . Under Constantine, however, the distinction between Church and State was abolished. The State became ecclesiastical, the Church became political. The combination of the divine and the secular dissolved the sense of fellowship and dissipated the freedom and independence of the Church. . . . We hold the amalgamation of the Church with the State (*Staatskirchentum*) to be an absurdity. An evangelical *Staatskirche* in which the monarch is the *summus episcopus* is a *contradictio in adjecto*. It is a further fundamental of the free church movement that the support of its work is on a voluntary basis."

However much controversial situations on the Continent may have involved the Methodist Episcopal Church,[34] its presence in Europe for nearly a century raised and kept alive the value and the ultimate validity of the fundamental necessity of voluntariness in the relation of man to God. The Methodists had never taken seriously the decision of the Eisennach Conference in 1855 to the effect that whatever is not a State Church is a sect. They preferred Professor Walter Köhler's statement: "Public law can never render a decision over things of a religious nature. The front no longer is between State Churches and sects, but rather between Christianity and anti-Christianity."[35]

Summarizing its history in relation to other continental churches, Bishop Nuelsen has said:

> We do not fight against the State Church. The Methodist Church does not live by the criticism of existing churches. The Methodist Church is not negative, it is positive. It does not deny. It affirms. It denies but one thing: sin. . . . As Methodists we are ready, according to the example of John Wesley, to form an alliance of offense or defense with every soldier of Jesus Christ who bears his name and wears his uniform. We confess ourselves still to the superb words of John Wesley: "Is thy heart like my heart? Then give me thy hand.[36]

Methodism in Central Europe, associated as it has always been with the Methodist Episcopal Church as a world ecclesiastical organization, gave a strength to the Free Church Movement on the Continent in a form which continually made religion more genuine, spontaneous, and voluntary. Though its influence in the regeneration of individual lives has been great, and though its ministries of mercy and charity have been far out of proportion to its numerical size and financial ability, the force of Methodism in keeping attention centered upon Christian freedom as a spontaneous fellowship of believers, unconcerned with the power of the State, must remain as one of the chief, if not the chief, of its contributions to the Old World.

European Conferences

Methodism's part in the Free Church Movement was strengthened by its system of organization. The establishment of Annual Conferences in Europe proceeded apace with the evolution in America. Methodism organized its advances on the Continent.

The preachers in Germany had met in Bremen on March 11, 1852, for their first annual meeting, the preachers being Jacoby, Doering, Nippert, Nuelsen, and Riemenschneider. They reported 232 members and 582 Sunday-school scholars. These annual meetings were continued until 1859.

The General Conference, which met in Indianapolis in 1856, encouraged by the presence of Jacoby, enabled the preachers in Germany to organize a Mission Conference of their own. Pursuant to this authority, the first Mission Conference assembled on September 10, 1856, Heinrich zur Jakobsmühlen, transferred from the Ohio Conference to Zurich, being present in addition to the missionary quintet. Bishop Simpson, the first member of the episcopacy to supervise the work in Germany, presided over the second annual session, held in Bremen in the late summer of 1857. He was accompanied by Nast, who was also a delegate to the convention of the Evangelical Alliance meeting a few days later in Berlin, and by J. A. Wright, American minister to the Prussian Court. At the session of 1858 the Mission Conference was divided into the Bremen, Oldenburg, South Germany, and Switzerland Districts. When in 1860 the Conference was held for the first time outside Germany in Zurich, encouraging reports were received from all fields. Three hundred converts had been enrolled during the year. The *Evangelist* and the *Children's Friend* had sufficient subscribers to cover publication costs.

The organization of the work as a Mission Conference proved increasingly unsatisfactory. In 1868 the General Conference accorded the German mission the rights of an Annual Conference. Pursuant to the action, Jacoby surrendered his office as superintendent and the presiding elders of the respective districts functioned in the same fashion as in America.

At the nineteenth session of the Conference in July, 1874, the Methodists celebrated the twenty-fifth anniversary of their work in Germany. They reported 7,022 members, 1,899 members on trial, 11,662 pupils in 262 Sunday schools. News of Jacoby's death in St. Louis came as the Conference adjourned. In 1885 the Methodists in Germany proposed to observe the centennial of the organization of American Methodism by a collection of a Jubilee Fund for the erection of a "Barbara Heck" chapel in Kaiserslautern.

The work in Germany had grown too large and unwieldy for a single Conference properly to handle. If Methodism was to organize its advances, a more satisfactory administrative setup was necessary. For one thing, the area from the Baltic Sea to Lake Geneva was too large. For another, the Swiss were really a people of themselves. The Annual Conference was divided in July, 1886, at Zurich into the "Conference of Germany" and the "Conference of Switzerland," the two Conferences maintaining a joint interest in the administration of the seminary at Frankfurt-on-the-Main, the Book Concern in Bremen, and the Preachers' Aid Society.[5]

"The Growth of Freedom"

If the Conference of Germany had a larger area, more preachers and churches than the Conference of Switzerland, the latter had stronger societies and a more concentrated Church body. When the former Conference met in Berlin in 1890, it reported an increase of 622 full members, and nearly 1,200 on trial. The work had expanded to the point where further organization was necessary. This step was taken on June 21, 1893, in Bremen, with the division of the Conference of Germany into the North Germany and the South Germany Conferences.

The North Germany Conference included a field which was hardly touched by evangelical religion. One reason for the tardy cultivation of these virgin fields was the belated recognition of religious freedom, in addition to economic difficulties. Work was begun in Hanover and pushed out to Breslau and Königsberg. By the merger with Wesleyan Methodism societies in Magdeburg, Halle, Kottus, Glogau, Gorlitz, and Vienna were added.

By 1895 a missionary, named *Robert Möller,* had been sent to Vienna. Supported by Frau Baroness von Langenau, he laid the foundations of a substantial work. In 1897 the prohibition against Methodist worship services was lifted. The conversion of a young man named Hawranek enabled a mission work among the Czechs and Slavs. In the prayer meetings German, Czech, Slav, and Bohemian, each in his own mother tongue, praised God at a time when Germans and Bohemians politically were militantly hostile to each other.

In 1900 *F. H. Otto Melle* gave up a successful pastorate in Dresden and went to the assistance of Möller to develop a work in Hungary. Despite governmental interference and Catholic opposition, Melle established a base and the societies of Austria and Hungary were organized into a district in 1907. The General Conference of 1908 passed an enabling act and pursuant thereto the work in Austria-Hungary was organized into a Mission Conference in the summer of 1911.

GROWTH OF THE MISSION TO THE GERMANS
IN CENTRAL EUROPE
1856-1886

Year	Members		Sunday Schools	Scholars
	Full	Trial		
1856	424	109	15	1,108
1857	558	216	16	1,125
1858	755	324	19	1,190
1859	828	491	24	1,585
1860	1,051	586	36	2,030
1861	1,354	827	40	2,254
1862	1,753	824	44	2,601
1863	2,126	1,249	51	2,844
1864	2,852	1,280	66	2,985
1865	3,465	1,151	82	3,953
1866	3,905	1,465	117	5,264
1867	4,302	1,626	139	5,668
1868	4,816	1,518	148	6,350
1869	5,396	1,560	161	7,434
1870	5,812	1,447	151	8,378
1871	6,092	1,369	207	9,216
1872	6,230	1,727	229	10,071
1873	6,642	1,871	244	11,260
1874	7,022	1,889	262	11,662
1875	7,348	2,319	273	12,395
1876	7,960	2,264	301	13,355
1877	8,537	2,270	314	15,283
1878	9,083	2,237	338	16,476
1879	9,224	2,112	360	17,953
1880	9,444	2,377	372	18,716
1881	9,717	2,237	380	19,359
1882	9,760	2,359	384	19,640
1883	10,058	2,408	404	20,707
1884	10,372	2,492	424	20,912
1885	10,713	2,665	426	21,569
1886	11,134	3,033	427	22,509

Methodist work in Europe by the turn of the century justified the General Conference of 1900 in assigning Bishop Vincent for a quadrennium to supervision of the continental work. Twenty-six thousand full members in Germany and Switzerland, together with Sunday-school scholars, gave the Methodists a work among probably 50,000 individuals. Bishop Vincent was succeeded by Bishop Burt, who for eighteen years had been directing the Methodist work in Italy.

The South Germany Conference organized itself in July, 1894, in

Strassburg with Bishop Newman presiding. It expanded along the Rhine and into the Saar. The Conference of Switzerland, after its separation from the Conference of Germany in 1886, was divided into two districts, the first session being held in Bern in June, 1887, Bishop W. X. Ninde presiding.

When Bishop Nuelsen went to Europe in 1912, German Methodism had about completed its organizational development. Ten German-speaking Conferences in continental United States, two Conferences in Germany, a Conference in Switzerland, a Mission Conference in Austria-Hungary, publishing houses in Bremen and Zurich, and a chain of deaconess hospitals and welfare institutions across two continents bore testimony to the soundness of the vision of Wilhelm Nast. The unexpected outbreak of the World War stunned the German Methodists as it did the Methodists in America. Bishop Nuelsen continued to be the instrument through whom faith was maintained despite the animosities and devastation of the conflagration. When war was over, Bishop Nuelsen, assisted by Otto Melle, preserved the intercontinental unity of Methodism until the organization of the Central Conferences.

CHAPTER IX

WOMEN IN CHRISTIAN SERVICE
THE DEACONESS MOVEMENT

That the Protestant Church should have an organized field of service for women was a fact belatedly recognized. That in Methodism the movement first should have developed in Germany is perhaps one of the most unexpectedly important results of the mission to the Germans. The reasons for the tardy appreciation of the value of feminine energy were largely historical.

In the beginning woman, according to the Scriptures, enjoyed the same status as man. The wholesome situation which existed in the early Church was corrupted by pagan contacts. Under the influence of Eastern monasticism, the Catholic Church took over the Egyptian name "nun" for virgins dedicated to the service of Christ. The vows of poverty, chastity, and obedience which created the orders religious into vital societies, however, received an interpretation as the years went by which created a gulf between the actual world and Christian service. As the idea spread that the vows could be kept only through constant restraint and years of practice, religion was transformed, as Christian Golder once remarked, from "inward to outward piety."

By 700 or 800 A. D. the historic deaconate had been completely corrupted and superseded by the societies of nuns. The originally benevolent movement of feminine service deteriorated into what Golder called "the sanctimonious austerity of convent life."[1] In the nine hundred years that followed, the New Testament conception was almost wholly obscured. The *women religious* locked themselves in their convents, built high walls behind which they lived, and inflicted a death penalty upon members of the order who married.

It was unfortunate that Luther at the time of the Reformation failed to provide opportunity for women to serve the Protestant Church. When he abolished the convent, he saw the need of the consecrated deaconate, observing that "the inclination to show kindness to others is more natural to women than to men." Yet Luther took no steps to enlist the energies of women in the development of the work of the Church.

The extent to which "outward" had been substituted for "inward" piety is shown in the religious ritual observed by Saint Douceline. She wore in secret a hard and rough shirt of pigskin which galled her to the quick so that she was often unable to remove it. When it was

131

taken off, it left her body torn and covered with sores. On one occasion the shirt was so ingrown into her flesh that it could not be torn off. She called her maid, who by main force drew off the garment by tearing her flesh away with the hide. Saint Douceline had a further custom of binding her waist so tightly with a knotted cord that worms would often breed where the knots cut into her flesh. Night and day she wore an iron hoop over which she showed fair and choice garments as though she loved gay styles. For penance's sake she lay on a little straw in the corner of her room. Fearful lest she should rest comfortably, she bound a cord above her bed with one end and tied the other end around her waist so that whenever she stirred the cord would drag and wake her. Then she would rise immediately to say her matins and to read.[2] This kind of ascetic attitude tended to overshadow the practical work of Christian love. Yet the nuns' hatred of luxury, worldliness, and pleasure-seeking, coupled with their self-denial and abstinence, gave them a deep and far-reaching influence upon the life of the Church.

The recovery of the apostolic deaconate was the product of two very different circumstances. At the end of the eighteenth and the beginning of the nineteenth century the cold theological rationalism, which had frozen affection as a force in spiritual life, began to break down through Europe as the leavening influence of the Pietist movement spread. An awakening consciousness of the necessity of Christian benevolence was evident. In Great Britain, and especially in the independent Churches of England, activities of Christian social service increased.

German influence was responsible to a large extent for the condition. For a good many years the Church circles in England had received a powerful influence from Germany. In 1707 Queen Anne called as her court chaplain an inspector from the orphanage in Halle. He served George I in the same capacity. The Moravians, having established a number of churches in England and especially in London, were exerting a profound spiritual influence. Their influence upon John and Charles Wesley was only one of the instances in which they were making impact upon the ecclesiasticism of England. The German evangelical passion was an antidote for the disease from which religion in England was suffering. The Anglican Church, so one historian wrote, "was an ecclesiastical system under which the people of England had lapsed into paganism."[3]

Just as Wesley had discovered the meaning of the religion of the "warmed heart" through the interaction of the Anglican tradition with simple German piety, so now the motive power for the revival of practical Christian benevolence came back on the rebound to Germany, chiefly from England. For the first time dissenters and established churchmen were aroused into a common effort for the development of Christian benevolent institutions.

From England came the Bibles and tracts with which Germany was furnished and from thence came also a large part of the money to form the auxiliary societies and benevolent institutions. In many ways England took part in the revival of practical Christianity in Germany at the close of the eighteenth and the beginning of the nineteenth centuries. As early as 1798 the London Missionary Society appealed to the Christians in Germany to co-operate with them, and the last year of the century saw the beginning of a common work.

The second circumstance which contributed to the development of practical Christian benevolence was an aftermath of war at the beginning of the nineteenth century. During the war a number of women's societies had sprung up for the amelioration of the suffering of the wounded soldiers. These organizations took part in the charge of the injured, sent provisions to the men on the field, cared for the destitute, and concerned themselves especially with the condition of the widows and orphans of the fallen soldiers. When peace finally came, these societies continued in existence, looking after the sick, the poor, and lying-in women.

The situation suggested almost simultaneously to the minds of Minister Karl von Stein and Amelia Sieveking the possibility of developing the societies into a Protestant Church sisterhood. Through the interest of a Prussian minister, E. von Bodelschwingh, their minds and plans were brought together, but death did not permit the woman to continue with the idea of a sisterhood mercy. Amelia Sieveking holds the honor, however, of being a pioneer in the great deaconess movement of modern times.

The real establishment of the deaconess work dates from the appointment of Theodor Fliedner to the pastorate of the little parish church in Kaiserwerth on January 18, 1822. The congregation was small, the community predominantly Catholic, and five weeks after the young pastor arrived the silk mills, upon which the village depended, went into bankruptcy. The government threatened to close Fliedner's church because it could not pay off a debt of $500. The young pastor was not easily beaten. He set out on a collection tour, soliciting $5,000 in Holland, $3,500 more in London, and in 1824 returned to Kaiserwerth with $9,000. He had enough money to pay off the debt and endow the church besides. But the result of his trip was an idea far more important than the collection of funds to save his church. Of the observations which he made he wrote:

> In both of these Evangelical countries, I observed a number of benevolent institutions for the care of body and soul—schools and educational institutions, asylums for the poor, and orphans, and the sick, prisons, and the society for the improvement of prisons, Bible societies, missionary societies, and the like; and I also observed that all these institutions and societies were called into existence and sustained by a living faith in Christ.[5]

The pastoral duties of his little parish being light, Fliedner interested himself in the welfare of the convicts in the prison in Düsseldorf. He preached to them fortnightly and became tremendously interested in what happened to the convicts when they were released. To the end of assisting their re-entry into social life, he decided to found an asylum. Lacking funds for the purpose, he began simply in his own garden house. He organized the Rhenish-Westphalian Prison Society. As the work developed, he became certain that his duty was to re-establish the apostolic deaconate. He began to work out his dreams by purchasing on August 20, 1836, a large house in the center of the town of Kaiserswerth for $2,300. On October 18, 1836, the first deaconess house was opened with Gertrude Reichard, a physician's daughter, as the first deaconess, and a servant girl as the first patient.

Fliedner was not just founding a benevolent institution; he was demonstrating at the same time the necessity of a divine vocation for women and showing how their capacities could be utilized in the service of the Church. By the revival of the apostolic deaconate, he gave to unmarried women of the evangelical churches a lifework that met with their highest expectation, expressing women's love and energy in Christian service.

It is worthy of mention in passing that in the year 1800 Germany gave two great leaders to the world. On October 26, 1800, General Field Marshal Helmuth von Moltke was born; on January 21, 1800, Theodor Fliedner. While von Moltke was winning his victories with brilliant strategy, Fliedner was enlisting an army of peace, commissioned to heal the wounds in bodies and souls.

Kaiserswerth became the model of all the deaconess institutions on the earth. The movement spread to five continents and expressed its service through vast institutions worth millions of dollars. By 1845 the State Church in Germany under the leadership of Friedrich Wilhelm IV of Prussia opened Bethany Institution in Berlin and Queen Elizabeth became its protectoress. At Bielefeld another great institution grew up under the leadership of Pastor Friedrich von Bodelschwingh. Bodelschwingh lived to become the first bishop of the German National Evangelical Church and the symbol of struggle between the National Socialist German Christians and the representatives of the historic Christianity organized into the Young Movement of the Reformation and later the Confessional Synod.

That the Methodists should take up the deaconess movement and develop it into the strongest institutional branch of German-speaking Methodism was a testimony to their leadership on the Continent. After many discouraging and abortive efforts in the decade following 1864, first because of the lack of efficiently trained nurses, and secondly because of the apathy of the Annual Conference, a beginning was made in 1873 which was substantial. In that year a committee was appointed to study the possibilities of founding an institution. When the Annual Conference met in 1874 in Schaffhausen, Switzerland, the friends of the deaconess cause presented a well-considered plan for taking steps. After a prolonged discussion of the report, the Conference voted to drop the whole matter and to proceed to the order of the day. Shortly after this vote was taken, four members of the Conference retired into an adjoining room. After a brief consultation they organized the free and independent "Bethany Society." This society was directed by a central board of managers, the members of which were required to be members of the Methodist Episcopal Church. The deaconesses were to be organized into a sisterhood under the direction of a head deaconess. All receipts from nursing were to flow into a central treasury, out of which the expenses of board, lodging, and clothing were to be paid. When the board adopted its constitution on July 9, 1874, it notified the Annual Conference the same day "that an independent society had been formed for the promotion of the deaconess cause." The society asked the Conference for an endorsement, which was enthusiastically given. Twenty-one of the sixty-four members of the Conference joined as paying members. The Bethany Society had been founded. Eighteen months passed before the deaconess work had developed sufficiently to conform to the principles which had been adopted.

The motherhouse of the Bethany Society developed at Frankfurt-am-Main. In the summer of 1875 Friedrich Eilers, one of the founders of the Bethany Society, was transferred to the church in that city. In the fall of 1875, Karl Weiss, chairman of the board of the society, had become acquainted with a deaconess who volunteered her services. In 1876 she moved to Frankfurt and took a room in the parsonage occupied by Eilers. The members of the board of the Bethany Society and several friends collected enough money among themselves to purchase a bed and table, the most necessary articles of furniture. The demands upon the one-roomed institution grew so that a second and a third deaconess were added to the staff. Several physicians in the city, in sympathy with the institution, gave their support to the enterprise. The rapid growth of the work made it necessary for the clergyman to vacate another room in his parsonage for the use of the deaconesses. It was not long before the volume of work forced the society to rent a small dwelling. One of the rooms was set aside for the sick and here the first operation was performed. When Eilers was moved from Frankfurt in 1879, the number of deaconesses had grown to seven. Although some looked upon this feeble work with misgivings, the Bethany Society continued its service and sent some of the deaconesses to the academic hospital in Heidelberg for advanced study.

Far from being discouraged, the board in 1878 extended its work to the city of Hamburg. The first deaconess was followed by a second and a third, all of whom lived in an attic room. It was all the society

could afford. In Hamburg as well as in Frankfurt the women voluntarily submitted to the greatest privations and at times suffered from
want of the necessities of life. The work in the Hanseatic city gained
an impetus by a fortunate circumstance. The four-year-old-son of one
of Hamburg's leading bankers had fallen ill with diphtheria. The
father, upon the instructions of the family physician, searched the
city in vain for a nurse until his attention was called to the sisters of
the Bethany Society. When he visited their attic home, only one sister,
herself convalescing from diphtheria, was available. Surrendering
to the urgent appeal of the father and "trusting in God," the deaconess
ventured to take charge of the boy. The child recovered and the parents
became warm friends of the deaconess work. Through their efforts
other influential friends joined in the promotion in March, 1884, of a
charity bazaar. The proceeds, 25,000 marks, were contributed to the
society for the erection of a deaconess home. From that time the work
in Hamburg had a remarkable growth.

By 1882 the deaconess work had grown to the point where a central organization with a superintendency was needed. At the same
time a small deaconess paper *Bethania* made its appearance. In February, 1883, the Bethany Society had begun work in Berlin with two
deaconesses. Two additional deaconesses were soon assigned to the
work, and the four lived together in a single room. In the spring
of 1885 a house, bought in 1883 in Frankfurt, was opened up as a
hospital. The cost of repairs were paid for by a door-to-door collection taken under a governmental permit. The collection netted 7,000
marks, and on April 25, 1885, the hospital was dedicated with nine
rooms for patients, eighteen beds, a small operating room, and necessary living and sleeping departments for twenty deaconesses.

By this time the work in Hamburg had attained such size that a
home for deaconesses was urgently needed. Many friends, won by
the work of the deaconesses, were ready to support the cause with
necessary funds had not a question of religious creed been raised.
"What is the Bethany Society?" asked some. "Is it not a Methodist
institution?" asked others. Many believed that the growth of sects
was not to be encouraged. At last civic leaders in Hamburg inter-
viewed the leaders of the Bethany Society. Declaring the information
that it was an independent organization, the deaconesses and officers
of which were members of the Methodist Episcopal Church, the
president of the Bethany Society said:

> Through its instrumentality [the Methodist Episcopal Church]
> we have come to a saving knowledge of the truth, and we love
> our Church.[6]

The civic leaders were satisfied. On March 11, 1886, a house was
purchased and fitted out as a deaconess home. This presently became
too small. In August of the same year the Bethany Deaconess Home

in Hamburg was publicly recognized as a charitable institution and granted charter privileges. This was an important event in the future development of the work. In August, 1885, the first course of instruction was begun in the society's own institution with four probationers. At the same time six deaconesses were being trained in the city hospital in Berlin.

After twelve years of Methodist deaconess work in Germany, sixty-six deaconesses were in service. Suggestions were now being made for the founding of a deaconess "rest home." The building was dedicated in June, 1889, in the village of Neuenhain. It was called *Erholungsstation Gottestreu.*

The work in Germany was now sufficiently strong so that the board could consider long-pending requests for the establishment of stations in other sections of Europe. In July, 1885, the Bethany Society answered the call from Saint Gallen, Switzerland. Two deaconesses were assigned to the station there. In the early part of February, 1887, the city of Zürich was taken up as the second field of labor in Switzerland with the assignment of three deaconesses. In the summer of 1890 two French-speaking deaconesses were assigned to a newly established station in Lausanne, Switzerland.

The work of the Bethany Society, widely appreciated on the Continent, received more than sixteen hundred requests for deaconesses to serve as private nurses in 1891. The Hamburg friends earnestly requested that the number of deaconesses in the Hanseatic city be increased. In other stations demand for services exceeded the meager supply of deaconesses. The ever-growing demand necessitated the establishment of a hospital as the center of the entire work where deaconesses might be trained under personal supervision.

In Hamburg the work was making rapid progress. Under the patronage of one hundred and fifty influential society women, a second charity bazaar was held in 1888, and a third in 1893. Through the generous sanction of the honorable senate and the citizens of Hamburg, a large and satisfactory building site was placed at the disposal of the Bethany Deaconess Home. Upon this lot the society erected two large buildings, a hospital, and a deaconess home. In the same year that the buildings were completed an epidemic of cholera broke out. The Bethany Society, placing thirteen deaconesses at the disposal of municipal authorities, assigned twelve more to nurse among the victims stricken by the disease, especially among the poorer families. For the work which the deaconess society performed during the epidemic, the municipal authorities presented as a testimonial the following sentiment emblazoned upon fine morocco:

> The Hospital Board of the Free and Hanseatic City of Hamburg thanks the Bethany Deaconess Institution for the self-sacrificing devotion of its deaconesses exhibited in the hospitals of Hamburg during the cholera epidemic of 1892.

During the rest of the decade the deaconess work continued to expand. On June 13, 1893, a deaconess home was purchased in Zürich, adjoining the Methodist Church on *Zeltweg*. Additional land was bought in Frankfurt looking toward the enlargement of the mother-house. On October 1, 1897, two deaconesses were assigned to a new station in Strassburg in Alsace. On November 1, 1897, the Bethany Society responded to a call from Vienna and assigned four deaconesses to the field. The Vienna work had been given over to the Bethany Society by the Martha and Mary Society, the deaconess association of the Wesleyan Methodist Church in Germany. The work in the Austrian capital prospered. Viennese physicians spoke of the Bethany nurses as the "technically best-trained deaconesses" in the country.

The Methodist ministry of healing by 1936, when the General Conference enabled the organization of a Central Conference, was doing its work in thirty-six German, Austrian, and Swiss cities in hospitals or stations adequately equipped and administered.[7]

The Methodist institutional work was strengthened when in 1897 the Wesleyan Synod in Germany was merged with the Methodist Episcopal Church and brought with it the institutions of the Martha and Mary Society. The Wesleyans, through the co-operation of G. J. Eckert and Sister Luise Schneider, had opened a hospital in a little room rented for twenty-five cents a week, on Fischer Alley in Nüremberg in 1889. In 1889 the Martha and Mary Society was granted charter privileges. From the motherhouse in Nüremberg it developed branch stations in Magdeburg, Munich, Heilbronn, and Vienna. The motherhouse of the Martha and Mary Society in Nüremberg is a large building situated in a beautiful garden. To the cost of 110,000 marks necessary to purchase it in 1893, Baroness von Langernau contributed 50,000. The Baroness contributed 22,000 marks to make the first payment on a 54,000-mark hospital in Magdeburg. In 1899, ten years after the deaconess home had been opened in Munich, a magnificent property was opened eight hundred meters from the council hall. The work in Heilbronn was opened as an affiliated institution in 1899. The rest home of the society was developed at Rupprechtstegen in Switzerland. Within twelve years after the work was begun in Nüremberg by Sister Schneider, the Martha and Mary Society owned property valued at 315,000 marks, and shortly after the beginning of the century had an annual income of 40,000 marks. Altogether seventy-five deaconesses were at work in the institutions. The superintendent was able to write: "If there were five hundred sisters at our disposal, they would all have quite enough to do."

The deaconess work began with a nursing ministry. That service continued to be its strength. Remuneration received from the rich helped to pay for serving the poor. In 1889 the Bethany Society, however, introduced a parish deaconate. For a small compensation deaconesses were assigned to different churches. They nursed the poor, assisted in the ladies' societies, the Martha Societies, and helped in other charitable and mission work.

In 1893 Leonhardt Weiss was appointed superintendent of the Bethany Society. His good sense, vision, and energy led to wholesome growth. At the end of the first year of the century, two hundred and forty-five sisters were working under the direction of Bethany.

The development of the deaconess work in America at a later date was largely due to the impact of the continental movement upon the Church in the United States. Women in America were still groping for a way of expressing their energies in Christian service when the work in Germany had already gained significant proportions.

For example, in 1872, Susan M. D. Fry wrote in the *Ladies' Repository:*

> When will the women of America awake to a sense of their responsibility? And what great soul, filled with love to God and man, shall open the way and prepare the means whereby we may be enabled to compete successfully with our sisters of Rome, not only as general charity women, educators, and succorers of the unfortunate, but especially as nurses of the sick—a department of such great good to soul and body, yet so long allowed to be monopolized by the daughters of Rome? Earnest thinkers upon the subject of "Woman's work in the Church" are looking to the Quakers and Methodists to move forward in God's name, smiting the waters of blind prejudice, and leading their daughters into the full possibilities of an entirely devoted Christian womanhood.[8]

In the 1860's, Bishop Simpson had become acquainted with the deaconess work in Germany. Upon his return to the United States he advocated the founding of deaconess institutions after the German models. It remained for Anna Wittemeyer, founder of the Ladies' and Pastors' Christian Union, however, the Amalie Sieveking of American Methodism, to pioneer in the deaconess movement in the Church. She had served in the hospitals during the Civil War and had organized bands of women to care for the wounded soldiers. When peace was established she endeavored to direct these labors of mercy into permanent channels. Together with Susan Fry, she traveled the country pleading for the expression of Christian benevolence in the founding of hospitals, orphanages, deaconess homes, homes for the aged, and other institutions. They were encouraged by Bishop Simpson, who was convinced that the time was ripe for the founding of institutions on the German model.

In the fall of 1872 Mrs. Wittemeyer went to Germany and visited Kaiserswerth. The articles which she wrote from Germany created an enthusiasm which prepared the way for the introduction of the deaconess work. Though the time was right, the growth of another movement postponed the development. When in September, 1874, the women in the United States suddenly became interested in the temperance movement and were drawn into the "crusade" originated in Ohio, the deaconess cause for the time was sidetracked.

The proposal was revived in 1886 when Bishop Thoburn returned from India to rest and regain his health. Always interested in the help of trained women on the mission field, he visited in Chicago the training school directed by Lucy Rider Meyer, to whom belongs the honor of having introduced the deaconess work in the Methodist Episcopal Church in the United States. The first deaconess home in American Methodism was opened in the unused rooms of the Chicago Training School in June, 1887. In the fall of the same year, a flat near by having been rented, Isabella Thoburn, sister of the Bishop, was appointed housemother, the name which dignified the office of matron according to the German fashion.

The development of the deaconess cause was furthered by the capable leadership of Jane M. Bancroft Robinson, of Detroit, secretary of the Deaconess Bureau of The Woman's Home Missionary Society. The daughter of a man who had resigned from the marines at thirty to become a preacher, she had been thoroughly educated at Emma Willard Seminary, Albany Normal School, and Syracuse University, where she took her Doctor of Philosophy degree. After serving as principal of Fort Edward Institute, she became dean of the woman's college of Northwestern University. Elected the first fellow in history in Bryn Mawr College, where she worked with Professor Woodrow Wilson, she went on to Zürich to study and later was the first woman admitted to the *Ecole des Hautes Etudes* in Paris. In the fall of 1886, while she was still in Zürich, Miss Bancroft became deeply interested in the deaconesses she saw working there. She had met them at services in the Methodist Episcopal Church on the *Zeltweg* and when she was told of their work, it occurred to her that the order ought to be introduced into the Church in America. She at once wrote to Mrs. R. S. Rust, corresponding secretary of The Woman's Home Missionary Society, describing in glowing terms her observations and impressions. Mrs. Rust at once caught a vision of the potential importance of the work and advised Miss Bancroft to make a special study of the deaconess cause so that on her return to America she could present the subject in its various bearings to the board of The Woman's Home Missionary Society with a view to inaugurating a similar movement in the United States. Following the instructions, Miss Bancroft went on to Kaiserswerth to study, ignorant of the fact that a beginning had already been made in Chicago and that there was a movement on foot to petition the General Conference to organize the deaconess work as an organic part of the Christian ministry. The General Conference of 1888 recognized the deaconess order as a church office.

In 1879, nearly a decade before this step was taken, *Christian Golder* returned from travels in Germany and read a paper on the subject before the North Ohio District meeting of the Central German Conference. Deep interest was aroused. The Central German Conference, to whose consideration the question was brought in 1881, would probably have been ready then to establish a home if the presiding bishop had not declared that the deaconess movement had no future in America and was "impractical and superfluous." Although the Conference was offered a house in Cleveland, in addition to a legacy of $25,000, and although a number of young women had presented themselves for this service, the Conference lost courage at the very time when work might have been begun.

The *Apologist* had in the meantime been drumming away on the idea of establishing a "motherhouse for deaconesses." It took hope when in 1888 the Elizabeth Gamble Deaconess Home was established in Cincinnati by English-speaking Methodists and the German Methodists were called upon to assist. Among the first group of young women to enroll was *Louise Golder*, who later was to play such a significant part in the development of the movement. In a short time fifteen German deaconesses had been admitted to the home.

In 1891, *Heinrich Liebhart*, who saw the importance of an exclusively German deaconess movement, wrote:

> Our mission is fully as significant in every respect as that of our English-speaking brethren. There is but one difference, and it is that we must accomplish it through the medium of the German language, and have regard for the education, views, and approval of the Church. German congregations, German Conferences, have arisen, and the German Epworth League was established. Why not, therefore, have German Deaconess Homes, especially as the Deaconess Movement is to be a lever for home missions work among the Germans? The best capital for an undertaking of this kind is young blood—consecrated Christian young women, who, for the love of Christ, are willing to perform the most menial Samaritan service for rich and poor, high and low, and this is worth more for the deaconess cause than many hundredweight of gold.[9]

The necessity for the establishment of a German motherhouse became more and more apparent to the entire Church. The need was seen when the Elizabeth Haas Home was opened on January 12, 1891, in Saint Paul, Minnesota. At the General Conference, which met in Omaha in 1892, the German delegates resolved to establish a German motherhouse in Chicago as soon as $25,000 could be raised for the purpose. While the committee was collecting funds and drafting a plan, a German Deaconess Institute was founded in Chicago. Though the $25,000 had not been raised, the institute made good progress. When General Conference met in Cleveland in 1896, the German delegates turned their attention to Cincinnati and agreed to build the motherhouse there if $25,000 could be raised by November, 1896. Cincinnati met the required conditions. The Central Deaconess Board, resolving to consider the Cincinnati institution as the motherhouse of German Methodism, required that future homes, as far as possible, be affiliated with it as branch houses and that the other established deaconess homes be considered "local institutions," having the same relation to the board as the motherhouse itself.

In the year 1894, an aged widow sent a check for $100 to the editor of *The Christian Apologist* as a first contribution to the erection of the deaconess motherhouse. The contribution was the primary gift necessary to precipitate action. On New Year's Day, 1895, John Kolbe, who later became the treasurer of the motherhouse, offered to give $1,000 for the same purpose. This gift was followed by a contingent gift of $5,000, provided $25,000 should be raised in the course of the year. The donor was *Frank Kreitler,* Pennsylvania, a former Catholic, a warm friend of the deaconess movement, and was the result of his acquaintance with and appreciation of the deaconess work while traveling through Germany. He gave during the rest of his life a large share of his means to support the work.

The gifts so far had come spontaneously. The Central German Conference, which met in Cincinnati in 1895, after a thorough discussion of the situation, passed the following resolution:

> While we rejoice in the success of the Elizabeth Gamble Deaconess Home and give it our fullest confidence, we are nevertheless convinced that our mission among the German churches would interest themselves much more for the Deaconess cause if we could establish an independent German Deaconess Home. We heartily commend this project to our well-to-do German Methodists.

The Elizabeth Gamble Deaconess Home and Christ Hospital had been the outgrowth of a meeting held in Cincinnati two days before Christmas in 1888. The Gamble family offered to give a large building, rent free, in the center of the downtown city in addition to a liberal sum of cash to give the program a start. Isabella Thoburn, who had been experienced as a housemother of the first deaconess home in the United States, was elected head deaconess. Against the wishes of the Gamble family, but to perpetuate the mother's name, the institution was named "Elizabeth Gamble Deaconess Home." The hospital was appropriately called Christ Hospital. A few years later the Gamble family bought a beautiful hilltop property on Mount Auburn, remodeled the female seminary occupying a four-and-a-half-acre campus into a hospital, and converted other buildings on the property into homes for deaconesses and probationers. The hospital became the hobby of *James N. Gamble.*

Gamble was born in Cincinnati on August 9, 1836, of parents who had emigrated from Ireland. James Gamble, senior, who like his wife Elizabeth, was an ardent Methodist, and whose home had been opened to Wilhelm Nast for German prayer meetings, was one of the founders of the Procter and Gamble Company. Young James, a thoroughly trained and ingenious chemist, devoted his career to the development of "Ivory Soap" to a high state of perfection.

With this work supported by the Gambles as an example of what could be done, pressure was exerted upon the delegates to the next General Conference to provide for the establishment of a German motherhouse. The Central German Conference named a committee with authority to collect funds and develop such a home as soon as circumstances justified the step. Through their connection with the Elizabeth Gamble Deaconess Home and Christ Hospital the German Methodist Churches of Cincinnati and Covington and Newport had acquired a knowledge and interest necessary for a broad support of the venture.

When several German deaconesses left that institution and a number applied for admission on probation, the committee resolved to request the management of the Elizabeth Gamble Deaconess Home to place at their disposal an experienced and capable deaconess to be the head of the German institution. The Board of Managers complied with this request and in the most magnanimous manner released Louise Golder to the German committee to lead the German work.

Miss Golder was a figure of appealing, steadfast faith unsurpassed in the whole history of German Methodism. She was born in Württemberg, Germany, in 1857. As an adventuresome, yet slight and painfully bashful girl of twenty, she had come to America in 1877, following the example of her six brothers and sisters. Four of the six children of that European home became distinguished American citizens. From childhood Miss Golder had longed to become a deaconess nurse. With this goal in mind she entered German Wallace College in 1879. There being no deaconess work in the German-speaking branch of the Methodist Episcopal Church, in 1899 she entered the Elizabeth Gamble Deaconess Home in Cincinnati, thus becoming the first German Methodist deaconess in America.

Still nourishing her childhood dream of becoming a deaconess nurse, she requested leave of absence for the purpose of traveling and studying hospitals and deaconess institutions abroad. She was gone nearly four years. In 1892 and 1893 she studied in Europe in the five great institutions located at Kaiserswerth, Bielefeld, Strassburg, Stuttgart, and Frankfurt. In 1894 she was studying in a nursing school in Berlin, and on her return in 1895 from Europe she entered Christ Hospital. In the next year a partnership was created between Miss Golder and her brother, Christian, in the development of the greatest single institution of German Methodism.

Christian, born in Württemberg, Germany, in 1849, had come to America at eighteen with his father's consent. His father, an independent and progressive thinker, was a member of the so-called Revolutionist Party and had carried a gun in 1848. The son had many of the characteristics of his father. Landing in New York in November, 1867, he went on to Columbus, Indiana, where his uncle lived. The uncle was a typical Methodist class leader, and through his fervent prayers at the family altar, Christian was awakened to a religious consciousness. Of his experience he wrote:

> After a period of true repentence, I was gloriously converted at a prayer meeting on January 30, 1868. I sang and prayed the greater part of the night. My joy was so great I could not sleep. The following day I wrote a twenty-eight-page letter to my parents, telling them of my wonderful experience. My parents felt so grateful that they immediately called all the relatives and friends together, and after reading the letter they decided to permit their eight other children to go then to America, hoping they too would make a similar experience. All but one crossed the Atlantic, and every one was converted at the Methodist altar.[10]

In 1870 Golder became a class leader and the following year was licensed a local preacher. His brief study at German Wallace College in 1870 was interrupted by his capitulation to the urgent demand for preachers. He consented to an appointment to Ann Arbor, Michigan, where he had the privilege of attending the university. After pastorates in Ohio and Pennsylvania, he was appointed to Pittsburgh. Here he was given orders by the Bishop to further the City Mission Movement throughout the country. He did. The movement printed and distributed at cost about three hundred different papers, both in German and English, in an edition of 250,000 monthly, mostly distributed in connection with the tracts of the Church. Other denominations joined the Methodists in the work. By 1921 more than fifty million of these papers—weekly, monthly, and quarterly—had been printed and distributed throughout the nation. In 1890 Golder was called to the associate editorship of the *Apologist,* where he remained until 1908, promoting the deaconess movement at every opportunity by his pen. During the eighteen years of his editorial work, he visited the Conferences in the United States, Germany, and Switzerland, addressed Epworth Leagues and Sunday-school conventions, assisted in camp meetings, visited schools and institutions, preaching every Sunday and frequently on weekdays. Through this experience he was ready, by an unusually wide knowledge of the Church and German Methodism in particular, to develop the deaconess work among his fellow Germans. A man of imposing appearance, well-proportioned, deep chested, with muscles of iron and nerves of steel, he was built for the prodigious labors which he performed. His services to German Methodism place him in the first rank with the elder Nast, Jacoby, Nippert, and Liebhart.

Golder's association in the deaconess movement with his sister, Louise, was one of the beautiful relationships in the epic of German Methodism. Miss Golder was so deeply humble in her service that her behavior at first acquaintance seemed to be characterized by un-necessary timidity. This attitude, however, sprang from her consci-entiousness and from a sense of responsibility in her sacred calling in which she sought so completely to heed divine guidance and rely upon divine strength.

A favorite saying of hers was:

> *Wo die Menschenverherrlichung anfängt, da hört die Gottes-verherrlichung auf.*[11]

Her serene and quiet poise was her professional strength. Albert Nast wrote of her:

> This genuine humility before God was the root and source of her inner prayer life. . . . Her inner confidence in God il-lumined her face and radiated from her eyes. I doubt whether she ever became really despondent, although at times disap-pointed but never discouraged. Therefore in her approaches to men for financial aid, she was rarely ever repelled. Her habitual smile and persuasive voice usually won a willing response.

In 1929 the columnist "Cincinnatus" in the Cincinnati *Post* paid this tribute to her:

> She built her own altar and served there thirty-two years. In a small rented house Louise Golder established the Bethesda Hospital in 1896 and by singular devotion caused it to grow to the great institution it is today. This was her altar and she made no end of serving at it almost to the last week of her long life. If one were to count the greatly achieving women of the city, the list would not be large but Louise Golder would be among them.[12]

In 1896 Christian and Louise Golder, with daring faith but little sympathy from the Church, rented a little house on the charming Cincinnati hillside known as Mount Auburn, and incorporated on April 13, 1896, the German Methodist Deaconess Home, which became the most typical German motherhouse in the United States, with the possible exception of the Mary J. Drexel Deaconess Home in Philadelphia. The six German nurses, who had been so graciously released by Christ Hospital with Miss Golder, performed a heroic service. Nursing often eighteen hours a day for the pittance of $5 or $10 a week, and more often with no remuneration at all, they paid a monthly rent of $40 out of a combined income that rarely exceeded $100. They received no salary but allowed themselves $6.25 a month for expenses.

In 1897 an organization was formed known as the Bethesda Society. For many years it was directed by Ida, wife of Christian Golder. Offering memberships for a dollar, the Society used its funds for the care of needy sick. By 1903 the income from these small contributions amounted to $1,500 annually. It was not alone by small contributions that the institution grew. The leadership of Bethesda during its entire history has been so able that vision commanded the support of wealth. Christian leadership and Christian wealth met in the development of the institution.

In April, 1898, just a little more than two years after the brother and sister had begun their partnership in Christian benevolence, they were able to purchase the well-appointed private hospital of Dr. T. A. Reamy for $55,000. The purchase seemed like too vast an undertaking, yet aided by a liberal donation from the physician, they made a payment on the day the property was transferred, and cancelled the entire indebtedness in the spring of 1901. Although the hospital was formally opened in September, 1898, it was not dedicated until May 16, 1901, when the properties were free from debt. In 1900 the plant was expanded with the purchase of Dr. Reamy's residence for $17,000 for use as a deaconess home. In 1901 a vacation home was purchased at Epworth Heights, a church resort outside Cincinnati. In 1902 a powerhouse and laundry were constructed at a cost of $35,000. In 1904 a maternity department was opened with eighty beds. This grew in 1913 into a $125,000 maternity hospital, at that time one of the finest in the country. In 1907 a fund left by John Kolbe, long treasurer and far-seeing financial adviser of the institution, was invested in the purchase of a deaconess rest home. A thirty-five-acre farm was bought in the suburb of Wyoming at a cost of $65,000, and named the Gertrude Kolbe Rest Home. In 1928 ten acres of this land were sold for $56,000, and the remaining twenty-six acres were offered for sale for $75,000. This transaction is only one example of the shrewd business foresight which went into the building of the Bethesda Institutions. In 1935 a new Deaconess Rest Home was opened within a half block of Bethesda Hospital, at a cost of $20,000, and dedicated free of debt.

In 1908, through the generosity of *E. H. Huenefeld and his wife,* the famous old Schoenberger mansion "Scarlet Oaks," located in a forty-seven acre park in the aristocratic Clifton section of Cincinnati, was given to Bethesda, together with an art collection valued at $50,000. The value of the property was $100,000. Used as a sanatorium from 1908 until 1916, it became a part of the medical hospital in the latter year, and in 1930 was devoted to the use of the Bethesda Home for the Aged.

The benefactions, begun by Huenefeld and his wife, were continued by their son Walter, who was treasurer of the Board of Managers. His business astuteness, together with his generosity, extended the Huenefeld tradition at Bethesda.

E. H. Huenefeld, born near Bremen in 1838, was brought to America by his widowed father at the age of seven. Enjoying but little schooling and subjected to many hardships and privations, and after working at whatever odd jobs his hand found to do, he started a stove business of his own in 1871. By business shrewdness, diligent effort, and a flare for salesmanship, his industry developed into a great concern. A man of good health and few words, he was fair but exacting with his employees. In 1884 he married Lena L. Diers, of Cincinnati. Mrs. Huenefeld was a modest woman, whose wealth never made her selfish. No beggar or representative of a benevolent cause was turned from her door without help. By the marriage of their son Walter to the daughter of Karl Riemenschneider, for nearly half a century president of Baldwin Wallace College, two of the leading families of German Methodism were united.

The development of the deaconess work shifted from the hospital in 1910 to the organization of the training school for deaconess workers. It was called the *Dorcas Institute,* offering training for the deaconess vocation, for social service, parish work as pastors' assistants, and more personal courses for Bible study, and larger usefulness in the home church. *August J. Bucher* was called from the Theological Seminary in Frankfurt to be its first principal. Bucher had been born in Zürich in 1862, had had a Methodist religious experience at the age of fifteen, and in his seventeenth year had migrated to America. Already well-educated, he entered German Wallace College and Nast Theological Seminary in 1893 and was graduated with high honors. After two years of missionary work in Wheeling, West Virginia, he returned to Switzerland to marry Maria Gebhardt, the daughter of the "Singer of Methodism." After pastorates in Akron and Cincinnati he was called to Frankfurt, where he remained seventeen years as a professor in the Theological Seminary. He was called from Germany to the principalship of Dorcas Institute and as rector of the deaconess motherhouse. A man of comprehensive knowledge, a linguist, an accomplished pianist and singer, he was equally at home in the fields of literature, science, art, or religion. Despite his wide erudition he never lost the Christocentric emphasis in his work. Gifted with a delightful sense of humor, he was in business and practical things as naïve as Nast, whose simple soul was described as being as "unsophisticated as that of a child."

Bucher was succeeded in 1912 by *John A. Diekmann,* who held the principalship for eleven years and was followed by the veteran German educator, Friedrich Schaub. Diekmann was born in Sandridge, Illinois, a village twenty miles southeast of Chicago, in 1872, the tenth child in the family. For seven decades his parents' home, charter members of the first German Methodist Episcopal Church in Chicago and founders of the church in Sandridge, had been a "hotel" for Methodist itinerants. When he was eight years old, according to his own story, he "struggled against the conviction of sin" and in his seventeenth year was converted. Capitulating to a conviction that he should enter the ministry, he studied at German Wallace College, was graduated from Nast Theological Seminary at the age of twenty-two, taught at the college for three years while taking his master's degree, and in 1898 did post graduate work at Drew Theological Seminary. In the fourteen years following he served three pastorates. Invited to the pastorates of leading churches, offered the presidency of three colleges, and important administrative posts in the Church, he remained at Dorcas Institute, and in 1922 was elected president of Bethesda Institutions. Despite the administrative demands of his work, he kept alive the evangelical passion in the true tradition of German Methodism and the spirit was contagious in all the many works in which he was concerned. A platform lecturer, a camp-meeting preacher, a Bible student, after-dinner speaker, and conversationalist, he loved the personalities and traditions of German Methodism with a passion unsurpassed by any German Methodist of his generation.

Even the World War did not interrupt the expansion of the Bethesda Institutions. The opening of the $125,000 maternity hospital in 1913 was followed by the organization of the Bethesda School of Nursing and registration with the Ohio State Medical Board in 1914, by the absorption of the $35,000 Ohio Hospital for Women and Children in 1915, and the purchase of a $5,000 frame house as the first unit in a Bethesda Home for the Aged in the same year. In 1916 a medical hospital was erected on the Scarlet Oaks grounds at a cost of $110,000. It became a unit of the Home for the Aged in 1930. In 1917 the new Deaconess Home and chapel building was erected.

For many years Bethesda had felt the need of such a meeting place. For half a decade it had been foremost in the plans of the leaders of the institution. One day Albert Nast asked Miss Golder what he might give Bethesda at Christmas. She replied,

"Oh, Dr. Nast, build us a new deaconess home."

The suggestion bore fruit in the dedication of the Fanny Nast Gamble Chapel and the Louise Golder Deaconess Home. The title to the institution fittingly joins the names of one woman who gave her life and another woman who gave her wealth for Christian benevolence. The daughter of Wilhelm Nast, Fanny had come into wealth by marriage into the Gamble family. She expressed her philosophy in an inscription to the memory of her husband on a tablet on a deaconess home in Kolar, India:

> To the memory of William A. Gamble, Cincinnati, Ohio, U. S. A., who practiced justice, was mild and forbearing and walked humbly before his God. He still speaks, although he is dead.

In 1917 a financial campaign for a quarter of a million dollars was successfully completed. In 1919 E. H. Huenefeld and his wife contributed a new $140,000 unit in the Bethesda Home for the Aged on the Scarlet Oaks grounds. In 1920 the Marjorie Louise Strecker Hospital for Children was opened at a cost of $35,000. In 1926, under the tireless leadership of Diekmann, a new hospital unit was opened at a cost of $1,127,500. In 1931 Dorcas Institute absorbed the Cincinnati Missionary Training School and continued its operations as the Cincinnati Training School.

In forty years the Bethesda Institutions had grown to a value of $3,000,000, free from debt. The hospital had served 139,976 patients, performed 73,284 operations, and witnessed 21,964 births. Its annual income, in 1904 $36,803.74, by 1937 had grown to $389,698.21.

The physical development of the Bethesda Institutions would have been of little value without the spiritual and technical skill of the deaconesses, doctors, and nurses who were a part of it. Their influence and reverence for life have given to Bethesda Hospital the reputation of having the lowest death rate of any hospital in the city of Cincinnati. Such men as Dr. Samuel Robert Geiser, chief of the medical staff for a quarter of a century; Dr. C. M. Paul, and Dr. C. E. Eha; such women as Louise Golder, Lillian Spicker, Minnie L. Draher; and such advisers and helpers as Jacob Krehbiel and his son, Charles S. Krehbiel, and the Huenefelds; and such feminine helpers as Ida Nippert, Katherine Weigele, and Sidonia Stueve, gave a distinctive character to Bethesda work.

The Bethesda Deaconess motherhouse developed and maintained branch homes in Chicago, Milwaukee, and Kansas City, Kansas. The home in Saint Paul was discontinued in 1917. It also maintains stations in Detroit; Terre Haute, Indiana; Los Angeles; and Akron, Ohio. The institutions located in Cincinnati comprise twenty-five separate buildings and eighty-five acres of land. The number of deaconesses was seven in 1896, rising to a high point of seventy-eight in 1916, and continuing at a level of seventy in 1938.

The development in Cincinnati, while perhaps the most prosperous of the deaconess foundations, is only an example of the evolution of benevolent work. A German Central Deaconess Board was organized at Cincinnati in 1897. In the beginning it was composed of one ministerial and one lay representative from each Annual Conference of the German-speaking branch of the Church, and one representative from each constituent institution. Up until the time of the dissolution of the German-speaking Conferences, these were the Bethany Deaconess and Hospital Society, Brooklyn; the Methodist Episcopal Deaconess Hospital, Louisville, Kentucky; the Emmanuel Deaconess Branch Home, Kansas City, Kansas; the Bethany Home for Young Women, Chicago; and the Milwaukee Branch Home. The deaconesses, excepting those related to the Brooklyn institution, have received their education and training at the motherhouse in Cincinnati, and are appointed to the various homes and stations from there. The deaconesses have always received, according to the rules, from $25 to $35 a month allowance, a room for life in the Louise Golder Deaconess Home, free care in sickness and old age, and a modest pension.

In 1908 the General Conference created the position of a general superintendent of German Deaconess work in America. Golder held the post from the time of its creation until his death in 1922. Since January, 1923, J. A. Diekmann has been the incumbent.

Although Bethesda Institutions became the most extensive project of German Methodism, the honor of establishing the first hospital belongs to the Bethany Deaconess Home and Hospital located in Brooklyn. A group of preachers of the East German Conference in the winter of 1893 organized the work in the upper story of a house at 1192 Green Avenue. Placing the supervision of the work in the hands of Sophie Nussberger, a deaconess of the Bethany Society in Hamburg, the provisional committee organized the Bethany Society in May, 1894. At the end of the first year Sister Nussberger, called back to Germany, was succeeded by *Martha Binder,* who for eight years had been in charge of the Bethany Deaconess Home in Zürich.

Sister Binder, born in Ebingen, Württemburg, in 1861, at the age of twenty decided to enter deaconess work. Writing to F. J. Hauser, father of Gustav F. Hauser, for many years superintendent, she was referred to Weiss in Berlin, who accepted her into the Bethany Society. Trained in Charité Hospital in Berlin and in the motherhouse in Frankfurt-am-Main until 1887, she was sent to Zürich to organize the deaconess home. Called to America, she became head sister in Brooklyn on November 1, 1894. She saw the institution grow during her long days of hard but happy work. Her day began before six in the morning and rarely ended before ten at night. Twice a day she made her rounds, visiting each patient's bedside. When a reporter asked her about her work at the half-century mark, she replied:

> The fifty years have gone quickly. That is, I suppose, because I have been busy. There is little room in a deaconess's life to think about the passage of time.

The work, begun by three deaconesses, "the grace of God," and the committee headed by Louis Wallon, grew. A gift of a $7,000 home by Anna Hartmann to the society on condition that she be privileged to use a few rooms until her death, encouraged the friends of the work. The donor died in 1895 and the entire property was devoted to the deaconess program.

In 1901, as a result of constant demands for hospital service, the deaconess work was broadened to include the hospital program. Borrowing $15,000 from the Harbor Mission Society, and acquiring a new site, the cornerstone for the new home and hospital was laid on November 4, 1901, and was dedicated September 16, 1902. The property was further expanded by the erection of a Deaconess Home, dedicated April 22, 1907. In forty years the value of the property held by the Bethany Society grew to nearly half a million dollars.

While German Methodists in the East German Conference were developing their own deaconess institution in Brooklyn, the Churches in Louisville, Kentucky, were no less active. On May 6, 1895, an interested group assembled at the call of Jacob Rothweiler, presiding elder, convened in Jefferson Street Church, Louisville, to discuss the problem. A committee was appointed to secure sponsors and the ministers pledged themselves to preach about the project. Just before Christmas in the same year, subscriptions totaling $672 were reported! Encouraged by this meager sum, the friends of the project organized themselves and proceeded to promote the cause against increasing difficulties. Hope revived, however, when in October, 1896, the faculty of the Southwestern Homeopathic College, under certain conditions, offered the Methodists a hospital. Accepting the offer, the committee assigned two deaconesses, Minnie Fischendorf and Luise Bockstahler, to start the work. This humble beginning caught the imagination of the Church. The demand for the service of the hospital increased to such an extent that on October 21, 1897, the well-shaded home of John P. Morton, on Eighth Street, was purchased at a cost of $12,000. Under the direction of Rothweiler, the hospital, well-equipped, was dedicated on February 24, 1898.

Experience proved that an old private residence, even when remodeled, is not a satisfactory hospital building. In 1900, therefore, a building fund was begun and actively solicited in 1902 by the appointment of John F. Severinghaus as financial agent and superintendent of the institution. In 1903 construction was begun upon the faith that God would provide the money. The building was dedicated on August 4, 1904, but the operation of the hospital continued to be burdened by the large indebtedness against it.[13]

The deaconess work of the German Methodists was a contribution of the social service of the Church. It flourished upon a formula: (1) a life consecrated to Christian service; (2) commands wealth from those who consider themselves its stewards responsible to God; and (3) produces a great institution.

The deaconess movement provided a career for Christian women. Such a program was a radical departure from the custom that "women ought to remain at home." Golder threw himself into the debate on the subject of a career for women with characteristic vigor. A wing of the movement promoting "woman's rights" asserted that "in order to emancipate woman one must first divorce himself from the Word of God." Golder took issue with this point of view.

> Women can no more be emancipated from the fundamental principles of the Holy Scriptures than from the eternal laws of nature [he declared]. . . . If a woman would honor her sex, she must remain womanly. . . . The slogan, "Equality of Sex," which the Woman's Rights champions have adopted, is a contradiction of terms, since sex presupposes inequality and difference, . . . There is in the present Woman's Movement an element which

might be properly designated "Andromania." Many women have lost the womanly ideal, and are endeavoring to be men. . . . We totally misapprehend the distinction of sex and the designs of God by asking: "If a man is entitled to this and that, why not the woman? . . . If the husbands go to war, why not the wives?" . . . The Scriptures give to us an entirely different idea of the essence of woman, and show us how the Creator assigned to each sex a particular sphere of action. If we would hold more to the Word of God, the woman question would be less complicated and easier to solve.[15]

Summing up his point of view on the function of women in Christian society, Golder held:

1. Woman is on a plane of perfect equality with man in the religious domain; that is, both sexes were redeemed by Christ, and have, as children of God, the common duty to build up the Kingdom as best they can. "There is neither male nor female: for ye are all one in Christ Jesus."

2. Woman has the mission in the gospel to build up the Kingdom according to her special gifts and faculties, particularly through the service of love. In this relation she is more like the Saviour and accomplishes greater things than man. The Church, in the Deaconess Work, has given the female sex a wide field of fruitful usefulness, even within its inner portals.

3. The order of creation has placed upon woman, on account of her natural endowments, certain restrictions which cannot be removed without injury to her highest interests. She should, therefore, not push herself forward and lord it over man. Neither in social nor commercial nor political relations can she usurp the lead without changing the nature of her being and forsaking her God-given vocation.

4. The calling best suited to womanly nature is that of wife and mother, and unto this the female sex ought to be specially educated, and man should have a conscientious care that their duties be not disregarded or depreciated.

5. Both the Scriptures and nature assign to woman the family circle as the principal sphere of her calling, and it is only from this standpoint that the woman question may be safely discussed. The scriptural passage, "The husband is the head of the wife," speaks only of his authority in the family circle, and determines nothing for public life.

6. The precept of the apostle, imposing "Silence" upon woman, was not at variance at that time with her highest interests, and while the necessity of her "silence" by the force of changed conditions has passed away, her highest interests may nevertheless be conserved. It is, however, certain that woman was debarred from ordination to the ministry, although the passages in question (1 Corinthians 14. 34, 35) say nothing of the boundaries within which woman is to move in public life.

7. It is clear that, if the world is to be saved, woman must at the present day be drawn into a much more expanded and general circle of activity, and it devolves upon the church in an entirely different manner than has happened for the past two

thousand years to return to the principles of Holy Scripture and the Apostolical Institutions. The Deaconess Movement opens up for woman a blessed usefulness outside of the home, and this in the direction of practical charity and service to mankind. When it is considered that the women of paganism can only be reached by female missionaries, that in the home churches two thirds of the membership belong to the female sex, and, finally, that their social and ecclesiastical relations, as well as their intellectual and educational progress, are far ahead of the apostles' times, it must be acknowledged that the Church needs in a great measure the enlightenment of the Holy Spirit on the question of the proper position and sphere of woman.[16]

CHAPTER X

THE GERMAN METHODISTS DEVELOP EDUCATIONAL INSTITUTIONS

Early in the winter of 1858 three young men sat in Jacoby's home in Bremen, discussing with him their preparation for the ministry. They had been converted by Methodist preaching, were clear enough in their conviction that they had been "called" to active Christian leadership, but were reluctant to take up parish work until they had been trained. Their earnest deliberation over adequate theological instruction was an expression of Germany's tradition of an educated clergy and was equally in harmony with the best Methodist experience. John Wesley had been educated according to the most exacting standards of Anglican churchmen. Perhaps more than any other evangelical denomination, the Methodists appreciated the importance of a "literate ministry."

Jacoby knew that the problem which the young men raised had to be faced. In the middle of February he called an informal committee meeting at his home. The ministerial triumvirate was present— Jacoby, Doering, and Nippert—together with three laymen, E. C. Poppe, H. Luersen, and H. J. Junker. The session was long, the discussion prayerful, and the outcome of unexpected significance. The men agreed among themselves that a Methodist educational institution should be founded for the purpose of training young men of twenty years of age and over "when they gave evidence of special talent and spiritual vigor." The committee was determined to make a prompt beginning. Before it adjourned the group contributed $75 for the venture. The Bremen congregation echoed its approval by assurance of its willingness to support such an institution.

On March 7, 1858, the little seminary opened in an unused attic room in the *Tractathaus* with three students and three teachers. Nippert was director and instructor in theology, the custom in Methodist schools at the time being that the school president personally supervised the training in the "Queen of the Sciences." F. Richter, a licensed pedagogue, taught German and English, and Poppe assisted both. The first three students were August Rodemeyer, of Vegesack, who became a great preacher and writer; Arnold Sulzberger, of Winterthur, Switzerland, who later took his Doctor of Philosophy degree at the University of Heidelberg, and became a teacher in the seminary;[1] and Martin Träger, of Braunschweig. In addition to their studies they performed four hours of manual labor each day to defray a part of their expenses.

The seminary was the first educational institution to be founded by the German Methodists. In many ways it was the most important. The hub around which central European Methodism revolved, it was the connecting link between Methodisms separated by the stormy waters of the Atlantic. Of unquestioned educational standards from the very beginning, it contributed not only a long line of distinguished clergymen and scholars to both America and Europe, but also created a practical but soundly scholarly enthusiasm in the German Church.

Hardly six months had elapsed before the school had outgrown its attic quarters and was moved to the chapel on *Steffensweg*. When Nippert presently was transferred to Berlin, Jacoby took over the direction of the school. The student body doubled and continued to grow until the chapel was outgrown. In the garden behind it the first seminary building, known as *"Mission House,"* was contructed and dedicated on October 1, 1860.

Jacoby continued as director of the institution until 1868. During the decade of his leadership the general character of the school was established as a scholarly but primarily practical professional school for the preparation of "preachers." Jacoby defined the program in these words:

> To train young men as plain, practical Methodist preachers who themselves stand in the grace of God and have sympathy with the necessity of reaching down to the lowest level to lead men to the Saviour of sinners.[2]

He did not want to educate just pastors, but rather shepherds "seeking the lost."

> Let us rather give up the work than to increase the numbers in the world of such men as are only willing to play pastors. We must pray and grow or else we cannot carry on our work. Beautiful sermons are not enough. We must preach penitence and faith. When we fail to show the way, how can men be converted?[3]

A distinguished line of professors was introduced in 1861 with the appointment of William F. Warren to the faculty. Warren continued to teach in Bremen until 1866, when he was called to a chair in the newly founded Boston University, of which he later became the president. The scholarly research which Warren was pursuing developed into his important volume, *Introduction to Systematic Theology.* Warren was associated at the seminary with *Friedrich Paulus,* who later went to America and contributed so much to the development of the theological seminary at German Wallace College, Berea, Ohio; and with Karl Riemenschneider, who served over fifty years as teacher and president at this institution. Professor Warren was succeeded by a young American scholar, *John F. Hurst,* who had just completed two years of study at the University of Halle.

The little seminary building in the garden behind the chapel by 1865 had become too crowded for effective work. What was to be done? The German leaders, taking advantage of the centennial jubilee of Methodism in America, appealed to the sympathy and generosity of the Church in the United States. Jacoby was successful in interesting his old St. Louis friend, *John T. Martin,* in the work. Martin's contribution of $25,000 at exchange made a sum of 72,000 marks for the development of the institution. News of the gift was received in Bremen on New Year's Day, 1867, and was hailed with rejoicing by the Methodists throughout Germany and Switzerland.

If the gift awakened enthusiasm, it also created a problem concerning the best location of the institution. Believing that a more central location was preferable to Bremen, and with the assurance of the Prussian Ministry of Culture that no legal complications would interfere with religious freedom, the Annual Conference in June of 1867 decided to purchase a lot in the east end of the city of Frankfurt-am-Main on the heights of Roederberg. Here the new seminary building was constructed and dedicated on January 17, 1869. Nippert, who succeeded Jacoby at this time and moved to Frankfurt with Hurst and Paulus, with characteristic evangelical vigor, declared at the dedication:

> The chief purpose of our institution is to educate men of God, men filled with faith and the spirit. We pray God that a man may never come into these halls who has not experienced the converting, enlightening, and saving strength of the spirit of God. And we entreat the brethren to send us no man, even when he has talent, who does not recognize Christ as the light of life.[4]

The school had hardly opened in its new quarters when Paulus in 1870 was called to Berea, Ohio, as professor of systematic theology. He was in the process of completing his work on *The Christian Life of Salvation.* Hurst followed him to America, having been called to Drew Theological Seminary as professor of church history. In 1884 he was elected bishop. The research which he had so industriously begun in Germany was continued throughout his lifetime and was made available in a series of publications on the history of the Christian Church.

Nippert continued as director of the seminary until 1886, when he returned to America. His diary is an important source document in the history of German Methodism. He was the author of two volumes, *Homiletics and Pastoral Theology* and *Principles of Christian Faith and Morals,* in addition to his studies on *Asbury's Life* and *The Life and Work of John Fletcher.*

An epoch in German Methodism was coming to an end with the death of the first generation of leaders. Jacoby, who had worked so strenuously in spite of his frail health, died in 1874. Nippert, after a brief eight years in America, died in 1894. Nast, who survived them all, brought the period to its close with his death in 1899.

Nippert was succeeded by Clément Achard, who continued as director until 1889, when he migrated with his family to America. His successor was *Heinrich Mann,* under whose leadership a fund of 75,000 marks was raised for the purchase of a lot adjoining the grounds. He was assisted in the solicitation by N. W. Clark, professor of English and church history, who at the time was in America. When Clark was called to the directorship of a theological school in Rome, his place was taken by *August J. Bucher,* who until his death in 1937, continued to be a leader in the second generation of German Methodist leaders and to exercise influence on two continents.

By 1895 the enrollment was approaching thirty. Heinrich Mann was succeeded by *Paul Gustav Junker,* editor of the *Evangelist.* The faculty was strengthened in 1909 by the appointment of *Emil Luering,* who had served two decades as missionary and teacher in India and the Orient. His practical experience in the mission field, together with his wide knowledge of languages (he was able to converse with ease in thirty different languages), made him an authority in his field.

By 1912 the enrollment of the seminary had grown to forty. Just before the World War the city of Frankfurt was making extensive alterations, which necessitated the moving of railroad yards and the construction of new streets. The seminary grounds and buildings were in the line of construction. The municipal authorities offered land near Pforzheim to the Annual Conference, but the Methodists were determined to keep the institution in Frankfurt for sentimental reasons. Chief among these was the fact that John Wesley's friend, Peter Böhler, had been born there on December 31, 1712. The city then offered a building site on *Ginnheimer Landstrasse,* near Ginnheim, a suburb of Frankfurt. Damages amounting to 160,000 marks were allowed for the condemned property. The buildings constructed with this fund were to be dedicated on the second Sunday in August, 1914. Delegates, scholars, and theologians from all sections of Europe and the United States had been invited to the celebration and were *en route* to the dedication when, as unexpectedly as a flash of lightning, war was declared on the first Sunday in August, 1914. The seminary students were ordered to report to the army. The new buildings themselves, never officially dedicated, were placed by Junker at the disposal of the military authorities. The beautiful halls and classrooms were turned into an army hospital and filled with beds on which lay wounded and dying soldiers. During the bitter years of fighting, theological instruction was abandoned until the sad months near the war's end when a few Swiss brethren began to take steps toward a new beginning. Two of Junker's sons were killed. The shock was too much for him to bear. This family loss was heightened by his mourning over his country's defeat. He died of a broken heart.

When Theophil Mann was called to serve the government in the work of dealing with war prisoners, the only remaining faculty member was Luering.

When the war was over and the beds had been cleared from the halls of the institution, the seminary was confronted with the problem of beginning almost anew. The little Methodist congregations scattered through Germany and Switzerland were weary and poor and struggling in their poverty to maintain even their own existence. At this critical time the board called *F. H. Otto Melle* to the directorship. He had for many years been the superintendent of the Methodist work in Austria and Hungary. He assembled a strong faculty, including J. W. E. Sommer, Theophil Spoerri, Paulus Scharpff, and later Theophil Mann. In his installation speech Melle, before the twenty-three students who had enrolled for work and guests, declared:

> The catclysms which have shaken the world of economic, intellectual, and spiritual life have given new tasks to the Church of Jesus Christ, and especially to the Methodist Episcopal Church.[5]

Melle promptly in 1920 sailed for the United States and again in 1921 to interest friends of wealth in the institution. He received assurance of gifts and returned to organize four endowed chairs of historic moment: the William Fairfield Warren chair of systematic theology; the Wilhelm Nast chair; a William Burt chair; and a Ludwig-Sigismund Jacoby chair. At the same time he purchased a large section of land adjoining the institution for purposes of expansion and other fertile fields for development as a farm. By 1924 eighty-three students were enrolled, not only from Germany, but from Switzerland, Austria, Hungary, Jugoslavia, Bulgaria, the Baltic countries, and Russia. Melle's ambition to make the seminary of service to all the countries of central and eastern Europe seemed about to be fulfilled.

One of the most valuable of Melle's many valuable services to the institution was his determination to establish co-operation between the Methodist seminary and the state universities. In promotion of this idea, he organized an annual three-day preachers' seminar, the first of which was held in the spring of 1922. Bishop Nuelsen lectured on "Methodism as a Religious Movement and as a Church." Professor Adolf Deissmann discussed the field in which he was an eminent authority, lecturing on "The Community of Paul With Christ." He also gave an illustrated lecture on the "Epistle to Philemon." Professor Otto Schmitz, of Münster, lectured on "The Idea of Freedom of Epictetus and the Freedom of Paul." The first seminar was given a historic importance in the relation of the Methodist Episcopal Church to the State Church and educational system when Professor Deissmann, in the name of the University of Berlin, conferred upon Bishop Nuelsen the honorary degree of Doctor of Theology.

The seminar at once became an accepted part of the Methodist program in Europe. With such professors as Julius Richter, of Berlin; Paul Feine, of Halle; Hans Schmidt, of Giessen; Karl Heim, of Tübingen; Gustav Entz, of Zürich, and others of equal scholarship, the program became an annual event of theological importance.

German Wallace College

Perhaps no institution founded by the German Methodists in America has had such a close relationship to the seminary in Frankfurt-am-Main as German Wallace College, which in August, 1913, was united with Baldwin University to become Baldwin-Wallace College.

In August of 1845 *John Baldwin* went before the North Ohio Conference of the Methodist Episcopal Church in session at Marion, Ohio, and offered a campus of five acres, a large three-story building, thirty village lots, and fifty acres of land in Berea, Ohio, for the founding of an institution of learning. The gift was accepted, a board of commissioners appointed, and on December 20, 1845, Baldwin Institute was chartered. In 1855 the institution was recognized and chartered as Baldwin University.

About the time that the university was being organized, Jacob Rothweiler was promoting the idea of organizing a German department in connection with the institution. Rothweiler had been a pioneer in founding schools of higher learning in the Mississippi Valley and in Ohio. He arranged an interview with John Wheeler, president of Baldwin. Assured that a German professorship would be established if the Germans were willing to make the necessary sacrifices in raising $10,000, Nast and Rothweiler brought the proposition before the Cincinnati and the North Ohio Conferences. The necessary approval was given. John Baldwin assisted the Germans by giving them Baldwin Hall as a dormitory for their students. In the fall of 1858 twelve German-speaking students were enrolled. The growth of the language work proceeded so rapidly that in the summer of 1863 a group of German preachers and laymen were called together in Berea to discuss the advisability of founding a German college. This was chartered on June 7, 1864, as German Wallace College. To Baldwin Hall was added Wallace Hall, the gift of *James Wallace*. The purpose of the institution was declared to be the promotion of "scientific education and biblical Christianity among the Germans in America." Wilhelm Nast was elected president; Rothweiler, vice-president and professor of German language and biblical literature; B. W. Mosblech, professor of ancient and modern languages; Albert Nast, teacher of piano; and Mary Hasenpflug, teacher of melodeon. Forty students were enrolled for the first year's work (1864-65).[6] By the small gifts of preachers and laymen, by a $25,000 campaign within the German Conferences for the endowment of a chair in theology, and by a growing enthusiasm for a language college, the institution underwent a substantial development. In 1868 *Karl Riemenschneider,* the first of the leaders of second-generation German Methodism, began his long career with the institution as professor of ancient languages and later as president.

The physical plant expanded as the student body steadily grew. In 1870 a "ladies' hall" was constructed, and in 1872 a college chapel. A triumvirate of teachers had been formed by this time by the association of Riemenschneider, Victor Wilker, professor of modern languages, and Julius O. Berr, professor of music. These three men continued for a generation as outstanding instructors. They were joined by C. F. Paulus, a brilliant and beloved instructor, who rendered a life of singular devotion to the institution between the years of 1874 and 1893. By 1873 the assets of the college had reached $90,000; 114 students were enrolled. When it was discovered that Old Baldwin Hall stood on a valuable quarry, it was sold in 1883 and a new student hall was built on the Wallace campus in 1884.

In 1893 Wilhelm Nast was forced to resign as president because of age, and Karl Riemenschneider was elected to succeed him. A period of peculiar trials now came upon the institution. Severe sickness attacked two of its teachers, Riemenschneider and Paulus. The former recovered slowly, while the latter died on November 27, 1893. A series of deaths among the trustees within a short period of time disorganized the board. Among them were R. A. W. Bruehl, Heinrich Liebhart (who since 1880 had been president of the board), Erhardt Wunderlich, and P. F. Schneider, the financial agent. *John C. Marting* at this time was elected to lead the financial affairs, and in 1939 was still active in the office. In 1896, thanks to a building fund completed by the work of Marting, a much-needed and long-anticipated building was dedicated.

The year 1899 was epochal for the institution. *Michael Dietsch* donated funds for the erection of a woman's building. Construction was immediately begun. Fanny Nast Gamble endowed the Wilhelm Nast chair of theology with a gift of $20,000. John L. Nuelsen was called from Central Wesleyan College as professor of exegetical theology. The theological department now became Nast Theological Seminary. Theodore Rodemeyer was called to teach Greek, and Professor Albert Riemenschneider became an instructor in music. The latter's promotion of Bach festivals contributed much to musical culture in Ohio. In 1900 Colonel H. A. Marting established a chair of practical theology, C. W. Hertzler being elected its first incumbent. In 1901 the first pipe organ was purchased. In 1902 the Commercial Department became the School of Commerce with W. B. Herms as principal.

By 1905 German Wallace College had three hundred alumni in the ministry and thirty teaching in colleges. Of its assets of $275,000,

$150,000 represented an endowment fund. The friendly development of German Wallace College and Baldwin University, performing identical functions side by side, made merger the only logical step in the development of both institutions. This step was taken in August, 1913, while Arthur L. Breslich was president of German Wallace. The united institution was called Baldwin-Wallace College.

The merger was a success from every point of view. Between 1913 and 1938, the student body increased from 247 to 767, the assets from $1,595,261 to $3,186,280. The erection of the *Emma Lang Hall* for women, the development of fraternity and smaller dormitory houses, the building of a second athletic field and the construction of a stadium, the erection of the *Kulas Musical Arts Building,* a $100,000 gift for the erection of a new dormitory for men, and plans for a new library building have all contributed to make Baldwin-Wallace the most important institution of higher learning in which German Methodists in America have been interested.

Breslich was succeeded in 1918 by *Albert Boynton Storms,* a pastor and educator of wide experience. He came to the president's chair at a time when the prejudices of war had broken the morale of the institution, and by establishing his administration in the public confidence brought the college through a difficult period in its development. He effected his task by keeping both the faith and support of the large German patronage of the institution. Storms was succeeded by Louis Clinton Wright, who, while pastor of Epworth-Euclid Church in Cleveland, had begun to lecture at the college in 1920.

The connection with German Methodism, following the merger of the German Conferences, was continued largely through the person of *John C. Marting,* who in 1939 was serving his forty-fifth year as treasurer of the college, and through twenty-two faculty members of German blood on the staff in 1938. A hundred and one missionaries were recorded as alumni of the institution. A majority of the preachers in all the German-speaking Conferences were educated within its halls.

Central Wesleyan College

If the Baldwin-Wallace College is the most flourishing institution in which German Methodists interested themselves, Central Wesleyan College, located in the small college belt of the Mississippi Valley, has a record of equally important service to the Church. The educational ambition of the German Methodists as shown in the program of German Wallace College, was to establish a German institution as a companion school of an English-speaking college. Pursuing this policy, they began an educational program in Quincy, Illinois, in 1854 in co-operation with the English-speaking Methodists. The school, struggling against difficulties and poverty, continued for nine years. The English-speaking department, disheartened and discouraged, dissolved.

German persistence, however, kept the German department in operation a few years more under the direction of *Hermann A. Koch*. Koch's effort to maintain an independent German-speaking institution called attention to the possibility of a development along that line. For the promotion of such an independent German school, a convention was called in Quincy in 1864. One of the great tragedies of the Civil War was the number of destitute orphans of fallen soldiers. The conference, called to consider an organization for training minds to be of service to the Church, turned its attention to the duty of the Church in caring for fatherless children.

The Quincy conference decided to deal with both obligations by the founding of an educational institution and an orphans' home. Selecting a location not far from Saint Louis, the committee began to realize its plans in Warrenton, Missouri. The population in the region was largely German. *Philipp Kuhl* was chosen president of the "twin institutions," which opened under the legal name of *Western Orphan Asylum and Educational Institute*. According to the charter, the school was to be co-educational and to admit all students of good moral character without regard to confessional affiliation. Classical, scientific, normal, and business courses were offered. Hermann A. Koch was brought to Warrenton from Quincy as educational principal, and George Böshenz was appointed superintendent of the home.

It became clear as the years went by that the educational would have to be separated eventually from the charitable work if both were to develop satisfactorily. In 1869 the name of the Warrenton project was changed to *Central Wesleyan College and Orphan Asylum*. The relative position of the two branches of the work was thus reversed.

Like all the small denominational colleges in the Mississippi Valley and along the Western frontier, Central Wesleyan's existence was threatened by inadequate buildings and downright financial embarrassment. The decade of 1870 determined the fate of the school. Kuhl, assisted by J. P. Wilhelm and Michael Röder, set out in 1872 to raise money for new buildings. Their success was realized on November 14, 1875, with the dedication of the new building. In the same year Louis Kessler, of Baldwin, Missouri, made a contribution of $10,000 for the establishment of a chair of German language and literature, provided the Church would raise $15,000 for an endowment fund. Röder, who had previously been so successful in raising money, accepted the offer by going into the field to raise the fund to satisfy the condition. H. Schrader, of Saint Louis, contributed $6,000 to the fund. It was set aside for the endowment of the Schrader chair of theology.

If the decade of 1870-80 proved that the college could develop, the remainder of the century demonstrated that neither wind nor fire could make the Germans quit. On May 9, 1881, a tornado razed the east wing of the new college building. Plans for rebuilding were drafted the next morning. The teachers, working with William Schutz, the local pastor, set out again to raise money. This was only the beginning of a program of expansion. In 1884 a $12,000 women's dormitory was erected. In 1889 two brothers in Saint Louis, W. F. and F. G. Niedringhaus, always benefactors of the institutions, gave $15,000 for the establishment of a second chair of theology, provided the church would raise $25,000 more for the endowment fund. J. L. Kessler, assisted by Ernst F. Stroeter, theological professor at Warrenton, went to the field and returned with money to qualify for the Niedringhaus offer.

The inevitable separation of the school and asylum took place in 1884 when both were organized legally as separate institutions. The divorce proved advantageous to both institutions.

In 1893 the women's dormitory burned to the ground. Kessler, who had done so much for the development of the school, lost his life in the fire. Just as the windstorm had encouraged development, so now fire was an incentive to improvement. The hall was rebuilt with brick and further plans were laid for a chapel and conservatory of music. Agents were sent out "into the field" and returned with funds enough to carry out the project. In memory of the man who had lost his life in the fire, the conservatory of music was named the *J. Louis Kessler Memorial Hall*. At the turn of the century a men's dormitory was constructed and named after Andrew Eisenmayer, who had been the largest single contributor.

Central Wesleyan continued as a four-year liberal arts college, offering also a four-year preparatory academy course until 1930. With the development of public high schools in Warrenton, and other towns of Warren County, Missouri, the need for the academy gradually decreased until it was discontinued. The financial crash of 1929 caused such a devaluation of the endowment of the institution that it was faced with two alternatives—either to close or to operate on a reduced budget as a junior college. The latter choice was made. The last four-year graduating class received its degrees in the spring of 1930. In the fall of the same year Central Wesleyan opened as a junior college. The University of Missouri promptly accredited the college, operating on the new program. That the institution did not close its doors during the serious year of reorganization was due to the sacrifices of the faculty and administrative officers and the loyalty of a small but devoted group within the Church.

Central Wesleyan, with a faculty of twelve and less than a hundred students, continues to serve the Middle West as the only college under the auspices of the Methodist Episcopal Church in the states of Missouri and Arkansas.

The junior college organization is very different from the four-year plan prior to its adoption. Central Wesleyan operated a preparatory department from the beginning. This included a grammar as well as a high school, offering college entrance courses and terminal work of a vocational or finishing school nature. The collegiate branch offered classical, philosophical, scientific, and literary work of the first quality. A normal department gave teachers training, granting first- and second-grade certificates recognized by the Missouri County Boards of Education. A commercial department, art department, conservatory of music, and military and gymnastics department completed the organization of the school.

The theological seminary at Warrenton had built up an endowment of $65,000 and had acquired $72,000 worth of real property. Forty students were enrolled in its classes. Five professors comprised the faculty in the school's most flourishing days. Central Wesleyan College itself by 1924 had an endowment of $350,000, property valued at $206,000, forty-four members on the faculty, and 252 students. The strength of the seminary at Warrenton compared favorably with Nast Seminary in Berea, which in 1924 had a special endowment of $131,000, six faculty members, and seventeen students. Of the 921 alumni of Central Wesleyan in 1924, 163 were preaching in German Conferences, 84 in English Conferences, 12 in other denominations, 32 were at work in mission fields or institutional service, and 228 were teaching.

The normal department of Central Wesleyan trained hundreds of public-school teachers for service in Missouri and the Middle West, and played a leading part in the teachers' institutes in all parts of the state. The influence of this branch of the institution was an outgrowth of the efforts of Heinrich Voshall, who for half a century directed its program. When Vorshall went to Warrenton he had already given distinguished service as a missionary of the Church in the development of the religious life of the great Northwest.

From the time that George B. Addicks succeeded Stroeter in 1900, he took an active part in the administration and financial direction of the college, becoming its president later. Addicks was followed in 1910 by Otto Kriege, who continued in the office until 1925, when he was called to the presidency of New Orleans University.

Mount Pleasant College

In 1909 Central Wesleyan absorbed Mount Pleasant German College. The organization of this institution was largely the result of a protest by the preachers of the West German Conference that the citizens of Warrenton did not show by their support their appreciation of Central Wesleyan College in their village. A committee was therefore appointed to study the advisability of moving the institution. The committee let it be known that it was agreeable to receiving offers from various cities for the relocation of the school. In the fall of 1872 the trustees of Iowa Wesleyan University, located in Mount Pleasant, offered the Conference in session at Quincy, Illinois, $10,000 as an endowment fund and a campus upon which to erect a building if the Conference would raise $20,000 as an endowment.

The Conference accepted the proposition. Details were worked out in a meeting held in Muscatine, Iowa. The school had the same relation to Iowa Wesleyan University that German Wallace College had to Baldwin University. They shared the same campus and pooled their resources. In addition to gifts amounting to $15,000, Iowa Wesleyan gave free tuition to all German students taking subjects which the university offered.

The purpose of the German college was soon defined as a practical theological school for training German preachers. Despite the usual financial difficulties, the institution thrived. Opening in 1873 with twenty-five students, the school grew to have an enrollment of more than a hundred and fifty. The endowment increased to $30,000. A dormitory was built in 1878 and a chapel in 1901.

Like most of the denominational colleges of the period, Mount Pleasant German College offered an academy course for those who had not completed their preparatory work. The college proper offered normal, commercial, theological, classical, and classical-theological courses leading to the degrees of Bachelor of Arts, Bachelor of Divinity, Bachelor of Science, and Masters of Arts and Science.

The burden on the Saint Louis German Conference in the support of the educational institutions at Warrenton and Mount Pleasant increased so heavily as the years went by that serious efforts began to be made looking toward the merger of the two colleges. In September, 1908, the Committee on Education reported to the Conference in session in Quincy, Illinois:

> We are especially rejoicing that at last the long-desired merger of our two educational institutions, the college at Mount Pleasant, Iowa, with Central Wesleyan College at Warrenton, Missouri, has at last become a joyful fact. The great work, which for so long and so earnestly has been prayed for, has through the grace of God allowed a peaceful and brotherly solution, for which we thank God.
> In this brotherly union we will as a Conference advance to achieve greater success for Christian education.[7]

The same committee in 1909 reported as follows:

> The union of the two schools is completed; we believe according to God's will and to their mutual benefit. May God give his rich blessing to that end.[8]

The college had a series of short-term presidents: Rudolf Havighorst (acting, 1872-74) ; G. F. W. Willey (acting, 1874-75, and 1877-78) ; Heinrich Schutz (acting, 1875-77) ; Wilhelm Balcke, who served as the first president (1878-85) ; John Schlagenhauft (1885-91) ; G.

A. Mulfinger (1891-93) ; and E. S. Havighorst, from 1898 until the merger of the institution.

Charles City College

The period directly following the Civil War was characterized by the development of Church institutions. The decade between 1868 and 1878 was, nevertheless, certainly a poor time to make a financial adventure. Religious enthusiasm, however, was not dampened by economic conditions. At the call of *Wilhelm Schreiner* a group of members of the Northwest German Conference met on October 26, 1868, in the German Methodist Church in Galena, Illinois, to discuss the advisability of organizing an educational institution. Proposals laid before the group by Schreiner were unanimously adopted and a Board of Trustees, headed by Schreiner himself, elected. On $6,000 of borrowed money the Marine Hospital in Galena was purchased and reconditioned for educational purposes. In December of the same year a primary school for children was opened in the basement of the church. The faculty consisted of a principal, a teacher of geography and history, of drawing and music, of mathematics, of German, of English and Latin languages, and an instructor in the primary department. When it appeared that a substantial beginning had been made, the institution was recognized as a Conference project and the property was legally transferred to the Conference trustees, who agreed to assume its debt. Ever-pressing financial problems forced the appointment in the fall of 1872 of a traveling financial agent, but the expenses of operation continued to exceed the income. Debts accumulated. The school at the time was known as the *Northwest German-English Normal School of Galena, Illinois*. Although the name was large, the school was small.

Small colleges typically live through periods when their right to existence is being determined. That period for Northwest fell between the years 1878 and 1890. The generous sacrifices of German Methodist preachers and laymen in the Northwest Conference enabled the board to pay off the debt on the institution. The endowment fund began to grow. A dormitory and library were constructed and the name was changed to *German-English College of Galena, Illinois*. A substantial theological course was introduced, thus placing the college in a grade with other German Methodist institutions.

In 1887 *Friedrich Schaub* was elected president. A graduate of the Galena school nine years before, he became its head at the age of thirty-two. His career followed the development of the institution in various capacities until the fall of 1921, when he went to Cincinnati as principal of Dorcas Institute. He estimated that in his thirty-seven years of educational work he taught sixty-five different courses.

The third epoch in the history of the school began in 1890. In 1889 the president raised the question of whether a better location could be found. It was customary in those days for a college which wished to move to advertise for offers. Municipality was thus played against municipality until the institution was promised the advantage it sought. The board of German-English College in this fashion let it be known in Iowa newspapers that it would consider moving its location if sufficient money could be promised to make the migration worth while. The final choice came between Storm Lake and Charles City, Iowa. *Charles City* won the competition by a promise of $30,000 and ten acres of land. This proposal was the result of the efforts of the Charles City German Methodist preacher, *Wilhelm H. Rolfing.*

The school was opened in the fall of 1891 in Charles City in the basement of the Baptist Church and in supplementary rooms on Main Street. The new building was opened in 1892, and the institution was henceforth known as Charles City College. The change of location seemed wise. Enrollment began to increase from the first. The whole indebtedness was paid off at the Annual Conference session in 1899 and an endowment fund started. In 1902 Henry A. Salzer, of LaCrosse, Wisconsin, already a generous benefactor of the institution, offered $10,000 upon the condition that other friends of the school would raise $15,000. While the fund was slow in coming, and upon the inauguration of a new president, in 1903, William F. Anderson, secretary of the Board of Education of the Methodist Episcopal Church, announced the offer of Andrew Carnegie to give the last $25,000 of a $75,000 fund. Fifty thousand dollars seemed to the Conference an enormous sum, yet at the annual session in 1909 the announcement was made: *Das Ziel ist erreicht.*[9]

In the meantime a gymnasium had been equipped on borrowed money. In 1910 George Föll, a member of the Church in Storm Lake, gave $6,000 for the purchase of a suitable president's residence. In 1911 two homes for professors were built. E. W. Henke worked weeks in this construction without pay. The women's dormitory, which burned in the winter of 1912, was rebuilt and dedicated a year later. In 1913 the property consisted of six buildings. The business and music department operated in rented rooms.

Despite its evidently strong position, Charles City College had increasing difficulties in meeting the rising educational standard set by the state authorities and the University Senate of the Church. As the board of trustees canvassed the alternatives open to it, it began to think favorably of merger. The trustees of Morningside College, located strategically in Sioux City, Iowa, in a thriving community at the juncture of the states of Iowa, Nebraska, and South Dakota, had repeatedly invited the trustees of Charles City College to discuss plans for merger. The board of the latter institution had come to the point where it was willing to negotiate. A commission of five trustees from each college began to discuss details of amalgamation. Charles City College at the time had a student enrollment of 186. A full college course was being offered in addition to a normal course, an academy preparatory course, and courses in schools of commerce and music. The terms of agreement were quickly agreed upon, and in the fall of 1914 Charles City College, having lost its identity, opened as a part of Morningside College. The net proceeds realized from the liquidation of the assets of Charles City College were created into a perpetual endowment found known as the "Northwest German Conference Endowment Fund of Morningside College."

W. C. Hilmer, president of Charles City College, was appointed professor of German literature and vice-president of Morningside at a salary of $1,500 a year and house rent. Friedrich Schaub was made professor of biblical and religious literature at a salary of $1,200. Three other members of Charles City's faculty were taken over, together with its library.

> We hope [said Hilmer in announcing the final terms of the agreement] that this epoch-making transfer was made under a guiding Providence, and that his favor and blessing may continually and more abundantly rest upon the Church and her educational work within the bounds of the Northwest German Conference.

Binn Memorial College

Interest in the development of educational institutions was not confined to the North. The efforts of the German Methodists in the South, however, were particularly discouraging. Their independence as a group on the question of slavery associated them with colored brethren of little or no education. Yet the demand for German preachers was larger than the supply, and the necessity of educating the men of Texas for the ministry was a present necessity, forcing the organization of a school. In 1876 E. F. Stroeter, pastor in Brenham, Texas, had opened a little school of eight pupils as Emmanuel Institute. Although the Conference elected the board of trustees, it assumed responsibility for only $300 of its expenses, plus $52.75 as allowance for equipping the institution. Although the Conference had more than a thousand members, they were poor. Unable to support the project, they were forced to close the school but the idea which prompted the experiment was not abandoned.

It was revived at the Annual Conference which met at Seguin in November, 1882, by William Pfaeffle. A board was elected and classes begun in the local church in 1883 with three students. Instruction was given in German language, world and sacred history, dogmatics, orthography, and exegesis. That a need for the institution existed was demonstrated by the growth of the school. The rooms in the church were soon too small. A house, constructed on a lot purchased in anticipation of the development, provided class facilities and four dormitory rooms for students. It was dedicated on September 9, 1883.

The Conference, so it seemed, had no well-defined educational policy. When in 1882 Ludwig Jauer offered seventy acres of good land to the Conference if the Conference would erect a "school of true Christian character" upon it, the gift was accepted. When it was unable to perform its part of the agreement, it accepted $800 as the equivalent of the land and used it as the nest egg for an endowment fund. In 1884 the school at Rutersville came under the control of the Conference and the Conference divided its interest between the two institutions. Unable to operate competition for its own educational interests, the Conference closed the Rutersville College, added new courses at Brenham, and employed a normal-school teacher. In 1885 the school was opened to women.

As the student body increased, the need for equipment and rooms grew apace. The board took the same step which all Methodist educational institutions had taken under similar circumstances. It appointed a financial agent. The function of this agent, William Pfaeffle, was to interest an individual of wealth in the development of the institution. He was successful.

Christian Blinn, of New York, was passing through Brenham. Pfaeffle met him and shortly announced that Blinn had donated a two-story building. Classrooms were on the first floor. The dormitory rooms were above. The gratitude of the board was shown when in 1889 the name of the institution was changed from Mission Institute to Blinn Memorial College.

The citizens of Brenham acknowledged the advance by a gift of $4,000 to the endowment fund, which in 1889 amounted to $20,000. The growth continued under the financially able administration of Carl Urbantke and John Pluenneke. When the board refused overtures of the city of Seguin to move the school there, the citizens of Brenham came forward with a gift of $10,000 in cash and property for the development of the school.

In 1906 Blinn made a further contribution of $16,200. This was followed by a $13,000 gift from Andrew Carnegie to complete a $35,000 fund for the construction of a new building, provided the Church would raise an equivalent sum for the endowment fund. In 1913 a three-story building was dedicated for dormitory purposes.

Despite the difficulties which the outbreak of the World War created for German Methodism, Blinn Memorial College continued to develop. In 1922 its grounds and buildings were valued at $134,257, its endowment stood at $67,580.

Although the institution was known as Blinn Memorial College, until 1937 is was only of academy rank. Competition with high schools forced the board, under the leadership of *Philip Deschner,* to organize a junior college. When the necessary financial support was not forthcoming, it was merged in 1930 with Southwestern University. This arrangement was not of long duration. In 1933 the Methodist Episcopal Church discontinued its support of the school. The citizens of Brenham, who had always so generously supported Blinn, forthwith incorporated a private nonsectarian junior college under the name of Blinn College. The control was placed in the hands of a board of nine regents. For a few years the property was rented from Southwestern University. When in the winter of 1937 the property was deeded back to the Brenham board, all connections with Southwestern University were severed. An election, held in Washington County, Texas, on June 8, 1937, resulted in a vote to recognize the school as a district junior college on a tax-supported basis. By this action Blinn College became the first county-district junior college in Texas. In 1938, 121 students were enrolled.

The Dorcas Institute

A constant demand for trained workers to assist in the program of the local church was recognized by the Bethesda Deaconess Board in 1910 by the organization of *The Dorcas Institute* in Cincinnati. Its purpose was to educate parish deaconesses. At first offering only a one-year course, the curriculum was soon expanded to a two-year program. In 1917 three years of work were offered. As the institution developed, a year of high-school work was added for the benefit of those qualifying for entrance to the Bethesda School of Nursing. The leadership of the institution began with the appointment of August J. Bucher as principal. He was succeeded in 1912 by John A. Diekmann, who in turn was followed in 1922 by Friedrich Schaub.

When the economic depression forced the consolidation of the educational interests of the church, the Cincinnati Missionary Training School was merged with The Dorcas Institute under the name of *The Cincinnati Training School.*

The Cincinnati Training School is "definitely a vocational school" offering a three-year course. Affiliated with Bethesda Institution, it operates in the former Bethesda surgical hospital building. Its religious position continues to be that of the German Methodists:

> The Cincinnati Training School takes the position that the Bible as a unified whole is the Word of God, and stresses the great facts concerning Jesus Christ; his divinity, his atonement for sin, his revelation of God through his life and teachings, and his saving power manifested through the work of the Holy Spirit in the world. We believe that the Christian life is based on a vital religious experience and a continuous growth into the fellowship with God.[9]

Accredited by the University Senate, the Cincinnati Training School owns property valued at $55,000, has a productive endowment fund totaling $40,000, and an enrollment of twenty students.

Saint Paul's College

Saint Paul's College was organized to serve the educational needs of the church in the Northwest. In the fall of 1887 the North German Conference, aware of the demand for a school, appointed a committee to find a location for the proposed institution and to solicit offers from localities interested in having a college in the community. In the fall of 1888 a board of twenty-one trustees was organized to accept an offer made to the Conference by the Saint Paul Park Improvement Company. In the spring of 1889 construction of the college building was begun in Saint Paul Park, Minnesota. Dedicated on October 1, 1889, by Bishop Mallalieu, it opened with thirty-five students. The student body grew during the first year to 103, and its highest enrollment was 138 students. The college work, due to increasingly exacting standards, was given up and the energies of the institution concentrated on the preparatory department. The academy course was recognized by the University of Minnesota and its program led to its rating as one of the best preparatory schools in the Northwest.

The years of the World War were difficult ones for all German Methodist institutions. Saint Paul's College was no exception. The Committee on Education reported to the North German Conference in September, 1917, that the college had eight teachers, property valued at $65,000, a $12,000 debt, and an annual operating budget of about $6,000. The committee, however, frankly confessed its concern over the future of the school and recommended the appointment of a committee to solicit the support of the two Minnesota Conferences. In the following year the committee recommended the acceptance of an offer of the Minnesota Conference to take over the college buildings as a Home for the Aged. An emergency hastened the liquidation of the interests of the college. Following a fire in the Home for the Aged in Saint Paul Park, the college offered its women's dormitory to the inmates. The event provided a way for the college to retreat from the field. Its endowment fund of $1,300 was turned over to the secretary of the Conference Claimants' Fund of the North German Conference. A surplus of $2,200 derived from the sale of the real estate for $15,500, was given to the treasurer of the Old People's Home in Minnesota Conference of the Methodist Episcopal Church. The twenty students enrolled in Saint Paul's were transferred to Parker College, Winnebago, Minnesota.

Enterprise Normal Academy and Commercial School

If the German Methodists founded some schools, they "took over" others. In the spring of 1896 the trustees of *Harrison Normal College,* Enterprise, Kansas, offered to the West German Conference the college building and 435 lots upon the condition that the Conference raise an endowment fund of at least $10,000 to assure the continuation of the institution. A commission, appointed to investigate the proposal, reported favorably to the Conference in session at Sedalia, Missouri, in the late summer of 1896. At the request of the Conference, the Bishop appointed H. S. Humfeld principal and the school opened under German Methodist control on October 6, 1896, with forty-four pupils.

The building which the Conference had taken over was a two-story limestone structure of thirteen rooms and a chapel. It was built upon a southern hill overlooking the town of Enterprise, Kansas, and was valued at $20,000.

The Academy operated, according to denominational custom, a preparatory department. A three-year academic course emphasized advanced English, German or Latin, higher mathematics, and natural science—work which anticipated the junior college. The normal-literary department offered one year in addition to the work of the academic department and granted a normal school diploma. The commercial department was well-developed for vocational purposes.

The educational program of Enterprise was a practical one and is one of the most interesting in the whole educational program of German Methodism. The student body in 1918 numbered seventy-four. The value of the property was estimated in the same year to be $60,000. Despite its years of service, Enterprise's Normal Academy was forced to discontinue its activities in 1917-18. The Board of Trustees was continued until 1920 to wind up the affairs of the institution. Hopes that the doors, closed in the fall of 1917, might be reopened with substantial Conference support were gradually broken down, and the affairs of the academy liquidated.

William Nast College of Central China

German Methodist enthusiasm spread to the Orient and because of the aggressiveness of its leaders in the missionary movement, developed its own institution in Kiukiang, China. In 1881 a mission school known as *Fowler University of Central China* had been organized in a few small rooms in the basement of a parsonage located in the British concession in Kiukiang. The growth of the project was so rapid that in 1885 the school was moved to the spacious compound within the city near the South Gate. Its rather imposing name was changed from "University" to "Institute." The development of the school, especially through the interest of the German Methodists, was so healthy between 1885 and 1901 that in February of 1902 it was raised, upon the recommendation of Bishop Moore, to the rank of a college and, having become the particular project of the German Methodists, was renamed *William Nast College of Central China*. The enrollment of the institution at the time was 152. The faculty, headed by *Carl F.*

GERMAN METHODIST EDUCATIONAL INSTITUTIONS, 1916[1]

| | PLANT | | | | | | | | | | |
| | Campus | | Buildings | | Total Value of Plant | Books in Library | Total Value Equipment | Total of all Funds | Total Income | Total Faculty | Total Students |
	Number Acres	Present Value	Number Buildings	Present Value							
Central Wesleyan College[2]	23	$40,000	7	$119,500	$159,500	10,500	$21,500	$209,000	$30,581	20	282
Baldwin-Wallace College[3]	25	60,148	10	390,000	450,148	16,880	72,413	575,102	46,447	50	733
Central Wesleyan Theological Seminary										4	32
Nast Theological Seminary										5	41
Blinn Memorial College					96,050		10,331	48,000	10,971	7	159
Saint Paul's College					63,900		3,175	10,000	9,241	9	113
Cincinnati Training School (1938)					55,000			40,000	5,000	13	20

[1] Data from General Conference Journal, 1916.

[2] The General Conference Journal of 1936 reported property worth $292,000, no endowment. A debt of $75,000, a faculty of eight, and 109 students.

[3] The General Conference Journal of 1936 reported property valued at $1,385,560, a productive endowment of $1,427,152, a debt of $96,793, a faculty of 44, and 643 students.

Kupfer, numbered 11, eight of whom were educated Chinese. All instruction was given in the Mandarin language.

Explaining some of the difficulties faced by the faculty, the *Yearbook* of 1902-03 spoke of the

> undue desire among all classes for a smattering of Western knowledge [making] it difficult to confine students to a pre-scribed graded course of study. . . . They are satisfied that a little veneering of Western science upon their Confucian knowl-edge is quite sufficient to fit them for the new conditions.

When Fowler Institute became William Nast College it had four buildings. The main hall was erected by the contributions of German Methodists. Beautifully located in the Yangtze Valley on a site slop-ing to the south, the campus looked toward an inland lake which lay below in a magnificent landscape looking toward the Lu Mountains. A serious problem faced the school in the ravages of consumption among the young men. Students had often been inadequately housed. Bishop Moore returned in 1903 from America with funds for the con-struction of a modern dormitory.

The school in Kiukiang had another difficulty to face. The catalogue of 1902-03 described it in this way:

> To meet the eager desire for Western education the Chinese government is establishing schools in all provinces, and is mak-ing the worship of Confucius obligatory upon all teachers and students. We have no grievance against the Chinese govern-ment for being zealous for their ancient religion, but we must make the highest education possible for all who desire it under conditions where liberty of conscience prevails.

Despite occasional internal difficulties and frictions not uncommon to the mission field, William Nast College flourished. Then came the World War, so disastrous in its effect upon all the German work. President Kupfer was unswerving in his loyalty to the cause of the Central Powers. Even after the United States entered the conflict he kept a portrait of the Kaiser upon the wall of his office, a fact which irked other missionaries. As the strength of German Meth-odism waned during the post-war days, William Nast College was given up as a special German-supported project and turned over to the Board of Foreign Missions.

The modest yet substantial achievements of German Methodism were actually triumphs of German faith and persistence. The German Church never exceeded 65,000 members. Its people as a whole were thrifty but not wealthy. The salaries of the preachers never averaged as much as they did in the English-speaking branch of the denomina-tion. Although the names of large benefactors are usually mentioned, the total contribution of many small givers, laymen and preachers alike, determined the development of the Conference projects.

Like most denominational colleges, the German schools were frontier institutions, for the small college found its congenial environment on the frontier. Their purpose was frankly to train a "literate ministry," and to meet the urgent demand for preachers at a time when available ministerial forces were inadequate to meet the demands of the outposts of the Westward advance. The institutions of German Methodism, like most of the frontier colleges, were founded for the explicit purpose of helping to solve the problem of ministerial leadership. The temptation always existed to draft into the ministry "robust men of religious earnestness and sound judgment but lacking in academic training."

The fact that German Methodists established schools for training their preachers is of special moment. The German Methodists clung to the reality of "religious experience" as no other group in the Church, but they wanted their preachers prepared. Perhaps it was because of the tradition of the Fatherland that clergymen should be educated. Perhaps it was just because of the good old German common sense. At any rate, the heart redeemed was united with the trained mind in the service of the Church by educational institutions.

The secularizing forces affected the German-Methodist schools far less than they did the colleges of the Church in general. Evangelical passion has continued to color the program of all the schools in the tradition of Wilhelm Nast and John Wesley.

CHAPTER XI

MINISTRY TO THE YOUNG AND AGED

Two Children's Homes and four Homes for the Aged testify to the earnestness of the social vision of the German Methodists. To the German Methodists belongs the honor of founding the first orphans' work under the direction of the Methodist Episcopal Church in America on March 2, 1864.

Children's Home in Berea, Ohio

Even the Civil War did not prevent the Germans from going ahead with their plans for the development of Church institutions. The opening of the home in Berea, however, was not a hasty action. A decade before *Wilhelm Ahrens* had contributed a series of articles to the *Apologist,* calling attention to the need of a Church program for the care of children, the aged, and worn-out preachers. A committee, appointed at the time and of which Ahrens was a member, selected Dayton, Ohio, as the proper location for an institution, but nothing more was done. Nearly ten years went by until in September, 1863, Ahrens was forced by poor health to leave the active ministry. Taking note of his plans, the Southeast Indiana Conference passed a resolution, praying that

> The Lord may crown Brother Ahrens with his rich blessing and long preserve him to our Zion that the project dearest to his heart may branch out into the founding of a children's home, the service of which may bless the Church.[1]

A month later the *Apologist* noted the gift of $10 from a preacher for Ahren's program, and a contribution of $25 from the Christian Aid Society of Newport, Kentucky. The *Apologist,* always so generous in its support of the causes of the Church, commented:

> Without any kind of solicitation, the Lord opened the hearts and hands of his children for this great undertaking. In his providence events have been so ordained that a man on whose heart this work has long pressed and in whose hands the Church has entrusted the leadership and administration of this project with unconditional confidence now finds himself in the circumstances to devote himself to this high calling.[2]

In the fall of 1863 Ahrens and his family moved to Berea, the seat of German Wallace College. Received generously by Rothweiler and given an apartment in Baldwin Hall, he was able before winter to report that through Rothweiler's efforts a commodious brick house and four acres of land had been acquired. The cost was $1,400, and $3,000 more were needed for furnishings.

In explaining his passion for social welfare work, Ahrens wrote:

The deplorable condition of orphans and old people, which I saw abundantly in the old country, awakened in me a deep sympathy with them which was intensified when, at my pastoral labors in our (German) Church—since 1841—I found similar cases. Old people, worthy members of our Church, suffering in poverty and want, and some of them on account of· their religion, were persecuted, neglected, and even cast off by their ungodly children, were forced to the county poorhouse, away from the privileges of their beloved Church; and poor widows, with more young children than they could provide for, delivering some of them to a Catholic orphanage. Others, for some reason, were driven to a marriage which drove them from the Church also. Yes, I saw heartrending cases of poverty and neglect of sick and wornout itinerants and their families. And all that in a Church where the preaching and profession of perfect love is pre-eminent!

Under my observation I got the idea that an asylum, in common for orphans, old people, and homeless superannuates and their families, erected and maintained by the Church, would be the best that could be done for the sufferers. For that purpose I wrote occasional articles in the *Christian Apologist,* and succeeded in getting the approval of my plan of my German brethren of the Cincinnati Conference, so that at a session about the middle of the fifties we appointed a committee to look up a suitable place, and to report at the next session. An excellent and reasonably priced place was found near Dayton, Ohio, but the opinion prevailed that the necessary money could not be raised among our people at that time, and that caused a halt.

When, in the fall of 1863, I was superannuated on account of broken health, and moved with my family to Berea, Ohio, where Brother J. Rothweiler, the circuit preacher, had just started the nucleus of our Wallace College, it seemed to me the circumstances and the place were suitable for my long-desired project, which I published in the *Apologist.* Right after that I got a letter from Rev. Fr. Schimmelpfennig, a member of my Conference, with one dollar, and the remark, "a brick for the asylum." That letter and money I took as a clear proof that the Lord was moving the cause, and reported such in the *Apologist,* telling the readers that if they would intrust their money to me, I should faithfully take care of it until further order.

From that time the greenbacks came flying to my address from all parts of our German Church, like "the doves to their windows," so that after a few months the practical undertaking of the work seemed to be insured. My opinion, which I published, that at a certain date the seven charges which then had contributed the most money, according to the number of members, should select each one man as trustee for the organization of the undertaking, was accepted and carried out. These men assembled in Berea, Ohio, in the spring of 1864, at which time they bought of Rothweiler a convenient house and four acres of land for that purpose, and paid for it in cash; and that is all Brother J. Rothweiler had to do with "the founding of the first orphanage of the Methodist Episcopal Church." By appointment of the trustees, my wife and self had the first management of the institution. We commenced with about a half dozen of orphans and a couple of old people. But these old people became ere long so homesick, that they left again. I found out that putting young orphans and old people under the same roof and at the same table is a mistake.[8]

The response to the Church was indeed encouraging. On November 28, 1863, Ahrens, through the *Apologist,* reported that he had received many letters enclosing one-, five-, ten-, twenty-, and hundred-dollar bills. On May 1, 1864, a twelve-year-old girl was received as the first orphan to be cared for in the institution.

The Central German Conference, meeting in Cincinnati, took note of the founding of the Home and asked the trustees to place it under the supervision of the Conference. Ahrens, after a year as father of the institution, turned over the administration to C. G. Lieberherr, an experienced Swiss children's worker, who continued in the position for thirteen years. In the first half-century of the Home's service it cared for nearly eight hundred boys and girls, all of whom were given a good Christian home and a sound elementary-school education.

With the exercise of the typical German business shrewdness, by June, 1866, a property valued at nearly $6,000 was owned free from debt. The Home, becoming too small for the growing group of orphans, was sold to German Wallace College and moved to a twenty-three-acre campus east of the college. Simultaneously with the decision of the trustees in 1866 to build a three-story home, Rothweiler was elected president of the Board of Trustees and continued in that position thirty-two years. The new building was opened in 1869. By June, 1870, the $25,000 property had only a $5,000 debt to carry.

The Central German Conference in 1867 officially recognized the Berea Home as a "church institution" under the "supervision of the Central German Conference." Patronized by the East and Northwest German Conferences, it received support from the Central, Chicago, and North German Conferences.

By the time the Central German Conference was dissolved in 1933, the physical property had increased to a value of three-quarters of a million dollars. Its campus had grown to a hundred acres. This progress was due in no small measure to the appointment in 1877 of *R. A. W. Bruehl* as treasurer of the Home. Despite the economic plight of the nation, he appealed to women's organizations, Sunday schools, youth organizations, and other groups to assist in the program. So satisfactory was the response that by 1893 Bruehl was able to show an operating surplus of $6,000. An endowment fund, started in 1880 by a hundred-dollar gift, continued to grow from numerous contributions to more than a hundred thousand dollars. The work of the Children's Home had caught the imagination of the Church public. The fact was demonstrated again when in 1890 a $15,000 building program was accepted by the board with only $5,000 in sight for construction.

Ten years later an appeal was made for $20,000 more for continued expansion. In the fall of 1901 a $38,000 building program begun. Fanny Nast Gamble contributed $10,000 to the fund, and the dining room and chapel were named for her mother, Margaret Eliza Nast.

The enthusiasm of the *Apologist* for the project was contagious. In 1907 *Mary A. Ott,* of Louisville, Kentucky, daughter of J. A. Klein, interested through the appeal in the paper, gave $45,000 for the construction of a building to house a program of industrial education and a gymnasium. She subsequently contributed $10,000 to help talented children obtain a higher education. In recent years the cottage plan has been developed under the leadership of *F. W. Müller,* the institution's able treasurer. In the first three-quarters of a century of the Home's existence, upwards of two thousand boys and girls were cared for through the interest of German Methodists.

Central Wesleyan Children's Home

While the Germans in Ohio were going ahead with their orphanage plans in the early spring of 1864, their brethren in Missouri were concerned with the same kind of a project. The growing number of destitute war widows and fatherless children as the Civil War continued spurred the Church on to realize a long-cherished dream of an orphans' home.

Upon the proposal of *Heinrich Fiegenbaum* at a meeting in Quincy, Illinois, on April 14, 1864, steps were taken to purchase for $15,000 a 940-acre farm located in Warrenton, Missouri. The program for the development of a children's home was a part of the plan for moving the German department of the school in Quincy to a location where an independent German educational program could be worked out. The college, while a part of the twofold program, was actually secondary in the minds of those interested in the whole project. They wanted first of all an orphans' home. The legislature chartered the institution under the name of *Western Orphan Asylum and Educational Institute.* The first child was received on July 20, 1864. That a home and institution of higher learning could not be permanently joined was increasingly evident. In 1869 the name of the project was changed by amendment of the charter to *Central Wesleyan College and Orphan Asylum.* By 1884 the two institutions had developed along such divergent lines that their administration as a common undertaking seemed longer unwise. The college and orphanage were therefore legally separated, each operating under the control of its own board of trustees.

George Böshenz was appointed the first father of the Children's Home. After a short term of F. W. Meyer, Philipp Kuhl took over Böshenz's work. Under his leadership the orphanage enjoyed substantial development. The growth continued under the leadership of H. A. Koch and Charles Heidel. Proposals for merger with the Berea Home were refused and in June, 1885, a new building was dedicated. This was followed in the next year by the construction of a schoolhouse. The two buildings were erected at a cost of $11,000.

When the institution celebrated its twenty-fifth anniversary in June, 1889, the Sunday schools of the patronizing Conferences came forward with $3,400 for the payment of the debt. The contribution was largely the result of the initiative of the treasurer of the Home, *H. H. Jacoby,* son of the first missionary to Germany.

The demand for the service which the orphanage rendered, chronically exceeded the capacity of the plant. The board voted, therefore, in the winter of 1888-89 to add a third floor to the main building at a cost of nearly $12,000. It was dedicated by Bishop Bowman in June, 1890. Under the able administration of J. H. Knehaus, beginning in 1895, the institution developed its cattle herd, its farms and gardens, and made improvements in the equipment.

In 1902 the number of orphans, pressing toward a hundred, necessitated the construction of a new schoolhouse by the enlargement of one wing of the main building at a cost of nearly $9,000. Capable of caring for about a hundred boys and girls, the home was valued at about a quarter million dollars, and owned 380 acres of land. The institution continued its program without substantial change, the number of children, as in the case of most denominational Homes, falling slightly to about seventy by 1936.

New York Harbor Mission

Contemporaneous with the founding of these two Children's Homes was a project which, if more ingenious in its program, was also less enduring in its service. The German Methodists had been concerned for a long time about the welfare of the immigrants arriving in New York. If only they could make a Christian contact in welcoming their fellow Germans to America, they believed they would be advancing the Methodist cause. On March 8, 1866, a self-appointed committee headed by John Ockershausen discussed the possibilities of a Christian lodging house near the docks. The committee proposed that if the New York and East New York Conferences would support the raising of a fund of about $30,000, it would buy the Hotel Shakespeare and open a Harbor Mission in New York.

The actual beginning of the work, however, was more modest. When the proposal was rejected, the friends of the project began in rooms located on Greenwich Street. Although the results were not encouraging, a property located at the corner of Pearl, Madison, and Roosevelt Streets was purchased for $65,000. On March 4, 1867, Adam Schuppan, succeeding Julius F. Seidel, became housefather and superintendent at a salary of $400 a year.

The program seemed excellent. The immigrants entered at Castle Garden. They would come to the mission and there they would be welcomed, lodged, furnished with tracts and good literature, led in

divine services in the chapel, and sent forth armed with letters of introduction to German Methodist preachers wherever they might go.
Although the city of New York twice encouraged the project with
gifts of $5,000, two circumstances prevented its success.   Between
1888 and 1898 the work was led by *George H. Simons.*

The first handicap was an unwise location.   It was too far from
Castle Garden, the port of entry.   The board tried unsuccessfully to
remedy the situation by trading its site.   The second difficulty was
the decreasing number of immigrants.   The need for the work grew
less and less.

The story of the mission became chiefly one of retreat.   The
property was finally sold for its debts.   The work was moved to
rented rooms, again on Greenwich Street, but it was still discouraging.
When Ellis Island was made the port of entry, the immigrants,
hastening on to their destinations by rail, seemed to have little need
for lodging while adjusting themselves to America.   The mission
office nevertheless was moved again to rented rooms on State Street
near the dock where the Ellis Island ferry landed, but the stream
of immigration had shrunk to a trickle of its former volume.   The
State Street rooms were finally given up and the work left to the care
of neighboring congregations.   In 1901 the Harbor Mission loaned
$21,000 of its funds to the Bethany Deaconess and Hospital Associa-
tion for the construction of a hospital.   On March 11, 1907, its
work was legally given up, its property and funds being transferred to
the trustees of the East German Conference.

Quincy Home for the Aged

If the program of work at the port of entry was unsuccessful, the
efforts of the German Methodists to aid the aged were eminently the
reverse.   The Saint Louis German Conference had felt the need for
a long time of an institution to care for the homeless Church members.   Indefinite discussion of the problem was crystallized when
Charles Pfeiffer, through his pastor, offered on September 9, 1889,
to give the Conference valuable property in the southern part of
the city of Quincy, Illinois.   The Conference promptly accepted the
offer, elected nine trustees to hold the gift, and incorporated the *Old
People's Home of the Saint Louis German Conference of the Methodist Episcopal Church.*

The first guest of the institution was admitted on May 6, 1890, and
the building was dedicated on May 15.   Within six months $11,000
was contributed to the program, proof that the program was needed
and appealed to the imagination of the Church.   The institution continued to expand to sixty-eight rooms.   The value of the property
has increased to over $300,000.   The Home has greatly expanded,
under the courageous leadership of Superintendent L. F. Buker.

Bethany Home for the Aged

The East German Conference felt the need for a similar institution. After the Bethany Deaconess Hospital and Home had been built in Brooklyn, interest turned to the founding of a Home for the Aged. On March 1, 1909, a committee, appointed for the study of the question, recommended to the Conference that the Home be developed as soon as possible and that the project form a part of the Bethany Deaconess Association, although its finances be handled independently.

The Home was chartered on September 7, 1909. The demand for its services necessitated expansion almost at once. In 1911 the board bought a two-story house on East Fortieth Street, Brooklyn, for $6,500, and six additional lots were acquired for an additional $3,000. The new Home was dedicated on October 5, 1911, caring for eighteen men and women.

The demand for the services of the Home continued to increase. More room was needed. In the fall of 1914 a building fund of sufficient size had been subscribed to warrant construction. On June 8, 1915, the new brick structure, accommodating forty, was dedicated, the property and endowment fund increasing to more than an eighth of a million dollars.

Pacific Home for the Aged

The development of the Home in Brooklyn was being duplicated by a more ambitious program on the Pacific Coast. A large number of German Methodists were moving West to enjoy the mild California climate. The thought that some of these would appreciate a Church home was brought to the attention of the California Conference by a $16,000 legacy of Margaret Amman. To promote the project the Camp Meeting Association donated three acres of land in South Hollywood. Under the Conference direction in 1912 a bungalow colony was developed, the guests increasing to seventy-five and the property value to $200,000.

The Home, which in time found its location in an exclusive residential section of Los Angeles, is one of the great institutions of German Methodism. Although the California German Conference merged with the Southern California Conference in 1927, thereby transferring the supervision to the latter Conference, it has continued in spirit a German institution. With assets exceeding $1,000,000, the property comprises nine bungalows, housing eight to twelve persons, and three magnificent new brick buildings. Margaret Hall, dedicated on March 8, 1936, serves as an infirmary. A dining hall, seating more than four hundred, was opened on May 16, 1937. An administration building, dedicated on February 11, 1938, provided 123 rooms, 13 de luxe suites, and a chapel.

Perhaps because of the kind of individual attracted to the California climate, perhaps because of the flat entrance fee of $3,000 so long maintained, perhaps because of the life-membership fees at age sixty ranging now from $5,500 to $7,100, the Pacific Home enjoys an unusual prosperity.   C. E. Leitzell is the able and successful superintendent.

Bethesda Home for the Aged

That a Home for Aged German Methodists should have developed in Cincinnati as a unit of Bethesda Institutions might have been expected.   *E. H. Huenefeld* donated Scarlet Oaks, the old Schoenberger mansion, to Bethesda in 1908 on the condition that some day a Home for Old People should be built upon the grounds.   Not until 1915, however, was the vision realized in a small way with the opening of a temporary Home on the corner of June and Peyton Streets in Cincinnati with five women as guests.   In 1919 Huenefeld's wish found expression in the construction of a $140,000 building with accommodations for fifty.   The building was the gift of E. H. Huenefeld and his wife.   In 1916 a medical hospital was erected on the Scarlet Oaks grounds at a cost of $110,000.   In 1930 this became a part of the Home for the Aged, completing the development of the institution.   In 1939 is was caring for a hundred guests, enjoying a debt-free million-dollar property under the direction of *Matthew Herrmann*.

By its concern for unfortunate children and its sympathy for old people, German Methodists demonstrated how Christian faith justifies itself by its performance.[4]

CHAPTER XII

A WORLD WAR STUNS THE CHRISTIAN CHURCH

"Christianity is supranational. In the kingdom of Christ
there are no trenches and no custom boundaries."—*Bishop John
L. Nuelsen.*

The decade and a half which followed the formal conclusion of the
war with Spain in 1899 was a period of exuberant paradoxes. That
such a contradictory epoch should culminate in America's entrance
into the World War, concealing the sordidness of commercial rivalry
under the banner of the ideal of "making the world safe for democracy," was an appropriate dénouement. It was a period of high idealism on the one hand and mad competition for foreign markets and
investments on the other. "Made in U.S.A." became as common a
trade mark in the markets of the world as "Made in Germany" had
been two or three decades before.

The United States was for the first time in American history
concerned with the problem of territory left in its trusteeship as
a fruit of victory. Beard describes the situation by saying that
"the Government at Washington was in a position akin to that
of the Roman Republic in 242 B. C. at the end of the Punic War." [1]
America was developing according to the policy of its "Manifest
Destiny." The Cubans, compelled to write the principles of the Platt
Amendment (1901) into their new constitution, assured to the United
States the substance of control but handed the actual sovereignty over
to an independent republic. Under the leadership of President Theodore
Roosevelt this program developed into a "moral mandate." The pres-
idential campaign of 1900 evolved into a national plebiscite on the
course to be taken in regard to the Philippine question. Theodore
Roosevelt, sweeping through the country as the "hero of the Rough
Riders," branded the opponents of the policy of imperial adventure
"mollycoddles." Republicans, renominating President McKinley, declared that

> it became the high duty of the Government to maintain its author-
> ity to put down armed insurrection, and to confer the blessings
> of liberty and civilization upon all the rescued people.

The process of subjugation organized a base for American economic
operations in the Far East and inducted the United States into a position of serious concern over events in the Orient. Taking advantage
of the Boxer Rebellion in China to give notice to the world of American

BISHOP JOHN L. NUELSEN

No Christian statesman ever served a quarter of a century through more trying days for the Christian Church.

"Our battle is against sin, the flesh, the devil, and his works. That is our sphere."

policies and ambitions in the Far East, American business hoped to command its share of Chinese trade by checking the greed of others. The program for such a purpose was negotiated by John Hay under the highly moral name of the "open door," a doctrine of "restraint and equality." Japan, by secret convention undertaking to respect American dominion in the Philippines in return for the promise of the President of the United States to accept the establishment of Japanese dominion over Korea by force of arms, was embarking on a program of continental expansion with American blessing. Japan, Russia, Great Britain, and the United States were competing for the benefits of rights in China.

If the annexation of Puerto Rico, the "moral mandate" over Cuba, the subjugation of the Philippines, and the active commercial entrance into the Orient extended America's economic interests, the same movement was only a prelude to the transformation of the policy of the nation with regard to lands along the Gulf of Mexico and the Caribbean. American business was marching "from victory unto victory" in Mexico, Central America, Colombia, and Venezuela. Loans were made; warships and marines sustained American authority. Manuel Guerrero, the Panama conspirator, and Philippe Bunau-Varilla, a French adventurer, received enough encouragement from President Roosevelt in Washington to go ahead with the revolt of Panama from Colombia which, within three days after the uprising, was recognized by Roosevelt as a member of the society of nations.

The entrance of the United States into world affairs with the victory over Spain was not just a sordid politically-administered commercial venture. It had its better side. All over the country men and women of idealism were believing in and working for the goal of universal peace. The idealism continued up to the very outbreak of the World War. At the suggestion of Nicholas Murray Butler, the New York Peace Society gave a medal to Kaiser Wilhelm II on the occasion of the twenty-fifth anniversary of his coronation. He was, so it was said, "a peace lord." Conferences, seeking to substitute arbitration for war as the technique for adjusting differences among nations, held at The Hague in 1899 and 1907, were acclaimed by naïve idealists as "omens of a new order." Churches and Sunday schools celebrated "peace Sunday." In 1907 the first National World's Peace Congress was held. In 1910 Andrew Carnegie gave $10,000,000 to found an "Endowment for International Peace."

Behind the surge of idealism, however, there was a justifiable skepticism. In the Episcopal Address to the General Conference of 1912, the Bishops warned:

> It is for mammon, not for righteousness, that thrones and parliaments are crowding the oceans with leviathans of battle, even while the people are praying for an end of war and pleading for international arbitration. . . . Save in the wars of the people

for freedom, the thrones and the honors have gone to the few, and thorns and horrors to the many. In the awful arithmetic of war it takes a thousand homes to build one palace, ten thousand lives of brave men to lift a pedestal for one man to occupy in lonely grandeur. . . . Ink is cheaper than blood. Law is better than force, and patience is a wiser diplomat than threat and bluster. But still the strategists are busy. Not content with drenching the soil and reddening the sea with blood, they are planning batteries that shall rain destruction from the clouds on helpless cities, and death on peoples who have no quarrel with each other until baited to battle by a painted lure labeled patriotism. . . .

Even while the churches are calling upon rulers to submit all international disputes to arbitration, our own republic answers with more doves of peace made of steel, breathing fire and winged with death. . . . If some suspect that treaties are held up at the signal of capital interested in steel plate for making more such doves, it cannot be denied that popular government has been perverted to such dastardly uses. The people can and must assert their nobler love of country by demanding that no American battleship shall disgrace its colors in a war for trade, or in any war, until every peaceful resort has been thoroughly tried.[2]

This anxious document analyzed with penetrating realism the dangerous paradox of the decade. It was a great utterance of a great Church, spoken hardly two years before the worst, which the Bishops feared, broke loose into the chaos of the World War.

By a strange irony of events the General Conference of 1912 assigned Bishop John L. Nuelsen to the superintendency of the Methodist work on the Continent. No man could have been better fitted for the position; no Christian statesman ever served a quarter of a century through more trying days for the Christian Church. The lives of Bishop Nuelsen (1867-   ) and his father, Heinrich Nuelsen (1826-89) span almost the entire history of the German-speaking Methodist movement. John L. Nuelsen was born in Zürich while his father was pastor of the church in that city. In 1883 the family moved to Bremen, where the father superintended the publishing interests. Educated in the gymnasiums in Karlsruhe and Bremen, the son took his Bachelor of Divinity at Drew Theological Seminary in 1890, and his Master's Degree from Central Wesleyan College in 1892. With further study at the Universities of Berlin and Halle, he was fully prepared for leadership in the fields of church scholarship and administration. After a year's pastorate at Sedalia, Missouri, in 1890, he taught ancient languages in Saint Paul's College. From this Minnesota institution he went for five years to Central Wesleyan College, Missouri, as professor of exegetical theology. In 1899 he was called to Nast Theological Seminary in Berea, Ohio, until in 1908, at the age of forty-one, he was elected a bishop of the Methodist Episcopal Church and assigned for the quadrennium to the Omaha (Nebraska) Area. In 1912 he sailed for Europe to continue the Methodist tradition which his father established during his thirty-eight years of service to his Fatherland. A master of languages, ancient and modern, a fluent linguist, a scholar of recognized international reputation, he had been in Europe scarcely two years when the World War broke out. The tragic years of the conflict were followed by the discouraging decade of an uneasy peace, financial despair, economic prostration, spiritual discouragement, a disintegrating world culture, and finally by a virile political cultural movement known as National Socialism. Through all these difficult years Bishop Nuelsen "kept peace" within the Church. No disaster was so destructive but that, to his way of thinking, its havoc could not be healed by the practice of Christian brotherhood.

The outbreak of war in 1914 was as shockingly unexpected to the German Methodists in America as it was to the Methodists in Germany who found plans for the dedication of the magnificent new theological seminary building in Frankfurt-am-Main so rudely interrupted in early August of 1914. The German Methodists, like the Methodist Germans, were, for the most part, modest people, concerned with their own neighborhoods, churches, and small trades and shops. That age-long rivalries should explode into this terrible calamity was a fact quite foreign to the thinking of the humble Germans on both sides of the Atlantic. Their interests lay chiefly in other directions. As a matter of fact, political relations between America and Germany had been "sociable."

> In those piping days of innocence and peace, few there were who looked with fear and dread upon the German Empire as a huge war machine prepared for "the day." On the contrary, the closest ties of friendship existed between the upper classes of Germany and prominent American citizens. German Americans who had wrung money from beer or pork or sugar found no trouble in breaking into the court at Berlin, and many Americans of native stock, sated with the culture of the local bourgeoisie, got thrills in the presence of His Imperial and Royal Majesty at Potsdam. Dinners in select New York circles were enlivened by choice bits of gossip straight from the entourage of the "All Highest." Professors were exchanged with much ceremonial. Prussian decorations of the second and third class were bestowed with lavish, yet, thoughtful, care upon a chosen regiment of American celebrities. Presentation to the Kaiser became as much an event as presentation to Edward VII or George V.
> No less a personage than President Theodore Roosevelt, when preparing for a European trip, fished for an invitation to Germany, caught the coveted prize, and thoroughly enjoyed the hospitality extended to him by Wilhelm II, especially the opportunity to review the German Army from the back of a mettlesome charger, with the Kaiser on his left. . . . In an outburst of enthusiasm, a distinguished university president, deeply impressed by the gracious beneficence of Wilhelm, declared that, if Germany were a republic, the people would unanimously elect the splendid

Hohenzollern president. The sober, respectable part of the American nation knew little about German politics and thought that little good as the great shadow fell athwart the eastern horizon.[8]

Upon the declaration of war, passion submerged objectivity for half a decade. The situation of the German Methodists, genuine Americans though they were, was not an enviable one. By inherited sentiments of affection they were naturally drawn by sympathy to the cause of the Central Powers, which, like the Allies, were secretly stimulating every friendly source to support propagandistic efforts. America was flooded with propaganda whipping up the factional controversy over the merits of the European belligerents into white heat. It was no longer a virtue to think; one must only strongly feel. The Allied propagandists soon discovered that Americans responded to stories of atrocities. By their invasion of Belgium, Germany had laid itself open to attack along these lines.

A stream of British clergymen filled American pulpits, wrote books, and portrayed the barbaric cruelty of the Germans in picturesque language. James Bryce signed his name to a report of the British Government, of dubious contents, and the document sent shivers up the American spine. Allied Belgian orphans, with ears or hands cut off, were described in the American press as examples of what the "Huns" were doing. During the days of President Wilson's neutrality the offenses against American intelligence by both Allied and Central Powers were revelations of the desperate designs pursued and venomous poison fed the public by interested partisans.

The "mythos" of the war was developed into a propagandistic creed to inflame emotions.

> It ran in the following form. Germany and Austria, under autocratic war lords, had long been plotting and preparing for the day when they could overwhelm their neighbors and make themselves masters of the world. England, France, and Russia on the other hand, all unsuspecting, had pursued ways of innocence, had sincerely desired peace and made no adequate preparations for a great cataclysm. When England and France were trying to preserve equal rights for all in Morocco, Germany had rattled the sword and now, taking advantage of the controversy over the assassination of the Austrian archduke, the Central Powers had leaped like tigers upon their guileless victims.
>
> To further their ends, the story for babes continued, the Germans had hacked their way through Belgium, a small and helpless country whose neutrality had been guaranteed by all the powers in their fond desire to safeguard the rights of little countries, and in cutting their way through this defenseless kingdom, the Germans had committed nameless and shocking deeds, crimes against humanity, offenses not justifiable in the name of war, horrors not usually incidental to armed conflicts. To crown their infamy, so ran the Entente articles of faith, the Germans did what no other Christian people would do; namely, employed the submarine, a new instrument of warfare against unarmed mer-

chant vessels, sending cargo, crew, and passengers alike to the bottom of the sea. Embellished in many details, embroidered with rumors and ghastly stories, this Entente war creed was pressed upon the people of the United States with such reiterations and zeal that in wide and powerful circles it became as fixed as the law of the Medes and Persians. To question any part of it in those spheres was to set oneself down as a boor and a "Hun" and, after 1917 as a traitor to America besides.[4]

On April 6, 1917, the United States declared war on the Central Powers. President Wilson, organizing a committee on public information for the purpose of "selling the war to America," placed George Creel in charge of American propaganda for Americans. No sentiment of loyalty, fear, love, or hate was left unstirred. The imprint of a bloody hand stared down at tens of millions of Americans from a poster bearing the legend: "The Hun, His Mark. Blot it out with Liberty Bonds."

When Americans sang in schools and churches and community mass meetings "Johnnie get your gun, get your gun, shoot a Hun," the thesis had burst into song. Every clergyman had a growing library of gratuitously supplied books and brochures. These included, for example, such volumes as *The German Terror in France,* by Arnold J. Toynbee, late fellow of Balliol College, Oxford. Page after page of similar incidents built up the stereotype of the "Hun." For example:

> On August 29th the Germans also burned seven houses and two barns at Framerville. Their methods show that the incendiaries of Framerville and Proyart were the same. "One heard an explosion," states the curé of Framerville, "and then the house took fire immediately. Each time a building was burning they played a pianola which they had taken from M. Francois Foucard's house." At Proyart, while M. Wable's house was in flames, they danced to the sound of a gramophone.[5]
>
> In the *Canton of Dinant* they destroyed 1,588 houses and killed 632 civilians in all; in the Canton of Florennes, 666 and 52. At Surice, in this Canton, they shot 18 men in the sight of their mothers and daughters and wives. There were five ecclesiastics among them, and boys of sixteen and seventeen. . . . Those who were not killed by the first volley were clubbed to death; the corpses were plundered; the whole village was sacked, and 130 houses out of 172 were burnt.[6]

So strong had become the emotion of patriotism that the burden of proof rested upon every German-American to show that he was not a secret agent of the Kaiser. When President Wilson turned to a Methodist bishop and asked, "Who are the German Methodists?" he was only raising a suspicion which was raised by Methodists themselves. The German Methodists were not allowed to preach or pray in German. *The Apologist,* forced to file translations of articles with postal authorities, preferred to publish war and political news in English for safety.

The bishops of the Church might have done in America what Bishop Nuelsen was doing in Germany—they might have insisted upon the supreme need of Christian brotherhood. Although a few general superintendents did stand by their German brethren, such Christian loyalty was not the dominant attitude. One bishop in a mid-Western area, suspecting one of his German-born young ministers of espionage, assigned, with the co-operation of the Government, a secret service man to gain the confidence of the clergyman. Tempting him to utterances considered by the bishop unpatriotic, he was promptly and severely punished. Another prominent churchman declared in a sermon in Cincinnati that "there are not enough telegraph posts in Cincinnati to hang all the German Huns that should be hanged," and still another churchman declared, "I would rather kiss a pig than shake hands with a Hun."

On one occasion secret service men called at the office of the superintendent of Bethesda Institutions in Cincinnati. "We are told that the superintendent has Bismarck's picture hanging in his office," they said. John A. Diekmann, who was at the desk during Golder's absence, replied:

> Gentlemen, I am an American, and not so familiar with these old German heroes; but you might look the pictures over hanging on the walls, and if you think Bismarck is among them, I shall be pleased to have you take him down.

They studied the photographs of John Wesley, Wilhelm Nast, and Bishop Walden. Pointing to the bishop's portrait, one of the agents exclaimed, "That's the fellow!" and took it down.

At one time Diekmann was lecturing in Nebraska. He was entertained by the parents of two prominent German Methodist preachers.

> Now, Brother Diekmann [said Mother Hohn], I have been wanting to hear you for many years; and now that you have come to our town, you are forbidden to speak in the German language and I don't understand English. Is it possible that our free country has sunk to such a level?
> Well [replied Diekmann], we'll have to fix that. You come over to the meeting and I will begin to talk in English and presently I will slip over into German while I am telling an interesting story, and nobody will notice the slip.
> Oh [said Mother Hohn], please don't do that, Brother Diekmann. There surely will be secret service men there tonight, and they will arrest you on the spot.

Diekmann gave most of his lecture in German and afterward learned that the two secret service men present had become so interested in his talk that one had said to the other, "I'll be damned if I will report that fellow to the Government."

The war cause was by this time receiving passionate support on the part of the Churches. Troy Conference declared in a resolution in 1918:

> We see the trembling lines above which float the Tricolor and the Union Jack, as the hellish Hunnish hordes beat against them to seize the panting throat of the world. We hear the cry, "Hurry up, America," and we go with fierce passion for world freedom to twine with Union Jack and Tricolor, the Stars and Stripes, and say to the sinister black eagle flag of Germany, "You shall not pass." We cannot do otherwise, God help us![7]

At Baldwin-Wallace College a hundred and fifty students petitioned for the removal of the president, alleging that he had failed to denounce "German crimes and atrocities," and that he had avoided mention of the war. Nine bishops, conducting an investigation while students staged a spectacular parade outside the conference room, recommended the removal of the college executive.

At Delphos, Ohio, where many Germans had settled, five business-men were seized by a volunteer vigilante committee, taken to the brightly lighted downtown street and forced to pay their respect to the flag under the threat of being hanged from a telephone pole.

The Baltimore Conference, fired by the same passion, declared,

> Not in personal hate, but in clean, white anger against a malignancy which can so threaten the peace of the world, we pledge our prayers, our purses, and our boys.[8]

On May 2, 1917, *The Western Christian Advocate,* discussing the "shame of the slacker," declared:

> Great conflicts make great men. What would Christ do in this situation? Would he be a slacker? Nay, never! Shame on the very thought! It is unbelievable. Patriotism and religion have always gone forward together. Man's heart rises toward his Lord and Master, if it responds to the appeal of the flag. Both are based on loyalty. A man cannot be highly intense in one without being as strong in the other. History proves that a great Christian is always a great patriot. He is by nature a shirk in whose unregenerate state God finds little pleasure and from whom is received small support in movements for the redemption of the world from human selfishness and age-long ignorance.

The Board of Bishops, assembling in semi-annual session in Grand Rapids, Michigan, in April, 1917, for "solemn and prayerful consideration of the position and duty of the Church in this our greatest war for human liberty" proclaimed:

> God himself makes peace. . . . There can and there ought to be no peace, until it stands squarely based upon righteousness. . . . We urge that your patriotism take on sacrificial forms and without the delay of an hour. . . . We stand with the President in his message to Congress where he said: "The right is more precious than peace. . . . The wrongs against which we array our-

selves are not common wrongs, they cut to the roots of human
life. The world must be made safe for democracy. Its peace must
be planted upon the trusted foundations of political liberty. . . .
We fight for such a concert of free peoples as shall bring peace
and safety to all nations and make the world itself at last free."

The German Methodists did not dissent from this kind of patriotism.
It is estimated that German Methodism furnished 5,000 soldiers, which
was a twelfth of the membership of the Church. The South German
Conference contributed alone 310. The Saint Louis German Conference printed in the Minutes of the 1918 session in the regular statistical
reports the contributions to benevolences and the purchase of Liberty
bonds and war-saving stamps as follows:

Benovelences	Liberty Bonds	War S.S.	Total
$43,621	$653,800	$90,837	$788,258

With their loyalty questioned by their own episcopacy and the Government alike, the German Methodists were in the position of having
the burden of proof of their patriotism placed on their own shoulders.
They did everything in their power to convince the officials of Church
and State of their thoroughgoing Americanism.

If German Methodists were distrusted in America because their
racial stock came from Central Europe, the Methodists in Germany
were in an equally embarrassing position because Methodism was so
closely connected with the culture of the United States. The position
of the Methodists in the Reich was as unfortunate as that of the
Germans in America. Until April, 1917, Bishop Nuelsen was able
to keep in close touch with his work. Then his position as an American
citizen became so difficult that he was forced to retire quietly into
Switzerland. He placed his administrative duties in the hands of
the district superintendents.[9]

He was forced to take this step for several reasons. In the first
place, it was necessary for the protection of the Methodists in the
Empire themselves to show the German government that the pastors
were not under the ecclesiastical direction of a citizen of an enemy nation. In the second place, orders of the United States Departments of
War and State prohibited any communication whatsoever with persons
in a country at war with America.

Propaganda was not absent in Central Europe. Just as France
had its *La Maison de la Presse,* supplemented by *Le Comité Catholique,*
Great Britain her Crewe House directed by Lord Northcliffe, and the
United States George Creel's Committee of Public Information, so
Germany had its *Pressekónferenz.*

People in central Europe were anxious to hear about the
latest French, Serbian, or Russian "atrocity"; about the cigars

filled with gunpowder which the Belgians were accused of offering to German soldiers, or the coffee and strychnine alleged to have been given by a French priest to a German sergeant. Faked photographs with the caption "the camera cannot lie" were circulated throughout the world, and "in Vienna an enterprising firm supplied atrocity photographers with blanks for the headings so that they might be used on either side for propaganda purposes." [10]

As the war wore on living conditions in Germany became so desperate that people could hardly satisfy their hunger and need for clothes and heat in winter time. School children were drafted to clean the streets and carry logs out of the woods to supplement the inadequate coal supply. Often school was held in unheated classrooms or adjourned for a week or more for a so-called "coal vacation" when no fuel was available. Before the last great offensive school children went into the woods, pulled down young trees, stripped them of their leaves, and sent the green fodder to the army to feed the horses. In 1917 an epidemic of dysentery proved fatal to thousands and so weakened survivors that they often contracted secondary ailments, such as heart trouble, because no strength-building food could be supplied to them. The following year three influenza epidemics in short succession sent a second wave of death across the land.

When the war broke out in 1914 the Church in America had shown a reasoned hope. "Look for the Builders," urged *The Western Christian Advocate* in its issue of September 2, 1914:

> The highway of Christian civilization is being broken up to be rebuilt. Ere long the chariot of the Prince of Peace will be driven where the lumbering armaments of men now crowd each other in their efforts to lead in the funeral march of Christian civilization.

The same issue of the *Western* talked about confronting a "warring world with the holy purpose of God" and printed President Wilson's proclamation, designating Sunday, October 4, 1914, as a day of "Intercessory Prayer," at which time the men should unite their

> petitions to Almighty God, that overruling the counsels of men, setting straight the things they cannot govern or alter, taking pity on the nations now in the paths of conflict, in his mercy and goodness, showing a way where men can see not . . . praying also to this end that he forgive us our sins, our ignorance of his holy will, our willfulness and many errors and help us in the paths of obedience to places of vision and to thoughts and counsels that purge and make wise.

"We are praying," declared Bishop Wilson, "that the Christian men of France may not lose their love for the Christian men in Germany."

The sentiments of Christianity thus expressed shine out like beacon lights in the mounting chaos of passion but they were forgotten as the battle lines stiffened.

The editor of the *Western* was right when he wrote in the issue of September 23, 1914:

> In this stupendous cataclysm not only have no adequate steps been taken by the forces of Christendom to meet the spiritual crisis presented, but in France it is reported that two hundred and fifty of the Protestant pastors have shouldered their rifles and marched to the front. In Germany nearly all Methodist preachers are bearing arms. The men who might be performing spiritual ministries are compelled to serve in the ranks of opposing armies.

The Methodist War Relief Fund was organized promptly to help the Church leaders better to serve the needs of the war-torn areas. American Methodism was also concerned with the confusing effect which the great conflict would have upon the heathen peoples of the mission fields, especially when the two great European nations who were foremost in foreign missionary activity—England and Germany—were at war. Missionary funds were being eaten up by war needs; only America could stem the tide of disintegrating Christian civilization.

Bishop Nuelsen knew that under the circumstances he was needed in Germany. When war broke, L. O. Hartman, fleeing from Germany to Switzerland, called Bishop Nuelsen on the telephone to ask his plans. "My place," said the bishop, "is here just now." He went on to describe the great task of reconstruction which the Church would have to face when war was over. That Methodism did not "snap" in the World War as it did in the prelude to the Civil War was the result of the tireless Christian passion of the "Bishop of Europe" who had remained at his post. His position was not an enviable one. The prejudices against the "Hun" which had been nurtured in America had their counterpart in Germany. The demand for separation from the Mother Church was a natural expression of patriotism.

Reporting to the General Conference of 1920, Bishop Nuelsen said:

> While the war was raging it seemed almost inevitable that Methodism in Germany would be compelled to sever its organic connection with an organization that emphasized so markedly its Americanism. I counseled moderation and delaying decisive steps until passion should cool down, judgments could be clarified, and the whole situation be normal again. . . . To my mind, it would have been a great pity if any branch of the Church of Jesus Christ, especially a Church that places the emphasis not upon externals but upon the spiritual message, should separate on national lines —while other agencies, some of them indifferent, even hostile to Christianity, strain every effort to extol the ideal of universal brotherhood above national issues.[11]

Bishop Nuelsen's penetrating analysis of the seriousness of resurgent nationalism was expressed in these words:

> Nationalism, unchecked by the ideal of international service, nationalism without the vision of the kingdom of God that has no frontiers, is a bane, a curse. . . . Nationalism that aims to develop the finest and best racial and national gifts and talents of mind and character in order to put them to the service of humanity; and internationalism, or better, supernationalism that unites the best and truest of every nation in a common agency for protection and uplift means the solution of the political and economic problems of today.[12]

Bishop Nuelsen was not only making these comments after the war was over. Before he had been forced to surrender his administrative leadership in 1917, while the movement for separation was rising to the crest, he had called the Methodists together and delivered one of the cardinal speeches in the history of the Christian Church:

> The power of the evil one will raise its head impertinently when peace comes [he warned]. But the battle against sin, against the lusts of the eyes and flesh will remain the same as before. . . . What must we do to render the greatest service to the German people and our Lord?[13]

Dealing directly with the problem of separation, he called attention to the fact that Methodism in Germany was still dependent upon America for financial support, that 30,000 Methodists could not hope to raise 136,000 marks just after the ravages of war, and that neither the German nor the Scandinavian work commanded the undivided sympathy of the Church in America. America would place nothing in the way of separation, he thought. It would welcome the step, probably, as most desirable. But, he said, "A realistic politics is necessary." Whatever sentiments anyone entertained, he could not avoid the "naked fact" that the Germans did not have enough money to run their own household. Other considerations were more important and less selfish. The bishop wondered in the second place whether German Methodism was yet ripe for independence. "I fear," he said, "that the separation from the great connectionalism will bring us to the greater danger of *Kleinigkeitskramerei*[14] and thereby to stagnation." Under such conditions he thought Methodism would assume more the proportions of a sect. Despite the momentary hostility to Methodism, he hoped to pave the way for a better understanding. He did not want the Germans to forget the importance which they exercised on the Mother Church.

Nuelsen then raised a final and "more important question." The clarity of his insight is all the more to be appreciated when it is realized that he was speaking in a nation at war, surrounded by armies battering at the gates of the state.

"One of the dangers which now threatens Christianity," he said, "is nationalism."

> There is no German Christendom, no German faith, any more than there is an English or an American. Christianity is supra-national. In the kingdom of Christ there are no trenches and no customs boundaries. Human beings are the same everywhere. They must be brought under the power of the spirit, purified and consecrated as human instruments to the service of God—not by isolation but by contact. It would be as much a tragedy for our German peoples as well as for Christendom if the many-sided and mutual relationships built up over so many years should be broken. I hold it for one of the most important tasks of peace to build the bridges again, to tie together the broken cords so that the Christians of different lands can learn to understand one another again, to win each other's confidence, to enrich our mutual contact. . . . The separation from America just at this time would have the effect of accelerating the divisions of Christendom.

Events of the succeeding two decades justified Bishop Nuelsen's analysis. He was seeking a means by which the unity of the whole Church could be preserved but at the same time so arranged that its work could be carried on with a more national organization. Methodism, he concluded, could work in any environment, with any government, among any people.

> We are [he said] the typical alliance people. We are found at all common meetings. Bigoted natures and church narrow-mindedness are foreign to us. *Our battle is against sin, the flesh, the devil, and his works. That is our sphere.*

German Methodism did not secede. If in America the animosities of war had struck a major blow to the continuation of German-speaking Methodism, in Germany the impoverished brethren took courage and continued "OUR BATTLE."

CHAPTER XIII

THE AFTERMATH OF WAR RELIEF AND RECONSTRUCTION

When the war was over, the world became seriously aware for the first time of the human tragedy among the civilian populations of Central Europe. For four and a half years a "hunger blockade" had slowly tightened its grip upon the precarious lives of millions of Germans and their allies. The suffering of the adults was exceeded by the physical and spiritual handicaps of the boys and girls. The tuberculosis rate among children in 1920 was twice that of 1914. According to official statistics the death rate of the civilian population in Germany increased year by year. In 1915 it was 9½%; in 1916 it had increased to 14%; in 1917 to 32%; and in 1918 to 37%.[1] Hunger, cold, and want of clothing broke the health and soul so that Ferdinand Sigg well says that there was "not a single child who did not bear an open wound or hidden weakness as a consequence of the war."[2]

The condition of the people, and especially the children in Germany, was brought to the attention of the public in Switzerland in 1919 by the circulation of an article appearing in the *Vossische Zeitung* on "Starving Children" (*Verhungernde Kinder*). The appeal did not fall upon deaf ears. Because Bishop Nuelsen had not left his post in Central Europe, he was ready to resume charge of the Methodist work in Germany and Austria in the fall of 1919. He took personal charge of the relief work, doing for the forces of peace what the generals in the preceding years had done for the organization of war.

The 1919 Annual Conference of Switzerland, meeting in Winterthur, adopted a proposal of the Sunday-School Commission, offering to bring fifty needy children from Methodist congregations in Vienna and Graz to Switzerland to be cared for in Swiss Methodist homes. Benjamin Niederhauser was commissioned to proceed with a program for carrying out the plan while Frau Suter-Mackert was put in charge of the Zürich committee for placing Austrian children in the same fashion. The Swiss had helped the people of Central Europe as best they could for several years. Now their activity in neighborly mercy became a passion. On June 25, 1919, a trainload of 850 children from Vienna, Salzburg, Graz, and other sections of German Austria arrived in Zürich. Where before the Swiss had seen prisoners of war and wounded soldiers, now they saw emaciated boys and girls with pinched faces getting off a special train, a tag hung around their necks giving their names, numbers, and Swiss home. Among this group were fifty children from Austrian Methodist homes. They were affectionately spoken of as "Our Vienna children" (*Unsere Wiener Kinder*). News followed that in the next month a large contingent would arrive from Germany.

Assistance to the human beings afflicted by the war was not a new activity to the Swiss Methodists. In 1917 they had begun to help the Austrians through F. H. Otto Melle, the superintendent of the Methodist work. The service of the Swiss Methodists was not forgotten, Melle reporting how in the dark of night the hungry civilians had come to *Trautsohngasse* to be given their share from the relief wagon of potatoes.

When the children began to arrive in Switzerland, a heavy administrative burden was placed upon the shoulders of Niederhauser and his assistants, Pastor and Frau A. Honegger, Zürich; Pastor and Frau E. M. Bauer, Basel; and Frau Suter-Mackert and G. Uebersax, Zürich. The local churches took up the work with Christian enthusiasm and devotion.

As soon as it was possible to send supplies into Germany, the Methodist Episcopal Church in America cabled funds to Nuelsen, who was able to purchase food and clothing in Switzerland and to send the first relief train of three freight cars into Germany. One carload of supplies was directed to the seat of the South Germany Conference and each minister, as he went back home from the annual session, carried with him such supplies as he could transport. These he distributed among his congregation to the neediest cases in the community. Other supplies were sent in from the north. The word circulated through Central Europe that the Methodist Episcopal Church, among all the Christian forces of the world, was doing its utmost to help suffering women and dying children. As far as possible the supplies were packed in standardized cases which were designed for kitchen cabinets, equipped with three shelves and hinge doors which could be used to great advantage by refugees. The first shipment of Methodist supplies included:

> 1,000 pounds of tea, 1,000 pounds of coffee, 1,500 pounds of cocoa, 16,200 pounds of corned beef, 21,600 pounds of bacon, 30,000 bars of soap, 7,200 cans of syrup, 600 cases of fats, 96,000 cans of evaporated milk, 48,000 cans of condensed milk, 1,000 women's coats, 2,520 suits of children's underwear, and quantities of shoes, men's suits, stockings, and overcoats.[3]

The sympathy of the German Methodists was aroused by appeals of leaders. The generosity of the Church was an amazing fact. To various relief organizations directed by *The Christian Apologist,* Judge Alfred K. Nippert, and J. A. Diekmann, more than a half million dollars, according to careful estimates, were contributed. Contributions poured through the central clearing offices of the German relief fund in Cincinnati in such volume that recording facilities broke down.[4]

The war was over; human sympathies in Christian mercies were extending hands of brotherhood, but the scars of hatred remained. The Ohio legislature passed a law that the

> German languages shall not be taught below the eighth grade in any of the elementary schools of this state.[5]

Governor James M. Cox (1917-21) recommending this statute to the legislature said that the teaching of German to American children was

> not only a distinct menace to Americanism, but it is part of a conspiracy formed long ago by the German government in Berlin.[6]

In Europe, Bishop Nuelsen was determined to demonstrate that the hatreds of war could not repeal the overarching sovereignty of God. He was concerned with a vital spiritual and social ministry at a time of extreme spiritual poverty and physical distress. What he could do to heal the scars of war, he was determined to perform. Unfortunately, the ecclesiastical leadership in America had neither his insight nor his vision. Despite the loyalty of the German Methodists, experiences of the war had struck a staggering blow at their faith in Christian brotherhood. One leader phrased the disillusion in these words:

> Our preachers lost faith in our leaders. Many of them were so utterly disappointed that they would have left the ministry but for the fact that that would have meant intolerable privations for their families. The war experiences reduced them to become bread servants; men, who formerly were most loyal and enthusiastic ministers of the gospel and patriotic citizens.

In America Bishop Nuelsen raised funds. In Europe he distributed relief. When Southern planters said they had no money but would contribute cotton, he solicited bales of cotton. Ships sailed from Galveston, Texas, to Hamburg, Germany, carrying the raw cotton to factories where it was manufactured for the Methodist relief agencies into clothing. The cost of transoceanic transportation was $19 a bale. Even this price did not deter the Bishop. With the promise of the Southerners to give the cotton, he went North and raised the funds to pay the cost of shipment. The South gave the goods; the North paid the freight.

Taking up the project of relief, Bishop Nuelsen captivated the Methodist imagination in America. He issued "Vacation Certificates" at $10 each, which entitled a needy child to a month's rest at the expense of an American family. These were beautifully executed by J. A. Bachmeier, of New York, and brought in large sums. Thirty-three thousand mite boxes were distributed to German-American families for the collection of their daily sacrifices for their continental brethren. Sunday-school classes and Epworth Leagues made their contributions.   Christmas offerings were sacrificially large.   Donations of food and clothing continued to stream into the destitute countries from the generous heart of America.   By the end of November, 1919, goods worth $50,000 had been dispatched to Europe.   The so-called "eleven-pound package" proved a popular way of solicitation and their volume swelled as the idea spread almost as a craze across the country.   A Methodist European Relief Office was established at 130 Mercer Street, New York.   In the meantime Magdalene Gamer, of Chicago, who had been stranded in Germany during the war, made a public appeal to the Methodist women of America for united support of the humanitarian movement of good will to overcome the shame of the havoc which the combat had played upon civilian populations.

The administrative problem involved in relief fell upon the shoulders of Continental Methodists, who themselves contributed generously to the program.   When the contributions were totaled, they had reached impressive sums.[7]

While the Swiss were doing their part in caring for the children, an offer came from the Scandinavian Methodists to do their share.   Denmark was prepared to take its quota at once.   Sweden was organized for similar action in the summer of 1920.   While Niederhauser was traveling through Saxony, he was so impressed by the pitiful condition of the people that he broadcast an appeal through the press.   The response was substantial.   From all sides food supplies and money began to come in.   Even the State Church in the canton of Bern voted to give Niederhauser half of its Sunday-school Christmas collection.

By April plans were completed to bring five hundred children from Saxony, the *Erzgebirge,* and Bavaria to Switzerland, and another five hundred from the big industrial cities of Central Germany.   The children were carefully selected between the ages of seven and fourteen from the Sunday schools of Methodist Churches.   By March of 1921, when the need for care of the undernourished children began to lessen, a statistical analysis showed the extent of the work to have been as follows:

In Switzerland—

	1919	1920	Total
Swiss Children	196	100	296
German Children	1234	816	2050
Austrian Children	50	—	50
Italian Children	36	15	51

In Denmark and Sweden—

Austrian Children	—	500	500
Assisted in their own homes (8)...	—	110	110
	1516	1541	3047

The work of the *Schweizer Ferienversorgung* was continued by the "Methodist Children's Aid" (*Methodistiche Kinderhilfe*). Bishop Nuelsen had declared in a letter to C. A. Binder, of Newark, New Jersey, on February 4, 1921, that the work of relief had to be organized into a "Foundation" (*Stiftung*). To carry out this purpose he appointed Heinrich Schaedel, a pastor in Stettin, director of the work. The constitution of the foundation was signed on June 2, 1921, by Bishop Nuelsen, Schaedel, and Richard Wobith. Declaring the purpose to give relief to needy children, the organizers stated their determination to found homes and raise an endowment of five million marks. The board included Bishop Nuelsen, F. H. Otto Melle, Wobith, H. Ramke, O. Göricke, Ernst Gideon Bek, H. Bargmann, and H. Schaedel. An advisory board named included E. Lienhard and Niederhauser in Switzerland, and A. J. Bucher, J. A. Diekmann, C. A. Binder, and Albert Klaiber in America.

The work began in earnest with the acquisition of the first home *"Auhof"* in Türnitz, Lower Austria. Bishop Nuelsen had received a wire from Melle that a home and farm could be acquired for $8,000. Arriving in New York, the Bishop went before the trustees of the First German Church in the city, who were meeting in a small prayer room. He returned to his hotel with checks for $10,500 in his pocket and cabled Melle: "Buy Türnitz."

Hardly had the purchase and development of the Türnitz property been begun when attention was called to the plight of youth in Vienna. Old and young were cold and hungry, poorly clothed, and suffering. The Methodist relief work acted promptly to establish a second institution, now known as *Erholungsheim Klosterwald* in Klosterlausnitz. The property had been a sanatorium and was well fitted for the relief work.

Bishop Nuelsen, cautious but determined, announced his intention of developing more homes when opportunity offered. In the middle of March, 1921, he proposed the opening of a home in Nagold in the southern part of the Black Forest. This was followed by the development of smaller institutions in Kelkheim, Blankenburg, and rest homes in Bansin and Freudenstadt, the last home being known as *"Teuchelwald."* The program of institutional development was extended to Hungary by the acquisition of property in Budakeszi. The impetus for the purchase of the project was given by a Christmas (1920) offering of Scandinavian Sunday-school children. On June 30, 1922, three new buildings in Budakeszi were dedicated. By the spring of 1925 ten thousand children were being or had been cared for by the Methodist homes serving the desperate needs of the postwar Europe.

The human crisis which had been the aftermath of war had hardly come under control when Germany was precipitated into another disaster which brought economic collapse. In 1923 inflation came in

Germany. It followed a political nightmare which swept over the nation when on January 11, 1923, the French troops occupied the rich Ruhr industrial section of the Reich. By fall the expansion of print-ing-press money had swelled to a volume which threw the nation into a panic. The process of destruction of the value of German money had been a gradual development since 1919. Few Germans realized that their money was becoming worth less and less. They did notice that prices were getting higher, but they were not generally aware of the statistics:

The Story of Inflation

Date	Paper marks given for one United States dollar
January 31, 1919	8.57
December 31, 1919	48.43
December 31, 1921	184
August 15, 1922	1,021
December 30, 1922	7,350
May 30, 1923	1,100,000
October 9, 1923	1,200,000,000
November 14, 1923	1,260,000,000,000
November 20, 1923	4,200,000,000,000

The value of German money became practically nothing. The cost of commodities soared. The winter of 1923-24 was a tragic one, to which the so-called *"Rübenwinter"* of 1917-18 seemed enviable in com-parison. By January 18, 1924, a pound of pork cost 1,000,000,000,000 marks; a loaf of bread 500,000,000,000 marks; and a quart of milk 360,000,000,000.

Bishop Nuelsen had hoped that the relief work would be wound up by the fall of 1922. In March of 1923, however, he wrote to friends in America that affairs were as bad as they had been a quadrennium before. The generosity of America had been taxed to the limit. Bishop Nuelsen had to strain his ingenuity to devise new ways of raising money. In April, 1923, he bought twenty-five thousand new one-mark notes for a dollar and sent them to friends in the United States with the following note:

Dear Friend:

Will you accept this brand-new one-mark note with my best wishes? Before the war it was worth twenty-five cents in Amer-ican money. Do you know what it is worth today? When you receive this letter I could get 80,000 for a dollar. But please tell your friends that for the twenty-five cents which this was worth before the war, I can give to hungry children two or three cans of condensed milk.

In November of the same year he dispatched a second letter to America. It began:

> Would you not like to be a millionaire? Then permit me to send you herewith a million. Today, when I write this I can buy 65,000,000,000 marks for a dollar. Fantastic, is it not? Surely, but the need, which exists among the people, the suffering, the hunger, the cold, all that is not fantastic; that is naked reality.

The Methodist Episcopal Church in Switzerland took official notice of the disastrous effect of the inflation upon the institutions in Germany. It expressed its concern over the situation of the homes and hospitals of the Bethany and Martha-Mary societies, which lacked fuel, foodstuffs, bandages, medicine, and clothing. The sisters with heroic devotion to their work, often underfed and working under demoralizing handicaps, remained at their posts.

The Church did not desert its duty in this situation. Clothing, stockings, potatoes, anything that would help, all these donations were collected at the various stations of the Bethany Society. The administration of the emergency collection was in charge of Alfred Honegger. In Basel alone the contribution included 500 boxes, 240 sacks, and other packages totaling 28,500 kilograms of freight. Even leather was collected and delivered to Pastor Klein in Planitz, Saxony, where a "Committee for the Establishment of Shoe Repair Shops" had been organized. Bishop Nuelsen, taking up the leadership of the "Committee for the Hungry People," dispatched 310 relief boxes of food supplies, valued at 12,330 Swiss francs.

As the distress and bitterness in the Ruhr region, which had been occupied, increased, the Methodists opened stations in Mannhein, Frankfurt, Bielefeld, and Kassel. In the spring of 1923 Bishop Nuelsen had personally conducted a survey of the situation throughout the territory. Need stalked the valley. The scarcity of milk was dangerous. A family with eight children received but a fourth of a quart of milk. Babies cried for milk. Under these circumstances the Methodists shipped boxes of condensed milk to central stations for distribution to families. Something more had to be done for the "Ruhr children."

Fortunately, the post-war development of children's homes gave the Methodists a useful equipment with which to meet the need. The homes were thrown open to the "Ruhr children" (*Ruhrkindern*). The Methodists in Switzerland took many more into their own homes. The same generosity was extended by the Methodists in Pomerania and East Friesland.

The social situation improved with the establishment of a new monetary standard. On August 30, 1924, the German currency was stabilized. Germany was beginning to live and breathe again, but it was a new and dismayed and impoverished nation. The middle classes had lost their savings. The Princes were reduced to scanty incomes. In their places stood the "new rich" who had come overnight into wealth.

The continuing crisis was over. For nearly a decade, through war and peace and the aftermath of war, the Methodist Episcopal Church had demonstrated its international organic unity. Bishop Nuelsen through all those sad years remained the ecclesiastical symbol of that unity. With deep sympathy, mature diplomatic poise, and administrative efficiency, he had led the Methodist Episcopal Church as an intercontinental fellowship from catastrophe through distress to a testimony of Christian unity. In the history of the Church no event exceeds this witness in its significance.

Methodism was faced with a problem in what should be done with the magnificent institutions which had been developed. The procedure followed in the solution of the problem has given to German Methodism a unique type of institution as far as the Church is concerned. In Freudenstadt the Teuchelwald was developed into a hotel (*Kurhaus*). A villa, purchased as an annex in 1926, gave Methodism an institution of 77 rooms and 120 beds, the property being worth 400,000 marks. In 1929 the *Kurhaus* cared for nearly two thousand guests. The rest home in Bansin on the Baltic Sea, purchased by the North Germany Conference in 1919, and *Klosterlausnitz* in Thüringen opened in 1921, continued to furnish rest and recreation to guests. The home in Kelkheim was sold eight years after it was purchased.

Developed largely since the end of the World War, Methodism had in Central Europe a welfare service with institutions worth more than a million and a quarter dollars. Despite constant political and economic difficulties, Methodism in Central Europe exercised an influence out of proportion to its membership. Its institutions of mercy are a continual reminder that Methodism carries out the injunction of John Wesley:

> Do all the good you can,
> By all the means you can,
> In all the ways you can,
> In all the places you can,
> At all the times you can,
> To all the people you can,
> As long as ever you can.

CHAPTER XIV

LIQUIDATION—THE MERGER MOVEMENT

The divided soul which the World War bequeathed to the nations of the earth was much like the condition of the heart and mind left in the wake of the Spanish-American War. High humanitarian idealism blossomed upon the smoldering fires of hates, prejudices, and commercial and political rivalries and antagonisms. The chief difference between the two periods was that both trends were much more pronounced in the latter.

Until the final breakdown of the Disarmament Conference with Hindenburg's calling of *Adolf Hitler* to *Wilhemstrasse* in 1933, a positive if weakening faith in the efficacy of an administrative apparatus for organizing peace had captivated the mind of liberal thought in all countries. The preamble to the Covenant of the League of Nations proclaimed the purpose of promoting "international co-operation" and achieving "international peace and security" by the acceptance of obligations not to resort to war, by the prescription of open, just, and honorable relations between nations, by the firm establishment of the understandings of international law as the actual rule of conduct among governments, and by the maintenance of justice and a scrupulous respect for all treaty obligations in the dealings of organized peoples with one another. The Permanent Court of International Justice, set up pursuant to Section XIV of the Covenant by the Council, anticipated a judicial settlement of the differences among nations much as the Court of Arbitration set up by the conventions of The Hague of 1899 and 1907 had presumed before it that a day of reason had dawned. Section I of the Articles establishing the International Labor Organization contained as exalted humanitarian sentiments the Western world had produced. It stressed the fact that "universal peace" could only be established when "based upon social justice." It continued:

> And whereas conditions of labor exist involving such injustice, hardship, and privation to large numbers of people as to produce unrest so great that the peace and harmony of the world are imperiled; and an improvement required . . . the High Contracting Parties, moved by sentiments of justice and humanity, as well as by the desire to secure the permanent peace of the world agree. . . .

In 1922 the Nine-Power Treaty was signed for "safeguarding the rights and interests of China." When the Locarno Pact was signed on October 16, 1925, between Germany and France and Germany and Belgium, the nerves of Europe should have been calmed by an international agreement binding the old enemies to *peaceful settlement of all disputes of all kinds* and promising that in no case would they attack or invade each other or resort to war against each other. The keystone in the arch of peace seemed finally to have been morticed into place with the signing of the Pact of Paris on August 22, 1928. By it the High Contracting Parties solemnly condemned "recourse to war for the solution of international controversies" and renounced "it as an instrument of national policy in their relations with one another."

If apparatus for international administration and adjudication and treaty assurances could usher in Kant's dream of *ewigen Frieden,* that day seemed to have arrived. Added to these instruments of peace was the growing habit of international consultation which was a kind of added insurance policy against war.

On the surface of international relations the peace appeared substantial. Germany was defeated. The Allied Powers were permanently in control of affairs. That the peace was a strategic one, however, and therefore temporary, became increasingly evident. The conditions of peace were repugnant to international friendship. Article 231 of the Treaty of Versailles had placed upon Germany

> the entire responsibility . . . of Germany and her Allies for causing all the loss and damage to which the Allied and Associated Governments and their nationals have been subjected as a consequence of the war imposed upon them by the aggression of Germany and her Allies.

The reparations bill of one hundred and thirty-two billion gold marks was from every point of view an economic impossibility. It was especially so in view of the restrictions placed on the Reich and the severing of important continental and colonial areas from the estate of the Empire. The economic impossibility of the task developed into open defiance of the restrictions imposed by the treaty.

The fact of economic impossibility did not concern the political makers of peace in the least. Passions were running high, and the public applauded the enormous financial burden on the "Huns." The height of enthusiasm was reached by Sir Eric Geddes in a reaction against the suspicion that he was not thoroughgoing enough in his vindictiveness. He declared:

> We will get out of her all you can squeeze out of a lemon, and a bit more—squeeze her until the pips squeak.[1]

Following the conference at Cannes in January, 1922, a first moratorium was allowed reparations payments. On January 11, 1923, France took possession of the Ruhr. The outcome was the report of the Dawes Commission's arrangement for payment of reparations on the installment plan after a short breathing spell. It proved unworkable. On June 7, 1929, an international committee of experts reported the Young Plan, which added new loans from abroad to those already made under the Dawes Plan. This plan likewise broke down, yet before Germany itself complained, President Hoover came forward with his plan for a general moratorium. The upshot of this was an international conference at Lausanne, where new proposals for new loans to Germany were made. This stage in checkmated diplomacy was ended by the rise to power of Adolf Hitler in 1933.

In the meantime Germany had justly been crying for a scientific adjustment of the reparations problem, for armaments equality, for general revision of the Treaty of Versailles, and even for some adjustment of the vast areas of colonies lost by the peace settlements. That Germany's plea was touching the hearts of the public in England and America in the decades following 1920 is certain. The fact was becoming evident that only a righteous and not a recriminatory peace could endure. The Churches listened favorably to Germany's petitions for justice. The Archbishop of York, preaching in Cathedral Church of Saint Pierre, Geneva, on January 31, 1932, at the opening of the Conference for the Reduction and Limitation of Armaments, declared:

> If the spirit that guides us is to be the Gospel, the War Guilt Clause must go—struck out by those who framed it.

On May 24, 1932, the General Conference of the Methodist Episcopal Church in session at Atlantic City, adopted a resolution in these words:

> We believe that the time has come for the world to acknowledge the fact that the sole guilt of the German nation for the World War cannot in justice be maintained.

The friendly attitude, however, developed too tardily. Germany was sinking lower and lower in economic, political, and social despair. Germans felt themselves on the verge of catastrophe. They spoke of Adolf Hitler with his program of defiant nationalism as *unsere letzte Hoffnung* (our last hope).

Such economic and political circumstances made the program of German-speaking Methodism as difficult in America as on the Continent. Under the wise guidance of Bishop Nuelsen, assisted by F. H. Otto Melle, the Conferences on the Continent began to build bravely upon the ruins left by the war. In America the reaction led to a program of merger of the German with the English-speaking Conferences. The language mission work begun by Nast in 1835 by 1924 was in process of liquidation.

The General Conference of 1924 established the policy that

> every effort be made to conserve the excellent results secured by our foreign language Conferences. . . . And that such foreign

language Conferences . . . be fostered and encouraged to continue so long as there is a constituency needing such special language ministry and supervision.[2]

Sociological forces of assimilation, even more powerful than the effects of the World War, however, were at work. Immigrants passed through a process of adaptation to American life. This fact was nowhere more apparent than in the manner of using a foreign tongue. During a period of transition the Germans were forced to use English in their trades, although their own tongue was the exclusive medium of social life. By the force of environment the Germans became bilinguists; second and third generations of children knew English better than the language of their parents and grandparents. Customs likewise were modified as children played and went to school with boys and girls speaking another language.

The result was inevitably neighborhoods in which both languages and the customs were mixed. In the same region of a city could be found strangers who had only recently arrived from Europe and who spoke only their native tongue, older people in various stages of language and custom assimilation, and children and grandchildren of parents speaking foreign languages, who were in the process of divesting themselves of the evidence of continental culture. A study of the language being used in the German Churches showed in 1924 that English predominated.

The use of English as the years went by and immigration fell off became an actual necessity. Children were not taught their mother tongue often at home and rarely in school. Intermarriage increasingly made it difficult for a husband or wife to understand if English were not used. Adults who had been many years in America acquired a thorough knowledge of English, although they preferred their native tongue for worship. In the associations of business and school English was an essential, even though German was still spoken in the home.

Bridging the gap between cultures, the Church made the inevitable capitulation first by using English partially in Sunday schools and Young People's Society meetings. The next evidence of the transformation was the appearance of an occasional English evening service on church calendars. As the process proceeded the language service was preserved in the morning, but all other services, with the exception of prayer meeting and the Adult Bible Class, were held in English. A final stage was reached when all the activities of the Church were carried on in English with the possible exception of a German Sunday class. This step was taken to give the Sunday-school children an opportunity to attend an English worship service in the morning. Sometimes this plan was varied by having language services on alternate Sunday mornings or by having a German service follow one in the English language. The final stage was reached when all the work

LANGUAGE USED BY GERMAN CONFERENCES*

Conference	No. of churches	No English in any service	German in all Services[1]	Mostly German[2]	Two-thirds English—Morning Service German	Mostly English[3]	All English	Percentage Predominantly German	Percentage Predominantly English
California	21	9	2	3	3	....	4	71.4	29.6
Central	108	3	9	6	32	18	40	26.9	73.1
Chicago	64	....	28	8	17	8	3	64.0	36.0
East	36	....	23	1	10	1	1	75.0	25.0
Northern	57	....	9	5	....	8	35	24.7	75.3
Northwest	41	....	8	1	10	10	12	29.3	70.7
Pacific	21	1	15	1	2	....	2	84.1	15.9
St. Louis	74	....	6	....	26	2	40	20.7	79.3
Southern	52	....	25	2	12	2	11	59.6	40.4
West	56	10	10	1	18	2	15	48.2	51.8
Total	530	23	135	28	130	51	163	43.0	57.0

[1]This classification permits partial use of English in Sunday school or Young People's Society.

[2]Sunday school and Epworth League in English or mostly so, with occasional English service.

[3]All services except morning service in English, but with occasional English morning service. Adult Bible class may be in German.

*Data from the Report of the Foreign Language Commission to the General Conference of 1924. See General Conference Journal, 1924, p. 1688.

of the Church, except the ministry to the older people, was conducted in English.

The maintenance of a class-conscious language group depends for its duration upon a continual stream of newly arriving immigrants, and immigration, under new Federal restrictions, began to fall sharply. The census of 1920 showed the population of the United States to be 105,710,610. Of this number 34.4% were foreign-born whites. More than a third of the people of America lived under direct foreign influence. If the population of the United States had marched past a reviewing stand in 1920, out of every thousand, 364 would have been of foreign birth. Of this latter number 97 would have spoken English, 82 German, 34 Italian, 24 Polish, 20 Jewish, 15 Swedish, 13 French, 12 Czechoslovakian, and 10 Norwegian.

The growth of German Methodism corresponded very closely to the curve of immigration. Between 1819 and 1882 records of immigration were kept by the collector of customs at the ports of entry. In 1820 the German arrivals numbered only 968. Between 1827 and 1850, the number grew so that by the latter date census figures showed 310,000 Germans in America. The revolution of 1848 sent increasing waves of refugees to the United States until in the year 1854 arrivals totaled 427,833. This was the high point until 1873. In the quarter of a century, 1847-72, the gain in full membership was 521%. The second twenty-five years, 1872-97, the rate of increase fell to 102.5%. While the gain in the third quarter-century, 1897-1922, was 1.8%, the loss in the decade, 1912-22, being 2%.

Percentage of Gain, German-speaking Methodism

Decade	Gain
1840-50	171.2%
1850-60	183.2%
1860-70 (immigration falling off)	48.2%
1870-80 (immigration rising)	52.1%

It is apparent from the Conference statistics that the membership of the ten German Conferences in the United States reached its peak in 1917 with a total of 60,544 members. The figure was significant by comparison with a membership in 1908 of 60,076. In nine years the Church had increased by only 468 members. In 1898 the membership was 58,125, which was only 74 less than the membership in 1921. The Sunday school showed a similar record. In 1896 the enrollment was only 240 less than it was in 1922. The gain in the Sunday school between 1857 and 1872 was 148.2%. In the twenty-five years between 1872 and 1897 it was 100.3%, but between 1897 and 1922 it was only six tenths of one per cent.

Other statistics testified to the growing ineffectiveness of the mission to the Germans. In 1890 the records showed 108 men in the Conference studies, but in 1922 only 26, and in the latter year only five men were received. Preachers increasingly sought transfer from German to English Conferences and between 1910 and 1922, 64 were so transferred. Even more serious than the fact that German-speaking Methodism was no longer recruiting its own leadership from its own ranks was the serious situation arising from the following age distribution of the effective ministers:

Age	Number
20-30	9
30-40	72
40-50	98
50-60	134
60-70	85
70-80	12

German Methodism had become an old people's Church. It had more effective preachers between the ages of 70 and 80 than between 20 and 30, and more between 60 and 70 than between 20 and 40.

It was clear enough that candidates for the ministry from families of German blood were studying in English theological seminaries and joining English Conferences. The young men had lost their linguistic patriotism. The reason was not hard to discover. Although German contributions to benevolences were large, the preachers' salaries were small. In 1922 the average salaries were as follows:

Conference	Salary
Chicago German	$1,407
Northwest German	1,310
North German	1,200
West German ⎫	
Central German ⎬ all between $1,000 and 1,100	
East German ⎭	
California German ⎫	
Southern German ⎬	900
Pacific German	$800- 900
Saint Louis German	517

Conference claimants payments were correspondingly small.

Another factor entered into the situation. Of 470 parishes studied, 62.7% were found to overlap English-speaking parishes, and in only 16% of the cases was the German Church stronger than the English. Duplication of effort and denominational competition with itself within a radius of five city blocks or five miles in a rural district was a serious administrative problem.

By 1922 it was evident that the operation of inexorable sociological law was bringing the Church in American society to a point where the language mission work must in all wisdom be given up. It was a difficult fact to be acknowledged by those who loved the German Methodist work with an unsurpassed passion. In 1922 the record of the German work was something of which to be proud. In America it was organized into ten language Conferences of 544 preaching points. Its full membership was 58,240. In its 574 Sunday schools, 71,130 scholars, teachers, and officers were enrolled. Its 614 church edifices and 446 parsonages were valued at 6,363,020, and its institutions at an equal figure.

The German mission had returned to the Church money on its investment. Since the time of their organization the ten German Conferences had received from the Board of Home Missions and Church Extension $1,241,315. During the same period the Church received in contributions from the Germans $912,173 more than that sum. This compared very well with the $91,051 received from the Swedish Mission in excess of missionary subsidy, and $50,584 from the Norwegians.[8]

In 1923 the per capita benevolent contribution of the German Methodists was $1.90. Up to that date the ten German Conferences had contributed the sum of $5,085,372 to the benevolent enterprises of the Church. The per capita benevolent contributions by Conferences in 1923 was: California German, $3.67; East German, $2.86; West German, $2.48; Northwest German, $2.38; Pacific German, $2.37; North German, $1.92; South German, $1.84; Central German, $1.57; Chicago German, $1.48; and Saint Louis German, $1.42.

The Centenary record of the German Conferences was one of which Germans were justly proud. Up to November 30, 1923, the annual per capita contributions to the movement were as follows:

Conference	Annual per Capita Contribution
Northwest German	$8.53
East German	8.10
North German	6.44
West German	6.40
California German	6.32
Pacific German	6.16
Central German	5.85
South German	4.73
Saint Louis German	4.18
Chicago German	4.01

In addition to the quarter million dollars raised directly by the Germans for post-war relief, the Centenary between 1919 and 1923 appropriated $481,502 for the assistance of Germany alone. This was in addition to $400,000 spent for relief during and immediately after the war.

The General Conference of 1924 took the step which began the painful process of the liquidation of the interests of German Methodism and their merger with the English Conferences.

The North German Conference was the first to go. By resolution of the General Conference of 1924 it was merged with the Minnesota Conference, the charges lying outside the boundaries of that Conference being transferred to the Conferences within whose boundaries they fell.[4] A series of enabling acts were passed at the same time.[5]

The Saint Louis German Conference was the second to surrender its identity. Because the process is typical of the subsequent merger of the other seven Conferences, its program deserves especial attention. The liquidation of the Saint Louis German Conference began with a memorial sent by it to the General Conference of 1924. The forty-fifth annual session of the Conference meeting in Saint Louis in early September, 1923, petitioned:

> We hereby memorialize the General Conference to grant an Enabling Act, whereby the Saint Louis German Conference may merge with the contiguous English Conferences, whenever it may deem it wise to do so.
> In view of the fact that all the Conferences of German Methodism may not be situated as is the Saint Louis German Conference, therefore we request the General Commission on Foreign-speaking Work of the Methodist Episcopal Church to do all it can for the welfare of the German Conferences, who contemplate a merger as well as those who do not.[6]

The General Conference in 1924 recognized the memorial by passing the Enabling Act requested:

> The Saint Louis German Conference, during the next quadrennium, may merge with the contiguous English Conferences whenever it may deem it wise to do so.[7]

Pursuant to this authority, the forty-sixth annual session of the Saint Louis German Conference, meeting in Mascoutah, Illinois, on August 28, 1924, created a commission of three to plan in detail all the necessary steps looking toward a merger with the contiguous Conferences. The Commission was instructed to report its findings for final action to the next Conference session and the contiguous Conferences were memorialized to appoint similar commissions. The proposal of merger was overwhelmingly approved by a vote of 47 to 8.

The problems which confronted the commissions on merger were not easy ones. The Saint Louis German Conference at the time had 50 effective, 4 probationary, and 48 local preachers; 10,000 members; nearly 12,000 Sunday-school scholars, teachers, and officers; 87 Sunday schools, 89 churches, and 62 parsonages valued at a million and a half dollars; 19 retired preachers; 26 preachers' widows; and $50,000 in the Preachers' Aid Fund. The Conference was further the patron of Central Wesleyan College, Central Wesleyan Orphans' Home, and the Home for the Aged in Quincy, Illinois. These human and material resources had to be absorbed by the Saint Louis, Missouri, Illinois, Southern Illinois, Central Illinois, Iowa, and Des Moines Conferences.

The Joint Commission on Merger reported on September 9, 1925, to the Saint Louis German Conference in session in Eden Church, Saint Louis. The proposal unanimously adopted by the Joint Commission was accepted by a vote of the Conference, the count being 53 to 2. The motion was made to make the vote unanimous and the Conference stood and sang "Praise God From Whom All Blessing Flow." The official declaration of merger was signed by Bishop Waldorf for the Saint Louis German Conference and by Bishop Hughes for the Saint Louis Conference. In old Union Church, Saint Louis, the brethren were called one by one and transferred to their new Conferences, after which the whole Conference stood and sang, "A Mighty Fortress Is Our God."

A cycle in the history of American Methodism had been completed by the liquidation. When the Saint Louis German Conference met for its first session in the Washington Street German Methodist Church, Saint Louis, on September 3, 1879, 71 ministers answered the roll call. When it dissolved in 1925, 76 were mustered out.

The general principles of merger set by the Saint Louis German Conference were followed by the subsequent liquidation of other Conferences. The geographical location of a congregation within the bounds of another Conference determined its official connectional relation. Requests of Quarterly Conference for bilingual pastors were to be given preference in the making of appointments. The Central Wesleyan Orphans' Home became the joint property of the Saint Louis and the Missouri Conferences, provided, however, that the patronizing and contributing German Conferences should continue to have representation on the board as long as they continued as official organizations of the Methodist Episcopal Church. The Quincy Home for the Aged became the property of the Illinois Conference. Central Wesleyan College was turned over to the Saint Louis Conference. All funds of the Saint Louis German Conference Preachers' Aid Society were given over to the Board of Pensions and Relief for actuarial and final adjustment. A commission was appointed to transact and complete all unfinished business. Eugene Weiffenbach, secretary of the Merger Commission, was largely responsible for the detailed factual studies which paved the way for the adjustments necessary to the liquidation of the language Conference.

The overwhelming vote in support of merger did not mean that the German preachers had lost their loyalty to their own Conferences. An almost universal regret was broken only by the acknowledged necessity of the movement. It was common knowledge that services in most of the German Churches were being held predominantly in the

English language.   German Churches could not fully man their own pulpits, nor could they fill their professional chairs with their own men.   For years the North German Conference had not received a candidate for the ministry on trial.   Since 1900 the Saint Louis German Conference had transferred eleven of its members to the other Gercan Conferences.   Of twenty-eight members of the younger faculty of Central Wesleyan College, only three in 1925 had been recruited from the ranks of German Methodism.   Even candidates for the ministry from German families matriculated at English-speaking theological seminaries and the enrollments in the German seminaries declined apace.

The logic of the situation seemed to dictate liquidation and merger as the course of wisdom.   F. W. Wahl, of the Saint Louis German Conference, summarized the point of view when he said:

> The real purpose of German Methodism was to bring the gospel message in the German language to the German immigrants and the German people of our country. . . . Our distinctive mission as a Conference was to preach the gospel in the German language to the German people in this country.   That work has been largely accomplished.   We were practically an English-speaking Conference.   It has never been the purpose nor the policy nor the program of Methodism that one English-speaking Conference should overlap or cover the same territory that seven other English-speaking Conferences cover.[8]

The issue of the conservation of man-power and money was a large one.   That two struggling Methodist Episcopal Churches should be receiving missionary money for the support of English and German preachers both on inadequate salaries seemed unwise from the standpoint of effectiveness, whatever may have been the sentimental attachments to the German-speaking Conferences.   The old adage that "in unity there is strength." held by the ardent advocates of merger, was true in the case of Methodist societies.

The liquidation of German Conferences proceeded rapidly.   In 1926 the West and South German Conferences dissolved.   In 1927 the California German Conference merged.   In 1928 the Pacific German Conference followed the fashion.   When the General Conference of 1932 met in Atlantic City only the East, Central, and Chicago-Northwest German Conferences remained.[9]

The Chicago-Northwest Conference, pursuant to an Enabling Act passed by the General Conference of 1932, was officially merged with nine English Conferences on August 27, 1933, when the merger declaration was signed by Bishops Magee, Waldorf, Leete, and Blake.

It might have been expected that the practical execution of the merger program would entail unforeseen difficulties and impose unmerited hardships.   By the time the idea of merger reached the Central German Conference a small but important opposition had developed, led chiefly by John A. Diekmann, superintendent of the Bethesda Institutions, August J. Bucher, editor of *The Christian Apologist,* and F. W. Mueller, of the Board of Home Missions and Church Extension.

The Central German Conference began its study of the advisability of merger at its session in 1929 by the appointment of a Committee on Conference Policy. The committee reported in 1930 and proposed a petition to the General Conference of 1932 for an enabling act.

The historical importance of the Central German Conference is so great and the standing of its opponents of merger so high that the carefully prepared and widely broadcast arguments against merger must be given. The mimeographed protest against liquidation read:

A careful survey of the present status of the Central German Conference will easily show that the Conference today on the whole—numerically, financially, and in point of Kingdom service —is quite up to the status of any former period of its history. In comparison with contiguous English-speaking Conferences its record in every way is most favorable, in spite of certain handicaps under which its work must be done.

Everyone concerned will readily concede that the proposed dissolution of this Conference by merging it with other Conferences is a step of such far-reaching and serious consequences that it should not be considered but for the most imperative and compelling reasons. From the survey made by the Conference Commission through a questionnaire sent to and answered by every pastor in the Conference, it is clearly shown that there are no such compelling reasons before us. The following are the facts:

In the majority of our churches the question of a Conference merger has not been a matter of interest or discussion. While several churches are favoring a merger, an equal number seriously object to it. The laymen, with but few exceptions, are not urging the merger. Most of the pastors report that, even if a Conference merger took place, their churches would not merge with neighboring English churches. The above facts certainly do not warrant so radical a step as the uprooting of so vigorous a plant of the Lord's own planting as is this great Conference.

Furthermore, we wish to bring the following considerations to the attention of the members of this Conference:

1. The disintegration of this Conference will inevitably hasten the dissolution of the remaining German Conferences. Many of their leaders have expressed that fear and are anxiously concerned. As the oldest German Conference, we must take serious and sympathetic cognizance of the grave responsibility such an act would necessarily involve.

2. Many of the wisest leaders of our Church, among them Bishops, Secretaries, and Editors, are expressing their grave apprehension at the present program of dissolving our German Conferences. They fear that with them a distinct and valuable type of Methodism will be lost, and they are particularly concerned that this Conference should continue for many years to come.

3. Logically with the dissolution of the German Conferences the days of the *Christian Apologist* will be numbered. This splendid paper today is the most powerful agency for Temperance

and Prohibition in Germany; it is also exercising a most whole-some influence for Evangelical Christianity in the church world and in the theological life in Germany. Then, too, the discontinuation of the *Apologist* will be a bitter disappointment to thousands of dear old people scattered all over the country, whose only connecting link with the Church at large, and in many cases, whose only means of edification and Christian upbuilding is the *Apologist*.

4. In eleven of our charges we still have German services every Sunday. Eleven others have German services on alternating Sundays. Three have an occasional German service and nine others have German classes in the church school. A total of thirty-four charges still use the German language to a more or less extent. This situation should make us very reluctant in urging a merger.

5. Our German Conferences have developed benevolent institutions of which the leaders of our Church tell us that they rank among the best in the Church. Those within the bounds of our Conference: Baldwin-Wallace College, William Nast Theological Seminary, the Orphanage in Berea, Ohio, the Emmanuel City Mission and Community House, Cincinnati, Ohio; the Louisville Hospital, Louisville, Ky.; the Goodwill Industry in Terre Haute, Ind., and our Bethesda Institutions in Cincinnati, Ohio. The leaders of these institutions have all, with one exception, expressed their fear that a merger with other Conferences by the dissolution of the Central German Conference at this time would create hardships for these institutions causing insurmountable difficulties. These institutions have been founded with much prayer and have been maintained with much sacrificial service. They are the direct outgrowth of the traditional record of German Methodism for liberal giving and loyalty of support. Most, if not all, direct access to the patrons and supporters of these important agencies would be cut off and their very existence would become jeopardized. In fact, a Conference merger for several of these agencies would amount to a tragedy. This Conference is in honor bound to further the present welfare and to safeguard the future of these institutions and to act with exceeding care in any program that threatens them with harm.

6. We still have among our members thousands of old people who joined the churches of this Conference in its earlier years. For most of them the disrupting of this Conference would be a great sorrow, and they will find it exceedingly difficult to adjust themselves to the new order of things. If a merger must ultimately come, for the sake of these fathers and mothers in Israel, who have borne heavy burdens in behalf of the Conference, it should be deferred until most of them have joined the Church Triumphant, which will not be so many years hence.

7. It should also be remembered that the dispersion of our preachers in contiguous English-speaking Conferences will bring no benefit to the majority of them. While a small number may be offered a better opportunity for the future, it must be clear to every thoughtful person that most of our present men will not fare so well in English-speaking churches as they do at the present time. The fact is, that in our English Conferences there is a perfect scramble among a large percentage of the pastors for

suitable places. It stands to reason that under such conditions, transfers by merger could and should not expect any special consideration.

8. Probably the most urgent reason for merging is the hope that thereby our retired men would be better cared for in the future. While this happily is the case in several of our former Conferences that have merged, we must be warned of the fact that according to an action of the last General Conference since January 1, 1929 (see *Discipline* of 1928, Par. 389, Sec. II), this expectation of better support in the future may easily meet with sad disappointment.

9. On careful reflection there will be no financial advantage in merging. The overhead will not be reduced since an equal amount, if not more, will be assessed for the larger salaries paid to superintendents in the English-speaking Conferences. The assessments for the Episcopal Fund, the Conference Claimants, the Conference Sustentation Fund will be the same, if not larger, since most of our present charges will continue as in the past, not merging with other charges.

10. Living in a democratic age, country, and church, it appears to us that so momentous a step as dissolving a Conference should not be undertaken unless the majority of our laymen so wish. They have had an equal share with the ministry in building up the Conference; their official voice should be heard in dissolving the same. This has not been done.

11. Finally, let us not overlook the fact that our Conference is a part of the wonderfully effective missionary factor as represented in our bilingual Conferences, having produced for Methodism a missionary product which is unsurpassed in its annals by any similar effort. It would appear a calamity should this missionary organization fade out of the life of the Church at large.

In the light of these considerations, and others which might have been specified, we earnestly believe no action should be taken at this session of the Conference in the direction of the proposed disruption of its organic Constitution. We believe that the question should be left open awaiting developments that will more clearly indicate what is the wisest and best course to take. Meanwhile our institutions will find time and opportunity to adjust their interests so that less hardships will be caused if a merger must ultimately come. To press it now would seem to be acting with unwarranted haste in so serious a matter.

That such an earnest appeal should have been made to the Central German Conference by the irreconcilable opponents of merger was an appropriate appreciation of the historic achievement of German Methodism. That the protest was futile was only recognition of the fact that the currents of circumstances were running so strongly in favor of merger that all argument was belated.

When the Central German Conference adjourned on August 27, 1933, its members went to their appointments in the Detroit, Indiana, Kentucky, Michigan, North-East Ohio, Northwest Indiana, Ohio,

Pittsburgh, and West Virginia Conferences. As the seventieth session closed, Emil I. Klotz, superintendent of the Ohio District, said:

> As the time draws near when the name of our dear Conference is to be wiped from the records of the Methodist Episcopal Church, a sadness creeps into my heart that I cannot express. You may call this a wedding, and possibly it is, but I have seen tears flow at weddings as well as at funerals. May I close with these words of Saint Paul: Finally, brethren, farewell. Be perfect, be of good comfort, be of one mind, live in peace and the God of love and peace shall be with you. The grace of our Lord Jesus Christ, and the love of God and the communion of the Holy Spirit be with you all. Amen.[19]

The *Apologist,* rushing an extra from the press on August 16, 1933, with news of the dissolution of the Central German Conference, pleaded:

> And last but not least, do not forget the *Apologist.* It is the last bond which still unites and holds into relationship the German Methodist family in America, Europe, and the world. Defend it, subscribe to it, otherwise it is consecrated to its demise.

Only the East German Conference remained to remind Methodism of the glory which had once belonged to the Mission to the Germans. A stage in the epic of America had been completed. The United States had taken to itself the people of Europe and made them its citizens. They in turn had contributed their efforts and their culture to the building of richly pluralistic American culture as the gift of one of the groups in the polyglot human structure of the New World. To hundreds of thousands of German-speaking immigrants, the Methodist Episcopal Church has proclaimed the gospel of a common Fatherhood, a universal brotherhood, and a common quest—the forgiveness of human sins by the grace of God, as Nast said, more abundant than man's needs.

VITAL STATISTICS OF GERMAN CONFERENCES, 1915

Conferences	Organized	Merged	Churches	Value	Parsonages	Probationers	Members	Sunday schools	Scholars	Total Disciplinary Coll.	Total all Collections
Central	1864	1933	134	$951,800	94	444	13,868	127	17,232	$15,207	$55,814
Northwest[1]	1864	1933	69	229,935	45	573	4,366	74	5,036	19,352	26,886
East	1866	.....	51	860,000	43	403	4,979	52	5,301	9,776	29,995
Chicago[1]	1872	1933	104	602,700	62	509	8,328	91	5,694	13,459	20,530
South	1874	1926	50	159,400	34	99	3,705	56	5,110	5,692	12,010
St. Louis	1879	1925	105	621,185	75	240	9,381	101	10,716	13,604	29,409
West	1886	1926	109	407,970	80	195	7,185	106	8,941	20,900	47,295
North	1886	1924	89	388,600	42	383	5,715	73	6,424	14,658	23,485
California	1889	1927	21	316,300	21	51	1,212	18	1,173	7,157	12,790
Pacific	1905	1928	29	107,940	21	93	1,532	25	1,670	3,485	7,297
Total	.....	.....	761	$4,645,830	517	2,990	60,270	723	67,297	$123,290	$265,511

[1]The Chicago and Northwest German Conferences were merged in 1924 to form the Chicago-Northwest Conference.

VITAL STATISTICS OF GERMAN METHODISM
BY DECADES, 1858=1928

GERMANY[1]

	1927	1920	1908	1898	1888	1878	1868	1858
Parsonages........	115	76	45	35	16	......	1	......
Churches..........	429	324	254	161	72	71	27	2
Value.............								
Baptisms..........	906	811	875	629	410	312	70	1
Sunday Schools.....	882	742	778	649	451	338	148	19
Scholars[3].........	27,946	56,625	50,307	40,932	25,945	17,856	6,966	1,327
Members[4].........	55,199	41,709	34,048	25,068	15,251	11,320	6,344	1,079
Epworth Leagues ...	20,168	16,375	......	......	......	......	......	......

CENTRAL

	1927	1918	1908	1898	1888	1878	1868	1858
Parsonages........	87	91	97	96	82	72	55	43
Churches..........	108	124	151	169	179	181	150	118
Value[2]...........	$2,006	$1,277	$1,128	$1,013	$846	$674	$440	$175
Baptisms..........	623	584	576	747	957	986	1,069	1,057
Sunday Schools.....	104	120	142	153	172	177	150	139
Scholars[3].........	20,026	19,779	13,477	15,037	14,707	13,138	9,617	6,326
Members[4].........	16,756	14,843	14,105	14,994	14,138	12,356	9,891	8,005
Epworth Leagues ...	2,731	3,858	......	......	......	......	......	......
Mission Board[5]......	$43,220	$12,649	$9,330	$7,707	$7,886	$5,828	$5,445	$3,329
Women's Missionary Society..........	$19,085	$6,327	$3,621	$877	$910	$25	......	......
Collections........	$82,980	$46,743	$34,085	$33,511	$23,719	$7,072	$6,157	$1,182
Salaries[2]...........	$166	$97	$85	$78	$69	......	......	......

ST. LOUIS

	1925	1918	1908	1898	1888	1878	1868	1858
Parsonages........	59	72	91	91	81	78	53	24
Churches..........	87	103	142	159	153	174	122	71
Value[2]...........	$1,103	$809	$754	$634	$508	$500	$374	$102
Baptisms..........	388	324	409	517	741	1,169	885	610
Sunday Schools......	82	99	126	152	154	230	137	55
Scholars[3].........	13,116	12,985	9,918	11,696	10,822	12,906	7,272	1,060
Members[4].........	10,487	10,011	11,044	11,700	10,061	11,365	7,729	3,515
Epworth Leagues ...	2,584	2,782	......	......	......	......	......	......
Mission Board[5]......	$18,178	$8,776	$7,762	$5,570	$5,603	$4,945	$3,628	$1,354
Women's Missionary Society..........	$8,803	$3,739	$1,609	$634	$418	$44	......	......
Collections........	$33,194	$29,338	$18,892	$19,972	$12,170	$3,856	$4,495	$721
Salaries[2]...........	$91	$69	$66	$63	$59	......	......	......

EAST

	1925	1918	1908	1898	1888	1878	1868	1858
Parsonages.........	33	42	43	45	35	24	17	3
Churches...........	38	51	61	66	57	41	30	10
Value[2].............	$1,154	$1,035	$1,014	$908	$658	$506	$331	$75
Baptisms..........	196	293	406	745	692	646	427	214
Sunday Schools.....	36	50	62	72	62	49	40	15
Scholars[3]..........	5,335	6,908	6,857	8,975	7,540	5,804	4,261	1,608
Members[4].........	5,059	5,668	5,248	5,541	4,931	4,710	2,805	1,010
Epworth Leagues ...	1,752	2,073	......	......	......	......	......	......
Mission Board[5]......	$15,645	$5,064	$6,996	$6,466	$7,104	$2,755	$1,423	$257
Women's Missionary Society...........	$6,938	$3,061	$2,030	$843	$486	$31	......	......
Collections.........	$44,109	$26,969	$25,859	$28,029	$20,096	$939	$759	$133
Salaries[2]............	$72	$55	$53	$49	$38	......	......	......

CHICAGO

	1927	1918	1908	1898	1888	1878	1868	1858
Parsonages.........	79	60	68	62	59	47	37	25
Churches...........	117	96	114	121	116	101	82	42
Value[2].............	$1,534	$766	$755	$570	$402	$245	$170	$85
Baptisms..........	457	334	428	537	628	608	644	411
Sunday Schools.....	104	81	104	122	119	113	109	59
Scholars[3]..........	11,516	7,957	7,618	9,661	8,500	6,449	5,307	2,475
Members[4].........	12,592	8,818	9,508	9,067	7,613	6,009	4,122	2,777
Epworth Leagues ...	2,596	1,427	......	......	......	......	......	......
Mission Board[5]......	$21,892	$5,451	$6,505	$4,556	$4,073	$3,142	$2,908	$739
Women's Missionary Society...........	$16,518	$3,157	$1,374	$406	$253	$10	......	......
Collections.........	$45,253	$19,734	$17,139	$16,210	$13,297	$5,148	$3,882	$260
Salaries[2]............	$139	$62	$54	$46	$36	......	......	......

NORTHWEST

	1927	1918	1908	1898	1888	1878	1868	1858
Parsonages.........	79	42	44	40	33	47	55	9
Churches...........	117	61	77	73	54	94	117	19
Value[2].............	$1,534	$411	$287	$204	$136	$206	$232	$27
Baptisms..........	457	206	240	308	373	669	885	278
Sunday Schools.....	104	65	77	87	96	143	137	27
Scholars[3]..........	11,516	5,670	4,941	5,408	4,602	6,132	6,960	918
Members[4].........	12,592	4,881	4,764	4,831	4,310	6,301	7,071	1,059
Epworth Leagues ...	2,596	1,385	......	......	......	......	......	......
Mission Board[5]......	$21,892	$7,315	$5,820	$3,271	$2,474	$2,762	$3,757	$361
Women's Missionary Society...........	$16,518	$6,688	$11,850	$691	$332	$112	......	......
Collections.........	$45,253	$9,530	$7,564	$6,100	$4,243	$4,502	$5,232	$154
Salaries[2]............	$139	$51	$31	$23	$18	......	......	......

CALIFORNIA

	1927	1918	1908	1898	1888	1878	1868	1858
Parsonages.........	16	18	19	14	7	4	3	2
Churches..........	17	19	19	19	13	5	4	4
Value[2].............	$426	$373	$329	$122	$119	$73	$20	$18
Baptisms..........	28	46	56	57	98	56	74	34
Sunday Schools.....	16	20	19	18	15	6	6	4
Scholars[3]..........	1,196	1,286	1,131	1,142	1,145	588	504	219
Members[4].........	1,229	1,298	1,172	934	735	333	188	85
Epworth Leagues ...	452	375	......	......	......	......	......	......
Mission Board[5]......	......	$2,077	$1,962	$981	$828	$189	$156	$257
Women's Missionary Society..........	......	$2,343	$1,344	$264	$35	$1.25	......	......
Collections.........	$13,284	$13,231	$3,639	$3,481	$3,019	$107	$82	$34
Salaries[2]...........	$27	$20	$16	$10	$10	......	......	......

SOUTH

	1924	1918	1908	1898	1888	1878
Parsonages......................	31	32	32	29	23	14
Churches.......................	49	50	50	47	35	24
Value[2].........................	$392	$231	$160	$111	$89	$39
Baptisms.......................	237	222	247	234	234	150
Sunday Schools..................	47	52	49	48	41	32
Scholars[3]......................	6,182	5,924	3,346	2,570	1,956	1,378
Members[4]......................	4,698	4,187	3,243	2,596	1,734	1,198
Epworth Leagues................	1,481	1,267	......	......	......	......
Mission Board[5]	$14,817	$3,476	$6,465	$1,784	$1,343	$1,118
Women's Missionary Society........	$2,250	$823	$553	......	$7	$11
Collections.....................	$9,692	$7,470	$4,323	$2,688	$1,671	$322
Salaries[2]......................	$40	$25	$17	$12	$9	......

WEST

	1926	1918	1908	1898	1888
Parsonages.........................	50	78	80	70	51
Churches...........................	61	107	114	112	90
Value[2]............................	$488	$541	$437	$311	$282
Baptisms...........................	251	302	415	478	547
Sunday Schools.....................	61	97	111	131	121
Scholars[3].........................	8,834	10,549	7,722	8,129	6,140
Members[4].........................	6,332	7,710	6,889	6,569	5,485
Epworth Leagues....................	2,147	2,831	......	......	......
Mission Board[5]	$19,337	$11,326	$12,512	$5,012	$3,454
Women's Missionary Society..........	$9,166	$7,678	$3,193	$1,258	$826
Collections.........................	$19,910	$19,451	$11,713	$8,853	$6,499
Salaries[2].........................	$70	$71	$55	$41	$32

NORTH

	1924	1918	1908	1898	1888
Parsonages..........................	27	39	46	49	37
Churches.............................	52	75	97	95	83
Value[2].............................	$408	$479	$420	$416	$265
Baptisms............................	174	253	285	384	388
Sunday Schools......................	46	63	96	109	102
Scholars[3]...........................	5,359	6,967	6,070	6,320	4,870
Members[4]...........................	4,318	5,840	6,234	6,026	4,693
Epworth Leagues....................	621	1,415	....	....	......
Mission Board[5]	$9,956	$4,687	$4,532	$2,422	$2,081
Women's Missionary Society...........	$5,261	$5,734	$3,219	$1,347	$671
Collections.........................	$10,120	$11,643	$8,782	$8,491	$4,850
Salaries[2]...........................	$37	$43	$36	$31	$24

PACIFIC

	1927	1918	1908	1898	1888
Parsonages..........................	17	22	20	15	4
Churches.............................	19	27	24	24	7
Value[2].............................	$106	$156	$119	$69	$20
Baptisms............................	55	44	77	81	16
Sunday Schools......................	17	25	30	24	11
Scholars[3]...........................	1,234	1,799	1,742	969	250
Members[4]...........................	1,256	1,599	1,569	861	220
Epworth Leagues....................	403	482	....	....	......
Mission Board[5]	$3,083	$2,102	$1,901	$859	$197
Women's Missionary Society...........	$1,323	$726	$398	$79	$6
Collections.........................	$3,860	$3,265	$2,454	$1,140	$138
Salaries[2]...........................	$16	$17	$13	$4	$ 1[6]

[1]Germany includes all Conferences in Germany, Switzerland, Austria, and Hungary.

[2]Thousand dollars. Add 000 to each figure.

[3]Scholars includes teachers and officers.

[4]Members includes probationers, full members, and nonresident members.

[5]Mission Board includes the contribution from Church and Sunday Schools for foreign and home missions, together with special missionary offerings.

[6]The statistics in this appendix were compiled by Max Dieterle.

CHAPTER XV

THE LITERATURE AND JOURNALISM OF GERMAN METHODISM

The publication of the *Apologist* was only the first step in the program of German Methodism's development of its journalism. It is more correct to speak of the German publications of the Church as "journalism" than as "literature." The books, like the periodicals, had a message to convey. Whatever form the printed word took, its purpose was to proclaim the good news of "grace more abundant than man's needs."

The Sunday School Bell
(*Die Glocke*)

Seventeen years after the *Apologist* appeared the insistent demand of the German constituency for Sunday-school papers was met with the publication of *The Bell*.[1] The first issue appeared as a monthly in October, 1856, a four-page illustrated sheet for "Sunday School and the World of Youth."

> We do not need to explain to you in the beginning why this paper is called the *Sunday School Bell* [the editor wrote]. The clear pealing of this bell shall summon all German children to Sunday school and to the house of God.[2]

The success of the publication was so great that its schedule became fortnightly and then weekly. As the demand for the German language periodicals increased Nast called Heinrich Liebhart to his office.

Born in Karlsruhe on December 5, 1832, and educated for the teaching profession in the Lyceum in his native city and at the seminary in Blaubeuren, Heinrich Liebhart attended the University of Heidelberg. Migrating to America at the age of twenty-two, he earned his living by the use of the pick, shovel, and wheelbarrow. While he was in Saugerties, New York, he was invited by a girl to attend Sunday school. Visiting church services and prayer meetings, he began to crave the kind of religious experience he heard about in the testimonies of others. He was converted at a Watch Night service which ushered in the year 1855. He united with the Church and began to preach. Liebhart had a systematic mind. Like a seasoned pedagogue, he prepared for every public address as if outlining a lesson plan for a class. The thoroughness with which he organized his materials always made a profound impression upon his audiences. Ordained in the New York Conference in 1857, he served pastorates in Poughkeepsie, Boston, Williamsburg, New York, and Baltimore before he was called to Cincinnati in 1865 to assist Nast in the editorial offices of *The Christian Apologist.* He succeeded Wilhelm Engel, who had become Nast's assistant in 1861.

Liebhart's great career of leadership began, however, when the General Conference of 1872 created a German Sunday School Department and elected Liebhart its secretary. In this capacity he served also as editor of *Home and Hearth* [4] and of German Sunday-school literature. He was perfectly fitted for the position. Under his direction *Home and Hearth* developed into a monthly family magazine which stood in the front ranks of both religious and secular language periodicals. Rudolf Eucken said of it that "no illustrated Christian monthly of its kind is on the German book market." [5] Despite the strenuous editorial duties of getting out the *Home and Hearth,* the *Sunday School Bell,* and the *Bible Student,* he found time to bring out a family library which contributed much to the education of German Methodists. He translated Stevens' *History of Methodism,* and edited books on missions, biblical history, and music. He brought out the first youth hymnal to be published in America with notes [6] and contributed a series of songbooks to the church. [7]

Editorial activity was only a part of his ministry. A leader of Sunday-school work, as he was the editor of its periodicals, he founded the youth society work among the German Churches. As college trustee, leader in his own Conference, delegate to General and Ecumenical Conferences, his experience and energy found the widest service. Yet Liebhart's own life was filled with personal tragedy which ended in his own sad death in 1895. In failing health, he left his family at the breakfast table on January 23, 1895, and started for his office. He did not appear at his desk. On January 25 his eldest daughter received a message from him telegraphed from Montreal, Canada, that he would be home on Saturday evening. Friday morning he boarded an express train in Montreal for Cincinnati. While passing between cars in a heavy snowstorm in the early morning, he lost his balance. He fell from the train and was flung by the howling gale against the cars. He was found dead on the tracks near New Haven, Michigan.

The Bible Student
(Der Bibelforscher)

The growth of the enrollment in German Sunday schools had been so rapid that a language lesson guide was necessary. The answer to demand was the publication of *The Bible Student.* This was a teachable lesson manual, appearing as a quarterly first in 1871 as a 24-page brochure with covers. Liebhart explained the editorial formula in the first issue as follows: (1) by the citation of appropriate Scripture lessons and (2) the giving of colorful and understandable explanations; (3) to raise leading questions; (4) and to answer them by a simple application which shows how the lesson can work upon the heart and conscience. *The Bible Student* never departed from this formula.[8] The lessons were further elaborated in the columns of the *Apologist*. Although the series of studies followed J. H. Vincent's *Berean Lessons,* Liebhart made his own use of the materials with great freedom.[9] This lesson leaf in 1939 was still being published in an edition of 4,200 copies.

Home and Hearth [10]
(Haus und Herd)

The *Apologist* was in its thirty-fourth year of publication when in January, 1873, the second leading periodical of German-speaking Methodism began publication. *Home and Hearth,* a "family magazine for young and old," was issued by The Methodist Book Concern pursuant to authorization of the General Conference of 1872. It appeared as a fifty-six page illustrated monthly, edited to appeal to the whole family circle.

The editor explained his formula by saying that the periodical was to

> publish articles of general interest, biographies, sketches, good travel descriptions and stories, history and natural history reports, as well as a few cultural and instructive articles on biblical, psychological, ethical, or social subjects; and as in the case of other monthly magazines, to be a mirror of the times.[11]

Giving special attention to the departments, "School and Education" (*Schule und Erziehung*), "Sunday School Lessons" (*Sonntägliche Bibellektionen*), and "News of the Day" (*Chronik der Gegenwart*), *Home and Hearth* continued the general lines of its editorial policy of its first issue until the day of its suspension of publication.

During its life the magazine was the mirror of the wide interests and literary charm of two of its editors, Liebhart and August J. Bucher. Liebhart in particular built his personality into the publication. He was a leader in his generation of German Methodists to be compared only with Nast, Adam Miller, Nippert, and the other leaders of the generation which preceded him. Tall, gaunt, and of powerful frame, with a face often compared by German Methodists to Abraham Lincoln, with a high forehead and pronounced nose, Liebhart was a man of imposing appearance and aristocratic bearing. He was a brilliant conversationalist, a powerful pulpiteer, and prolific author. His inquisitive mind approached fields of knowledge with the tastes of the average man and the sensitivity of a skillful editor. Liebhart was assisted in the editorial offices by H. A. Schröter, and his son, H. W. Liebhart. Upon his sudden death *F. L. Nagler* succeeded him until his own untimely fatal illness in 1900. Nagler had called *Friedrich Munz* to his side in 1897 to follow Otto Gilbert, and trained him as his assistant. He assumed the editorship in 1900 and continued in the office until 1912, when he was succeeded by August J. Bucher. *Home and Hearth* was fortunate in having a series of scholarly and efficient editorial assistants: J. J. Hoffmann (1900-01); Friedrich Cramer (1901-4); Albert Cramer (1904-09); and Carl Fritz (1909-19).

Home and Hearth was struck a fatal blow by the World War. In April, 1918, the Book Committee voted to merge the magazine with the *Apologist* in July. Bucher, writing its valedictory, declared:

> The war throws its waves on all shores. Its disturbing influence is felt in few areas so seriously as in the field of publications. A large number of newspapers of all languages have fallen its victim all over our land.[12]

The German language Sunday-school materials increased both in number and circulation. *The Bell,* after five years of publication, became a bi-weekly, and later, in 1887, a weekly. Pictorial cards and teaching aids were published in large volume.[13] A small paper *For Little People,*[14] first published in 1879, died after three years. The five-year life of the *New Bell,*[15] dating from 1882, was another vain effort. The appearance in July, 1897, of the four-page *Little Bell*[16] was more successful. Although a monthly, it was published in as many numbers as the month had Sundays. It contained the Sunday-school lesson, poetry, materials to emphasize the study work, and items of entertainment.[17] The *Little Bell* succumbed, along with other German publications, to the fatal atmosphere of the war in 1918.

Guide to Holiness
(*Wegweiser zur Heiligung*)

The wing of German Methodism which leaned to "holiness" was given a voice when on January 7, 1885, the *Guide to Holiness* appeared under the editorship of *Hermann A. Grentzenberg,* formerly assistant in the *Apologist* office. Ill health had forced him to retire from the active ministry but he edited and published the paper until 1910.

The *Apologist* greeted the 24-page monthly as, for many, "a good and desirable curiosity," and urged preachers to support it by soliciting subscriptions.[18] The theme symbol of the *Guide* was a Cross within a Crown, beneath which the legend was printed: "Without holiness no man will see the Lord."

By the end of the century German Methodist journalism was in its golden age. In 1893 the circulation of the official publications was reaching new heights and were still going up:

	1893	1912
Apologist	20,231	15,876
Home and Hearth	9,150	7,876 [1]
The Bell	29,948	15,000 [2]
Bible Student	44,500	42,000
The Little Bell	....	6,300

[1] Foreign Circulation, 579.
[2] Foreign Circulation, 1,140.

The sales of German literature had become by 1893 an important item in the business of The Methodist Book Concern. In that year the gross income from the *Apologist* amounted to $42,470.34; the *Home and Hearth,* $15,975.31; the *Sunday School Bell,* $9,390.93; and the *Bible Student,* $3,382.82.

The regular publications of German Methodism were supplemented by a series of tracts edited successively by Nast, Liebhart, Nagler, and Munz. The systematic publication of German tracts had begun in 1848, following the organization of the first German Tract Society in the Illinois Conference. The following year the German preachers in the Ohio Conference followed the example of their brethren in Illinois. By the fall of 1849 forty-nine different tracts were being distributed. In 1850, fifty tracts were published for children. By 1900, fifteen thick volumes of leaflets represented the output of the tract material.

Books

The periodical literature developed by German-speaking Methodism was no more important in its influence nor superior in quality than the books which were published as a part of its technique of influencing the human will and heart "to save man's soul for its eternal destiny." In the course of the century in which German Methodism flourished, The Methodist Book Concern published more than three hundred and fifty volumes. The subjects covered a wide range—theology, inspirational sermons, popularizations of science and history, biographies, stories for young and old, and hymnals.

The German books fell into three general classifications. The first was the group of publications dealing with the mechanics of faith and Church doctrinal discussions, ritual translations, discipline, articles of faith, hymnals, and treatises on theology and biblical subjects. The second group was edited to inspire the hearts of converts by sermons, especially those of John Wesley, biographies and experiences of holy living, and stories. The third class of books was a kind of library for adult education.

The sales of German books, manufactured under the supervision of H. C. Dickhaut, in charge of the German department, like the sale of the periodicals, were a substantial item in the income of The Methodist Book Concern at Cincinnati. A few figures taken from the peak years will emphasize the fact.

German Department Sales
Methodist Book Concern, Cincinnati

	Books	Periodicals
1892	$43,434.41	$66,152.87
1898	42,233.39	63,652.46
1906	46,354.19	55,526.07
1911	25,319.71	59,794.43

Of the teaching and worship materials none were more important than the hymnal and the catechism. For four years after Nast began his missionary work in Cincinnati, the people sang without songbooks. In 1839 Nast and Peter Schmucker collaborated in editing a book for worship. Despite the demands of their regular duties, they finished the work within a half year and in the late summer the hymnal was on the market. For a century the compilation continued to furnish the substantial part of subsequent German hymnals. The volume, a book of 451 pages, included 369 songs, selected from both German and American hymnals. Nast chose the words. Schmucker, a good singer and an accomplished musician, wrote and chose the melodies. Both collaborators were agreed on the soundness of the editorial advice of Martin Luther, "Prefer poor words with an arresting melody to splendid words with a flat tune."

The melodies were partial to the English taste, which preferred four lines to six, and livelier songs to the slower chorales. Because the volume was to be used by Germans, however, a sufficient number of songs of longer verse were included. Introducing a new style into German singing, the hymnal was enthusiastically received and widely used. Its publication had been considered as the most pressing necessity after the publication of the *Apologist*. By 1846 it was being published in its third edition. In 1860 the General Conference appointed a committee, headed by Nast and including C. Jost, Rothweiler, Mulfinger, and J. H. Barth, to prepare a new hymnal. The product of their work during the quadrennium was laid before the General Conference in 1864 and appeared in 1865. In the same year the *Zion Singers* [19] was published and included the notes. The third German Methodist hymnal was placed on the market in 1888. Its 792 songs were arranged for the first time so that the words and music appeared on the same page.

The church hymnal was supplemented by a series of songbooks. In 1839 a 40-page pamphlet, including ten songs, appeared to serve the need evident in the conduct of the first German Sunday school in Cincinnati. A standard youth hymnal was not brought out, however, until 1850.[20] It was a compilation, without notes, of 184 songs. Not until 1878 did the edition contain notes.[21] The German hymnal was edited for the last time in 1905 by Munz.[22] The fact that the notes were so belatedly added to the hymnals, according to the German custom, placed special emphasis on a usable memory knowledge of tunes. German Methodists knew their hymns.

Almost as important to the life of the Church were the catechism volumes edited by Nast and first appearing, with the confirmation of the General Conference, in 1868.[23] Nast outlined the principles by which the volumes had been prepared: (1) "faithful representation of the doctrinal consciousness and experimental verities held by the denomination"; (2) "embracing, as an organic whole, all that is essential to the Christian faith"; and (3) designed as "one of the chief means for training the young for an active part in the life of the Church." [24] Nast drew generously upon *The Christian Catechism of Dr. Philip Schaff,* a source which he gratefully acknowledged.[25]

The Germans of the Methodist Episcopal Church were probably its best-trained members. Thorough drill in the catechism was a venerable German tradition. Just as they mastered their songs, so they knew the doctrine of their faith. Nast's catechism ranks as one of the major documents in influence in all the activities of the Church. It began:

1. *What should be your chief concern in this life?*
    To save my soul.
2. *In what does the salvation of your soul consist?*
    In the remission of my sins through Jesus Christ, and being born again, to the end that I might be in union with God in time and eternity.
3. *Where are you taught the way of salvation?*
    In the Bible.[26]

The whole purpose of the catechism was not a mere drill in Methodist doctrine; it was much more to develop attitudes of confidence in God and in his love and grace.

God's providence was stressed in the following words:

62. *Is there, then, any such thing as chance?*
    No, nothing can occur in the world without the knowledge and permission of God.

[The doctrine of God's providence does not for a moment admit of any possible *chance* as entering into the events of our lives. God's wise plans for the well-being of his creatures would otherwise be seriously endangered by so-called accidents. (Example: The lightning which struck Luther's friend at his side; the child, John Wesley, in the burning house of his father, etc.) But while, on the one hand, it is impossible to reconcile mere chance with the belief in Divine Providence, it is by no means to be understood, on the other hand, that the events of our lives are so irrevocably appointed from eternity that God himself is not able to bring about a change, or that there is no room left for the free agency of man. The Bible in its teachings leaves nothing to chance, but places everything under the government of God; yet in such a manner that the freedom of the human will is by no means neutralized. Especial stress should be laid upon the evidence that God not only controls the general destiny of mankind as a whole, but watches over and protects us in the most minute circumstances of our lives. Human short-sightedness may distinguish between events as more or less important, but for God who sees through the course of our lives from beginning to end, there is no such distinction. The most important matters spring frequently from apparently most insignificant causes. Had, for instance, the merchants who carried Joseph into captivity in Egypt come only a little later, Joseph in all probability would have been brought back to his father by Reuben, and all would have been different with the family.]

63. *What application should you make of the fact that God is the Creator, Preserver, and Ruler of the world?*

This, that I, myself, owe my life and all that I enjoy to the special providence of a gracious, All-wise, and Almighty God.

[A lively faith in the first article of the Apostles' Creed, as Dr. Luther has beautifully shown in his catechism, consists in a personal appropriation to ourselves of what God has done for the whole world. It should be the object of the teacher to awaken in the minds of those committed to his care, similar personal reflections. For instance, God is *my* Creator, because I should not have been brought into existence had it not been the particular will of God, that just such a person as I should live. To his goodness I further owe the power I have of seeing, hearing, understanding, and speaking; for had not he bestowed upon me these gifts, I might like many others be deprived of them. For these and all other benefits I ought devoutly to thank God, obey and serve him, remembering that each moment of my life is preserved by his power; that I could not draw a breath, raise an arm, or speak a single word, should he for a moment withdraw his arm.] [27]

Nast's treatment of prayer indelibly impressed upon the mind the reality of the intimate fellowship which man enjoys with God:

300. *What is indispensably necessary on our part in order to enter the way of salvation and continue therein to the end?*

Prayer.

301. *What is prayer?*

The uplifting of the heart and voice to God.

Psalm 29. 14. Let the words of my mouth, and the meditation of my heart, be acceptable in thy sight, O Lord, my strength and my redeemer.

The catechism was nothing if not direct. It ended:

362. *What should we be moved to do in view of that which awaits us in the world to come?*

We should be moved without delay to seek that change of heart without which we cannot see the kingdom of God, and, after having obtained it, to press toward the mark for the prize of the high calling of God in Christ Jesus, bearing with patience the cross and rejoicing in hope of the glory of God.

363. *What, then, is the sum and substance of religion?*

To be in blessed union with God the Father, the Son, and the Holy Spirit, in time and in eternity. [28]

This blessing may God, in his mercy, grant us through Jesus Christ our Lord! Amen.

The hymnals and the catechism books were supplemented by a library of popular literature unduplicated in the history of any other Christian movement. By 1848 the so-called *ABC* books for children were introduced to the market. Between 1849 and 1865 fifty volumes of a "Youth Library"[29] were published, an editorial performance unparalleled in any other Methodist publication program. During the same period the "Library A for Small Children"[30] grew to a shelf of sixty books.

The popularization program received a new impetus when in 1865 Liebhart was called to the editorial offices to assist Nast. His genius for simplification while maintaining scholarly respectability led to the increasing of the "Youth Library" to a hundred volumes. The publication of four picture books, three small "Pocket Libraries" of ten volumes each, and the "Treasure Chest" of twelve volumes performed an educational service of no mean importance in the Christian Americanization of the German homes. The "Columbia Series" of ten books, was developed for older boys and girls. The publishing program was made complete, by bringing out an eighteen-volume "Family Library."

The appearance of Nagler on the Methodist literary scene gave a new direction to the popularization work. A consummate storyteller, he was equally at home and equally interesting whether writing *A Short Theory of Nature, Biographical Sketches From Sacred History, Biographical Portraits From Secular History,* or *The Future of Christ.*

Perhaps the influence of no single popularization was more profound than *George H. Simons' Life Compass for Old and Young.*[31] In homes which could afford it—and it was the ambition of almost every German family to own it—Simons' volume held a place of importance second only to the Bible. By a comprehensive, graphic, and simple exposition of the Christian way of life, it dealt with four major themes:

(1) How one becomes a Christian; (2) how one grows in the Christian faith; (3) how Christianity is revealed; and (4) what dangers the Christian has to avoid.

The influence of the book was due in no small measure to the directness of its illustrations. German Methodists did not quickly forget their impressions of the "Four Fateful Steps—debt (Romans 13. 8); lying (Ephesians 4. 25); stealing (Exodus 20. 15); and murder (Isaiah 59. 7). This course to destruction was pictured as a man forced to descend four labeled steps under the pressure of a great burden. In the distance a gallows threatened its punishment. The whole illustration was given even greater authority by the citation of such verses as: "The wicked borroweth, and payeth not again: but the righteous showeth mercy, and giveth" (Psalms 37. 21); "The wicked worketh a deceitful work; but to him that soweth righteousness shall be a sure reward . . . he that pursueth evil, pursueth it to his own death" (Proverbs 11. 18-25); and "Then when lust hath conceived, it bringeth forth sin: and sin, when it is finished, bringeth forth death" (James 1. 15). The graphic representation of the inner condition of a man who serves sin and lets the devil rule in him was made by a heart enclosing symbolic animals ranging from the peacock to the serpent and representing haughtiness, envy, hate and gluttony, indolence, covetousness, unchastity, and anger. The scriptural authority for the illustration was taken from Matthew 15. 19, "Out of the heart proceed evil thoughts, murders, adulteries, fornications, thefts, false witnesses, blasphemies." Pictures of families, gathered in the home around the family altar, men, women, and children on their knees, and neighbors showing mercy according to the example of the Good Samaritan, together with powerful exhortation to total abstinence and exposition of the tragic effect of the saloon upon the happiness of the family, played their part in building a Christian character which elevated the *mores* and created standards which were so necessary for stabilization of the evolving American culture.

Taken as a whole, the literature of German Methodism was designed for popular consumption. Yet for the more advanced German Methodists, for pastors, local preachers, and students, a considerable number of scholarly works was published. These included, in addition to the technical materials necessary for the conduct of the Church and the rituals, lives and sermons of John Wesley, Nast's commentaries, Church histories, and histories of Methodism, biographies and autobiographies of leaders in the movement, and a number of penetrating theological studies.

The printing press played a vital part in the development of the Mission to the Germans. The emphasis upon reading material—tracts, books, and magazines—was even more pronounced than in the Methodist Episcopal Church's general English language work. If its influence in awakening and sustaining the Christian life must be reckoned as a primary force, the educative power of the Methodist German language press in fitting the immigrant mind and soul into American society must likewise be judged as equally important in secular history.

CHAPTER XVI

THE CHRISTIAN APOLOGIST CELEBRATES ITS CENTENNIAL

The editorship of the *Apologist* was handed down from father to son. After more than a half-century at the desk, Wilhelm Nast at the age of eighty-six laid down his pen. He had reluctantly continued in the office for a number of years. In announcing his retirement in May, 1892, he wrote to the General Conference:

> Dear Fathers and Brethren:
>
> In response to a unanimous request of the German delegates four years ago, I suffered myself to be renominated as Editor of *The Christian Apologist,* and the General Conference did me the great honor of electing me by acclamation. This action was prompted by the generous desire that I might complete the fiftieth anniversary of my editorial service. In retiring from the position I have held so long, I wish to give a brief expression, however inadequate, to my unspeakable gratitude toward Almighty God for his unbounded mercies to me personally during my more than fourscore years, but more especially for that form of vital and experimental religion and branch of his church which found and followed me when in the meshes of German rationalism and the darkness of unbelief, and led me into the glorious light, peace, and liberty of the blessed gospel of Jesus Christ. For nearly sixty years the Methodist Church has gently led me and borne me up in her patient arms, notwithstanding my frequent inner conflicts and imperfections. But I have felt through all these years that she did it not unto me, but unto my German brethren, and for this loving and earnest evangelical care for my fellow countrymen, I thank God through our Lord Jesus Christ daily, and pray that all needed wisdom and grace may be vouch-safed for the future guidance and enlargement of the German work.

Nast had been aided in his editorial work by a happy selection of seasoned pastors and capable journalists. The list of assistant editors of the *Apologist* is a distinguished one. Heinrich Liebhart (1865-72) developed in its office into the brilliant journalist of *Home and Hearth.* He was followed by Hermann Grentzenberg (1872-76), the founder of the little journal, *The Guide to Holiness.* Grentzenberg was succeeded by *Jacob Krehbiel* (1876-90), an industrious scholar of sympathetic character, wide knowledge, and deep conviction. Often representing Nast at meetings of the Book Committee, he knew personally most of the leaders of the Church. Krehbiel was followed by *Christian Golder* (1890-1908). As assistant editor Golder was responsible

235

for instructing Albert Nast in the details of the work, the general features of which he knew so well from his lifetime of close association with Nast's father.

Albert J. Nast was forty-seven when he succeeded his father. Scholarly by family tradition, he was well educated at Wesleyan University. A year's experience in the editorial offices of *The Methodist* in New York had given him an acquaintance with Methodism and Methodist personalities which supplemented the same wide knowledge which he had acquired through his association with his father. Nine years in city pastorates in Cincinnati, Cleveland, Pittsburgh, and Columbus had given him first-hand training in the work of the local church. Five years of college language teaching had given him the feeling of the academic mind. Eight years in Cincinnati as editorial assistant to his father completed his preparation for the sixteen years of his editorship. As unimpressive a public speaker as his father had been before him, he was no less a scholar. Under his direction the editorial policy of the *Apologist* underwent a gradual transformation. The leading articles dealt less with abstract theological questions and points of Methodist doctrine and more with Church actions, personalities, and national questions. He focused his policy upon the consideration of problems of practical life. Under the editorial leadership of Albert Nast the *Apologist* achieved the honor of being the most widely read paper in Methodism in proportion to its field of service. One out of every four members of German-speaking Methodism was a subscriber.

When Golder left the editorial office to found Bethesda Hospital with his sister, Louisa, Nast called to his assistance Frank T. Enderis (1908-18), an experienced pastor and leader among young people who not only devoted himself to the difficult problems of the editorial office but also with his wife contributed so much to the life and leadership of the Salem Church in Newport, Kentucky.

The conditions under which Albert Nast and his capable assistants worked were made more exacting by the outbreak of the World War. The German soul, so it seemed, must be torn between two allegiances. The German Methodists were first of all Americans and only secondarily Germans, yet it was natural that their sympathies should tend to follow the course of events in the Fatherland. The Christian statesmanship of the *Apologist's* editorial policy will remain one of the enduring testimonies to the sanity of German Methodists in the crisis. The position of the *Apologist* was even more difficult because from the beginning *The Western Christian Advocate* threw its entire influence without qualification upon the side of the Allies.

The *Apologist* was more interested in the question of prohibition than in the outbreak of war. In the issue of August 12, 1914, it published before the war news a magnificent article on the "Prohibition Election" in Ohio. War news was treated by a full, lucid, factual account, and on August 19 maps and fuller details were added, which made the record of the war in the pages of the *Apologist* accurate and complete. On August 26, 1914, the *Apologist* wrote:

> It is now useless to ask who bears the chief guilt for this world conflagration. No human power can check the awful human slaughter. The civilization of the world today has suffered a collapse. It had to crash so long as the leading world powers believed in the power of weapons and placed their hopes in them. The commandment, "Thou shalt not kill," is as valid for nations as for individuals.

When the United States entered the war the situation became delicate and obviously strained. In the *Apologist* of April 25, 1917, Bishop Henderson, located in Cincinnati, declared in a proclamation:

> Methodism has always been bound up with patriotism. In the darkest days of the American Republic, Bishop Simpson was the confidential adviser of Abraham Lincoln. Methodism and Americanism have always been synonymous. In this hour of national as well as international crisis, every Methodist preacher will be a patriotic leader and every Methodist congregation a flock of true patriots. While I detest war more than all else save sin, yet I believe that justice is greater than peace.

"America," he said, referring to the German Methodists, "shall have first place in their hearts." As a confession of loyalty and patriotism he asked every church and Sunday school to display the Star-Spangled Banner.

Yet there was no reason to doubt the loyalty of the German Methodists. The editorial policy of the *Apologist* was so sane and so thoughtfully Christian that it was difficult for frenzied leaders to appreciate its stand. On April 25, 1917, the *Apologist* said:

> Our land has not needed for a long time the influence of a sound, vital Christianity as at the present moment. That Christianity cannot be exercised if in this crisis the love of God among the children of God cools. Let us also in this crisis above all follow the course which best serves the cause of peace. For the church of God and above all for the preaching in these times, it will depend in first line upon whether a people heeds the voice of God and recognizes what serves the cause of peace. The church will be grown to such a task only when it fits itself to seek the throne of grace.

Even at this critical time the problems of the war were secondary in the minds of the German Methodists to the fiftieth Jubilee of the "Freedman's Aid Society." In subsequent issues it was more concerned with the progress of the work against *"König Alkohol"* (King Alcohol) and the demand for national prohibition. The progress of the war, editorially, was always secondary to the progress of the

9

Church and the advancement of moral issues. It dealt with the war in graphic, reliable, and factual accounts of events. The *Apologist* took the occasion on Memorial Day, 1917, to say in a leading editorial:

> The god Mars must be dethroned as well as Baal. As Americans we must give ourselves, although separated from the masses, to the realization of this ideal. Humanity must stand above the nation and over all nations must stand the God of nations.

The general suspicion of disloyalty of anything German took definite political form on October 6, 1917, when Congress passed an act which required a true translation of war reports to be filed with the postmaster at Cincinnati. From that time on much of the war news and political comment was given in English. The *Apologist* began publication under Permit No. 442 of the Federal Government. Nast's position was increasingly difficult.

On January 2, 1918, Bishop Nuelsen, who had remained at his post in the war-torn central areas, concerned about not having enough fuel to keep him warm through the winter, wrote,

> I have the firm conviction that God's hand will finally use this mighty world crisis to lead us to a better understanding of his will and our relations to him, that powerful forces may be joined to the demands for the realization of justice and love.

By the spring of 1918 Nast's editorial position had become untenable. His resignation was forced by an unusual incident. Nast had a great faith in human nature and was given to efforts to reclaim all kinds of fallen men. One of the derelicts who won his sympathy was a former Austrian journalist, a member of a titled and wealthy continental family. Nast picked him up in the gutter, took him home, and fathered him. The journalist was a brilliant writer with an apparently precise knowledge of European events. Nast gave him the opportunity of writing for the *Apologist,* with unfortunate results in such a period of tense suspicions.

Nast was seventy-two and had eminently earned retirement. On May 8, 1918, the first issue appeared under his successor, August J. Bucher. Bucher introduced himself in these words:

> "We be brethren!" And the world shall see it and know it! As we stand united under the banner of Jesus Christ, we stand and will stand united under the flag and behind the government of this blessed land of ours, the United States of America.

Nast's voluntary retirement eased the situation. Bucher was Swiss by birth. In the pastorate, as a professor in the theological seminary in Frankfort-on-the-Main, as rector of the Bethesda Institutions in Cincinnati, and as editor of *Home and Hearth* for four years, he was prepared for his new responsibilities. He had not been under attack, and he demonstrated a positive Americanism in his new position.

In the issue of November 13, 1918, which had gone to press before the news of the Armistice was cabled, he wrote in the *Apologist:*

> Not power but nature and right will determine the borders between nations. After the present rulers, who had proven themselves such poor leaders, shall have abdicated, the civilians will secure the rights so long denied them. According to his well-known slogan, the Emperor placed Germany's future "on the seas." It was a bad foundation; the dream was drowned. The German people will be better builders.

The first issue after the signing of the Armistice appeared on November 20, 1918. Beneath the front page picture of a husbandman cradling grain was the caption:

Der Arbeit Frucht (The fruit of labor).

It was a silent testimony to the value of the economy of peace as contrasted with the economy of war. Writing on "Peace," Bucher said:

> Perhaps never before in the history of the world has the magic word "Peace" had such monumental meaning as today. . . . The military power of Germany, the pride of her rulers, the bane of her people, and the terror of the world, is broken. . . . God finally used America, the most unmilitaristic nation of the earth, to free Germany from her unbearable burden and the world from its menace. . . . But the victory that was made possible by us, and what we helped to achieve is accompanied by serious problems and grave duties. May God help us properly to recognize and solve and fulfill them, as they relate to our own nation, and to our fellow victors, and to the conquered.

Bucher's editorship was noticeably different from that of the Nasts. His prose and verse were as eloquent as his preaching and his conversation. His comprehensive knowledge of German art and literature added a grace to the evangelical passion from which he never departed. His sense of humor developed the departments of the paper devoted to entertainment, and the poetry and beauty of the cover illustrations became a weekly experience. The journal's circulation reached its zenith under his leadership, and in a period of dying language publications was generally considered the foremost German religious publication in America.

Bucher was assisted by F. W. Schneider (1918-29), Enderis having left the office with Nast. Schneider was succeeded by A. J. Loeppert (1920-23). Loeppert was followed by Christian Baumann (1923-33), a Swiss scholar who had served successfully in a half dozen city pulpits. He served humbly and effectively as an able second to Bucher until the financial conditions under which the *Apologist* was published forbade the employment of an assistant editor.

From the standpoint of policy, Bucher's problem was conserving the values of German Methodism and soliciting the co-operation of the English-speaking Methodists in the task. His position required tact and vision. The World War, for one thing, had broken the unity among the German Americans. The teaching of German in schools and colleges was dropped and only slowly regained its right to be a part of curriculums. By 1923 the talk of the merger of the German with the English Conferences was gaining substantial support. Immigration, both as a result of the war and of quota restrictions, was curtailed. English had become the common language of most of the German homes, and services in English were being held with increasing emphasis in the German churches. In the administrative circles of the Church there was little enthusiasm for the continuation of the *Apologist*. Its future was determined by the friendship of *George C. Douglass,* the publishing agent at Cincinnati, who with a broad vision of the Church, felt that the publication still had a mission in the difficult days of the inevitable merger of Conferences. "We have him to thank more than any other person for the continuation of the *Apologist,*" the editor wrote. "He alone came to our aid." Douglass and Bucher, supported by Diekmann and a group of loyal German-Methodist laymen, worked untiringly together in the interests of Methodism to keep the *Apologist* in action until its work was really done. The age of its subscribers, the constant inroads of death upon its circulation, and the economic hardships of many sections of the country, necessitated constant retrenchment in editorial and publication costs. Bucher, his faithful assistant, Christian Baumann, and devoted and efficient secretary, Amanda Heitmeyer, accepted these economies and attacked their problems with increasing vigor. By the spring of 1934 the first appeal to the public was made for help in the open letter to the friends of the paper.

Dear Friend of the *Apologist*

As you have already read in the editorial article in the issue of May 23, the *Apologist* stands in direct peril of being discontinued at the end of this year.

Its continuation is simply a problem of money. Our publisher has shown a willingness to go more than halfway. But the publisher can no longer bear the continued deficit of over $5,000 under the present business conditions.

In view of this emergency situation what shall be done?

We have the feeling that a courageous attempt must be made to preserve the life of our valued *Apologist*. It would be disloyalty if we do not do that, for the *Apologist* is the single messenger which brings to thousands of our old German members the Word of God and entertainment and encouragement in the mother tongue. It is a moral obligation to keep such an essential publication alive as can be done.

The following can and ought to happen

If we can raise $2,500 and lose no more readers, the Book Concern proposes the continuation of the *Apologist* until the end of 1935. Before then some better scheme may develop.

How is this sum to be raised?

Everyone who has an interest in this noble and urgent matter and wants to see the *Apologist* live must at once make a pledge to underwrite the above-named sum. Gifts from $1 to $100 will be thankfully received.

Payments can be made at any time up to July 1, 1935. But the underwriting must be reported unconditionally to the editor on June 26. The decision must be made during the next week. Therefore, fill out the enclosed card, and drop it (it needs no postage) as soon as possible in the post box.

Already two promises of $100 each have been received. We hope that the friends of the *Apologist* will heed this notice and lose no time in answering the call. Please do your part at once. The life of our paper depends upon you.

While Douglass extended the deadline of the *Apologist's* fate from November 25 to December 9, 1934, Bucher pleaded with his readers for the fund to enable publication of that monthly edition, which for the sake of economy was to continue the weekly edition *"bei weitem nicht erreicht."* The response to the appeals pledging support for the continuance of the *Apologist,* however, was heartening as well as heartbreaking.

Never before had it been realized what deep affection for the paper existed in the hearts of its subscribers.

One reader from Riga wrote:

Shall this paper, which we cannot get along without, come to an end? What can I do to prevent it? I have nothing left. I sold my engagement ring to help pay the rent of a poor woman. I gave my silver teaspoon to another poor woman to pay her rent. What have I still? Then a voice said to me: "You still have your silver soup spoon which you received as a wedding present." I rejoiced. Yes, the *Apologist* shall have it! I can just as well eat my soup with a tin spoon; it makes no difference to me. When I think that Jesus shed his blood for me so that I could have new life, then I want to give everything which his Kingdom demands. Today my husband will sell it and send the money to you.

A reader from Salem, Oregon, wrote how sixty years before in Kendallville, Indiana, in the coldest winter weather he had walked six miles "to fetch" the *unentbehrlich* (indispensable) paper.

The adjective which most of the readers used to describe their paper was *unentbehrlich.* Most of the letters which came into the editorial office were written in German script and faltering pen.

From Granite City, Illinois, Frau M. E. Fix wrote:

> I am enclosing my birthday dollar to help in the *Apologist* crisis. I am eighty-six years old and feel I just cannot get on without it.

"I read for my blind mother, stone blind for forty years," wrote a daughter from St. Louis. "We did not like to miss our *Apologist*. We have received the *Apologist*, I think, sixty-nine years and can't do without it."

From Plainfield, New Jersey, came this note:

> I am enclosing $5 for the upkeep of the precious *Apologist*. I don't know how I could get along without it. My parents had it in their home when I was only a little girl. Now I am almost eighty. How much it has helped me all these years! . . . I am sending this by air mail so that you will get it in time.

Others wrote:

> Am enclosing a widow's mite to help keep the dear old friend for years to come, which may not mean but a few more for me as I am in my eighty-ninth year.

> Yesterday morning after services [Emmanuel Methodist Episcopal of Newark, N. J.] a widow, member of our church, handed me one dollar for the continuation of the *Apologist*. This dollar means a real sacrifice as Frau Schneider has no means and has to work hard for a living, and it is very difficult for her to obtain work in these times.

From Chicago came a letter with a contribution saying that:

> Mother told us the other day that her parents were readers in 1854 and that my uncle sent his copies to his native *Malterdigen* where my father, then a mere lad (1858) became acquainted with this messenger of the Church.

From New Ulm, Minnesota, came a check for $5 with this note:

> I would like to send you more but my whole family has had bad luck since the failure of the banks. I put some of my money in three different banks and they have all failed. My one daughter at Chicago lost hers in a bank; the one who is a nurse in California put some in a building and loan association and did not get a cent out of it. Eighteen months ago my wife's mother was taken sick and put her money in two banks, which were two I think that failed. I have paid for the paper for how many years I do not know, but it must be more than sixty years. I believe it was in our family before I was born and I am past eighty-three. Excuse my mistakes as I had hardly any school from my eighth year. I had to begin to plan as my father was a cripple.

From London, England, came an English pound note from a regular reader since 1890. From Elgin, Illinois, came a note saying:

> I grew up with the *Apologist* and the evil report of its possible death pains me. I do not know what paper can substitute for it.

There is only one *Apologist*. My sister is a widow who must work with her hands for her little daughter. She wants to subscribe to the *Apologist* for Rev. Fritz Belkner, *Annabert-in-Erzgebirge,* and for Rev. Fritz Mueller, Vegesack *a. der Weser.*

The loyalty of the subscribers was adequate for the crisis. The *Apologist* began the year of 1937 as a monthly, but its editorial policy was not altered by the publication program. Still the paper was fighting a losing battle. While its readers still numbered about ten thousand, its circulation was falling steadily:

December,	1934	4,686
"	1935	4,356
"	1936	4,181
"	1937	4,175
"	1938	4,143

The subscription list had decreased steadily since January 1, 1920, when the circulation was 9,847, the first year that it had been under ten thousand. Subscribers were dropping off at about the rate of three hundred a year. The Book Concern had published the *Apologist* at a loss for years. In 1918 the deficit was $2,117.08; in 1919 it had grown to $5,861.25. By 1932 it had reached the alarming sum of $9,856.57. The deficits between 1928-31 amounted to $34,665.50; and between 1932-35 to $20,917.22. By careful cost accounting and prudent retrenchment planned by Douglass with the co-operation of Bucher, substantial reductions in the deficit were made. By 1933 he had cut it to $5,071.37; by 1934 it stood at $2,478.75.

The strain of the situation had begun to tell on Bucher. On November 9, 1936, the *Apologist* announced that after Christmas the editor would retire as he approached his seventy-fifth year. On December 7, Bucher suffered a breakdown and edited the next issue of the paper from a hospital room. He did not rally from the illness.

Under the pressure of journalistic activity, Bucher had made a definite contribution to German religious literature. The range of his interests and the depth of his writings were apparent when in 1934 a selection from his contributions was published in a single volume.[1] The title theme of the work appeared in a poem summarizing the course of life of a German Methodist.

Meine Vaterländer

Drei Vaterländer nenn' ich dankbar mein;
In jedem trug man meinen Namen ein.
Im ersten einst als Kind zur Welt geboren,
Hab' ich das zweite selber mir erkoren.

Aus Himmelsfernen winkt das dritte mir;
So bin trotz jener ich nur Fremdling hier.
Das erste liegt, umsäumt vom Alpenkranze,
Wie ein Smaragd im Firn—und Gletscherglanze.

Das zweite, reich und ein gewaltig Land,
Dehnt von Alaska sich zum Tropenbrand.
Durch beide ist mein Lebensstrom geflossen;
In beiden habe ich viel Glück genossen.

In beiden auch vergoss ich Trän' und Schweiss
Als Kind, als Jüngling und als Mann und Greis.
Doch keins von ihnen kann mich dauernd halten,
In beiden muss mein Wanderzelt ich falten.

Drum schau aus ihnen ich hinaus, hinaus:
Im dritten nur bin wahraft ich zuhaus.
Es liegt, O Glück, hoch überm Sternenzelt
Fern, ewig fern dem Wechsel dieser Welt.[2]

With literary charm Bucher was able to put into verse the cardinal principles of the German Methodist faith. For example, he wrote:

Mein Glaube

Ich glaube nicht, dieweil ich muss:
Wer wollte mich denn dazu zwingen?

.   .   .   .

Wer zwang den Adler je zum Flug,
Und wer die Nachtigall zum Singen?
Wer peitscht die Schwäne auf den Wanderzug?
Kein äuss'res Muss,—ein inn'res Dringen,
Des Deutung kein Verstand vermag,
Weckt jedes Lied und jeden Flügelschlag.

So ist mein Glaube, ohne Zwang
Mein freies Denken, Fühlen, Wollen,
Ist meinem Ursprung zu ein Drang,
Ein seliges, tief inn'res Sollen.[3]

Scattered through Bucher's editorial columns were such restful thoughts as this:

Gebet um Schlaf

Gib mir nach des Tages Last,
Herr, in süssem Schlaf nun Rast;
Dass ich nicht auf heissem Pfühle
Nutzlos mir den Kopf zerwühle
Ohne Frieden, ohne Ruh—
Vater, drücke mir die Augen zu!

Leg' mir deine Hand aufs Haupt,
Dass mir nichts den Schlummer raubt—
Weden Liebes noch auch Leides—
Dir befehle ich nun beides.
Kurz ist mir die Nacht bemessen.
Gib mir seliges Vergessen.[4]

Bucher's artistry gave a beauty to German Methodist faith in its maturity. It even gave heaven a new beauty.

The older I become [he wrote] the more I see that my short days on earth are not sufficient for all the work which has challenged my energies. I begin to reach out toward the possibilities of work on the "Other Side." . . . I have felt that a heaven without work, at least for me, would be no heaven . . . and I have begun to rejoice in the hope of heaven as a place where I shall work with my transfigured spirit.[5]

By his translation of classic thoughts from other languages into German, Bucher performed a service to literary intercourse among peoples. Perhaps the most distinguished of these translations was that of Edwin Markham's *The Man With the Hoe*. Any linguist taking pleasure in comparative analysis must respond to the German words:

> *Ist das der Mensch, den Gott der Herr einst schuf*
> *Zum hohen Herrscher über Land und Meer,*
> *Zum Sternenforscher, Kräftezähmer—tief*
> *Im Herzen das Gefühl der Ewigkeit?*
> *Ist dies das Bild, das dem einst vorgeschwebt,*
> *Der Sonnen, Monden rief, sie weislich lenkt?*
> *Nein . . .* [6]

Bucher could turn his artistic mind as well to stinging political irony. No better example of this is available than his verse *"Die Friedensstifter von 1919,"*[7] a lengthy poem ending with these two stanzas:

> *Die Ernte reift. Vor ihrem Tag*
> *Mag wohl die bange Welt erzittern.*
> *Schon naht er, und zückt Schlag um Schlag*
> *Der Blitz aus Gottes Zorngewittern.*
>
> *Ein hassgeborner Friedenspakt*
> *Kann nichts, als Hass und Krieg gebären,*
> *Ist mit der Hölle ein Kontrakt;*
> *Auch der von Versailles wird das lehren!* [8]

The General Conference of 1932 had abolished the *Apologist* editorship as a four-year tenure. The editor was elected by the Book Committee "to serve for such period of time as the Book Committee shall continue the publication." [9] Bucher's retirement left the office vacant, to be filled by younger men. Diekmann, foreseeing the situation, had introduced a resolution before the General Conference of 1936, asking that the *Apologist* might be kept alive to observe its centennial, a very rare event, even in the field of secular journalism. He wrote:

> Its continuation under the direction of the Book Committee is of great, even vital importance to a large part of our work. . . . Of the ten German-speaking Conferences, nine recently have been merged with English Conferences. Many tender ties have been strained, that, for awhile, will need careful nursing; educational and benevolent institutions have lost overnight . . . long-time loyal and liberal constituencies, so that they find their future seriously threatened.
> In two years the *Apologist* will celebrate its hundredth anniversary of loyal and royal Kingdom work.[10]

Bucher's work was taken over without salary by Diekmann, superintendent of Bethesda Institutions, and A. J. Loeppert, pastor of Fowler-Clifton Church, in Chicago, Illinois. Frau Heitmeyer had borne a large part of the editorial burden during Bucher's last years, and under the new organization performed a great service. The continuation of the *Apologist* to celebrate its hundredth anniversary of publication became to Diekmann a prime necessity for the preservation of the German constituency of the Church and the maintenance of a necessary loyalty in support of German Methodist institutions. With his assumption of the editorial duties with the issue of January 13, 1937, Volume 99, Diekmann became the acknowledged leader of the thinning group of German Methodists concerned with the preservation of the German tradition of the Church. His long years in the pastorate and his successful leadership of the Bethesda Institutions had given him the wide experience and contacts necessary for the kind of leadership he was now called upon to perform. His conversational prose, like his popular preaching, was fitted for the occasion. Despite his administrative duties, which taxed his energies to the maximum, he never considered himself anything but a "German Methodist preacher." Constantly preaching, in summers going from camp meeting to camp meeting, he symbolized the forces trying to conserve the German Methodist heritage.

This fact was not alone evidenced by his determination that the *Apologist* should live and serve a hundred years.[11]   It was also demonstrated in his personal interest in the improvement of the Museum of German Methodism which Golder had founded. Housed in adequate quarters in Bethesda Institutions, staffed at the expense of Bethesda by competent attendants, it includes all publications, books, minutes, records, journals, letters, hymnals, pictures, and historical objects which diligent search can discover.

The *Apologist* did live a hundred years. The first issue in 1939 featured the centennial, as it entered its second century. The publication was directed by a committee composed of Bishop Nuelsen, Douglass, Enderis, J. C. Marting, Alfred K. Nippert, Wilhelm Weiler, E. Edelmaier, Loeppert, and Diekmann. The editors called attention to the fact that subscribers were dying at the rate of about four hundred a year, but declared their determination to produce a paper satisfactory to the best editorial standards of Nast and Bucher for as long a period as the German constituency of Methodism might demand.

CHAPTER XVII

METHODISM IN CENTRAL EUROPE

When the World War was over and in peace churchmen were able to survey the situation around the globe, they became aware of a fact of deep implication. The international organic unity of Methodism was cracking everywhere under the strain of nationalism. No one knew this better than Bishop Nuelsen, whose ecclesiastical statesmanship was again called upon to deal with perhaps the greatest crisis of Christianity during his long career.

In 1933 Germany reeled through a National Socialist Revolution into the Third Reich. During the nervous early days after the NSDAP, the Party of Adolf Hitler, absorbed the State, the Methodists maintained a status of co-operative understanding with the new leaders. At the time of the event Methodism in the Reich was organized into five Annual Conferences recognized in nine different States as nine separate legal corporations. Under the political circumstances it seemed advisable to amalgamate these into one national corporation recognized by the government in Berlin according to German law. Despite the confusion of the summer and fall the Methodists in the Third Reich remained loyal to the Methodist Episcopal Church. As assurance of freedom was given and in good faith carried out by the Government, each one of the five Annual Conferences voted in favor of remaining in organic union with the parent movement. The South German Conference embodied the thought in a resolution:

> WHEREAS, We are guided by the sincere desire to remain in the future in connection with the Methodist Episcopal Church, we petition the General Conference to appoint representatives who, in collaboration with ours, shall find a way in which this connection may be maintained, duly considering the peculiar conditions now prevailing in Germany.

The resolution subsequently adopted by the Central Germany Conference differed only in the last words, "which will allow the Methodist Church in Germany to remain in connection with the Mother Church, while at the same time meeting the requirements of the German law." That not a single speech was made in any of the Conferences by ministers or laymen in favor of separation was a testimony to the common loyalty of Methodists reaching beyond national borders and towering above political chaos. With characteristic tact, Bishop Nuelsen admonished Methodist brethren in England and the United

States, who were inclined to be critical of what they believed to be too intimate a friendship between the Methodists in Germany and the National Socialist State, to "have patience" and refrain from hasty comments. Only time and experience could dictate the course of wisdom.

The General Conference of 1936, taking cognizance of the situation, passed an enabling act authorizing the five Conferences to organize a Central Conference of Germany and to elect a bishop pursuant to the provisions of the Discipline. Summoned into session in September, 1936, in Frankfurt-am-Main, the Central Conference was organized and on the first ballot almost unanimously elected F. H. Otto Melle, president of the Theological Seminary in Frankfurt, its bishop. He was consecrated by Bishop Nuelsen and Bishop R. J. Wade, of the Stockholm Area, with the assistance of F. W. Lofthouse, of Birmingham, England, a former president of the Methodist Church in Great Britain, whom the English Conference had sent as official pastoral delegate to the installation ceremony. The episcopal residence of the newly elected bishop was quite properly fixed at Berlin. The Central Conference included the former Annual Conferences of *Central Germany,* which organized the work in Saxony and Thuringia, the province of Silesia, and Halle and Dessau; the *Northeast Germany,* comprising the work extending to the eastern boundary of the Reich; the *Northwest Germany,* comprising the work extending to the western boundary of the Reich; the *South Germany,* comprehending the work within the geographical boundaries of Bavaria except the Palatinate and Württemberg; and the *Southwest Germany,* covering an area running south of Lippe from Wesel to Hamm, east to Marburg and Pforzheim to Lahr, and west to the boundary of the Reich.

The enabling act under which the Central Conference was organized provided also that upon its organization the Central Conference of Middle Europe, to which the five Germany Conferences had belonged, should be dissolved and cease to exist. (*Discipline,* Paragraph 1379). The organization of the Central Conference removed from the jurisdiction of Bishop Nuelsen, located at Geneva, Switzerland, the greater part of Continental Methodism. When he turned over his work in Germany to Bishop Melle, the Conferences remaining in his charge were the *Austria Mission Conference,* the *Bulgaria Mission Conference,* the *Hungary Mission Conference, Italy,* the *Jugoslavia Mission Conference,* and *Switzerland.* The result of the reorganization of the administrative structure in Europe was to leave the Annual and Mission Conferences of the Geneva Area without connection with any Central Conference. Of these the Austrian Mission Conference and the Switzerland Annual Conference are German-speaking Conferences; while the Hungary and Jugoslavia Mission Conferences are predominantly German-speaking. Only the work in the Italy Annual Conference and the Bulgaria Mission Conference is

BISHOP F. H. OTTO MELLE

Elected Bishop of the Central Germany Conference
in September, 1936

carried on in the Italian and Bulgarian languages respectively without a bilingualism which includes German.

The organization of the Central Conferences was an administrative concession to the rising tide of Nationalism. Political and social developments in China and India led to the creation of this new wheel in the ecclesiastical machinery of Methodism. The Central Conference was designed as a result of the effort to give as large an area as possible to the national indigenous churches and yet to maintain an ecclesiastical unity. In Mexico and Japan this system did not prove itself to be workable because governmental restrictions and demands interfered with the proper establishment of Central Conferences. As a result it was necessary in those two countries to organize the Methodist work into independent bodies, only loosely federated with the parent Church. Whether the organic relation of the Central Conference of Germany to the Methodist Church as an integral part will continue depends upon the attitude of the Reich Government toward Free Church organizations and their international connections. Political events have greatly influenced Methodism's administrative system.

The program of the Third Reich for a "Greater Germany" began to be realized when on March 13, 1938, Germany absorbed Austria. The union of the two German-speaking nations of Central Europe was welcomed by Methodists in both states. Protestants in Austria had never represented five per cent of the population. The politics of the *Fatherland Front* under the Catholic national leaders, Dr. Schuschnigg and Dr. Dollfuss, had pressed heavily and intolerantly upon the religious minorities. The hope of a greater degree of religious freedom under a government at war with the Roman Catholic Church and favoring the Free Church movement appealed to Austrian Methodists.

The merger of the political states of Germany and Austria necessitated changes in Methodist organization. Bishop Nuelsen promptly transferred the five pastors of the Austria Mission Conference to the South Germany Conference under the jurisdiction of Bishop Melle and left the pulpits to be filled by Bishop Melle. On April 21, 1938, the Board of Foreign Missions announced the official dissolution of the Mission Conference.

In the process of reorganization Bishop Nuelsen turned over to Bishop Melle a revolving fund of a quarter million marks, the remainder of an account which he had personally effectively administered for the welfare of the ministers and churches under his supervision.

The establishment of the Central Conference in Germany and Austria seemed an inevitable post-war development. The General Conference of 1924 extended the powers of the European Central Conferences so that they were something more than Church conventions making the Continental churches "only colonies of the American

Church." When Bishop Nuelsen called the Central Conference of Middle Europe to order in Freudenstadt on October 7, 1925, eight Annual Missions and Conferences of Austria, Bulgaria, Hungary, Jugoslavia, North Germany, Russia, South Germany, and Switzerland were represented. The effect of the Conference was to co-ordinate the work on the Continent and to develop a sense of Methodist fellowship and unity among the varied racial and language groups.

On September 23, 1930, the second session of the Central Conference of Middle Europe was held. The General Conference of 1928 had made some changes in the structure of the Conference. It had joined the Russian work with the Stockholm Area, and put Jugoslavia and Bulgaria in the Paris Area. After this redivision of the Continental work the two Conferences in Germany were divided into five Conferences. The arrangement was such that, despite their common language and cultural unity, the Germans were brought more and more into an administrative unity.

The third session of the Central Conference met in Freudenstadt on September 22, 1935. Bishop Nuelsen discussed the situation of the five Conferences in Germany with their 286 preachers and 43,283 members as the dominant part of the Central Conference, the rest of which was composed of 104 preachers and 14,801 members. He discussed the reasonableness of the Germans in demanding of the General Conference of 1936 their own Central Conference and the right to elect their own bishop. Analyzing the legal situation under the National Socialist Government, the bishop told the Conference that from the standpoint of German public law the organization of the Methodist Episcopal Church in Germany was already an accomplished fact. From the standpoint of church law, the General Conference still had to take action. The General Conference did take such action.

On September 17, 1936, Bishop Nuelsen called the first Central Conference of Germany to order. "No longer," he declared, "can the Methodist Church in Germany be called an 'alien plant,' a colony of a foreign organization. The Methodist Episcopal Church in Germany is from now on exclusively under German leadership. German Methodists can now look their racial comrades in the eye and say, 'Methodism is German.'" Having arrived at ecclesiastical maturity, the Methodist Episcopal Church of Germany continued its work as before under the episcopal leadership of Bishop Melle.

Tent Mission Work

Methodism in Germany celebrated the anniversary of John Wesley's Aldersgate experience by a renewed emphasis on evangelism. From the beginning Methodists had held revivals in dance halls, chapels, farmhouses, and private rooms. After the World War the preaching was carried to busy centers of urban life by two tent missions. A generous contribution toward the purchase of the first canvas was given by John Schaum, a clergyman of Eustis, Nebraska. The Methodist tents are pitched for five months during the summer in market places, gardens, fields, and even cemeteries. Handbill invitations by the tens of thousands are passed out and all forms of billboard advertising are utilized. The tent missionaries face any emergency. In 1932 a Communist invited the tent to an industrial center to debate the subject "Christ and Communism." The Communists took care of the publicity and crowded the tent. A former member of the Communist Party told of his Christian conversion. This was matched by a party leader who was hostile to Christianity. The meeting, earnestly facing facts, turned into a revival service.

Temperance Work

The fight against alcohol began with the appearance of the Methodist Mission in Germany. Although the first temperance societies in the Reich were organized in 1831 under British and American influence, the first total-abstinence societies were established in 1877 in Lausanne, Switzerland, by *W. Cornforth,* and in Strassburg, Germany, by *Ernst Gebhardt.* In 1882 Gebhardt founded the *Temperance Friend,* the first total-abstinence periodical in the German language. Since 1924 it has been edited by Melle. Methodism also publishes *The Christian Abstinent.*[1]

One of the most important events in the history of the anti-alcoholic movement in Germany was the campaign for local option in 1926. Under the direction of the National Committee for Local Option, headed by Melle, all the German temperance societies combined to promote the common program. One of the results of the work was a petition signed by two and a half million persons. Melle headed a delegation which delivered these names, bound into two hundred volumes of ten thousand signatures each, to the Reichstag in Berlin.

Germany, in the meantime, assisted the temperance organizations in Austria, which at one time polled a prohibition vote of 120,000. Methodists in 1930 had twenty thousand abstainers enrolled in eighteen organizations. It is estimated that they have distributed about a half a million pages of tracts on temperance. In Germany more than two hundred thousand pledges for total abstinence have been taken.

The Methodists have become enthusiastic over the stand of Chancellor Hitler on tobacco and alcohol.[2] The National Socialists founded a *National Association Against Intoxicating Poisons,* which combines most of the temperance societies and has local branches in even the smallest parishes. The thirty temperance secretaries working under the direction of the Methodist Conferences found a congenial association in the moral reform wing of the National Socialist Party. Methodist influence in temperance work has been one of its most important contributions to social welfare.

Youth Work

Methodism in Germany found favor with youth from the beginning of the mission. The reorganization necessitated by the victories of the Third Reich caused the Methodists to restate their youth program. The provisions of the agreement were that the Church recognize: (1) the totalitarian political educational ideal of the National Socialist State and acknowledge the Hitler Youth as the custodian of that ideal; (2) that no boy or girl under eighteen belong to a church youth society unless first a member of the Hitler Youth; (3) that out door sports, gymnastics, and political education be confined solely to the Hitler Youth; (4) that the members of church youth societies wear the service uniform of the Hitler Youth; and (5) that two afternoons a week and two Sundays a month would be reserved for church youth activities. These regulations, explicitly enforced, were serious matters for the church societies to deal with.

Methodist youth societies, like all other similar organizations, dissolved. The work was continued without constitutional form in the following way: the pastor, held responsible for the program of his youth, appointed a leader who was again responsible to him and to the Quarterly Conference. Since the new program was introduced, most Churches have held weekly youth meetings, concerned of necessity with Bible studies, prayers, and testimonies of religious experiences. The *Council of Work With Young People of the Methodist Church,* meeting in Frankfurt on February 8, 1934, assented to the government's program. *The Guiding Star (Der Leitstern),* a twenty-four-page monthly Methodist youth magazine, perhaps better edited and more constructive in its editorial policy than any Methodist periodical of similar type in the United States, continued to exercise an important influence in the new situation. Working no longer as a society but as young people of the local church (*Gemeindejugend*), youth performs a substantial service in the local parishes. Deprived of those vigorous social and physical activities characteristic of youth organizations and limited to a circumscribed sphere of spiritual discussion, the Methodist Youth Societies have gained a deeper spiritual insight and a more vital appreciation of their major and common interests.

Political events, however, had little effect upon the Sunday schools. In 1938, 2,402 teachers were instructing 26,339 scholars in 582 Sunday schools.

Homes for the Aged

Methodists in Germany have been fortunate in the development of their institutions for the aged. Stimulated by a gift of five thousand marks, preachers of South Germany met under the leadership of *W. Kleinknecht* in 1902 to organize a society to develop a Home for the Aged. In August, 1903, the work was begun in a rented house. Solicitation of funds and careful selection of paying guests enabled the society to open *Home Nagold*. A new building was dedicated on June 12, 1905. The sale of the property in 1921 to a children's aid association enabled the development of a new institution in *Schwarzenberg bei Liebenzell*. In the new location, surrounded by beautiful forests, the home expanded to a value of 150,000 marks.

The Home for the Aged in Northern Germany developed later. In 1922 Bishop Nuelsen returned to Germany with fifteen thousand marks for the founding of an institution. A fortunate sale of the institution in Bansin to the Children's Aid Society enabled in 1924 the purchase of an estate, *Schwarzenhof*, near Rudolstadt. The Home opened in the spring of 1925, but was burdened with a debt of a hundred thousand marks, which was systematically and successfully liquidated. These institutions, in addition to the rest homes, *Kurhäuser*, and children's homes, give to Methodism in Germany a substantial position. With 1,196 deaconesses carrying on their own ministry of mercy, the work of the Church has a broad and effective scope.

German-Speaking Methodism in Other European Countries

The numerical and financial strength of German-speaking Methodism was of course in Germany. It is obvious therefore that the organization of the Annual Conferences of Germany into a separate Central Conference created a difficult situation for the work and institutions of German Methodism in the countries outside Germany. The only self-supporting Conference beyond the Reich is the Switzerland Conference, the Mission Conferences in Austria, Hungary, and Jugoslavia being dependent upon outside financial assistance. Difficulties in the European work became acute because the Churches in Germany for many years had liberally supported the wider European interests by their missionary collections. As economic conditions in Germany became severe and the National Socialist Revolution established new standards of international relationships, the gifts from the German Churches were completely terminated by decrees of the Reich Government, which prohibited funds or collections from being sent out of the country. This was not the only factor. A number of Swiss Methodists, upon solicitation, had loaned considerable amounts of money to churches and institutions in Germany, Austria, and Hungary for the acquisition of property. With the establishment of the National

Socialist regime, these investments were "frozen" inasmuch as payment of interest and the repayment of the principal of the debt were prohibited by the German authorities. These "frozen" loans totaled about $110,000. More than $50,000 of this amount was loaned by the Swiss Bethany Deaconess Institution to the Methodist Deaconess Institutions in Germany. When the loans were made there was a reasonable expectation that they could be repaid within ten years; but when the annual appropriation of the Board of Foreign Missions was cut down from $20,000 to $2,000, and when neither a missionary collection nor a repayment on the loans could be made from Germany, the financial situation became serious.

The Methodist work in Austria and Hungary, however, did not suffer because valuable properties had been acquired, the income from which remained in those countries and was used for the maintenance of the work, virtually at the expense of the Swiss Methodists. The work in Jugoslavia, on the other hand, would have had to have been given up if the Swiss Methodists had not come forward and in a superb manifestation of missionary devotion accepted the challenge. The Swiss Missionary Society assumed the support of the work in Jugoslavia. When the Swiss creditors relinquished one-third of their claims, the Conference, with the help of Bishop Nuelsen, took over the remaining two-thirds of the debt and repaid those creditors who had advanced their savings in good faith, but were now in need of money as a result of the financial depression. This action of the Swiss Conference is unparalleled in the annals of Methodism and deserves the unstinted praise of churchmen around the world.

The behavior of the Swiss Methodists in this emergency situation is a testimony to the quality of their faith. Swiss Methodism is virile, evangelistic, progressive, and self-sacrificing. Undaunted by political unrest and economic uncertainty, the 16,000 Swiss Methodists continue to proclaim the gospel in 284 towns and villages, partly in their own buildings, partly in rented halls, or in private residences. Led by 90 preachers, assisted by 151 local preachers and exhorters and 348 class leaders, the work is carried on. In the 265 Sunday schools nearly 17,000 scholars are enrolled. They are instructed by 1,115 teachers. In 1939 the boys and girls enrolled in catechism classes numbered 1,186. The Swiss Woman's Missionary Society supports three women missionaries in China in co-operation with the Woman's Foreign Society in America, one in Pingyang, one in Malacca, and one in Macedonia. In addition to this, the Swiss contribute toward the support of two Swiss missionaries sent out by the Board of Foreign Missions.

The work of the *Bethanien Verein* of Swiss Deaconesses, discussed in a previous chapter, performs a recognized ministry of healing and social service, while the Methodist Publishing House in Zürich brings out a high quality of Christian literature, and under the leadership of Ferdinand Sigg in 1939 was becoming a financially sound institution. The Swiss Methodists own and operate a Home for the Aged at Horgen, known as *Tabeaheim,* established in 1913. In 1930 a Home for Aged Men was opened at Eschlikon. A Home for Young People, Victoria, is located at Hasleberg in the beautiful mountains above Bern. Here in the summer vacation Bible schools are conducted and leaders' training courses held. In winter skiing and other winter sports are sponsored. Hundreds of young Swiss Methodists spend their vacations in the invigorating atmosphere of Methodist vacation camps.

By their church life and their social ministry the Swiss Methodists have won a recognized place in the religious and community life of the Nation. The Methodist Church is the only Free Church which has been admitted to membership in the Swiss Church Federation. In the performance of their mission they co-operate with the national agencies, especially in their temperance efforts. Following the example of John Wesley, the Swiss have collected funds to assist members in temporary economic needs, and since 1919 have applied more than $50,000 to this purpose.

In Hungary Bishop Nuelsen led the movement for the development of a Children's Home which was located at Budakeszi, a suburb of Budapest. This developed into a sanatorium for tubercular patients. A part of the premises are devoted to the care of subnormal and epileptic children. The work is carried on by German-speaking deaconesses, the children's department being subsidized by the government.

The Jugoslavia Mission Conference is, like the Jugoslavian state itself, a composite affair. In the north the German provinces of Banat and Batschka were taken from Hungary after the war and incorporated into the new kingdom of Jugoslavia. On the south the same disposition was made of the larger part of the Bulgarian province of Macedonia. The result was that six Protestant societies, formerly affiliated with the Congregational Church in Bulgaria, were torn from their previous connection. At the request of the American Board the Methodist Church agreed to shepherd them and they were integrated into the Mission Conference of Jugoslavia. This little Conference, in addition to the German-speaking congregations in the north, includes the Serbian-speaking churches in the south. During the postwar period of reconstruction the Board of Foreign Missions acquired a valuable property in Novi-Sad, one of the principal cities in the German section, and established a school. When the government, by the promulgation of a new educational policy, took charge of all educational institutions, the school had to be given up. It was transformed into a hospital and sanatorium in charge of German-speaking deaconesses supported by the Swiss Deaconess Association.

The Methodist Church in Europe, by its devotion to the Free

Church idea and by its magnificent performance in the field of social service and the ministry of healing, carries on an important work despite political difficulty and economic uncertainty. The Methodist program in Central Europe may well be summarized in the words of Georg Neumark's hymn which begins, *Wer nur den lieben Gott lässt walten,* and ends,

> *Wer Gott dem Allerhöchsten traut,*
> *Der hat auf keinen Sand gebaut.*[3]

CHAPTER XVIII

GERMAN METHODISTS

What have been the human products of German-speaking Methodism? The question is a valid one. Methodism did affect attitudes, direct ambitions in channels of human service, and produce a kind of character peculiar to itself.

This biographical note appears in *International Who's Who:*

> Spoerri, Theophil, Ph.D.; Swiss literary historian; b 90, Professor of French and Italian Languages and Literature, Zürich Univ. Publs. Präludium zur Poesie 30, Französische Metrik 30, Die Götter des Abendlandes 32. Zürich 7, Haselweg 1.[1]

The influence of Methodism on the Continent is in no case more apparent than in the brilliant writings of the Swiss literary historian, Theophil Spoerri, professor of romance languages in the University of Zürich.[2] Pursuing the thesis of the Crocian school of aesthetics, Spoerri holds that art in its essence is lyric.[3] Analyzing poetry as a phase of art, Spoerri holds that in the area of human life, poetry is the purest voice which in memory calls a lost world into harmony with the divine.[4] He sees our age as suffering from the creation of idols, the result of the secularization of God and the deification of the world, of the humanization of God and the deification of man. The growth of this paganism begins when man severs his connection with the divine.[5] Spoerri sees in life what he sees in the art of poetry. Confusion results when man willfully separates himself from God.

Man's life, too, is confused until man establishes his connection with the sustaining center of existence. Here is the point where Spoerri's theory of aesthetics reaches out into life and summons man himself into harmony with the divine. He speaks quite openly of sin, the "something between," the *"etwas dazwischen,"* the "wall between me and God." "Sin is the separation of man and God." "Sin means that man stands in his own light." The solution of sin is reconciliation with God, *"Versöhnung mit Gott."* Christ has broken through the sin of the world. At this point the light of God shines again in our darkness.

> *Welt ging verloren,*
> *Christ ist geboren,*
> *Freue, freue dich, O Christenheit.*[6]

In his most recent volume, which he considers brings to sharpest focus the substance of his own thought, Spoerri sees life as seeking form and declares that the decisive adventure of every man is to "find his form." [7]

What Spoerri has discovered as the fundamentals of aesthetics by his brilliant philosophical researches into the meaning of literature, he has discovered in his heart as the experience of an humble German Methodist. When in the afternoons he comes out of the university building on its high hill and looks off to the snow-capped peaks lighted by the reddening sinking sun above the city of Zürich, Methodism's Swiss capital, he praises the God whom Wesley and Nast have praised before him, the "sustaining center of existence."

> Why am I a Methodist? Because here I have found a vital community [answers Professor Spoerri].[8] The fellowship can be compared to a great family. . . . Men have things to do with other men. One person is concerned about other people. One knows something of others. Sickness and death, weddings and births are a common experience. Each individual participates in the common life. Acceptance into the fellowship demands a conscious act from him as well as from the group which accepts him. In all kinds of offices and effective relationship one is active. The individual knows that he is not alone. So people come closer together. One says "Brother" and "Sister." . . . All the common experience stands in the light of the gospel. The everyday world reaches into the great lines of the history of salvation. And vice versa: the Word which is proclaimed from the pulpit receives a weight and greater reality when it is not for individuals alone but for individuals in a fellowship. The individual hearer must be in earnest. He must not keep the Word within himself but make it visible in the fellowship. . . . How differently "Our Father" sounds when I say it together with the other sons and daughters of the Father, now really "Our" Father, not just "My Father."

> How is the enormous influences emanating from Wesley to be explained? Not through the special contents of his theory, but because of the special emphasis which he gave it. He showed how man can take the Word in earnest. . . . When I see my brothers and sisters, living in the pressure of the everyday world, in the factory, behind the counters of the stores, tempted among agnostic comrades being earnest with the Word, simple men with tired faces and hard hands which ring with the whole strength of their souls for salvation for a change of the heart— then I see the seriousness of everyday life against the earnestness of the Word; then I learn what it means to be in earnest. I know that there are vital fellowships and serious Christians. Because I found this life and this earnestness among the Methodists, I remain thankful and by conviction with the Methodists and pray to God that he may preserve our Church in earnestness and in bondage to the Word which became flesh.

In Education [9]

The service of scholars of the German branch of the Church to the cause of education was especially broad because the Germans spoke two languages fluently. The German preachers, with few exceptions, were college men with seminary training. They were students of the Bible and many were versed in French, Greek, Latin, and Hebrew, as well as in English and German. More than the average number were acceptable, if not always accomplished, musicians.

Mark Twain, who attended Methodist services in Hartford, Connecticut, with his daughters so that they would not forget their foreign languages, observed, so the story goes, that the preachers spoke German in such a manner as to make their preaching an aid to a liberal education.

The deference to scholarship in German Methodism was never a substitute for evangelical enthusiasm. Both went hand in hand. As a result of this attitude the Germans contributed a large contingent to the teaching ranks. Few Methodist colleges did not benefit by the contribution.[10]

German Methodists served as deans of some institutions. Homer Albers, graduating from Central Wesleyan College in 1882, became dean of Boston University Law School in 1912, after having declined an appointment as judge of the Massachusetts Superior Court. Henry H. Meyer, graduating from Baldwin-Wallace College in 1900, was elected dean of the School of Religious Education and Social Service in Boston University in 1929, having previously served fifteen years as the distinguished editor of Church School Publications of the Methodist Episcopal Church. William Frederic Hauhart, taking his doctor of philosophy degree from Columbia University in 1909, became director of the School of Commerce of Southern Methodist University in 1921. Karl Stolz, graduating from Baldwin-Wallace in 1907, was appointed dean of the School of Religious Education in the Hartford Seminary Foundation in 1927. Otto E. Kriege, who served as professor and then president of Central Wesleyan College between 1899 and 1925, became president of New Orleans University in 1925.

Some of the leading professors of the passing generation came from German Methodist homes. Edward L. Schaub, beginning his studies at Charles City College, became professor of philosophy in Northwestern University in 1913. Editing *Imanuel Kant, 1724-1924,* translating Wundt's *Elements of Folk Psychology,* and editing, since 1926, *The Monist,* he has been recognized as a philosopher of the first rank. Henry F. Nachtrieb made the department of zoology in the University of Minnesota an important academic discipline. William A. Heidel, graduating from Central Wesleyan College in 1888, became professor of Greek in Wesleyan University in 1905, and research associate of the American Council of Learned Societies and the Carnegie Institution of Washington in 1928. As associate editor of *Classical Philology* and member of the managing committee of the American School of Classical Studies at Athens and as editor of a series of brilliant monographs on Greek life and literature, he was easily for a generation one of America's foremost scholars.   John T. Buchholz, graduating from Iowa Wesleyan College in 1909, was elected head of the department of botany in the University of Arkansas in 1919 and in the University of Texas in 1926, going to the University of Illinois in 1929.   Thomas Nixon Carver, the internationally famous Harvard University economist, who became professor of political economy in 1902, found time, despite his fundamental contributions to the theory of distribution, to write volumes on *The Religion Worth Having, Essays in Social Justice, The Conservation of Human Resources,* and *Government Control of the Liquor Business in Great Britain and the United States.*   John F. L. Raschen, coming to the United States from Germany at the age of fourteen, was graduated from Baldwin-Wallace College in 1895 and from Nast Theological Seminary in 1898.   He became professor of Germanic language and literature in the University of Pittsburgh in 1914 and wrote a series of modern language texts known as the *International Modern Language Series.*   William B. Herms, taking his degree from Baldwin-Wallace College in 1902, became professor of parasitology and head of the division of etomology and parasitology in the University of California in 1920.   As a scientist he distinguished himself in the field of public health, frequently directing public health programs of the United States Government.

The list of German Methodist contributions to the acknowledged group of leaders in American education is too long to allow adequate treatment.   Carl C. Sauer, graduating from Central Wesleyan College in 1908, became map editor of Rand-McNally Company in 1912, and chairman of the department of geography in the University of California in 1923.   As correspondent of the *Gesellschaft für Erdkunde zu Berlin,* and the *Geographische Gesellschaft in Wien,* he became an intellectual bridge between two continents.   Joyce O. Hertzler, taking his bachelor's degree from Baldwin-Wallace College in 1916, was appointed chairman of the department of sociology in the University of Nebraska in 1928 and recognized as an authority in the field of social institutions.   Walter H. Bucher, son of the former editor of the *Apologist,* became professor of geology in the University of Cincinnati in 1925 and has become internationally famous for his studies in the field of structural geology.   Daniel Starch, educated at Morningside College in the class of 1903, after teaching psychology in the University of Wisconsin and Harvard University, was appointed director of research of the American Association of Advertising Agencies, and is an advertising consultant of the first rank.   Albert Kuntz, graduating from Morningside College in 1904, was appointed professor of microanatomy in the Saint Louis University College of Medicine in 1919. Charles H. Handschin, educated at Baldwin-Wallace in the class of 1897, became professor of German in Miami University in 1905. Wesley D. Zinnecker, graduating also from Baldwin-Wallace in 1903, was appointed professor of German in Cornell University in 1922, and became secretary-general of the New York University School of Fine Arts in Berlin in 1927. Julius E. Kammeyer took his degree from Central Wesleyan College in 1886, and was appointed professor of economics in Kansas State College in 1904. Herbert W. Schneider, professor of religion in Columbia University, and one of the outstanding members of the younger generation of philosophers, was accepted as an authority on the subject of Italian Fascism following the publication of his volume on *Making the Fascist State* in 1928. George A. Mulfinger, son of the pioneer preacher, after graduating from Baldwin-Wallace College in 1884, became president of German Wesleyan College, Mount Pleasant, Iowa, in 1890, and in 1892 accepted a professorship in Heidelberg University. Eleonore Nippert, daughter of the pioneer missionary, has been teaching German for many years in the University of Cincinnati. Ernest W. Winkler, educated at Blinn Memorial College, became librarian of the University of Texas in 1923. John L. Nuelsen, Jr., is on the teaching staff of the American University in Washington, D. C.

In speaking of the Theological Seminary in Frankfurt, E. H. Luering deserves special mention because of his unusual linguistic abilities. One of the world's most erudite linguists, he spoke no less than thirty languages. His services as interpreter for the World Sunday School Convention held at Zürich, Switzerland, in 1913, attracted universal attention. His mastery embraces Oriental as well as European languages. After only a year's sojourn in China, he outwitted the natives by serving as interpreter between Chinese of different dialects. Malaysian, Persian, Japanese, and Turkish afford him no more difficulty than his mother tongue. When the Turkish sultan visited Germany, Luering welcomed him to Frankfurt in the sovereign's own language, receiving from him special recognition in the form of a gold medal.

It is obviously impossible to enumerate the list of German Methodists who have entered the field of American education. The persons mentioned in preceding paragraphs are representative of the rich contribution of the Germans influenced by the Methodist tradition. In the public school, the college, the graduate school, the vocational and professional college, and in research the Germans have made a rich gift to the development of the American mind.

Journalism

In literary activity it is always better to speak of German Methodist writings as journalism rather than as literature, because it characteristically was a purposive expression with the definite objective of influencing the will. The Germans, under religious inspiration seemed to take as naturally to the writing of poetry as an eagle takes to the sky. Much of this was of the type written by Peter Schmucker in

1851 upon the death of a grandson. *The Little Straw Hat* was a poem
loved by all generations of German Methodists:

> 'Tis a dear little hat that hangs there still—
> And its voice of the past bids our heartstrings thrill;
> For it seems like a shadow of days passed o'er,
> Of the bright little one, who has gone before.
> 'Tis a dear little hat, for each simple braid
> Tells that oft o'er each plaiting those fingers played,
> And many a wreath for its crown hath been twined
> To the grateful taste of his youthful mind.
>
> Yes; there silent it hangs with its curling front,
> Still as playfully rolled as had been its wont;
> But the golden ringlets which waved below,
> Have curled their last clusters long ago.
> Aye, the hat is the same, but it shades no more
> Those light blue eyes as in days of yore;
> And the sunlit smile that danced o'er that brow,
> Can but light up our hearts' sad memories now.
>
> Sad memories they are; o'er their quivering strings
> Each breath of the bygone a tremor flings,
> And joys that we fain would waken again,
> In memory are wreathed with a thrill of pain.
> Then recall not the past—though the dimpled hand
> May never again clasp the braided strand,
> Though the breeze no longer may bear the tone
> Of the ringing laughter of childhood's own.
>
> Ah! think of him now with a glittering crown
> O'er his heavenly forehead resting down,
> While his fingers stray o'er the golden wire
> That blends with his voice 'mid the cherub choir.
> Aye, I see him now with the holy light
> Pouring broad on his brow with radiance bright,
> And I hear the tones which in heaven have birth—
> O! call him not back to this saddened earth.

The hymn was a natural channel of poetic expression. Wilhelm
Ahrens sang *O Blessed Sabbath, Thou Day of My Lord*.[11] John Lyon
wrote *Jehovah, Lord of the World*,[12] *Joyful, Joyful, Go I Forth*,[13] and
We Are Only Pilgrims and Strangers Here.[14] Perhaps the favorite
hymn of German Methodists was written by C. F. Paulus, *Homeland,
O Homeland, How Beautiful Thou Art*.[15] Ernst Gebhardt, introduc-
ing the English hymn into Germany as an instrument of evangelism,
did much to lighten the heavy German chorale by the influence of the
folk song. He wrote hymns himself, such as *I Know a Stream*.[16]
Among the other poets of German Methodism were Gustav Weiler,
Franz Nagler, John Reitz, John F. Horst, Karl Keck, Karl Eisler,
Wilhelm Esslinger, G. E. Hiller, August Flammann, Louis Wallon,
Wilhelm Schwarz, August Reicker, and Frau Anna Spoerri.

In the field of pure poetry perhaps only two names are outstanding.

Emil Dörnenberg ranks with the best of the German-American literary talent.[17]   The other writer of importance is Helene Margaret, the granddaughter of E. C. Margaret, a German preacher and himself a contributor of poetry to the Church press.   Her narrative poem, *The Trumpeting Crane*, was effective in presenting the Middle West as an essential part of the American scene.

A voluminous literature, chiefly of importance to the German branch of Methodism, developed in the fields of biblical interpretation and exploration of the areas of religious living.   The outstanding writers of permanent importance, however, are fewer in number.   Herbert W. Schneider, of Columbia University, one of the editors of *The Journal of Philosophy*, by his studies of the Puritan mind and religion in various cultures, by his researches into the philosophy of Fascism, and more recently by brilliant philosophical papers, stands undoubtedly in the first rank.   Second to him must be placed Karl R. Stolz, of the Hartford Seminary Foundation, whose studies of the psychology of prayer and of religious living are important.   His researches have done much to join the best in science and religion in the service of the Church.

Bishop Nuelsen's enduring contributions to religious literature, made despite his busy life of Christian statesmanship, place him in a class by himself.   As one of the editors of *The International Standard Bible Encyclopedia* (1915) he helped to make available one of the best of the reference works on the Scriptures.   He crowned his literary activity with monographs of historical importance and exacting scholarship on *The Ordination in Methodism* and on the influence of the German Church hymn in the religious experience of John Wesley.   From 1897 to 1908 he edited the *Deutsch-Amerikanische Zeitschrift für Theologie und Kirche*, the leading German language theological publication in the United States during the period.

William A. Heidel's volume, *The Day of Jahweh*, is a work of erudite scholarship into which the author poured his heart's blood.   It is a monument in the field of historical research into a religious concept.

By his volume, *The Church in History*,[18] Arthur W. Nagler, associate professor of church history in Garrett Biblical Institute, established his reputation as a historian, probably in a class with Bishop Nuelsen, whose volume on the *History of Methodism* appeared a decade before.[19]

The volumes digesting the scientific researches of German scholars are too numerous and too generally important to be mentioned in detail. Typical of the group is the work of Edward O. Ulrich, educated at German Wallace College, a distinguished Paleontologist, who began in 1884 to contribute an extensive series of monographs to his field.   In 1930 he was awarded the Mary Clark Thompson Medal.

Textbook writing and editing has been the contribution of a number of other scholars, such as Wesley D. Zinnecker, author of *German for Beginners*, and editor of the "Prentice-Hall German Series."

In the field of music Henry E. Krehbiel was a critic of international importance on the staff of the New York *Tribune*. Despite a busy newspaper and lecture schedule, he wrote seventeen volumes on subjects ranging in interest from a discussion of the folk songs of the American Indian and the Negro through the technics of the violin and discussion of Beethoven and Wagnerian drama to the preparation of encyclopedias and histories of music. When Krehbiel died in 1923, he had served forty-three years as a New York newspaper critic. Granted by Yale University an honorary degree, he was also made chevalier of the French Legion of Honor.

Guido Enderis, chief of the Berlin bureau of the New York *Times,* probably held the most difficult newspaper assignment continuously since the outbreak of the World War. Throughout the years of the conflict, through the years of German reconstruction in the 1920's, and during the trying days of the National Socialist Revolution he continued to give to America the most reliable and impartial reports available, at the same time keeping the confidence of his German sources. That a German Methodist should be the channel of intercourse for a quarter of a century in the most trying days American and German relations have ever known is an honor not to be esteemed lightly.

In the field of general literature German Methodists have made some contributions. Walter E. Havighurst's *Pier 17,* a story of a longshoremen's strike in Seattle, caused him to be compared with Joseph Conrad. Arthur E. Hertzler's *The Horse and Buggy Doctor* caught the national imagination and in 1938 was a best seller and Book-of-the-Month Club selection.

Among the German Methodist newspaper journalists two are of major importance. Charles Nordhoff served as assistant editor of the New York *Evening Post* under William Cullen Bryant, and was made editor of the New York *Herald* by James Gordon Bennett. Guido Enderis holds an even greater claim to enduring fame.

Music

In the field of music the Germans furnished a useful leadership, especially on the organ. Albert Riemenschneider, Dean of the Northern Ohio chapter of the Guild of American Organists, and moving spirit in the famous Bach festivals, has been for many years a master of the instrument. Edwin Kraft is the Dean of the Guild's Georgia chapter. Walter Keller holds the same position in Illinois, and Oliver H. Kleinschmidt a similar part in the Eastern Oklahoma chapter. The piano was another instrument upon which the Germans were especially proficient.

In the field of composition there were many efforts, many of them centering around hymn writing, although Walter Keller and Edward Hubach have done some important works.

The Germans made numerous contributions in the field of architecture. Waldemar Ritter did creative work in planning a church tower design in Baltimore. William Magly prepared the plan for the first skyscraper in Cincinnati, the Cincinnati Art Museum, and many of Cincinnati's business houses.

Medicine

In the field of medicine the Germans made a very significant contribution. Edmund J. Doering, son of the pioneer missionary, has served since 1891 as editor of the *Chicago Medical Recorder*. A consulting physician of the Chicago Lying-in and Michael Reese Hospitals, he has for nearly half a century been an important figure in the field of organized medicine. Augustus Jonas, a pioneer in American surgery, for twenty-nine years chief surgeon of the Union Pacific Railroad, served on the staff of the Methodist and Wise Memorial Hospitals in Omaha. Arthur E. Hertzler, of Halstead, Kansas, author of more than thirty books on medical subjects, is a national figure. J. Wesley Faust, in Kansas City; Arthur Mahle and Henry Dueringer, on Mayo Brothers' staff; Paul Morf and George Apfelbach, in Chicago; and S. R. Geiser, in Cincinnati; Louis Nippert, in Minneapolis and Henry Nippert are but a few of the names of those who have served so well in the history of healing.

American Industry

German frugality, persistence, and ingenuity created an independent, self-respecting segment of American society. Some of the immigrants and their descendants grew wealthy. Many more became comfortably fixed; and most, though living on meager incomes, were nevertheless honest, clean, and useful.

In the process of westward migration and settlement a good many became prosperous farmers. Gottlieb Hauser, of Big Springs, Nebraska, owns thirty-five sections of land; Simon Winter, with twenty-five quarter-sections on the Kansas-Oklahoma line; Charles Sauter, with a ranch in Duel County, Nebraska; Edward Meyer, rancher, in Nebraska and Oklahoma; Henry Timken, with extensive lands in Kansas and citrus groves in California, are but a few examples of the real estate accumulated by German Methodists.

The Germans had an inborn appreciation of good stock. William Buehler, of Sterling, Nebraska, became one of the nation's leading Chester White hog breeders. Louis Thieman developed a noted Polled Shorthorn breed. L. M. Monsees, of Smithton, Missouri, was for many years one of the leading mule breeders in America.

Forests were appreciated by those who knew of the careful culture of trees on the Continent. F. X. Kreitler, of Nebraska City, Pennsylvania, and Phil Buehner, of Portland, Oregon, owned vast timberlands in northeastern and northwestern United States.

A large number of German Methodists or their descendants became major captains of industry: Among this number were F. G. and William F. Niedringhaus, Missouri industrialists; Charles E. Allinger, Detroit manufacturer of drilling machines and steam engines; E. H. Huenefeld, Cincinnati stove manufacturer; Louis Rueckheim, creator of Crackerjack; J. B. Meyers, New Orleans molasses and syrup dealer; Christian Bernet, Saint Louis textile mill owner; the Saint Louis Timkens, manufacturers of bearings; the Rech Brothers, New York bankers; Phil Buchner, lumber magnate; Simon Kruse, chain hotel proprietor; William Rodenberg, lawyer and politician, who became wealthy in South America; and Edward Meyer, investor in Western lands.

It was not surprising that the German talent for business should find opportunity for expression in banking. Nelson Lampert became a vice-president of the Fort Dearborn Bank, Chicago, while his brother, Wilson Lampert, was appointed to a similar position in the Commercial and Continental Bank in the same city. Wilson Lampert later organized the National Bank of Commerce and became its first president. In Arkansas City, Henry Thane was a leading banker. In Minneapolis, George N. Bauer rose to be president of the East Hennepin State Bank. In Saint Louis, John C. Rodenberg headed the Laclede Trust Company. In 1907, Benjamin F. Salzer was elected president of the Central National Bank in Denver.

In the shrewd purchase of lands in the West the Germans accumulated wealth. Anton Classen, for example, with a small group of German Methodists, bought up land surrounding the village of Oklahoma City. When the town grew into a city, he made rich gains.

In the baking field the Germans found an industry for which they were well fitted. Henry Schust started a small bakery in Saginaw, Michigan, which grew into the flourishing Schust Baking Company. Candy manufacturing was an equally good field. The Rueckheim Brothers, in Saint Louis, made a fortune by the manufacture of Crackerjack, and developed one of the largest candy concerns in the West. E. H. Huenefeld's benefactions to German Methodism were made possible by his stove and oven works. F. W. Dietrich became president of the Elgin (Illinois) Stove and Oven Works. F. H. Wolterstorff was for many years president of the Wolterstorff Range Company, Saint Paul, Minnesota. John W. Miller headed the Malleable Iron Range Company at Beaver Dam, Wisconsin. The Niedringhaus Brothers founded the rolling mills at Granite City, Illinois. Since 1919 George W. Niedringhaus has been president of the concern. In the bearing field, the Timken family became outstanding.

It might have been expected that the Germans would have become active in milling. Christian Hoffman built the second flour mill to be erected in Kansas. The Eisenmayers in Trenton, the Albers family in Warsaw, the Huegeles in Nashville, and the Postels in Mascoutah, Illinois, identified their names with successful milling.

In the fields of printing and paper manufacture, in textile production, in wholesaling, in retail establishments, as dry-goods merchants, as grocers, as technicians, as builders and contractors, and as leaders of trade associations and welfare organizations, the Germans made a stimulating contribution to American life.

Church Life

German Methodism was generous in the lives which it gave to the leadership of the denomination. John L. Nuelsen, elected bishop in 1908, has been for a quarter of a century the leading Christian statesman of Methodism and was properly called by Bishop Francis J. McConnell "one of the most noted men that our Church has produced in the course of the present century." Emil Luering, for twenty years a pioneer missionary in Malaysia and Borneo, was nearly elected a missionary bishop by the General Conference in 1920. George A. Simons, appointed superintendent of Methodist work in Russia, was awarded the Russian Red Cross, made a *Chevalier of the Order of the White Rose* in Finland, and honored by the Republic of Latvia as a knight in the Order of the Stars. France decorated him with the *Palms d' Officer de l' Instruction Publique*. Julius Hecker, one of the early leaders in the *Living Church* movement in Soviet Russia, and often persecuted, turned Communist and accepted a professorship in the University of Moscow. F. H. Otto Melle has been a link between the Methodisms separated by the Atlantic Ocean, and was elected bishop of German Methodism. Henry H. Meyer, as editor of Church School Publications, exercised a primary influence upon the educational work of the Church for a decade and a half. W. E. J. Gratz became editor of *The Epworth Herald* in 1924. Edward D. Kohlstedt, elected president of Dakota Wesleyan University in 1922, became corresponding secretary of the Board of Home Missions and Church Extension in 1927. Fred W. Mueller was appointed superintendent of the Church Extension department of Kohlstedt's board in 1928. As the leader of the *Save the Sanctuary* movement, he did much to prevent foreclosure on Church properties during the serious years of economic depression following 1930. John A. Diekmann has rendered a long and constructive service on the Board of Hospitals, Homes, and Deaconess Work. To pulpit and parish work the Germans contributed a group of leaders so important that even English-speaking Methodism must pay its tribute to the German mission work. To the mission field the German families sent a stream of devoted workers.

Politics

German Methodist religion, although it created a strong personal faith and a keen sense of social responsibility, did not encourage activity in politics. The German Methodists were as a rule indifferent to office holding. Their influence, however, was not negligible in this field. Since the Civil War twelve German Methodists have served in Congress: William Rodenberg, of the twenty-second Illinois district, was appointed by President McKinley a member of the Civil Service Commission. F. G. Niedringhaus, Saint Louis, championed the protective tariff as a member of the House of Representatives. Harry Gahn, Ohio, led a fight over the Ship Subsidy Bill, and W. F. Kopp, Iowa, was one of the leaders of the "farm bloc." Homer Hock, Kansas; L. C. Dyer, Missouri; Theodore Hukriede, Missouri; D. C. Smith (Schmidt), Illinois; Charles O. Lobeck, Nebraska; Charles E. Winter, Wyoming; Florian Lampert, Wisconsin; and Henry Niedringhaus, Missouri, served their states in Washington.

In the field of diplomatic service German Methodists were not absent. Michael J. Cremer, brother-in-law of President Grant, was appointed minister to Denmark in 1871. Charles C. Eberhardt was sent as minister to Nicaragua. In 1922 he was made consul-general for Eastern Europe. W. K. Herzog went to Berlin as consul, and Paul Meyer to Nanking, China.

Charles Nordhoff was entrusted to Wilhelm Nast's care when his father died. Following the Civil War he published a book, "The Cotton States," which exposed the Republican misrule in the South.

Edward W. Hoch was twice governor of Kansas, serving his first time in 1904. His political leadership in the interests of prohibition and his tact in handling the controversy between the State of Kansas and the Standard Oil Company, which flared to a crisis during his administration, made him a worthy descendant of one of Nast's first converts. Carl Nippert, son of a pioneer preacher, became lieutenant-governor of Ohio, and Alfred K. Nippert was a judge of the Ohio Court of Common Pleas.

As state treasurers, commissioners, public service commissioners, state legislators, and city councillors, the Germans were active and useful citizens. In the cause of prohibition, as supporters of the Anti-Saloon League, they did much to mitigate the evils of liquor which other Germans were brewing and distilling. A. L. Koeneke, for example, while a member of the Northern German Conference, served as president of the Minnesota Anti-Saloon League.

In the legal profession German Methodists were also active. William A. Rodenberg became attorney for the Interstate Commerce Commission. William F. Broening, Baltimore; Harry G. Gahn, Cleveland; Charles Winter, Wyoming; William Schlagenhauf, Quincy, Illinois; Alfred K. Nippert and C. S. J. Walker, Cincinnati; Milton F. Schwind and F. A. Boehmer, Lincoln, Nebraska; William Hoersch, Davenport, Iowa; William Vosholl, Missouri; B. E. Sattler, Indianapolis; H. A. Schroetter, Covington, Kentucky; John Kaste, Portland, Oregon; Albert E. Nuelsen, son of Bishop Nuelsen, New York; and Royal Wilke, Los Angeles, have been but a few members of the bar of first rank.

German Methodism in American Life

It is always dangerous, and often unfair, to mention a few names in discussing the influence of a movement. To take typical individuals as representatives of a group to make a general discussion concrete, however, is a justifiable procedure. The personal discussions in the preceding paragraphs are only evidence of the outcome of a great human drama and social phenomenon of European migration and the building of America.

The historical event in its human aspect deserves emphasis. From crowded and chaotic Europe, the hearts of millions of people of all classes, but chiefly the middle classes, longed for the congenial haven of America. Carl Schurz expressed it in the spirit of one who had experienced the pageant:

> I, born in a foreign land, pay my tribute to Americanism. Yes, for to me the word Americanism, true Americanism, comprehends the noblest ideas which ever swelled a human heart with noble pride.
>
> It is one of the earliest recollections of my boyhood that one summer night our whole village was stirred up by an uncommon occurrence. I say our village, for I was born not far from that beautiful spot where the Rhine rolls its green waters out of the wonderful gate of the Seven Mountains, and then meanders with majestic tranquillity through one of the most glorious valleys of the world. That night our neighbors were pressing around a few wagons covered with linen sheets and loaded with household utensils and boxes and trunks to their utmost capacity. One of our neighboring families was moving far away across great water, and it was said that they would never again return. And I saw silent tears trickling down weather-beaten cheeks, and the hands of rough peasants firmly pressing each other and some of the men and women hardly able to speak when they nodded to one another a last farewell. At last the train started into motion, they gave three cheers for America, and then in the first gray dawn of the morning I saw them wending their way over the hill until they disappeared in the shadow of the forest. And I heard many a man say how happy he would be if he could go with them to that great and free country where a man could be himself.[20]

America had a meaning to the immigrant soul. Millions left their Fatherland under conditions which Carl Schurz described. They came to a vast country spreading between two oceans and from the tropics to the snows. It was a land of moving geographic, spiritual, commercial, and intellectual frontiers. Those who were active along these front lines were pioneers. The pioneer society is a social organization of energy but not stability.

It was precisely at this point that the Methodist mission to the Germans was so influential as a factor in Americanization. It took

10

the seething enthusiasm of the frontier and gave it the balance of a soul. Men might seek their liberty and their fortune but God still reigned. That fact the German Methodist preachers proclaimed in no uncertain terms. Because of their presence, homes became different. Communities felt the gravitational influence of Christ, swinging human life into new orbits. Churches raised their voices in the shadow of saloons. Institutions developed for practical Christian service. Minds were trained.

A study of *Who's Who in America* reveals a representative fact. In the biographies, the notation appears over and over again: *German Wallace College; Central Wesleyan; Charles City College; Baldwin-Wallace College; Blinn; Saint Paul's College; Nast Theological Seminary.*

What are the meaning of these data? The small Christian college was playing a vital part in the development of American culture. The immigrant home found a center in the Church. The Church was ambitious to train the minds of its youth, hence the progression through the Church to the church school was natural. American culture was built from the interaction of immigrant souls on the national frontiers. From immigrant homes flowed the stream of youth to become the substance of American life.

The German was particularly fitted to take advantage of his bilingualism. From the small American college, hundreds went to Germany to study at the greatest universities in the world. German-American scholarship broke open and held open the channels of intellectual intercourse and scientific investigation.

In the great epic of the building of the American soul, the German Methodist played a vital rôle. "What do the Methodists want?" The *Swiss Evangelist* answered the question:

1. Personal fellowship with Christ.
2. The evangelical experience of full salvation.
3. The complete and invincible zeal for service which flows from a wholly consecrated heart.
4. The inner fellowship of a spiritual brotherhood.
5. The feeling for a world-wide and world-renewing mission.
6. The courage of faith of a great national testimony.
7. The striving toward that great unity of the soul through which all sectarian hostility shall be overcome."

German Methodism was an important agency of Americanization. It was something more. It was a part of America. It helped to make American culture. It joined the mind, culture, and soul of two continents in the Christian home and gave to life a purpose which is only created by genuine faith and conviction.

CHAPTER XIX

THE NATURAL HISTORY OF GERMAN METHODISM

"We and God have business with each other: and in opening
ourselves to his influence our deepest destiny is fulfilled." [1]

Methodism touched a chord in the pietistic German nature almost
as naturally as the eagle takes to the skies. Within the German-
speaking branch of the Methodist Episcopal Church the ardor and
simplicity of Methodism burned as deeply and continued longer than
in any other section of the denomination.

Like Methodism itself, German-speaking Methodism was in its first
stage a religion of experience. The natural history of a German
Methodist began with a condition of the consciousness which was real,
vivid, dated, and impelling. The Aldersgate experience of John Wesley, when at a quarter past nine he felt his heart strangely warmed,
was continually an experience verified at the altar and the "mourner's
bench." Wilhelm Nast testified that

it was on the *18th day of January, 1835*, that I was born again,
unto a lively hope, with joy unspeakable and full of glory to an
inheritance incorruptible and undefiled.

Ahrens witnessed the same discovery:

There was glory above me and glory beneath me and glory
around me and glory in my soul. This was the *17th day of
August, 1839*.

Koeneke could say,

From such a miserable life God delivered me in 1834.

Nippert had witnessed the same awakening,

In 1840, the *fiteenth year of my age*, I, too, was awakened
under the preaching of Brother Riemenschneider.

The religious experience was so real that its vivid memory enabled
the Methodists to name the exact place, day of the week, hour of the
day, and emotional transformation which came over them. The
experience was the *first stage* in the natural history of German Methodism.

William James tried to analyze this kind of experience in the
Gifford Lectures on Natural Religion which he delivered at Edinburgh

in the winter of 1901-02. His comment is well worth recording. He said to the students:

> Revert, then, for a moment more to the psychology of self-surrender. . . . When you find a man living on the ragged edge of his consciousness, pent into his sin and want and incompleteness, and consequently inconsolable, and then simply tell him that all is well with him, that he must stop his worry, break with his discontent, and give up his anxiety, you seem to him to come with pure absurdities. The only positive consciousness he has tells him that all is *not* well, and the better way you offer sounds simply as if you proposed to him to assert cold-blooded falsehoods. "The will to believe" cannot be stretched as far as that. . . . There are only two ways in which it is possible to get rid of anger, worry, fear, despair, or other undesirable affections; one is that an opposite affection should overpoweringly break over us, and the other is by getting so exhausted with the struggle that we have to stop—so we drop down, give up, and *don't care any longer*. Our emotional brain centers strike work and we lapse into a temporary apathy. Now there is documentary proof that this state of temporary exhaustion not infrequently forms part of the conversion crisis. So long as the egotistic worry of the sick soul guards the door, the expansive confidence of the soul of faith gains no presence. But let the former faint away, even but for a moment, and the latter can profit by the opportunity, and, having once acquired possession, may retain it. Carlyle's *Teufelscroeckh* passes from the everlasting yes through a *"Centre of Indifference."* [2]

James had difficulty to make academic the experiential injunction of Willbur Fisk to Wilhelm Nast.

> You need only to go to Christ that you may have light and strength.

The vividness of the life-changing experience developed as the Methodist personality type grew into a definite theological consciousness. Section IX of the Articles of Religion had a critical importance:

IX. *Of the Justification of Man*

> We are accounted righteous before God only for the merit of our Lord and Saviour Jesus Christ, by faith, and not for our own works or deservings. Wherefore, that we are justified by faith only is a most wholesome doctrine, and very full of comfort.

The testimony of God through the life and death of Christ that God takes the initiative in seeking reconciliation with sinful men because he has the heart to it was no idle fancy to the Germans. That the willing God seeks to bring unwilling men to his holy fellowship was to them the heart of the Scriptures. His motive was free grace and the question of merit was irrelevant when men in faith accepted Christ, whose grace was "more abundant than their needs."

Christ was, therefore, the *central fact* and German Methodists were stubbornly and theologically conscious that to be "saved by the grace of God" was a cardinal event. *They were practical theologians.* They substantiated their experience by a homely philosophical theory. The universality of sin, the corruption of human nature, and the universality of the grace of God were fundamental concepts, "vital matters of life and death."

Sin to the German Methodists was a fact; it was not just a functional aberration. It was living life against the will of God; its consequence was punishment. As Bishop Nuelsen has so well phrased it:

> No man stands exclusively under the influence of sin, but also under the free and universal grace of God which can operate on every man if he but wills. Every man, corrupt though he is, is constantly placed through continuing grace in such a situation that he can accept or deny the salvation through Christ. His own free relationship toward the Holy Spirit determines the result.[3]

Sin—Christ—Reconciliation—that was the unvarnished theme which German Methodists proclaimed. Their clergymen were preachers, not just pastors. They referred to them as *Prediger,* never as *Pfarrer.* Their field of preaching was not a wide one; it was circumscribed with telling effect in that evangelical formula. The German Methodists were concerned with the same vital problem which concerned Wesley when he said that his mission was to spread "scriptural holiness" over the land. Yet the Methodists, insistent though they were upon this vital fact of sin, did not base Christianity upon theological or dogmatic religious grounds. They merely held it essential that in all circumstances and at all times the sin-redeeming power of God is at work transforming men that they may be perfect even as their Father in Heaven is perfect.

German Methodism was *first* of all a *religion of experience.* The nature of that experience made the Methodists uncompromising only at one point—that *sin is a fact* and that the *complete surrender of the will to God* is the means of being reconciled with *him.* These two principles were united in a third. Methodists, and German Methodists in particular, were *uncompromising Protestants.* That meant first of all that they were *not* Roman Catholics. Methodism continued in the tradition of the Reformation. The Methodists were concerned with putting the theory into operation in practical life. The battle which they waged was not against dogmas or theories but against the "godless life," and any ecclesiastical system which stood in the way of man's opening directly his contrite heart to God's loving mercy and forgiving grace. The vitally important rediscovery of Luther of the nearly forgotten conception of the loving, forgiving character of God and his slowly developing conviction that sinful man is made just or righteous before God simply and solely by trust in the Father's love as manifested in Christ's sacrificial life and death became the common conviction of the German Methodists. These ideas, together with *insistence on the Bible* as the sole authority for the Christian in religious teaching and practice, completed their religious system. Perhaps the Germans, by national tradition deeply concerned with a clear-cut distinction between Protestantism and Catholicism, were better oriented by historic experience to appreciate and take pride in their Protestant heritage. Adam Miller saw the salvation of men from Catholicism was almost as important as the regular missionary work. He wrote:

> While these missionaries were laboring in distant fields, supported by the prayers and contributions of their Christian friends at home, the Church, watching the openings of Providence, so as to be able to make further advances to the territories of moral darkness, beheld the situation of the thousands of Germans who annually come to seek a home for themselves and their families in the land of freedom. She saw the hand of an all-wise Providence opening the way; and, following this opening, she sent her servants to preach to this people in their own native tongue, to invite them to come and partake of a full and free salvation by faith in the atonement of Christ. Numbers have already heard and obeyed the invitation; and, with humble joy, they now can testify that "Christ has power on earth to forgive sins"; and that they have "found redemption in his blood, even the forgiveness of their sins." *Among those who have thus been brought to a saving knowledge of the truth, are members who were Roman Catholics; and instead of counting their beads, instead of paying a considerable part of their income to be saved from purgatory or to have their time therein shortened, instead of calling upon departed saints to pray for them, they now come directly to a throne of grace, in the name and through the merits of Jesus Christ; and in this, the only right way, find "peace and righteousness and joy in the Holy Ghost."* [4]

In the fourth place, Methodism strongly influenced the morals and standards of the Germans in both America and on the Continent. Methodist injunctions against worldliness played havoc with the traditional *Gemütlichkeit* of the beer garden, the gambling table, and the dance hall. It gave a new emphasis to the Sabbath. Converted Germans, who formerly enjoyed their drinking, under the influence of Methodism became ardent workers in temperance movements. Men who had formerly broken most of the Ten Commandments on Sunday now began to distribute tracts for its strict observance. The wholesome corrective influence of the German Methodist moral standards cannot be underestimated. Although the German Methodists were only a small minority in the great mass of immigrants, their forthright declaration of their principles called attention to a simpler and higher plane of living.

In the next place, the German Methodists showed *a capable deter-*

mination to express their religion in social service. The energies which they had formerly dissipated in their *Bünde* (federations) and their *Vereine* (societies) now were collected and directed in the institutional activities which they developed in a scope all out of proportion to their numerical strength. The support of hospitals, children's homes, schools and colleges, and havens for the aged was the motive which brought the German Methodists together in their Christian *Geselligkeit* (sociability). They had a good time. No English-speaking Methodist ever attended a German Methodist function but that he realized how good a time the Germans did have. But their common purpose was making the experience of the heart visible in concrete Christian service ministering to the needs of social life.

And, finally, *the Germans were loyal.* Loyalty was a first German virtue. It was a quality native to the German soul, cultivated in a national tradition as *die alten Soldatentugenden, Treue, Gehorsam und Pflichterfüllung—die Richtschnur Eures Handelns.*[5] *Connectionalism meant something to them.* It meant their common association in a gigantic crusade in which unity and leadership were of telling importance. It was not by accident that during the Centenary the old Northwest German Conference contributed $8.64 per member, an expression of faith so generous that the Conference set a record for other Conferences in Methodism. They did in the Centenary only what they had been doing in the whole history of German Methodism.

That the mission to the Germans, so modestly begun in 1835 in Cincinnati, should have contributed so many scholars to the Church, so many preachers, so much humble generosity of joyfully witnessing hearts; that it should have reared such a monumental network of ministering institutions across two continents is in part a testimony to the high character of the Germans themselves, but even more witness of the fact that the mission to the Germans was the instrument for joining the native piety of the Teutonic soul, which had first awakened the British heart of the Anglican John Wesley, with Anglo-Saxon culture for the quickening of the religious life of England and the expansion of the spiritual frontiers in the youthful and polyglot America.

"A Methodist," said John Wesley in an attempt at a definition,

> is one who lives according to the method laid down in the Bible. He is one who loves the Lord with all his heart, who prays without ceasing and in everything gives thanks. His heart is full of love to all mankind, and is purified from envy, malice, wrath, and every unkind affection. He keeps all God's commandments from the least unto the greatest. He follows not the customs of the world. He cannot speak evil of his neighbor any more than he can lie. He does good unto all men, neighbors, friends, and enemies. These are the principles and practice of our sect. These are the marks of a true Methodist. By these alone do Methodists desire to be distinguished from other men.

When Wilhelm Nast was in his ninety-second year he took his pen in hand and wrote his valedictory:

"This is a faithful saying, and worthy of acceptation, that Christ Jesus came into the world to save sinners; of whom I am chief." (1 Timothy 1. 15.)

This promise helps no man until he applies it to himself. May every reader of the *Apologist* test its validity in his own life.

Wilhelm Nast's work was done. The mission which he as an instrument of God had helped to organize was now an intercontinental program of Christian evangelism and Christian social service. His wife, who had been his companion for sixty-two years, died in September, 1898. Lonely, having survived his generation, he lived quietly with his daughter, Fanny Nast Gamble, until in early May, 1899, he fell ill with pneumonia. In the presence of his faithful children, he prayed:

"O Herr, tu mir auf die Gnadenpforte. Ich glaube, sie ist aufgetan." ("O Lord, open the door; I believe it is open.")

At his request deaconesses were summoned from the Motherhouse to sing to him. They began the well-known hymn, "Saved by Grace." In feeble affirmation, the old man muttered from his bed:

"Es ist wunderbar! Es ist wunderbar!" ("It is wonderful, wonderful!")

The sisters nodded their understanding and sang so softly:

> *Christ, the blessed One, gives to all,*
> *Wonderful words of Life;*
> *Sinner, list to the loving call,*
> *Wonderful words of life.*
> *All so freely given,*
> *Wooing us to Heaven:*
>
> *Beautiful words, wonderful words,*
> *Wonderful words of Life.*

The Door opened. The date was May 16, 1899, in the afternoon.

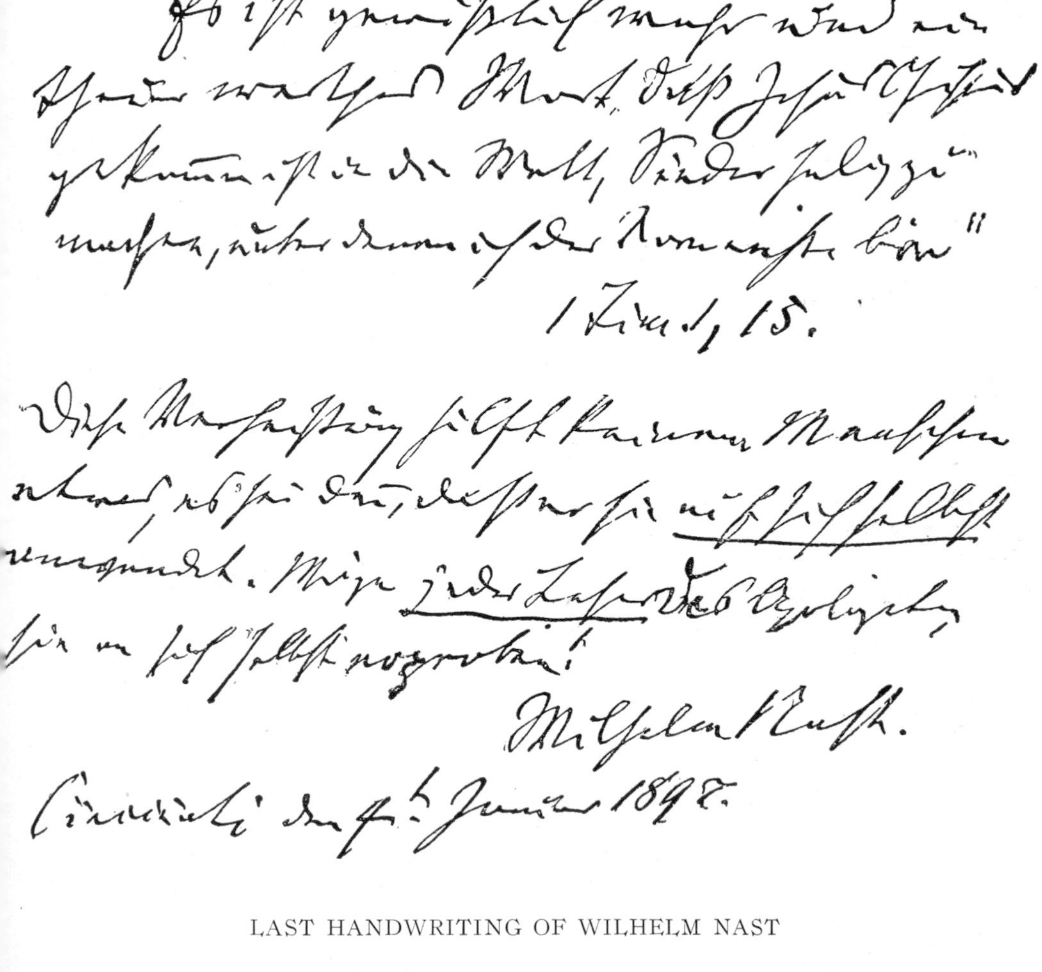
"Das ist gewißlich wahr und ein theuer werthes Wort, daß Jesus Christus gekommen ist in die Welt, die Sünder selig zu machen, unter denen ich der vornehmste bin."
1 Tim. 1, 15.

Diese Wahrheit hilft keinem Menschen etwas, als bis daß er sie auf sich selbst anwendet. Möge jeder Leser des Apologeten sie an sich selbst erproben!

Wilhelm Nast.

Cincinnati den 9ten Januar 1898.

LAST HANDWRITING OF WILHELM NAST

NOTES

CHAPTER I

[1] See A. M. Carr-Saunders, *World Population: Past Growth and Present Trends.* Oxford: Clarendon Press, 1936. Pp. 336. *Population.* London: Oxford University Press, 1925. Pp. 111.

[2] In 1900 the census showed that the German population was more evenly distributed over the territory of the United States than any other immigrant group. At the turn of the century natives of Germany constituted a little more than a quarter of the entire foreign element (25.8 per cent). Save for the following exceptions, all the states of the Union had a larger native German population than any other foreign stock: Maine and Michigan (Canadian-English); Vermont and New Hampshire (Canadian-French); Massachusetts, Rhode Island, Connecticut, and Delaware (Irish); Florida (Cuban); Louisiana (Italian); Texas, New Mexico, and Arizona (Mexican); Utah, Idaho, and Wyoming (English); Montana and Washington (Canadian-English); Nevada (Irish); Dakotas (Norwegian). The predominantly German areas constituted a vast and progressive continental belt.

[3] *The Rise of American Civilization.* New York: The Macmillan Company, 1930. Vol. I, p. 641. Used by permission.

[4] *Immigration of Germans by decades:*

$$1830\text{-}1839 — 150,000$$
$$1840\text{-}1849 — 434,000$$
$$1850\text{-}1859 — 951,000$$
$$1860\text{-}1869 — 822,000$$
$$1870\text{-}1879 — 811,000$$

[5] Albert Bernhardt Faust, *The German Element in the United States.* Boston and New York: Houghton Mifflin Company, 1909. Vol. II, p. 337.

[6] "Work makes life sweet."

[7] German societies and clubs.

[8] Gymnastic clubs.

[9] Choral congresses.

[10] 1607-1676.

[11] "The world is a laugh to me, with its great wrath."

[12] Eugene Holloway Rosebloom and Francis Phelps Weisenborger, *A History of Ohio.* New York: Prentice-Hall, Inc., 1934. Pp. 189-191.

[13] *Ibid,* p. 177.

[14] "He who does not love wine, wife, and song, remains a fool his whole life long."

[15] Outings.

[16] *Western Christian Advocate,* March 13, 1835.

[17] *Ibid.*

CHAPTER II

[1] Joseph Holdich, *The Life of Willbur Fisk, D.D., First President of Wesleyan University.* New York: Harper and Brothers, 1842, p. 269.

[2] *Ibid.*

[3] *Ibid,* pp. 267, 268.

[4] Adam Miller, *Experience of German Methodist Preachers.* Cincinnati: Printed at The Methodist Book Concern, 1859, p. 82.

[5] Holdich, *Life of Willbur Fisk,* p. 266.

[6] Financial counsellor.

[7] Her husband was Friedrich Gottlieb Süsskind, *Studien-Direktor und Prälat in Stuttgart.*

[8] *Origin and Progress of the German Missions in the Methodist Episcopal Church.* Cincinnati: S. F. Wright and L. Swormstedt, 1843. Pp. 138

[9] *Ibid.*

[10] *Ibid.*

[11] *Ibid,* p. 139.

[12] *Ibid.*

[13] *Faith, the Old and the New.*

[14] *Experience of German Methodist Preachers,* pp. 79, 80.

[15] *Origin and Progress of the German Missions,* p. 140.

[16] Born at Wildbad in 1798 and died in 1828. Educated at the University of Tübingen, he became a celebrated German divine and preacher, noted for his personal piety, earnestness, and orthodoxy. His published sermons enjoyed a large sale, and the volume was found in almost every German Methodist home in America.

[17] *Ibid,* pp. 141, 142.

[18] *Origin and Progress of German Missions,* p. 141.

[19] *Ibid,* pp. 141, 142.

[20] *Experience of German Methodist Preachers,* p. 64.

[21] *Origin and Progress of the German Missions,* p. 142.

CHAPTER III

[1] *Origin and Progress of the German Missions,* p. 26.

[2] *Experience of German Methodist Preachers,* p. 90.

[3] *Ibid.*

[4] *Ibid.*

[5] *Ibid,* p. 91.

[6] *Origin and Progress of the German Missions,* pp. 27, 28.

[7] *Ibid,* p. 28.

[8] *Experience of German Methodist Preachers,* p. 46.

[9] *Ibid*, pp. 48, 49.

[10] Mother church.

[11] *Origin and Progress of the German Missions*, p. 28.

[12] *Ibid*, pp. 35, 36.

Chapter IV

[1] *Experience of German Methodist Preachers*, pp. 112, 113.

[2] *Ibid*, p. 114.

[3] *Ibid*, pp. 116, 117.

[4] *Origin and Progress of the German Missions*, p. 85.

[5] *Experience of German Methodist Preachers*, pp. 119, 120.

[6] *Ibid*, pp. 121, 122.

[7] *Ibid*, p. 122.

[8] *Origin and Progress of the German Missions*, pp. 87, 88.

[9] *Experience of German Methodist Preachers*, pp. 123, 124.

[10] *Ibid*, p. 92.

[11] *Origin and Progress of the German Missions*, pp. 90, 91.

[12] *Ibid*, pp. 97, 98.

[13] *Ibid*, pp. 101, 102.

[14] *Experience of German Methodist Preachers*, pp. 158-162.

[15] *Origin and Progress of the German Missions*, pp. 107, 108.

[16] *Ibid*, pp. 109, 110.

[17] *Ibid*, p. 111.

[18] *Origin and Progress of the German Missions*, p. 130.

[19] *Experience of German Methodist Preachers*, p. 140.

[20] *Experience of German Methodist Preachers*, p. 125.

[21] *Ibid*, p. 126.

[22] Heinrich Mann, *Ludwig S. Jacoby, Sein Leben und Wirken*. Bremen: Verlag des Traktathauses, 1892, pp. 13-16.

[23] *Ibid*, pp. 135-138.

[24] *Ibid*, pp. 27, 28.

[25] *Origin and Progress of the German Mission*, p. 127.

[26] *Ibid*, p. 129.

[27] *Ibid*, pp. 133, 134.

Chapter V

[1] *Origin and Progress of the German Mission*, p. 36.

[2] *Ibid*, pp. 36, 37.

[3] *Ibid*, pp. 38, 39.

[4] *Ibid*, pp. 41, 42.

[5] *Ibid*, pp. 43-45.

[6] *Ibid*, p. 46.

[7] March 19, 1838.

[8] *Origin and Progress of the German Mission*, pp. 64, 65.

[9] August 14, 1838.

[10] *Origin and Progress of the German Mission*, pp. 69-80. The letter was signed by L. L. Hamline and William H. Raper. It was dated January 4, 1839.

[11] *Verhandlungen und Berichte der ersten Sitzung der Central deutschen Jährl.-Conferenz, 1864*, pp. 26, 27.

[12] *Verhandlungen und Berichte der ersten Sitzung der Nordwestlichen deutschen Conferenz, 1864*, pp. 21, 22.

Chapter VI

[1] The appointments to the twelve charges on the Cincinnati District were: Cincinnati, W. Ahrens; Lawrenceburg, Christian Wittenback; Madison, Charles Shelper; Louisville, E. Riemenschneider; Evansville, Henry Koenecke; Perry County Mission, Indiana, to be supplied; Dayton, George Breunig; Portsmouth, John Hoppen; Chillicothe, John Bier; Columbus, John H. Barth; Delaware, to be supplied; and Sidney, John Zwahlen. The appointments to the eight charges on the Pittsburgh District were: Pittsburgh, John Miller; Wheeling, Michael Mulfinger; Monroe, John M. Hofer; Marietta, John Guyer; Chester, Henry Koch; Zanesville, to be supplied; North Ohio, John H. Bahrenburg; and Canal Dover, to be supplied. The appointments to the St. Louis District were: North St. Louis, G. Dancker; South St. Louis, C. Jost; Hermann Mission, C. Koeneke; Pinckney Mission, Fr. Horsman; Versailles Mission, Seb. Barth and H. Nuelsen; Belleville Mission, W. Hemminghaus and Jos. Steinhauser; Beardstown Mission, P. Wilkens; Washington Mission, D. Brestel; Quincy Mission, Phil. Barth; Leadmines Mission, W. S. Schreck; and Iowa Mission, J. Mann.

[2] *Kalender für das Jahr 1860*, pp. 28-34.

[3] *Minutes of the Cincinnati Conference* for the year 1863, pp. 22-25.

[4] *Souvenir der West Deutschen Konferenz.* Cincinnati: Jennings und Graham, 1906, p. 30.

Chapter VIII

[1] Bishop Nuelsen discusses the influence of the German song upon John Wesley in an exhaustive monograph, *John Wesley und das Deutsche Kirchenlied.* Bremen: Anker Verlag, 1938.

[2] Op. cit., p. 34.

[3] *Ibid*, p. 54.

[4] *Ibid*, p. 57.

[5] Heinrich Mann, *Ludwig S. Jacoby, Sein Leben und Wirken.* Bremen: Verlag des Traktat hauses, 1892, pp. 36, 37.

[6] *Ibid*, p. 37.

[7] *Ibid*, p. 39.

[8] *Ibid*, p. 41.

[9] *Ibid*, p. 44.

[10] *Ibid,* pp. 46-48.

[11] May the grace of our Lord Jesus Christ be with you.

[12] *Die Christen lieben ihren Herrn,*
(The Christians love their Lord)
Der sie zuerst geliebet;
(Who first loved them)
Von ihnen wird mit Lust und gern
(By them gladly and with zeal)
Das Christentum geübet.
(Is Christianity practiced)
Ein jeglicher Befehl von Gott
(Every command of God)
Ist ihnen heiliges Gebot.
(Is to them a holy command)

[13] Feuerwasser.

[14] Some of the adjectives used are expressive in the German:

"Alcohol=*Feuerwasser.*"
"*Aergster Widersacher.*"
"*Grösste Feind der Menschen.*"
"*Abscheulichste Ruhe- und Friedensstörer.*"
"*Der Verderber unserer Jugend.*"

[15] For example: Ein Mann, namens Michael Daicy, wurde in Boston tot gefunden. Seine Kleider hatten, da er betrunken war, Feuer gefangen, und auf diese Weise kam er um.

[16] The tracts available included two volumes of John Wesley's sermons, a collection of spiritual songs for church and home, "containing not only many German hymns, but also translations of glorious English songs," a brief defense of the Methodist Church, refuting various unjust accusations, the Articles of Faith, and the General Rules.

[17] *Experience of German Methodist Preachers,* p. 199.

[18] *Ibid,* pp. 200, 201.

[19] *Ibid,* pp. 201, 202.

[20] Popular orator.

[21] *Ludwig S. Jacoby: Sein Leben und Wirken,* p. 55.

[22] *Experience of German Methodist Preachers,* pp. 338, 339.

[23] *Ludwig S. Jacoby: Sein Leben und Wirken,* p. 72.

[24] *Ibid,* p. 73.

[25] E. F. Wunderlich, *Glaubenskampf, oder Freud und Leid eines Missionars in Deutschland.* Cincinnati: Walden and Stowe, 1882, p. 132.

[26] Quoted by Bishop Nuelsen. *The Christian Apologist,* September 28, 1893, from page 84 of the Journal of John Wesley.

[27] *Ibid.*

[28] Quoted by Bishop Nuelsen, *The Christian Apologist,* September 28, 1893, *Neustaedtel, den 22. April 1886. Der Stadtrath.*

[29] *Ibid, Königliche* Amtshauptmannschaft Auerbach, den 10. April 1880.

[30] "Woe unto you, scribes and Pharisees, hypocrites! for ye compass sea and

land to make one proselyte, and when he is made, ye make him twofold more the child of hell than yourself."

[81] *The Christian Apologist,* September 28, 1893.

[82] The story of the development of the work in Switzerland is summarized in L. *Peter's Geschichte der Bischöflichen Methodistenkirche in der Schweiz.* Zürich: Christliche Verlagsbuchhandlung, 1906, p. 91

[83] *Das deutsche Freikirchentum und seine Sendung* Bremen: *Verlagshaus der Methodistenkirche,* 1928, p. 36.

[84] *Wesen und Recht der Sekte im religiösen Leben Deutschlands.* Giessen, 1930, pp. 5-25.

[85] *Die Methodistenkirche im religiösen Leben der Schweiz.* Zürich: Christliche Vereinsbuchhandlung, pp. 21, 22.

CHAPTER IX

[1] Christian Golder, *History of the Deaconess Movement in the Christian Church.* Cincinnati: Jennings and Pye, 1903, p. 26.

[2] Coulton, *A Medieval Garner.* London: Constable, 1910, p. 320f.

[3] *History of the Deaconess Movement,* p. 34.

[4] *Ibid,* p. 36.

[5] *Ibid,* p. 47.

[6] *Ibid,* p. 138.

[7] The work is organized through the *Union of Deaconesses' Associations of the Methodist Episcopal Church.* This federation is composed of the Bethany Deaconess Association of North Germany, the Bethany Deaconess Association of South Germany, the Mary and Martha Deaconess Association and the Bethany Deaconess Association in Switzerland. The following statistics are useful to give an overview of the extent of the work:

UNION OF DEACONESSES' ASSOCIATIONS

NORTH GERMANY CONFERENCE

	Date of Establishment	Number of Licensed Deaconesses	Probationers
Bethany Deaconess Association of North Germany;	1910	....	....
Motherhouse, Hamburg.......	1887	184	84
Berlin.....................	1883	41	3
Chemnitz..................	1904	8	5
Dresden...................	1912	16	1
Leipzig....................	1911	10	5
Plauen....................	1910	7	1

SOUTH GERMANY CONFERENCE

	Date of Establishment	Number of Licensed Deaconesses	Probationers
Bethany Deaconess Association of South Germany:			
Motherhouse, Frankfurt.......	1876	154	64
Darmstadt...................	1913	4	1
Esslingen...................	1926	2	....
Heidelberg.................	1911	3	....
Karlsruhe..................	1903	7	3
Kassel.....................	1920	2	1
Ludwigsburg................	1915	2	2
Mannheim..................	1915	4	1
Pforzheim..................	1900	8	2
Pirmasens..................	1913	2	2
Saarbrucken................	1912	3	1
Budapest...................	1913	4	4
Strassburg..................	1896	4	....
Vienna.....................	1890	12	3

MARY AND MARTHA DEACONESS ASSOCIATION

	Date of Establishment	Number of Licensed Deaconesses	Probationers
Mary and Martha Deaconess Association:			
Motherhouse, Nurnberg.......	1889	215	77
Donndorf..................	1911	11	1
Dusseldorf..................	1908	5	1
Halle......................	1912	3	3
Köln......................	1902	8	3
Magdeburg.................	1892	12	5
Siegen.....................	1904	7	3
Stuttgart...................	1905	19	5
Wiesbaden.................	1911	7	1
München..................	1889	22	11

BETHANY DEACONESS ASSOCIATION IN SWITZERLAND

	Date of Establishment	Number of Licensed Deaconesses	Probationers
Bethany Deaconess Association in Switzerland:			
Motherhouse, Zurich..........	1887	152	62
Basel......................	1917	14	3
Bern......................	1915	16	3
Geneva....................	1908	17	3
Lausanne..................	1890	25	2
Luzern....................	1911	12	....
Saint Galen	1885	16	1

Data from Journal of the General Conference, 1936, pp. 1122, 1123.

[8] Quoted by Golder, *History of the Deaconess Movement*, p. 305.

[9] *Haus und Herd,* December, 1891.

[10] *In Memoriam,* Christian Golder, p. 8.

[11] When one begins to glorify himself, he ceases to glorify God.

[12] Quoted in *In Memoriam,* Louise Golder, 1857-1929, p. 30.

GERMAN DEACONESS HOSPITALS IN AMERICA

	Date Established	Value of Property	Endowments	Debts	Value Free Service
Bethesda Hospital.....	1898	$1,829,996	$193,266	$40,000	$57,229
Louisville, Kentucky...	1896	175,000	....	41,792	5,082
Brooklyn, Bethany....	1894	414,400	20,000	37,000	15,926

GERMAN DEACONESS HOSPITAL IN AMERICA—*Continued*

	Number Beds	Number Patients Treated	Number Licensed Deaconesses	Number Nurses
Bethesda Hospital.....	239	6,518	38	71
Louisville, Kentucky...	75	1,068	....	29
Brooklyn, Bethany....	90	1,525	12	4

[14] The Elizabeth Haas Deaconess Home, founded in St. Paul, Minnesota, in 1891, as the first German Methodist institution of its kind, closed its doors in 1898. The Emanuel Deaconess Society, of Kansas City, Missouri, was organized on Thanksgiving Day, 1897, in Chicago, and upon the invitation of the Deaconess Board of the West German Conference, moved to Kansas City in

1901. In March, 1903, the work became a branch station of the Motherhouse in Cincinnati.

A hospital, owned by the First German Methodist Episcopal Church, Los Angeles, and valued at half a million dollars, is operated under lease.

[15] *History of the Deaconess Movement*, pp. 526-533.

[16] *Ibid*, pp. 545, 546.

CHAPTER X

[1] 1870-1895.

[2] F. H. Otto Melle, *Das Walten Gottes im deutschen Methodismus*. Bremen: Kommissionsverlag, 1925, p. 221.

[3] *Ibid*, pp. 221, 222.

[4] *Ibid*, pp. 225, 226.

[5] *Ibid*, p. 235.

[6] Fanny Nast (her given name was really Francisca) was one of the first two graduates in June, 1866. The other was C. F. Morf.

[7] *Kalender für 1909, St. Louis Deutschen Konferenz*, p. 93.

[8] *Kalender für 1910, St. Louis Deutschen Konferenz*, p. 81.

[9] "The goal has been reached."

CHAPTER XI

[1] *Geschichte der Zentral Deutschen Konferenz*, p. 177.

[2] September 14, 1863.

[3] *Western Christian Advocate*, June 22, 1898.

[4] According to the General Conference Journal of 1936 the statistics relating to institutions founded by German Methodists were as follows, pp. 1110-1115.

HOMES FOR AGED

	Pacific Old Peoples Home	Quincy Home for Aged	Bethany Home for Aged	Bethesda Home for Aged
Date Established.....	1910	1889	1911	1915
Location............	Los Angeles	Quincy, Ill.	Brooklyn	Cincinnati
Value of Property....	$100,000	$300,000	$100,000	$131,000
Endowments.........			$71,000	$309,975
Capacity............			35	100
In Home During Year.	60		26	73
Value of Free Service.	$1,500		$5,996	

CHILDREN'S HOMES

	Central Wesleyan Orphans' Home	German Methodist Orphans' Home	Emanuel Home for Girls	William Nast Home for Young Men
Date Established.....	1864	1864	1924	1912
Location............	Warrenton, Mo.	Berea, Ohio	Cincinnati	Cincinnati
Value of Property....	$262,000	$750,000	$70,000	$20,000
Endowments.........		$102,000		
Capacity............	80	102	60	27
In Home During Year.	71	102	34	13
Value of Free Service.	$8,628	$19,860	$361	$748

CHAPTER XII

[1] *The Rise of American Civilization.* New York: The Macmillan Company, 1930; II, p. 481. Quoted by permission.

[2] *General Conference Journal,* 1912. New York: The Methodist Book Concern, 1912; pp. 216, 217.

[3] *The Rise of American Civilization.* II, pp. 612, 613. Quoted by permission.

[4] *Ibid,* II, pp. 617, 618. Quoted by permission.

[5] *The German Terror in France.* London: Hodder and Stoughton, 1917; pp. 17, 18. Distributed with maps to clergymen "with the compliments of Professor W. MacNeile Dixon, of the University of Glasgow."

[6] *Ibid,* p. 123.

[7] *Troy Conference Minutes,* 1918; pp. 74, 75.

[8] *Baltimore Conference Minutes,* 1918; pp. 70, 71.

[9] According to provisions of Paragraph 190, Section II, of the *Discipline* of 1916.

[10] Walter Langsam, *The World Since 1914.* (Third edition.) New York: The Macmillan Company, 1936; pp. 74, 75. Quoted by permission.

[11] *Journal of the General Conference,* 1920; p. 960.

[12] *Ibid,* pp. 964, 965.

[13] *Der Methodismus in Deutschland nach dem Krieg.* Bremen: Buchhandlung und Verlag des Traktathauses (undated); p. 29.

[14] A trinket shop, a church stunted by its own insignificance.

CHAPTER XIII

[1] The work of the Methodist Episcopal Church in post-war relief and reconstruction is discussed in a detailed monograph in manuscript: Ferdinand Sigg, *Unsere Hilfsaktinonen. Ihre Veranlassung, ihre Durchfürung und ihr Ergebnis,* p. 79.

[2] *Unsere Hilfsaktionen,* p. 3.

[3] *Journal of the Twenty-ninth Delegated General Conference,* p. 1837.

[4] For example: Nast reported that up to December, 1915, he had raised $24,509.86 by his special appeals in the columns of the *Apologist.* The Christmas Fund, which he reported in the same year, amounted to $9,653.23. At the same time Bishop Nuelsen reported Christmas gifts received by him totaled $5,133.28. Bucher, soliciting for the fund for the relief of German children, reported on February 10, 1915, collections amounting to $4,352.21. Contributions received after that date taxed the capacity of the clerical staff in his office so that the funds were not totaled after that date. Gifts and clothing reported by Diekmann and Golder during 1919 up to March 3, 1920, were $49,751.12 in cash and $25,478 in clothing. Bucher in the meantime reported that in 1919, 1920, and 1921 up to November 16, 1921, he had received $198,185.51.

[5] *108 Laws of Ohio,* pp. 614, 615.

[6] *History of Ohio,* pp, 488, 489.

[7] Between 1914 and 1929 a total of $1,380,202.27 passed through the offices of the relief work in Zürich. Computed in Swiss francs the sum amounted to 7,177,051. Goods solicited by Bishop Nuelsen, coming from America, Switzer-

land, Denmark, Norway, and Sweden amounted to 1,370,000 francs more, making the relief funds, in cash and commodities, total 8,547,051 Swiss francs. See Sigg, *Unsere Hilfsaktionen,* p. 80.

[8] *Ibid,* p. 8.

Chapter XIV

[1] Josiah Stamp, *The Financial Aftermath of War.* London: Ernest Benn Limited, 1932; p. 94.

[2] *Discipline* of 1924, Paragraph 571, Section 6.

[3] *General Conference Journal,* 1924; p. 1670.

[4] *General Conference Journal,* 1924; p. 577.

[5] These included power to the St. Louis German Conference to merge with contiguous English Conferences during the next quadrennium, authorization the Chicago and Northwest German Conferences, power to the St. Louis Conference, of a merger of the California and Pacific German Conferences, and the Chicago and Northwest German Conferences power to the St. Louis Conference to absorb the work of the St. Louis German Conference in the counties of Warren, Lincoln, Montgomery, and St. Charles, and power to the West German Conference to discontinue its organization at any session by a three-fourths vote. See *Discipline* of 1924, Paragraph 518, Sections 3, 4, 16, 20, 23, and 24.

[6] *Official Record: Minutes and Historical Review of the St. Louis German Conference, 47th Annual Session.* P. 126.

[7] *Ibid,* p. 30.

[8] *Ibid,* p. 149.

[9] Pursuant to authorization of the General Conference of 1924, the Chicago German and Northwest German Conferences had been merged. The first session of the Chicago-Northwest Conference was held at La Crosse, Wisconsin, September 27-31, 1924.

[10] Official Journal, Central German Annual Conference, 1933; p. 192.

Chapter XV

[1] *Die Glocke.*

[2] Vol. I, No. 1, p. 2.

A poem from the first issue shows the didactic method of the paper.

Herr, Lehre mich beten.
Herr, Lehre mich beten,
Wecke Herz und Sinn,
So vor dich zu treten,
Dass ich Heil gewinn!

Samm'le die Gedanken,
Dass sie hell und rein,
Auf dich ohne Wanken
Nur gerichtet sein!

Deine Macht und Liebe
Lass die Seele schauen;
Wecke Ehrfurchtstriebe,
Glauben und Vertraun

Vol. II, p. 3.

Gieb mir aus der Höhe,
Deinen heil'gen Geist,
Dass ich stets nur flehe,
Was du selbst mich heisst.

Lehr' mich sauft und stille
Stets wie Jesus flehen:
"Vater, nicht mein Wille,
Dein Will soll geschehen."

[3] *Der Bibelforscher.*

[4] *Haus und Herd.*

[5] *Haus und Herd,* June, 1918, p. 381.

[6] *Jugendharfe.*

[7] *Harfenklänge, Psalter und Harfe, Liederlust,* and *Die Perle.*

[8] The first Sunday's lesson for January 1, 1871, set the pattern:

> Lektion—über die Anbetung Gottes, 1. Bezügliche Schriftstellen: Joh. 4, 19-26. 2. Schriftstelle zum Hauptinhalt: Gott ist Geist, und die ihn anbeten, die müssen ihn im Geist und in der Wahrheit anbeten. 3. Erklärende Bemerkungen. 4. Fragen. 5. Anwendung.

[9] He emphasized the cardinal points of Christian faith. The subjects covered in the first quarter included:

1. Ueber die Anbetung Gottes.
2. Die Sünde der Menschen.
3. Das Heil.
4. Reichthum.
5. Das eine Pfund.
6. Der Heilige Geist.
7. Hass.
8. Der Gebrauch der Zunge.
9. Das Gebet.
10. Charakter.
11. Die unbekannte Sünde.
12. Der Himmel.

[10] *Haus und Herd.*

[11] *Haus und Herd,* erster Band, erstes Heft, January 1873, p. 1.

[12] June, 1918, p. 381.

[13] *Bildersaal* and *Kleine Lehrbilder.*

[14] *Für Kleine Leute.*

[15] *Neue Glocke.*

[16] *Die Kleine Glocke.*

[17] The poetry was often heavy verse for small children. The "Morning Prayer" appearing in the issue of July 25, 1897, is an example:

Gott, unter deiner Vaterhut
Hab' ich die Nacht so sanft geruht,
Dass ich erquickt nun in die Höh,
Der Morgensonn' entgegenseh.

Wohin ich blicke, redest du
Mit Wohlthat mir und Güte zu;
Mein erster Hauch sei Lobgesang,
Mein letzter Atemzug sei Dank.

Nur deine Hand teilt Segen aus,
Giebt Segen in mein kleines Haus;
Lass gern mich nützen jedermann
Und willig helfen, wo ich kann.

Der Erde köstlichter Gewinn
Ist frohes Herz und frommer Sinn,
Und diese, Vater, schenke mir,
So wall' ich ruhevoll vor dir.

No. 4, B. I, p. 15.

Questions and answers in the same issue show how direct the teaching was. Following the lesson on Paul's preaching at Athens this sequence was printed:

5. What did he preach?
   God does not dwell in heathen temples.
6. What more did he preach?
   We shall seek God.
7. How can we do that?
   When we are converted and believe on the Lord Jesus Christ.
8. Who will judge the world?
   Jesus Christ.
10. What then shall we do?
   We shall believe in the Lord Jesus.

[18] January 5, 1885.

[19] *Zionsänger.*

[20] *Der neue Liederschatz für die Jugend und zum Gebrauch in Sonntagschulen.*

[21] *Liebhart's Die Jugendharfe.*
The youth hymnals which Liebhart edited during the following fifteen years made a cardinal contribution to the life of the church:
Die neue Harfe, Harfenklänge, Psalter und Harfe, Liederlust und Psalter und Perle.

[22] A series of prayer-meeting songbooks was also published:
Der Kleine Psalter and *Der Neue Kleine Psalter.*
The final development of this series was the edition known as *Pilgerklänge.*

[23] *Der Kleinere Katechismus für die deutschen Gemeinden der Bisch. Methodisten-Kirche mit Genehmigung der General-Conferenz.* Cincinnati: Cranston and Curts.
Der Grössere Katechismus. Cincinnati: Hitchcock and Walden, 1869.
The Larger Catechism (English Edition), Cincinnati: Hitchcock and Walden, 1869.

[24] *The Larger Catechism,* pp. 5, 6.

[25] Philip Schaff (1819-1893), was a Swiss-born church historian who ended his career at Union Theological Seminary. A follower of Neander, he combined critical scholarship with evangelical piety.

[26] *Larger Catechism,* p. 9.

[27] *Ibid,* pp. 34-36.

[28] *Ibid,* pp. 147-149.

[29] *Jugendbibliothek.*

[30] *Bibliothek für kleine Kinder·*

[31] *Lebens-Compass für Alt und Jung.* Cincinnati: Jennings and Pye, p. 508 Illustrated.

CHAPTER XVI

[1] August J. Bucher, *Unter drei Sonnen.* Bremen: Anker-Verlag, 1934, pp. 176.

[2] *Unter drei Sonnen,* p. 9.

My Fatherlands

Three fatherlands I gratefully call my own;
In each my name is enrolled.
In the first I was born into the world as a child;
The second I chose myself.

From heaven distant the third beckons to me,
So I, despite that, am only a stranger here.
The first lies hidden by an Alpine Crown,
Like an emerald in the *névé* and the glacial splendor.

The second, rich and powerful land, spreads from Alaska to the tropics.
Through both my streams of life has flown,
In both have I enjoyed good fortune.
In both have I shed tears and sweat, as child, as youth, as adult and old man.

Yet none of them can hold me fast; in both I must fold my wander's tent.
I look from them away, away..
In the third am I only truly at home.
It lies, O fortune, high above the canopy of stars.
Far, eternally far, from the vicissitudes of this world.

³ *Ibid*, p. 45.

My Faith

I do not believe because I must·
Who could compel me to do that?
What drives the eagle to his flight,
And who makes the Nightingale to sing?
Who whips the swans upon their procession?
No external Must—an inner urge
Whose meaning no reason knows—
Awakens every song and wing.

So is my faith, without coercion,
My free thinking, feeling, willing,
It is an urge toward my origin,
A hallowed, deep, and inner shall.

⁴ *Ibid*, p. 55.

Prayer for Sleep

Give me after the burden of the day,
Lord, rest in sleep so sweet,
That I may not on heated pillows
Vainly twist my head,
Without peace, without rest—
Father, close my eyes.

Put Thy hand upon my head
That nothing rob me of my sleep—
Neither body nor sorrow—
I order both now to Thee.
Short to me the night is measured,
Let me now forget it all.

⁵ *Ibid*, p. 97.

⁶ *Ibid*, pp. 62, 63.

Is this the thing the Lord God made and gave
To have dominion over sea and land;
To trace the stars and search the heavens for power;
To feel the passion of Eternity?
Is this the dream He dreamed who shaped the suns
And marked their ways upon the unknown deep? . . .

⁷ "The Founders of Peace of 1919."

⁸ *Ibid*, pp. 39, 40.

The harvest ripens. Before the day
The anxious world well may tremble.
It nears already and draws blow by blow
The lightning from God's angry thundering.

A peace pact born of hate
Can bear but hate and war,
It is a contract with hell,
The peace of Versailles will teach us that.

⁹ *Discipline*, 1932, Paragraph 403, Section 2.

¹⁰ *General Conference Journal*, 1936, pp. 314, 315.

¹¹ The *Apologist* as an agent of the Church was supplemented by a group of German Conference and regional papers. The most important of these were the *Hausfreund* of the Northwest German Conference (1901-1924); the

Familienfreund of the East German Conference (1883-); the *Famielien-freund* of the Chicago German Conference (1891-1928); *Am stillen Meer* of the California German Conference (1904-1925); the *Hausfreund* of the Pacific German Conference (1901-1918); the *Texas Stern* of the Southern German Conference (1892-); the *Hausfreund* of the St. Louis German Conference (1899-1914); and the *Hausfreund* of the West German Conference (1886-1926). The missionary paper of German women, *Heiden Frauenfreund,* established in 1886, was discontinued in 1926.

CHAPTER XVII

[1] *Zeitschrift für Enthaltsamkeit und Volkswohlfahrt,* founded in 1883.

[2] For example, they quote often his comment: "Fundamentally any man will have to admit this, that alcohol is a detriment to humanity. What alcohol has destroyed in worthful men or made worthless to the nation is far greater in a century than the loss on all the fields of battle in an equal space of time. Let no one be deceived: that people which first succeeds in cutting this poison out of its life may perhaps have stiff resistance and bitter accompanying phenomena, but that act will be only the beginning of a great act of blessedness for later humanity. Probably therewith will be founded a domination over another world which was not ready to take the same step."
Methodists also enthusiastically applaud the principles laid down by the National Socialist Party:

1. Abstinence from the use of alcohol and tobacco until the sixteenth year of age.
2. Abstinence of pregnant and nursing mothers from the same.
3. Abstinence for all workers performing functions involving the safety of human life.
4. Control of tobacco and liquor advertising.
5. Prohibition of advertising of tobacco and liquor as beneficial to health and happiness.
6. Education of the nation in the effects of alcohol and narcotics.

[3] "He alone who lets God rule his life
He who trusts in God above,
That man has not built upon the sands."

CHAPTER XVIII

[1] 1937 edition, p. 1020.

[2] *Die drei Wege des Erkennens in Wissenschaft, Dichtung und Offenbarung.* Berlin: Furche-Verlag, 1926.
Präludium zur Poesie—Eine Einführung in die Deutung des dichterischen Kunstwerkes. Berlin: Furche-Verlag, 1929.
Die Götter des Abendlandes: Eine Auseinandersetzung mit dem Heidentum in der Kultur unserer Zeit. Berlin: Furche-Verlag, 1931.
Die Sünde. Bern: Buchhandling der Evangelischen Gesellschaft, 1933.
Vom befreienden Glauben. Berlin: Furche-Verlag, 1934.
Der Herr des Alltags: Von dem Wunder der Begegnung mit Christus. Berlin: Furche-Verlag, 1934.
Revolution in Genf? Sonderdruck aus der "Nuen Schweizer Rundschau," Oktober 1935.
Kurze Anleitung zur Tat: Eine Antwort auf Frages: Was sollen wir denn tun? Berlin: Furche-Verlag, 1936.
Die Formwerdung des Menschen: Die Deutung des dichterischen Kunstwerkes als Schlüssel zur menschlichen Wirklichkeit. Berlin: Furche-Verlag, 1938.

[3] *Die drei Wege des Erkennens,* p. 36. For comparison with the point of view see Croce, *Breviario* di Estetica, Nuovi Saggi di Estetica, Laterza, Bari, 1920.

[4] *Die Götter des Abendlandes,* p. 129.

[5] *Ibid,* pp. 9-12.

[6] *Die Sünde,* pp. 10, 11.

[7] *Die Formwerdung des Menschen,* pp. 11, 12, 189.

[8] *Warum ich ein Methodist bin?* Schweizer Evangelist, 20. Juni 1931; pp. 398, 399.

[9] For the names used in the following pages the author is indebted to Zwingli F. Meyer, who for fifteen years cataloged material on the achievements of German Methodists. In 1935 Meyer had a manuscript of a hundred and fifty pages entitled "A Century of German Methodism" ready for publication. For various reasons the volume was not published and Meyer, with a great generosity, contributed his material for such use as the author of the *History of German-speaking Methodism* might make of it· This footnote is in no way adequate acknowledgement of his work.

[10] A list of German Methodist teachers in Methodist colleges, by no means complete, follows:

Albion College: Fred Lutz, Henry Battenhouse, Remmt Luebbers; *Allegheny College:* George Mulfinger, Fred Henke, Daniel Matthaei; *Baldwin-Wallace College:* Albert Riemenschneider, P. E. Bauer, H. C. Beyer, M. Wicke, Ruth Beyer, A. L. Breslich, J. C. Marting, C. W. Hartzler, H. T. Ficken, Carl Stiefel, Fred Cramer, Fred Roehm, E. C. Unnewehr; *Boston University:* M. J. Cremer, Homer Albers, H. H· Meyer, J. Schlagenhauf, Jr.; *College of Puget Sound:* Paul Rader, Paul Schilpp; *College of the Pacific:* W. W. Guth, J. W. Riedemann, Paul Schilpp; *Cornell College and Upper Iowa:* H. P. Lotz; *Dakota Wesleyan University:* E. D. Kohlstedt, E. C. Paustian, Noble C. Nagler; *De-Pauw University:* Chas. Nordhoff, William F. Swahlen; *Dickinson College:* M. J. Cremer; *Drew University:* M. J. Cremer; *Evansville College, Goucher College:* W. W· Guth; *Hamline University:* Paul Rader, E. C. Buehler, George Muhlemann; *Illinois Wesleyan University:* A. J. Nast, W. A. Heiden, Otto J. Baah; *Iowa Wesleyan University:* G. F. Willy, W. H. Heppe, H. G. Leist, John Helmers, E. S. Havighurst, Emelie Havighurst; *Inter-Mountain Union College:* N. C. Nagler; *Kansas Wesleyan University:* W. F. Swahlen, Edward Mueller, H. P· Lotz; *Lawrence College:* F. C. Havighurst, Gottlieb Cast; *Mc-Kendree College:* D. S. Wahl, O. H. Kleinschmidt, Wesley Kettelkamp; *Missouri Wesleyan:* H. J. Dueker, F. C. Havighurst; *Montana Wesleyan College, Morningside College:* F. W. Schneider, William Hilmer, S. C. Steinbrenner, Fred Schaub, Laura Fischer, Mrs. F. W. Schneider, F. O. Barz, A. B· Gehrig, Benjamin F. Schwartz; *Northwestern University:* F. L. Schaub, Frank Bernstorf, E. T. Asling, Ernst Lauer, A. W. Nagler, F. W. Lesemann, O. J. Baah, P. A. Schilipp; *Ohio Wesleyan University:* William Herms; *Oklahoma City College:* George Marquardt; *Simpson College:* W· C. Hilmer; *Southwestern College:* Henry Limper, Dale Liese; *Syracuse University:* Zeno Nagel, George Marquardt; *University of Chattanooga:* Godfrey Tietze; *University of Denver:* E. F. Stroeter; *University of Southern California; Wesley College:* Karl Stolz; *Wesleyan University:* W. A. Heidel; *West Virginia University:* Reemt Luebbers, Aaron Repking; *Willamette University:* D. A. Schulze; *University of Wisconsin:* Wm. J. Keller.

[11] *O Seliger Sabbath, du Tag meines Herrn.*

[12] *Jehovah, Herr der Welt,*
Wie lieblich und wie schön.

[13] *Freudenvoll, freudenvoll, walle ich fort, Hin zu dem Lande der Seligen dort.*

[14] *Wir sind nur Pilger und Fremdlinge hier.*

[15] *Heimatland, Heimatland, O wie schön bist du!*

[16] *Ich weiss einen Strom.* Other hymns included: *Auf Ewig bei dem Herrn; In dem Himmel ist's wunderschön;* and *Wann Schlägt die Stunde.*

[17] Among his poems are the better-known *Herz und Heimat, Kain und Abel, Wilhelm Raabe und Dickens, De Profundis,* and *Lieder eines Einsamen.*

[18] The Abingdon Press: New York, 1929.

[19] *Geschichte des Methodismus von seinen Anfängen bis zur Gegenwart.* Bremen: Verlag des Traktathauses, 1920.

[20] Quoted in Jesse Lee Bennett, *The Essential American Tradition.* New York: George H. Doran Company, 1925, pp. 301-30.

CHAPTER XIX

[1] William James, *The Varieties of Religious Experience.* New York: The Modern Library, 1936, p. 509.

[2] *Ibid,* pp. 208, 209.

[3] John L. Nuelsen, *Kurzgefasste Geschichte des Methodismus.* Bremen: Buchhandlung und Verlag des Traktathauses, 1920, p. 744.

[4] *Origin and Progress of the German Missions,* pp. 8, 9.

[5] "The old soldierly virtues—loyalty, obedience, and performance of duty—the rule of conduct for your behavior." A favorite saying of General von Hindenburg.

APPENDIX

WESLEYAN METHODISM IN GERMANY

Nearly two decades before Ludwig Jacoby returned to his native land as a missionary of the Methodist Episcopal Church, Wesleyan Methodism had begun a modest work in southwestern Germany. Less fortunate in a trained and native leadership, the Wesleyan Methodists did not grow in the fashion that the efforts of the Methodist Episcopal Church enjoyed. The result of two unassociated Methodist missionary programs was a happy merger in June, 1897. By the union the Methodist Episcopal Church received 29 traveling preachers, 6 preachers on trial, 189 local preachers and exhorters, 2,414 full members, 89 members on trial, 79 Sunday schools, 219 officers and teachers, and 4,395 scholars. At the same time the institutions of the Martha and Mary Society became projects of the Methodist Episcopal Church.

This early consolidation of Methodist work demonstrated the practicability of organic association. Two difficulties which arose in the course of the merger negotiations, which began in 1894 between the Missions' Committee of the Wesleyan Methodist Church in London and the Mission Board of the Methodist Episcopal Church in New York, were solved by a generous gift from Baroness von Langenau, the most influential and wealthiest member of the Wesleyan Methodist persuasion on the Continent. The first problem arose over the adjustment to be made for valuable property which had been acquired, largely free from debt, as the result of generous missionary grants from England. The Wesleyans were reluctant to withdraw from the field without some compensation for their investment in chapels and parsonages. The second problem arose because the Methodist Episcopal ministers were reluctant to accept the Wesleyan preachers as claimants on their pension funds inasmuch as the Wesleyan preachers' aid annuities were smaller. Both difficulties were resolved when Baroness von Langenau gave a quarter million marks to the Missions' Committee in England as compensation for the surrender of its property claims, but upon the condition that the Committee in return should contribute 70,000 marks to the united pension fund. On June 22, 1897, Bishop Goodsell formally declared the union of the two branches of the Methodist Church, saying, "Now we are one in love, in doctrine, in government, and in body."

Wesleyan Methodism was born in Winnenden, a citadel of German Pietism. It happened in this way: In 1810 *Christoph Gottlieb Mueller,* reluctant to serve under the flag of Napoleon Bonaparte, fled to England. Finding little satisfaction in the activities of the German colony in London, he occasionally visited the services of the Methodists in the chapel on Great Queen Street. Here the fervent prayers and direct sermons awakened him to the necessity of seeking God's grace. He joined the Church. Recognized by the pastor as a young German of talent, he was soon granted local preacher's orders. Homesick and wishing to see his father again before he died and to testify to his relatives about his religious experience, he returned to his native Winnenden. His father, a *Herrnhuter,* was still holding meetings in his home. Mueller visited these and when occasion offered itself, he related the story of his conversion. He spoke with such conviction of his certainty of forgiveness that the meetings which he attended grew. Although his witness kindled an enthusiasm among a growing circle of followers, he returned to London. Pleas to move to Germany fell on his deaf ears. His friends, however, appealed to the Missions' Committee of the Wesleyan Methodist Church. On November 15, 1830, *Imanuel Strubel,* a mechanic in Winnenden, pleaded with the Committee with such vigor that London influence finally encouraged Mueller to return to Germany. His wife and three children followed him to the Continent.

Mueller had religious enthusiasm but only an elementary-school education. His awareness of his scant schooling made him reluctant to enter the active field. When he gave his first witness on March 13, 1831, however, there was no doubt of the fact that he was the leader whom the humble folk had awaited. As demands came for him to preach in Stuttgart, Backnang, Marbach, Leonberg, and Tuebingen, he insisted that he had not come to found a church nor to proselyte. Harassed by the police upon complaint of the clergy of the State Church until the police themselves were disgusted, Mueller's circle of influence widened. In 1835 he had 23 helpers and 326 followers. At the end of 1839 the movement had 600 members and 60 helpers. Chief among these was *Christian Gottlieb Hiller,* a twenty-six-year-old nailmaker, who had but an elementary-school training. Hiller had been converted in solitude and became an enthusiastic evangelist. In 1867 he was accepted as a preacher. Another of the assistants was *Johann Gottlieb Steinlen,* a young man educated at the Latin School in Schorndorf, who at sixteen had migrated to America. After working as a farmer, teacher, and sailor, and having taken part in Evangelical and Quaker meetings, he returned to his native land. Affected by Mueller's preaching, he became his assistant in 1848, preaching throughout the forests in southwestern Germany. *Michael Wiedmann,* a lame boy with the added handicap of stuttering, was accepted as a preacher in 1861. He too had come into his religious conviction through solitude. Reluctant to talk in public, he discovered during prayer that his tongue was released and he could speak fluently. In 1862, *Jakob Klenk,* a shoemaker, took his orders, having come in contact with the Wesleyan Methodists thirteen years before.

The first fraternal relationships between the Wesleyan Methodists and the Methodist Episcopalians began in 1844 when Wilhelm Nast visited Mueller in Winnenden. He wrote Peter Schmucker about the watch-night service he attended in the home of Mueller, which "was so full that all those present could not kneel down during prayer." He noted that the consciousness of awakening, conversion, and growth in grace was uncommonly clear in the fellowship.

Mueller suffered from asthma. By 1848 ill health forced him to relinquish most of his active duties. The fellowship had grown to 1,100 members and preaching was being conducted in 67 places. When he died in 1858, he was succeeded for a year by Steinlen, who proved to have neither the energy nor the organizing ability necessary for the leadership of the work. Despite its reluctance to send an English preacher to Germany to take command, the Missions' Committee in 1859 appointed *John Lyth* to the Continent. He took up his residence in the little village of Stetten, beautifully situated in the *Remstal*. Lyth was eminently successful. In six years he added 784 members to the fellowship and had 60 more on trial. Sensitive to the need for literature, he founded and edited in 1863 *The Sunday Guest (Sonntags-gast)*. Within the first year of publication it paid expenses. In his own study he founded a seminary with a student body of two young men. He also moved his residence to Waiblingen, which for a quarter century continued to be the center of Wesleyan Methodism in Germany. In 1865 he returned to London and was succeeded by John C. Barratt, a man of vision, organizing talent, diplomatic ability, and scrupulous respect for the State Church and for ecclesiastical formalities. For eight years he had been a successful missionary in the West Indies. Lyth had often been taunted with the fact that the Wesleyan Methodists had no "doctors of theology." He had always replied that the Methodists needed none of them because they already had a sound and healthy doctrine. It was true nonetheless that Wesleyan Methodism was concentrating its efforts in a ministry to small town and forest folk of humble station. Barratt wanted to extend his ministry to larger communities and to other classes. He studied German industriously and within two years could preach in the language acceptably. He maintained good relations with the State churchmen by requiring his helpers to attend the State Church services and sacraments. His program of expansion met with modest success. In 1867 he opened services in a rented room in Stuttgart. In 1870 work was begun in Vienna. Preaching places were opened in Munich, Augsburg, and Kladno.

Although the Wesleyan Methodists, especially under English leadership, had striven against the establishment of a Church, they were unable to avoid this consequence of their growth. The first communion was administered by the group to about a hundred members in Stuttgart on January 6, 1873. Two years later, on June 17, 1875, a class of eight candidates for the ministry was ordained. Wesleyan Methodism had become a church against its own inclination. The growth of the church had been so substantial that in 1873 *The Sunday Guest* became a fortnightly journal with enlarged format and a new name, *The Methodist Herald (Methodisten Herold)*. In 1875 a fortnightly paper for children, known as *Grains of Seed for Young Hearts (Sämenkörner für jungen Herzen)*, was introduced. The first chapel had been built two years before.

At the end of 1875 twenty-nine preachers and 88 local preachers and exhorters were holding services in 209 chapels and rooms, and caring for 2,344 members. Fifty-one Sunday-school teachers and officers were training 2,731 scholars. In 1876 the scope of the work was widened to include points in Silesia, Bavaria, and Westphalia. On September 2, 1882, Wesleyan Methodism observed its quarter-century anniversary in the mission garden in Waiblingen. As a monument a church was dedicated at Winnenden on September 11, 1883.

The Wesleyan Methodists felt the need of providing a career for women in the Church. A committee was appointed in 1887 to study the problem. Under the leadership of *G. J. Ekert,* a deaconess hospital was established in Nuremberg in February, 1889, with two nurses, one of whom was only a domestic. In September of the same year the Martha and Mary Society was chartered and the deaconess work extended to Munich, Vienna, Madgeburg, Heilbronn, Cologne, Siegen, Stuttgart, Halle, and Wiesbaden. The development of the Wesleyan Methodist deaconess work was promoted by the influence and generosity of Baroness von Langenau. The widow of a former ambassador to the Russian court and a lady-in-waiting in the Austrian court, she first visited a Methodist meeting on November 10, 1889. Her soul was ready for the specific tonic which the Methodists were administering, and she became an active member of the church. The royalty which she entertained was invited to the Methodist meetings held in her home. Her wealth was dedicated to the promotion of Christian work. She opened her own doors to a class of more than 100 Sunday-school scholars and cared for unfortunate children.

When Barratt completed twenty-five years of leadership in 1890, the membership of the Church had grown to 2,308, the enrollments of the Sunday schools to 2,573, the number of preachers to 30, and the value of chapels and parsonages to 600,000 marks. By 1892 the German Church was strong enough to send a foreign missionary to Togoland, Africa. Home missionary work to the Slovaks and Bohemians was being carried on in Vienna. The Methodists had begun to feel a unity which raised the question of merger to the level of serious discussion. When Barratt was succeeded by *Edmund Rigg,* a missionary returned from Ceylon, in 1892, as the leader of Wesleyan Methodism, negotiations looking forward to union proceeded rapidly. Methodists became one people in Germany on the second day of summer, 1897.

PART II

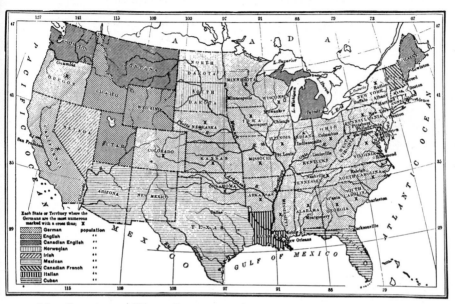

MAP SHOWING IN WHAT STATES THE GERMANS WERE MORE NUMEROUS
IN 1900 THAN OTHER NATIONAL STOCKS

(Reprinted by permission from Albert Bernhart Faust, *The German Element
in the United States.* Boston and New York: Houghton Mifflin Company,
1909. Volume I, p. 576.)

During the nineteenth century Europeans, for the first time in human
history, began to migrate by the millions to America, "the asylum for the
oppressed of every land." The Census of 1900 reported that the population
of the United States included 7,310,604 persons of German blood and
German parentage among the thirty-five million immigrants who were
pressing out the frontiers of the nation and developing a richly-varied
American culture. [Pages 1, 2, 9]

I

Mounted on his horse, his saddlebags filled with Bibles, tracts, and Christian literature, the Methodist circuit rider rode west with the moving frontiers of the "Awakening Giant" of America, ministering, as Theodore Roosevelt said, "to the frontiersman's spiritual need and seeing that his pressing material cares and the hard and grinding poverty of his life did not wholly extinguish the divine fire within his soul." Where the German immigrants settled, the German Methodist missionary promptly followed.

[Page 56]

THE METHODIST CIRCUIT RIDER

No leader of the Church was more alert to the imperativeness of a mission to the German settlers than T. A. Morris, editor of *The Western Christian Advocate*. Living in Cincinnati, focal center of the Teutonic invasion, he threw open the columns of his paper to the promotion of the German language mission. "We have waited too long for Providence to do the work without co-operation," he thundered with his pen. "Let the question be put directly: 'Who will go for us?'" [Pages 7-9]

T. A. MORRIS

2

WILHELM NAST AND TWO OF HIS CHILDREN

Albert (*left*) succeeded his father as editor of *The Christian Apologist.* Fanny (*right*) married William Gamble and gave her wealth to Christian philanthropy.

The call which Editor Morris uttered was answered by Wilhelm Nast, a young German scholar who had migrated to America because he heard that in the New World the demand for language teachers was greater than the supply. Becoming librarian at the United States Military Academy, West Point, and subsequently doing college teaching, he was converted on the frontier by the ever-present Methodist circuit rider. "I found a city of refuge in the Methodist Church," he said. In America he raised his family. [Pages 9-21]

Wilhelm Nast's
father, Johann, a
government fiscal
officer, himself
the son of a dis-
tinguished Ger-
man educator,
died when the
boy was fourteen.
[Page 13]

JOHANN WILHELM NAST

His mother was
the daughter of
Egidius Friedrich
Böhm, a war
counsellor. She
died when he was
seventeen.
[Page 13]

LUDOVIKA BOEHM NAST

4

FRAU DR. FRIEDRICH GOTTLIEB SUESSEKIND

Wilhelm Nast, bereft of father and mother in adolescence, made his sister, Wilhelmina, his confidant. She, like two other of her sisters, was the wife of a Lutheran clergyman. [Page 13]

5

MARGARET ELIZA McDOWELL NAST
[Photograph in late life]

On August 1, 1836, Nast married a young school teacher named Margaret Eliza McDowell, a girl of Scotch descent and formerly Presbyterian persuasion. She taught school while he rode his circuit, earned his hundred dollars a year salary, and returned every fifth week to his bride. [Page 27]

6

At the end of Nast's first missionary year in Cincinnati (1835-36), he reported only three converts. Number three was John Zwahlen. He was typical of the first German Methodists. Born in Switzerland, he migrated to the Queen City, was "awakened" under the influence of Nast's second sermon, and testified: "On my knees, while praying to God, I for the first time felt the love of God powerfully shed abroad in my heart." [Pages 23, 24]

JOHN ZWAHLEN
[Photograph in late life]

When Nast was appointed editor of *The Christian Apologist* in the fall of 1838, Peter Schmucker succeeded him as German missionary in Cincinnati. An experienced clergyman, he distributed tracts at the Ohio River wharves, preached passionately, and led a revival, which added eighty members to the Methodist Society.
[Pages 34, 35]

PETER SCHMUCKER

7

Migrating from Hanover to West Virginia, Heinrich Koeneke found his spiritual home by organizing a neighborhood Christian Society in Wheeling. It flourished. In 1840 the first German Methodist Episcopal Church edifice in the world was dedicated in Wheeling. [Pages 42-44]

HEINRICH KOENEKE
[Photograph in late life]

William Koeneke followed in his father's footsteps and for decades was the outstanding leader in the Saint Louis German Conference. Albert Koeneke, his grandson, continued the distinguished tradition into the third generation.

WILLIAM KOENEKE

8

BIRTHPLACE OF LUDWIG NIPPERT, GOERSDORF, ALSACE

In 1826 the Nippert family migrated from Goersdorf, Alsace, to Captina, Belmont County, Ohio. First the mother, and then the father was converted by the preaching of the circuit rider, Engelhardt Riemenschneider.

[Page 108]

Although the son, Ludwig, protested that he "could not bear to be called a Methodist," he confessed: "In 1840, the fifteenth year of my age, I, too, was awakened under the preaching of Brother Riemenschneider." A devoted leader of the Church, he gave as the formula of his effective sermons: "I sought to preach as if I were in the presence of God."

[Pages 108, 109]

LUDWIG NIPPERT
[Photograph about 1858]

9

LUDWIG SIGISMUND JACOBY
"I grew in the knowledge of things divine"

Methodism was carried West from Ohio by Ludwig Sigismund Jacoby, a young Jew who had been converted under the influence of Nast's preaching in 1839. Marrying Amalie Theresa Nuelsen, a Catholic girl who had experienced the "grace of God" while living with the Nasts in Cincinnati, he went by river boat to Saint Louis where large numbers of Germans were settling. [Pages 48-53]. He was the first missionary to Germany. In 1849 Jacoby, in poor health and with a wife reluctant to return to the Continent, arrived in Bremen to carry out the commission of the General Conference. He began a work which in large part laid the substantial foundations of a "Free Church" movement in Europe. Converted souls built great institutions of Christian mercy in Europe.

[Pages 101-127]

MISSIONARIES TO GERMANY
[Photograph about 1859]

Heinrich Nuelsen   Ludwig Nippert   Wilhelm Schwarz   K. H. Doering
      Engelhardt Riemenschneider   L. S. Jacoby

Jacoby's missions met with success. The work developed so encouragingly that he was in need of assistance. Despite the prejudice of the State Church against the Methodist preachers, they continued to expand the area of their ministry. America sent back to Germany as evangelistic leaders some of the most stalwart leaders which Europe had sent to the New World as immigrants. [Pages 101-127]

11

JOHN SCHNEIDER

In America the German missionaries, riding their horses over plains and mountains, advanced westward with the moving frontiers. In 1864 German-language Conferences were first organized to furnish adequate administrative leadership for the work. John Schneider was the first presiding elder of the Louisville District of the Central German Conference.
[Page 80]

When the Northwest German Conference was organized in September, 1864, George Mulfinger, a powerful figure in the expansion of Methodism, was appointed presiding elder of the Chicago District.
[Page 81]

GEORGE L. MULFINGER

12

The Southwest German Confer-
ence was the third to be organized.
It met for the first session in Saint
Louis in September, 1864. Philipp
Kuhl was appointed one of the five
presiding elders.

[Page 82]

PHILIPP KUHL

Heinrich Lahrmann was another
presiding elder of the Southwest
German Conference. The other
three were Gerhard Timken, Friedrich Fiegenbaum, and Michael
Schnierle.

[Page 82]

HEINRICH LAHRMANN

13

Washington, October 31st, 1804.

Reverend & Dear Sir:

It is with feelings of cordial gratification, that I acknowledge the reception of your
communication of the 20th of October covering the Resolutions of the Central German Conference of the Methodist Episcopal Church adopted at their recent session.

I have not been unprepared for this definite and
unequivocal statement of the continued loyalty and
devotion of the Church you represent to the free institutions of the country of your adoption.
The conduct of your people since the outbreak of
this desolating rebellion has been the best proof of the
sincerity of your present professions.

I trust it is not too early for us to rejoice
together over the promise of the speedy removal of that
blot upon our civilization, always heretofore a standing
menace to our peace and liberties, whose destruction so long desired by all friends of impartial
freedom, has at last been rendered possible
by the crimes of its own reckless friends.

I am very truly,
Your obedient servant,
A. Lincoln

Reverend William Nast

While the nation was divided over the issue of human slavery, the
German Methodists took their stand for freedom and supported the
Union cause with enthusiasm. President Lincoln acknowledged the sup-
port of the Central German Conference in a personal note to Nast.

[Pages 68, 69]

14

German Methodism was carried East by Nast, Karl Doering, Johann Lyon, and Adam Miller. On April 11, 1866, the East German Conference held its first session in New York. John Zwahlen and Heinrich Kastendieck were appointed presiding elders.
[Pages 82, 83]

HEINRICH KASTENDIECK

More than half a decade elapsed before the Chicago German Conference was organized in September, 1872. Bishop Janes appointed C. F. Loeber, J. J. Keller, and George Haas presiding elders.
[Page 83]

J. J. KELLER

15

KARL URBANTKE

The position of the Germans in the South was difficult. Loving freedom, they were branded sympathizers with the North. When they became Methodists, they were terrified by organizations of Germans called *Lateiners*. After the war carpetbaggers added their nefarious influence to the scene. Only men of deep conviction could submit themselves to the abuses and humiliations to which Methodists were subjected. The thirteen charter members of the South German Conference, organized at Industry, Texas, in January, 1874, were stalwart characters whose faith had been tested by fire. Karl Urbantke was one of these. He exercised a large influence in the development of Blinn Memorial College. [Pages 83-87]

Another charter member of the South German Conference was Ernst Stroeter, who was later called to a chair in Central Wesleyan College. His mind and pen stimulated the thinking of German Methodism. For many years he traveled around the globe lecturing on the Bible. For twenty years he edited *Das Prophetische Wort*. His daughter, Luella, married the young professor, John L. Nuelsen. [Page 86]

ERNST STROETER

HEINRICH FIEGENBAUM

Other Conferences were organized. In 1879 the Southwest German Conference was divided into the Saint Louis and the West German. In 1887 the North German Conference held its first session. Heinrich Fiegenbaum traveled a district that was 400 river boat miles long before the Northwest German Conference was divided. In 1891 the California German Conference was organized. The Pacific German Conference first met in 1905. [Page 88]

On two continents Methodism grew through the zeal of converted men. Typical was the career of Hermann zur Jakobsmühlen, converted through the preaching of Nippert. Migrating in 1851 to America with most of the other Germans in his community who had become Methodists, he returned to Germany in 1856 and was appointed to Zürich to build a society in Switzerland.

(Pages 122, 123]

HERMANN ZUR JAKOBSMUEHLEN

17

12

On New Year's Day, 1859, a young German named Ernst Gebhardt followed the example of his mother and joined the Methodist Church. Upon Jacoby's invitation he began to preach.

[Page 120]

ERNST GEBHARDT
[At the time of his conversion]

He wrote hymns, sang to the souls of men, and led the movement for total abstinence in Central Europe. In 1881 he visited America with his daughter, Maria, who later married August J. Bucher. On the trip he traveled 3,600 miles by coach, buckboard, and sleigh through thirty-two states and sang in over one thousand meetings.

[Page 121]

ERNST GEBHARDT
[As American Methodism knew him]

Converted women found a career of Christian service in the Deaconess movement. For more than a half century Sister Sophie Hurter has served in the Deaconess Hospital in Zürich, Switzerland.

SOPHIE HURTER

18

Humble homes in Europe often made large contributions to American life. Such a home was that of the Golder family in Württemberg, which sent seven children to the United States. Five of the seven became distinguished American citizens, and all were prominent in the Methodist Church. [Page 143]

LOUISE GOLDER

One of these children was named Louise. She nourished a childhood dream to be a deaconess nurse. Going back to Europe to study, she joined the Christ Hospital staff in Cincinnati in 1895. In 1896 she formed a partnership with her brother Christian. With six German nurses she formed the nucleus of Bethesda Hospital, which developed to be the greatest single institution in German Methodism. [Page 143]

19

LOUISE GOLDER
[In a typical pose]

"She built her own altar and served there thirty-two years. In a small rented house Louise Golder established the Bethesda Hospital in 1896 and by singular devotion caused it to grow to the great institution it is today. This was her altar and she made no end of serving it almost to the last week of her long life. If one were to count the greatly achieving women of the city, the list would not be large, but Louise Golder would be among them."—*Cincinnati Post.* [Page 145]

CHRISTIAN GOLDER

Christian Golder came to America when he was eighteen. His character had much of his father's strength. The latter, an independent and progressive thinker, had been a member of the Revolutionary party in 1848. Christian was converted at a family altar in Indiana. Preacher, editor, administrator, he was his sister's partner in the development of Bethesda Institutions. In creative power he was the outstanding man in German Methodism.

[Pages 143, 144]

21

Lives consecrated to Christian service merited the stewardship of wealth. German immigrants, converted at Methodist altars, gave generously to institutions of the Church. No benefactor was more lavish in his gifts than E. H. Huenefeld. Born in Bremen in 1838, left fatherless at seven, he became a captain of industry but never lost his faith in God and devotion to his fellow men.

[Pages 146, 147]

E. H. HUENEFELD

His wife encouraged him in his benefactions. No representative of a worthy cause was turned from her door without assistance.

[Page 147]

LENA L. DIERS HUENEFELD

22

Lillian Spicker succeeded Louise Golder as head deaconess of Bethesda Motherhouse. Bethesda Institutions in two decades had grown into new, magnificent endowed buildings.

[Page 149]

LILLIAN SPICKER

FANNY NAST GAMBLE

Fanny Nast, daughter of Wilhelm Nast, married William Gamble, and gave lavishly of her wealth to Christian institutions. "I am but the stewardess of my wealth, it belongs to God and his kingdom." At the time of her death she distributed $3,000,000 among Methodist institutions.

[Page 148]

In his first years in Cincinnati Wilhelm Nast had been encouraged by James Gamble, an Irish soapmaker, who opened his home for German prayer meetings. James N. Gamble, his son, an ingenious chemist, became immensely wealthy by perfecting the formula for Ivory Soap. Between the Elizabeth Gamble Deaconess Home and Christ Hospital, which Gamble supported, and Bethesda Institutions, there was close co-operation. His daughter, Maude, married Alfred K. Nippert.

[Pages 142, 143]

JAMES N. GAMBLE

SCARLET OAKS

In 1908 the Huenefelds gave to Bethesda the famous old Schoenberger mansion, a castle set in a forty-seven-acre park on a Cincinnati hillside. Purchased for $100,000, it housed an art collection valued at $50,000. This was but the first of the Huenefeld benefactions. [Page 146]

BETHESDA MATERNITY
HOSPITAL

In 1913 a $125,000 maternity hospital was dedicated, then one of the finest in the country.
[Page 146]

BETHESDA SURGICAL HOSPITAL

In 1926 a new surgical hospital was opened at a cost of more than a million dollars. The buildings are typical of the $3,000,000 Bethesda Institutions. [Page 149]

24

JOHN A. DIEKMANN

In 1912 John A. Diekmann came to Cincinnati to succeed August J. Bucher as principal of Dorcas Institute and rector of the Motherhouse. Converted when he was eight, he was educated in German Methodist Colleges. After fourteen successful years in the pastorate, he entered the field of institutional leadership. In 1922 he was elected president of Bethesda Institutions. Under his dynamic leadership Bethesda continued to grow. During the period of the merger of the German Conferences, he led the movement to conserve the German traditions of the church. Serving as editor of the *Apologist* without salary, he also was the leader of the committee to raise funds for its publication. [Pages 147, 148]

FANNY NAST GAMBLE CHAPEL
AND THE
LOUISE GOLDER DEACONESS HOME

In 1917 Fanny Nast Gamble gave Bethesda the chapel and deaconess home. The name of the new building fittingly joined the names of two distinguished Christian women. One gave her wealth, the other gave her life. [Page 148]

Jacob Rothweiler was the presiding elder who led the movement for the Louisville Deaconess Home and Hospital. To his faith and industry German Methodism was indebted for other institutions. [Pages 150, 151]

JACOB ROTHWEILER

LOUISVILLE GERMAN METHODIST DEACONESS HOME AND HOSPITAL

In the spring of 1895 a group of German preachers discussed the possibilities of founding a deaconess home and hospital in Louisville, Kentucky. By Christmas they had raised $672 for the purpose! Encouraged by this meager sum, they continued by faith and in 1898 the hospital was dedicated. [Pages 150, 151]

BETHANY HOSPITAL, BROOKLYN

The first German Methodist Deaconess Home and Hospital, however, was founded in 1893 in the upper story of a house at 1192 Green Avenue, Brooklyn. It was known from the beginning as "Bethany." In forty years it grew to be a half-million-dollar institution.

[Page 150]

Martha Binder was called to Brooklyn in 1894 to be the head deaconess at Bethany. Trained in Charité Hospital in Berlin and in the Motherhouse in Frankfurt-am-Main, she organized the deaconess work in Zürich. During a half century of service at Bethany, she saw the institution grow. Her day began before six in the morning and rarely ended until ten in the evening. Twice each day she made her rounds, visiting each patient's bedside. "There is little room in a deaconess's life to think about the passage of time," she said on her fiftieth anniversary in America. [Page 150]

MARTHA BINDER

28

Fliegeraufnahme
Krankenhaus Bethanien, Zürich.

DEACONESS HOME AND HOSPITAL, ZÜRICH, SWITZERLAND

The German Methodist ministry of healing on the Continent was begun earlier than in America and developed more institutions. In Hamburg, Berlin, Frankfurt-am-Main, Nuremberg, Vienna, and other important centers, the Methodist Homes and Hospitals of the Bethany and Martha and Mary Societies render their service of mercy. The Methodist Deaconess Home and Hospital in Zürich, Switzerland, is typical of these institutions. A magnificent site was purchased on the Zürichberg overlooking the city and the lake. In addition to the general hospital a new three-story maternity hospital and separate home for deaconesses were erected in 1930.

[Page 137]

THEOLOGICAL SEMINARY, FRANKFURT-AM-MAIN

In the winter of 1858 the Methodists in Germany felt the need for an institution to train preachers. On March 7 of that year a little seminary was opened in an unused attic room. Three young converts formed the student body. The school joined evangelical passion with sound scholarship. In 1869 this first educational institution founded by German Methodists was moved to Frankfurt-am-Main. The seminary has contributed its graduates to the leadership of the Church in Europe and America.

[Pages 154-159]

THE FACULTY, THEOLOGICAL SEMINARY, FRANKFURT-AM-MAIN
[Post-War Period]

Emil E. Luering	Theophil Mann	Paulus Scharpff
Theophil Spoerri	F. H. O. Melle	J. W. E. Sommer

From the first the seminary had a distinguished faculty. William F. Warren became president of Boston University, John F. Hurst became a church historian and bishop. This was but a beginning.

30

LUDWIG NIPPERT
First Director of the Theological Seminary, Frankfurt-am-Main

A gift of $25,000 by John T. Martin made possible the erection of an adequate building in Frankfurt-am-Main. Ludwig Nippert was the first director. His spirit was contagious. At the dedication Nippert said in characteristic manner:

"The chief purpose of our institution is to educate men of God, men filled with faith and the spirit. We pray God that a man may never come into these halls who has not experienced the converting, enlightening, and saving strength of the spirit of God." [Page 156]

In 1870 Friedrich Paulus was called from Frankfurt-am-Main to German Wallace College, Berea, Ohio. A brilliant writer, teacher, and preacher, he exercised a profound intellectual and spiritual influence upon German Methodism in America and Europe.

[Page 155]

FRIEDRICH PAULUS

In 1889 Heinrich Mann became director of the seminary. He raised a fund of 75,000 marks to enlarge the campus.
[Page 157]

HEINRICH MANN

After twenty years as a missionary in India, Emil Luering joined the faculty of the seminary, bringing his experience and wide knowledge into the service of the preacher-training program. He could converse with ease in thirty different languages. [Page 157]

EMIL LUERING

32

GERMAN WALLACE COLLEGE, BEREA, OHIO

Jacob Rothweiler and Nast conceived the idea of founding a German Methodist College. German Wallace College was chartered in 1864. It shared the campus of Baldwin University. In 1913 the two institutions were merged, being known as Baldwin-Wallace College. No American institution was in closer association with the seminary in Frankfurt-am-Main. Its contribution to the church in trained leaders was great.

[Pages 159-161]

BLINN MEMORIAL COLLEGE

Among other colleges founded was Blinn Memorial College, located in the South at Brenham, Texas. [Pages 161-164]

13

33

KARL RIEMENSCHNEIDER

Came to German Wallace College in 1868, serving for fifty years as professor and president. He was the first of the leaders of second-generation German Methodism. His son, Albert, continued the tradition into the third generation as the distinguished professor of music and organist at Berea. [Page 160]

34

Arthur L. Breslich

German Wallace College was merged with Baldwin University while Arthur L. Breslich was its president. He continued as head of the institution until 1918.

[Page 161]

In 1893 John C. Marting came to Berea to direct the financial affairs of the college. His success in the office was the chief cause for the sound development of the institution. He was still active in 1939.

[Page 160]

John C. Marting

CENTRAL WESLEYAN COLLEGE

At Warrenton, Missouri, the German Methodists founded twin institutions—an orphan asylum and a college. [Pages 161-164]

36

George Addicks became president of Central Wesleyan in 1900. He was welcomed throughout German Methodism as a great preacher on anniversary occasions.
[Page 164]

GEORGE ADDICKS

Otto Kriege succeeded Addicks as president of Central Wesleyan, serving from 1910 until 1925, when he was called to New Orleans University. Like Addicks, he was eminently successful as a college administrator and leader of his Conference. [Page 164]

OTTO KRIEGE

Friedrich Schaub was a leader in German Methodist education. In 1887 he became president of German-Englsh College, Galena, Illinois. In 1921 he went to Cincinnati as principal of Dorcas Institute. [Page 166]

FRIEDRICH SCHAUB

37

CHARLES CITY COLLEGE

In the Middle West the German Methodists developed a college at Charles City, Iowa. In 1914 it merged with Morningside College.

[Pages 166-168]

CHILDREN'S HOME, BEREA, OHIO

[Partial view of cottages]

The German Methodists built homes for aged and the orphans. Among these important institutions is the Children's Home at Berea, Ohio.

[Pages 176-179]

38

HEINRICH LIEBHART

In 1865 Heinrich Liebhart went to Cincinnati to help Nast edit the *Apologist*. In 1872 he became secretary of the German Sunday School Department and editor of *Home and Hearth*. A popular scholar gifted with editorial sensitiveness, he developed a popular and constructive German-language literature. [Pages 225, 226]

39

ALBERT NAST
Succeeded his father as editor of the *Apologist* in 1908.
[Page 236]

40

Friedrich Munz   Herman Grentzenberg   Christian Golder
A. J. Nast   Wilhelm Nast   F. L. Nagler

GERMAN METHODIST EDITORS
[About 1895]

41

August J. Bucher succeeded Albert Nast in 1918 as editor of the *Apologist*. After the World War German Methodism began to liquidate its interests. The tradition of its unity was kept alive by the continuation of the *Apologist*. The publication of the paper was made possible through the efforts of John A. Diekmann and Adam J. Loeppert, co-editors after Bucher's retirement in 1936.
[Pages 238, 239]

AUGUST J. BUCHER

A. J. Loeppert had been assistant editor from 1920-23. From 1922-26 he served with much success as national secretary of the German Epworth League. He was a recognized leader of the former Chicago German Conference, serving in prominent pulpits and as superintendent. Under his wise guidance the merger of this Conference with contiguous English Conferences was consummated to the satisfaction of all concerned. Four times his brethren elected him delegate to the General Conference.
[Pages 239, 246]

ADAM J. LOEPPERT

42

As T. A. Morris in 1835 had devoted himself to the organization of a mission to the Germans, so in 1935 George C. Douglass, publishing agent in Cincinnati, gave his services to keeping alive the traditions of German Methodism. Following Bucher's death, he became president of the Board of Bethesda Institutions.
[Page 240]

GEORGE C. DOUGLASS

PUBLISHING HOUSE AND PRINTING PLANT OF THE METHODIST
BOOK CONCERN, ZÜRICH, SWITZERLAND

In Bremen and Zürich, publishing houses were built.
The Concern in Zürich is typical.

[Pages 254, 255]

43

BISHOP JOHN L. NUELSEN   A. J. NAST   ALFRED K. NIPPERT
Post-war Relief Workers

The World War left human tragedy in its wake in Central Europe.
Methodists in America and Switzerland promptly developed a relief program. [Pages 197-204]

After the war, Methodism in Germany developed important children's
homes, *Kurhäuser*, and homes for the aged. Typical of these was the
Home for the Aged, *Schwarzenhof, bei Rudolstadt*. [Page 253]

44

One of the American leaders
interested in the development of
German Methodist institutions
was Jakob Krehbiel, an assistant
editor of the *Apologist,* one of the
beautiful spirits of the Church.
[Page 235]

JAKOB KREHBIEL

J. G. Schaal had the honor of being
a member of the Central German
Conference from the time of its organization until its dissolution. His
faith was kept vital by close association with the camp meeting at Santa
Claus, Indiana. Approaching his
ninety-sixth birthday (September,
1939), he is probably the oldest living
German Methodist preacher in the
world.

J. G. SCHAAL

45

GERMAN METHODIST EPISCOPAL CHURCH
RACE STREET, CINCINNATI

The first German-language Conference was quite appropriately organized in the historic "Mother Church" on Race Street, Cincinnati. It was equally appropriate that T. H. Morris should be the presiding bishop.

[Page 80]

METHODIST CHURCH, DAVOS, SWITZERLAND

On two continents Methodist churches bear witness to the enduring work begun by Wilhelm Nast as an instrument of God. The edifice in Davos, Switzerland, is representative of temples of worship in Europe. Hospice Bethany is shown at the left.

47

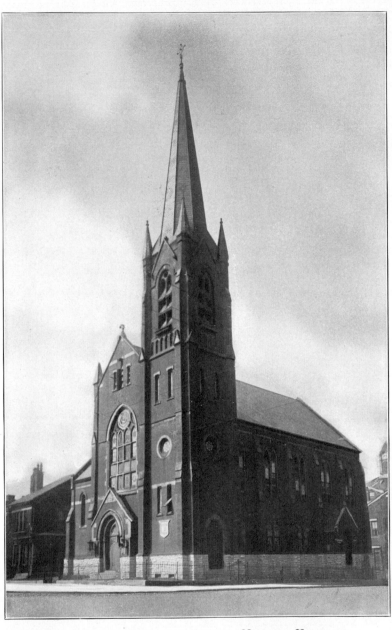

SALEM GERMAN METHODIST CHURCH, NEWPORT, KENTUCKY
[A typical edifice]

Through the Methodist Church, the German soul made
its testimony to God.

48

BIBLIOGRAPHY

THE LITERATURE OF GERMAN METHODISM

The volumes listed below are the books which in the summer of 1939 were catalogued and in the archives either of The Methodist Book Concern in Cincinnati or of the Historical Museum of German Methodism located in the Bethesda Institutions, Cincinnati. Where the date of publication is missing in the citations, no date could be established.

About 250 books were translated into the German language. These are not listed here. They contain many of John Wesley's writings and sermons; many story books of a religious nature, and some theological works. The volumes found a wide distribution and rendered a distinct educational service.

Ahrens, Wilhelm: *Der Universal-Konflikt zwischen Gut und Böse*, 1902. Cincinnati ;* pp. 184.
Die Taufe im Lichte der Bibel, 1869. Cincinnati; pp. 160.
Betrachtungen über die biblische Geschichte, 1852. Cincinnati; pp. 256.

Breunig, G. A.: *Von Rom nach Zion*, 1884. Cincinnati. Illustrated; pp. 246.

Bruehl, R. A. W.: *Des Soldaten Freund im Feldlager und Hospital;* pp. 112.

Bucher, A. J.: *Wie ich ein Seemann wurde*, 1891. Cincinnati; pp. 196. *Ein Sänger des Kreuzes*, 1912. Kober: C. F. Spittlers Nachfolger; pp. 241. *Unter drei Sonnen*, 1934. Bremen: Anker-Verlag; pp. 176.

Breiter, H. J.: *Echo*, 1876. Bremen: Druck von C. H. Doering; pp. 300. Columbia Series, *General Gordon*, 1891. Cincinnati; pp. 222. *Der Gottesdienst der Römischkatholischen Kirche*, 1861. Cincinnati; pp. 114.

Diekmann, J. A.: *Die Gebetsheilung, Lehre und Irrlehre*, 1907. Cincinnati; pp. 47. *In Memoriam Christian Golder* (1849-1922), 1922. Pittsburgh. Pittsburgh Printing Company; pp. 51. *In Memoriam Louise Golder* (1857-1929), 1929. Pittsburgh. Pittsburgh Printing Company; pp. 47.

Eisele, Karl: *Der Methodismus, ein Element des Fortschrittes innerhalb des Protestantismus*, 1924. Bremen

Esslinger, W.: *Die Mission der Bischöfl. Methodistenkirche in der westlichen Welt*. Zürich.

Fotsch, W.: *Glaubenshelden*, 1893. Cincinnati; pp. 678. *Von Krippe und Kreuz zum Thron*. Cincinnati; pp. 716. *Denkwürdigkeiten aus der Neuen Welt*. Cincinnati. Zwei Bände; pp. 365 and 367.

---

*All books designated "Cincinnati" were published by The Methodist Book Concern.

Galen, P.: *Percy,* oder: *Der Irre von St. James.* Revidiert von F. L. Nagler; pp. 286.

Golder, Christian: *Die Geschichte der weiblichen Diakonie,* 1901. Cincinnati. Illustrated; pp. 506. *History of the Deaconess Movement,* 1903. Cincinnati; pp. 614. *Deaconess Motherhouse,* 1907. Pittsburgh. Pittsburgh Printing Company; pp. 155.

Golder, Gottlieb: *Klänge aus stillen Stunden,* 1916. Pittsburgh. Pittsburgh Printing Company; pp. 111.

Griewe, William F.: *Primitives Südamerika,* 1863. Cincinnati. Illustrated; pp. 251.

Grob, R. Ernst: *Die Bischöfliche Methodistenkirche in der Schweiz,* 1931. Zürich: Christliche Vereinsbuchhandlung. Illustrated; pp. 664. *Ein Jahrhundert Methodistischer Mission.* Zürich. *Hans Jakob Breiter.* Zürich.

Grünewald, J. P.: *Ein Heldenleben,* 1914. Bremen: Kommissionsverlag Buchhandlung und Verlag des Traktathauses. Illustrated; pp. 80.

Guth, George: *Das Buch Hiob,* oder: *Rechtfertigung der Göttlichen Weltregierung,* 1900. Cincinnati; pp. 208.

Hertzler, C. W.: *Die Religiös sittliche Erziehung der Kirchlichen Jugend,* 1908. Cincinnati; pp. 371.

Hiller, G. E.: *The Christian Family,* 1907. Cincinnati; pp. 326. *The Great Question,* 1924. Indianapolis: The Promise Company; pp. 292. *A Believer's Critique of the Bible,* Indianapolis: The Promise Company; pp. 233.

Hildenstein, J. G.: *Immergrün Kern und Liebeslieder der Christlichen Kirche,* 1901. Cincinnati; pp. 231. *Wohltäter,* oder: *Lebensbilder berümter Männer und Frauen,* 1896. Cincinnati; pp. 208.

Hug, Ed: *Handbüchlein für Probeglieder der Bischöfl. Methodistenkirche.* Zürich. 1909.

Jacoby, Ludwig S.: *Christliche Geschichten,* 1857. Bremen: J. G. Heyse's Verlag; pp. 304. *Christliche Geschichten, Die Bibel.* Bremen: Traktathauses; pp. 293. *Christliche Geschichten für Jung und Alt.* Bremen: Verlag des Traktathauses; pp. 330. *Christliche Geschichten, Hilfe in der Noth.* Bremen: Traktathauses; pp. 268. *Geschichte des amerikanischen Methodismus,* 1870. Bremen: Verlag des Traktathauses; pp. 476. *Handbuch des Methodismus,* 1855. Bremen: Im Verlag der Traktat-Gesellschaft der Bischöflichen Methodistenkirche; pp. 376. *Kurzer Inbegriff der Christlichen Glaubenslehre,* 1855. Bremen: Im Commissions-Verlag von J. G. Heyse; pp. 109. *Letzte Stunden,* 1874. Cincinnati; pp. 272. *Predigt—Entwürfe über freie Texte,* 1858. Bremen: J. G. Heyse's Commissions-Verlag; pp. 272.

Junker, Paul Gustav: *Ein Lebensbild,* mit Vorwort von Bischof F. H. Otto Melle. Anker-Verlag, Bremen; pp. 224. *Der Glaube im Leben der Väter.* Zürich. 1903. *Reformation im Hinterwald. Ein Charakterbild von P. Cartwright und seiner Zeit. Die Aufgabe des Methodismus in Deutschland.* Bremen. 1913. *Was mir am Methodismus besonders wertvoll erscheint.* Bremen. 1910. *Der Klassführer als Seelsorger.* Zürich. 1903.

Keck, Karl: *Wie die Lerche singt,* 1896. Cincinnati; pp. 194.

Keller, John J.: *Saatkörner aus Gottes Wort,* 1909. Bearbeitet von C. F. Morf; pp. 576.

Keller, Wm. J.: *Goethe's Estimate of the Greek and Latin Writers,* 1916. University of Wisconsin; pp. 161.

Klüsner, F.: *Mitteilungen aus meiner Reise im Morganlande,* 1881. Bremen: Traktathauses. Illustrated; pp. 128. *Töne aus der Halljahrsposaune,* 1879. Bremen: Verlag des Traktathauses; pp. 170. *Menschenpläne und Gottesführungen.* Bremen.

Kopp, Fr.: *Charakter Bilder aus der Geschichte des Methodismus,* 1881. Cincinnati. Illustrated; pp. 325. *Das verborgene Leben mit Christo,* 1876. Cincinnati; pp. 167. *Die Deutsch-amerikanische Kanzel,* 1882. Cincinnati; pp. 586.

Kriege, Otto E.: *Geschichte des Methodismus,* 1909. Cincinnati; pp. 262.

Krehbiel, Jacob: *Perlen Christlicher Weisheit,* 1875. Cincinnati: Krehbiel Printing Co.; pp. 167.

Liebhart, Heinrich: *A. B. C. Buch und Lese-Uebungen,* 1881. Cincinnati; pp. 64. *Bibelstudien,* 1883. Cincinnati; pp. 318. *Biblische Geschichte,* 1882. Cincinnati. Illustrated; pp. 318. *Bilder aus dem Thierleben,* 1871. Cincinnati; pp. 119. *Daheim,* 1871. Cincinnati; pp. 231. *Das Buch der Gleichnisse,* 1876. Cincinnati; pp. 588. *Das Leben und Wirken in der Heidenwelt,* 1879. Cincinnati; pp. 344. *Deklamier Stücke.* Cincinnati; pp. 120. *Der Chorist,* 1889. Cincinnati. *Der Hinduknabe,* 1868. Cincinnati. Illustrated; pp. 279. *Der Hundertjährige Bestand des Amerikanischen Methodismus,* 1866. Cincinnati; pp. 128. *Die drei Könige von Jerusalem,* 1871. Cincinnati; pp. 207. *Die Familie Schönberg-Cotta,* 1868. Cincinnati; pp. 398. *Die Perle,* 1894. Cincinnati; pp. 224. *Die Reformation im Hinterwald,* 1873. Cincinnati; pp. 335. *Drei Weihnachtabende,* 1869. Cincinnati; pp. 293. *Edle Frauen,* 1871. Cincinnati; pp. 310. *Familienbuch,* 1884. Cincinnati. Illustrated; pp. 304. *Frisch, Fromm und Frei,* 1871. Cincinnati; pp. 256. *Geschichte einer Bibel,* 1870. Cincinnati. Illustrated; pp. 304. *Handwerk hat einen goldenen Boden,* 1871. Cincinnati; pp. 136. *Im Jugenkreis,* 1885. Cincinnati; pp. 448. *Lesebuch für die Christliche Jugend,* 1881. Cincinnati. Illustrated; pp. 128. *Lesestunden,* 1871. Cincinnati; pp. 134. *Moody's Leben und Wirken,* 1877. Cincinnati; pp. 408. *Reisebilder,* 1871. Cincinnati; pp. 189. *Sam Jones,* 1886. Cincinnati; pp. 312. *Winter-Abende,* 1871. Cincinnati; pp. 143. *Zum Feier-Abend,* 1872. Cincinnati; pp. 691. *Liturgie der Bischöflichen Methodistenkirche,* 1878. Cincinnati; pp. 148.

Loebenstein, A.: *Predigten,* 1874. Cincinnati; pp. 283.

Loeppert, A. J.: *Modernism and the Vatican,* 1911. Cincinnati; pp. 324.

Lyon, Johann Chr.: *Kurze Erklärung der Offenbarung St. Johannis,* 1859. Cincinnati; pp. 248.

Mann, Heinrich: *Ludwig S. Jakoby,* 1892. Bremen: Verlag des Traktathauses. Zürich: Buch- und Verlagshandlung; pp. 274.

Melle, F. H. Otto: *Das Walten Gottes im Deutschen Methodismus*, 1924. Bremen: Traktathauses; pp. 356.

Messmer, J. J.: *Im Strom der Zeit*, oder *Kapital und Arbeit*, 1883. Cincinnati; pp. 324. *Kurze Geschichte der Bischöflichen Methodistenkirche*, 1889. Cincinnati; pp. 74.

Miller, Adam: *Experience of German Methodist Preachers.* Edited by D. N. Clark, 1859. Cincinnati; pp. 430. *Origin and Progress of the German Mission in the Methodist Episcopal Church*, 1843. Cincinnati; pp. 249. *Then and Now, A Sixtieth Anniversary Sermon*, 1891; pp. 31.

Mann, Theophil: *Fünfzig Jahre Diakonissen Arbeit*, 1914. Bremen.

Möller, Robert H.: *Heilsbotschaften*, 1937. Bremen: Anker-Verlag. *Uwikopun*, 1938. Anker-Verlag; pp. 95. *Johannes Wesley*, 1914. Bremen.

Mitter, George: *Das richtige Heilverfahren*, 1903. Cincinnati; pp. 288.

Mölling, Peter: *Golfblumen.* Cincinnati; pp. 160.

Mulfinger, Julius A.: *Georg Leonhard Mulfinger, Ein Lebensbild*, 1889. Cincinnati; pp. 238.

Munz, Friedrich: *Bilder aus der alten Morgenländischen Geschichte.* Cincinnati; pp. 60. *Das Buch der Bücher*, 1911. Cincinnati; pp. 191. *Der Kreuzzug für unsere Zeit.* Cincinnati; pp. 34. *Dreihundert Biblische Kernsprüche*, 1909. Cincinnati; pp. 88. *Homiletik, eine Darstellung der Predigt auf biblischer Grundlage*, 1897. Cincinnati; pp. 260. *Pilgerklänge*, 1907. Cincinnati; pp. 164. *Verborgene Klippen*, 1899. Cincinnati; pp. 128.

Nagler, Franz L.: *Allgemeines Handwörterbuch der Heiligen Schrift*, 1889. Cincinnati; pp. 504. *Bilder aus der Weltgeschichte*, 1899. Bremen: Verlag des Traktathauses; pp. 350. *Biographische Bilder aus der Heiligen Geschichte* (Dritter Band), 1899. Cincinnati. Illustrated; pp. 310. *Biographische Bilder aus der Heiligen Geschichte* (Vierter Band), 1899. Cincinnati. Illustrated; pp. 320. *Die Unsterblichkeit der Seele*, 1888. Cincinnati; pp. 330. *Die Würde des Lammes*, 1877. Cincinnati; pp. 226. *Die Zukunft Christi*, 1879. Cincinnati; pp. 222. *Eine kurze Naturlehre*, oder *Die Wunder auf dem Gebiete der Physik*, 1896. Cincinnati. Illustrated; pp. 92. *Geistliche Erweckungen* (Mit einem Vorwort von Jakob Krehbiel), 1883. Cincinnati. Gedrukt und gebunden bei C. J. Krehbiel; pp. 300. *Jerachmeel*, oder *In grossen Stürmen*, 1892. Cincinnati; pp. 320. *Neue Historische Bibliothek* (Vier Bände), 1897. Cincinnati. Illustrated. *Poesie und Prosa*, 1896. Cincinnati; pp. 250. *Neue Predigtstudien*, 1893. Cincinnati; pp. 344.

Nast, Wilhelm: *Allgemeine Einleitung über das Neue Testament*, 1860. Cincinnati; pp. 152. *Ein Kommentar über die Evangelien Matthäus und Markus*, 1870. Cincinnati; pp. 1224. *Kommentar über das Evangelium Johannes.* Cincinnati; pp. 189. *Das biblische Christentum und seine Gegensätze*, 1883. Cincinnati; pp. 256. *Die Aufgabe der christlichen Kirche im neunzehnten Jahrhundert*, 1857. Cincinnati; pp. 155. *Christologische Betrachtungen*, 1866. Cincinnati. *Ein Biblischer Katechismus*, 1847. Cincinnati; pp. 76. *Der kleinere*

Katechismus für die Gemeinden der Bischöfl. Methodistenkirche, 1869. Cincinnati; pp. 96. *Der Grössere Katechismus für die deutschen Gemeinden der Bischöflichen Methodistenkirche*, 1869. Cincinnati; pp. 156. *Theologische Betrachtungen*, 1867. Cincinnati; pp. 275. *Lautir- und Lesebuch* (No. 1), 1858. Cincinnati. Illustrated; pp. 133. *Philosophie des Erlösungsplanes*, 1859. Cincinnati; pp. 226. *R. J. Wurst's Deutsche Sprachdenklehre*, 1852. Cincinnati; pp. 172. *Was ist und will der Methodismus?* 1855. Cincinnati.

Nippert, Ludwig: *Beweise für den göttlichen Ursprung der Heiligen Schrift*, 1881. Bremen: Traktathauses; pp. 171. *Das Walten der göttlichen Vorsehung in Johann Wesley's Leben und Wirken*, 1876. Bremen: Verlag des Traktathauses; pp. 85. *Geschichte und Bericht der Martin M. E. Kirche in Frankfort* (1858-1866). Bremen: Traktathauses; pp. 15. *Praktische Theologie: Homiletik und Pastoral theologie*, 1879. Cincinnati; pp. 460. *Leben und Wirken von Bischof F. Asbury*, 1885. Bremen. *Auszüge aus dem Tagebuch und den Briefen der seligen Adelheid Nippert*, 1869. Bremen.

Nuelsen, John L.: *Das Leben Jesu im Wortlaute der vier Evangelien*, 1904. Cincinnati; pp. 220. *Luther, the Leader* (Men of the Kingdom Series), 1906. Cincinnati; pp. 255. *Die Ordination im Methodismus*, 1935. Bremen. *Der Methodismus in Deutschland nach dem Kriege*. Bremen: Buchhandlung und Verlag des Traktathauses; pp. 29. *Die Bedeutung des Evangeliums Johannes*, 1902. Berlin: Edwin Runge in Lichterfelde; pp. 24. *Die letzten Schritte zur Selbständigkeit der Bischöflichen Methodistenkirche in Deutschland*, 1936; pp. 87. *John Wesley und das Deutsche Kirchenlied*, 1938. Bremen: Anker-Verlag. Zürich: Christliche Vereinsbuchhandlung; pp. 222. *Jugend, Kirche und Staat*, 1896. Cincinnati; pp. 32. *Some recent Phases of German Theology*, 1908. Cincinnati; pp. 114. *John Wesley und die Soziale Frage*. Bremen: Anker-Verlag; pp. 56. *Der Methodismus als religiöse Bewegung und als Kirche*, 1924. Bremen. *Der Methodismus im kirchlichen Leben Europas*, 1925. Bremen. *Reformation und Methodismus*, 1917. Zürich. *Jean Guillannine du le Flecheri* (John William Fletcher), 1929. Zürich. *Ausgewählte Predigten Wesleys,* in "Die Predigt der Kirche" (Bänd XI), 105. Dresden. *Das Heilserlebnis im Methodismus*, 1938. Zürich: *Christliche Vereinsbuchhandlung;* pp. 45.

Nuelsen, John., und Mann, Theophil, und Sommer, J. J.: *Geschichte des Methodismus*, 1924. Bremen; pp. 875.

Paulus, C. F.: *Das Christliche Heilsleben*, 1890. Cincinnati; pp. 370. *Das Leben Jesus*. Cincinnati; pp. 54. *Durch Kampf Zum Sieg*, 1893. Cincinnati; pp. 178.

Plüddemann, R.: *Der kleine Korporal*, 1891. Cincinnati; pp. 218.

Pritzlaff, Paul: *Weckstimmen, Betrachtungen zur Beförderung wahren Christenthums*, 1891. Bremen: Verlag des Traktathauses; pp. 217.

Peter, L.: *Geschichte der Bischöflichen Methodistenkirche in der Schweiz*, 1893. Zürich: Christliche Vereinsbuchhandlung; pp. 299.

Runck, Carl L. Chr.: *Polyhymnia, Sammlung Christlichreligiöser Gesänge*, 1891. Cincinnati; pp. 128.

Rexroth, G.: *Jakob Ekert.*

Riemenschneider, E.: *Mein Lebensgang*, 1882. Bremen: Verlag des Traktathauses; pp. 237.

Rösch, F.: *Die Methodistischen Klassenversammlungen*, 1912. Bremen.

Rodemeyer, A.: *Beispiele und Aphrorismen zu den Psalmen*. Leipzig: Verlag von Ferd. Riehm; pp. 408. *Beispiele und Erzählungen* (Erster und zweiter Band). Bremen: Verlag des Traktathauses. *Biblische Heiligung*, 1879. Bremen: Verlag des Traktathauses; pp. 299. *Blumenstrauss*, 1876. Bremen: Traktathauses; pp. 208. *Die verschiedenen Religionsparteien*, 1887. Bremen: Traktathauses; pp. 559. *Dr. Martin Luthers Leben und Wirken*. Bremen: Verlag des Traktathauses. Illustrated; pp. 104. *Frauen der Bibel*, 1893. Bremen: Verlag des Traktathauses; pp. 280. *Predigt-Entwürfe*, 1893. Bremen: Verlag des Trakttahauses; pp. 224. *Wegweiser für die Jugend*. Bremen: Verlag des Traktathauses. Illustrated; pp. 224.

Röhl, Karl: *Kurze Geschichte der Vereinigten Staaten*, 1890. Cincinnati; pp. 56.

Roser, Elias: *Allerlei Leute*, 1913. Cincinnati; pp. 265. *Der Knabenbund von Waldorf*, 1894. Cincinnati; pp. 210.

Schwarz, William: *Vortrag über den Methodismus in Bern*, 1866. Bremen und Zürich.

Schaal, J. G.: *Biblische Erzählungen des Alten Testamentes*, 1904. Cincinnati. Illustrated; pp. 206. *Kurzgefasste Bibelkunde*. Cincinnati; pp. 70.

Sommer, J. J.: *Wesleys Einfluss auf die Welt*, 1914. Bremen.

Sommer, F. W. Ernst: *Aus der Morgenröte des Methodismus in Deutschland*, 1924. Bremen. *Wesley Predigten*, 1938. Bremen: Anker-Verlag. *Der Methodismus in Deutschland*, 1914. Bremen.

Schlagenhauf, J.: *Meine Bibel*. Cincinnati; pp. 52.

Schneider, F. W.: *System der Christlichen Lehre*, 1908. Cincinnati; pp. 552.

Schneider, Peter F.: *Die Lebenserfahrungen von Johannes Schneider*, 1860. Cincinnati; pp. 326.

Schuckai, H. J.: *Seelengewinnung*, 1913. Cincinnati; pp. 301.

Schuetz, H.: *Ein Handbüchlein über das volle Heil in Christo*, 1875. Cincinnati; pp. 96.

Schuh, Karl: *Die Macht des gläubigen Gebetes*, 1883. Cincinnati; pp. 272.

Spoerri, Theophil, Prof.: *Präludinun zur Poesie*, 1929. Zürich. Berlin: Furche-Verlag; pp. 331.

Spoerri, Theophil, Lic. Theol.: *In der Schule des Leidens*. Zürich: Verlag der Christlichen Vereinsbuchhandlung. *Der Mensch und die frohe Botschaft*, 1939. Zürich: Christliche Vereinsbuchhandlung; pp. 331.

Scharpff, Paulus: *John Wesleys Tagebuch*, 1938; pp. 310.

Simons, George H.: *Christlicher Ratgeber,* 1892. Cincinnati; pp. 118. *Lebenscompass für Jung und Alt,* 1888. Cincinnati. Illustrated; pp. 595.

Ströter, E. F.: *Die Judenfrage und ihre göttliche Lösung.* Kassel: Druck Verlag von Ernst Röttger; pp. 227. *Reisebilder aus dem Morgenlande.* Zürich; pp. 111. *Das Königreich Jesu Christi,* 1909. Bremen: Verlag der Missionsbuchhandlung; pp. 150.

Stevens, Abel: *Geschichte der Bischöflichen Methodistenkirche* (Frei aus dem Englischen übersetzt von H. Liebhart), 1867. Cincinnati; pp. 868.

Sulzberger, A.: *Der Methodismus und die Christliche Kirche des ersten Jahrhunderts.* Zürich und Bremen. *Christliche Glaubenslehre vom Methodistichen Standpunkt,* 1887. Bremen: Traktathauses; pp. 536. *Die Heilige Geschichte,* 1891. Bremen: Traktathauses; pp. 285. *Erklärung der Glaubensartikel und Hauptlehren der Methodistenkirche,* 1879. Bremen: Traktathauses; pp. 197. *Leitfaden zur Christlichen Glaubenslehre.* Bremen: Traktathauses; pp. 64.

Urbantke, C.: *Aus meinen Lebensführungen,* 1902. Cincinnati; pp. 169.

Völkner, W.: *Der verlorene Bruder,* 1892. Cincinnati; pp. 240.

Weiss, C.: *Zur Abwehr,* Eine Abhandlung über die Verhältnisse des Methodisten zur Landeskirche. Bremen.

Wesley, Johannes: *Sammlung auserlesener Predigten* (Aus dem Englischen übersetz von Wilhelm Nast), 1847. Cincinnati; pp. 767.

Werler, P. J.: *Biblische Aonen- und Hoffnungslehre,* 1938. Bremen: Anker-Verlag; pp. 126.

Worthman, D.: *Dit und Dat,* A volume of Poems in the Low German Language, 1938; pp. 70.

Wuhrmann, J. U.: *Am Häuslichen Herd.* Zürich: Christliche Vereinsbuchhandlung; pp. 100. *Blumen aus Gottes Garten.* Bremen: Christlicher Volkschriften Verlag; pp. 192. *In Jesu Schule,* 1891. Bremen: Verlag des Traktathauses; pp. 148. *Kornelius,* 1899. Zürich: Druck und Verlag der Christlichen Vereinsbuchhandlung; pp. 360.

Wunderlich, C. F.: *Glaubenskampf,* oder *Freund und Leid eines Missionars in Deutschland,* 1882. Cincinnati; pp. 267.

Wunderlich, J. F.: *Mein Leben,* 1896. Bremen: Traktathauses; pp. 92.

ANNIVERSARY VOLUMES AND CONFERENCE HISTORIES

Chicago Deutschen Konferenz, Jubiläumsbote der, von A. J. Loeppert, 1921. Chicago. Illustrated; pp. 96.

Nordwest Deutsche Konferenz der Bischöflichen Methodistenkirche, von E. W. Henke, W. H. Rolfing, Friedrich Schauf, L. J. Brenner, und J. F. Hartke, 1913. Charles City, Iowa. Illustrated; pp. 429.

Nördlichen Deutschen Konferenz der Bischöfllichen Methodistenkirche, Wegweiser der, 1903, von W. H. Miller, Faribault, Minnesota: Hawson Brothers. Illustrated; pp. 160.

Ost-Deutschen Konferenz der Bischöflichen Methodistenkirche, Geschichte der, herausgegeben nach Anordnung der Konferenz, von H. Mueller, G. Bobilin, J. J. Messmer, J. Lange und J. Suter, 1916. Illustrated. New York; pp. 194.

St. Louis German Conference, Fortieth Anniversary and Patriotic Number, 1918. Edited by Eugene Weiffenbach. Cincinnati. Illustrated; pp. 314.

West Deutschen Konferenz der Bischöflichen Methodistenkirche, Souvenir der, 1906. Cincinnati; pp. 407.

Zentral Deutschen Konferenz, Geschichte der. Einschliesslich der Anfangsgeschichte des Deutschen Methodismus. Herausgegeben nach Anordnung der Konferenz von C. Golder, John H. Horst, J. G. Schaal. Cincinnati. Illustrated; pp. 447.

Südlich-Deutschen Konferenz, Kurze Geschichte der, von B. C. Breihan, A. A. Leifeste, C. F. Schüssler, Wm. Mahowski und Wm. Buehrer, 1922. Illustrated; pp. 104.

German Methodism, Souvenir of the Ninetieth Anniversary of, 1928. Cincinnati. Illustrated; pp. 64.

St. Louis Deutschen Konferenz, Jubiläumsbuch der, hereausgegeben nach ihrer Anordnung zur Feier ihres Funfzigjährigen Bestandes, 1904. Cincinnati; pp. 429.

Deutschen Methodismus, Fünfzig, Jahre des, von J. J. Messmer, 1885. Rochester: Druck des Rochester Volksblatt; pp. 88.

Bethesda Institutions, Fortieth Anniversary (1896-1936), by J. A. Diekmann. Cincinnati: Krehbiel Printing Co.; pp. 57.

Santa Claus Campmeeting, Historic Sketch of, by E. Meyer.

Seminars der Bischöflichen Methodistenkirche, Festschrift zur Feier des 75jährigen Jubiläums des Prediger—Herausgegeben von Direktor Dr. F. H. Otto Melle, 1933. Bremen: Traktathauses. Illustrated; pp. 104.

Martins Missions Anstalt, Eine Festgabe zur Einweihung des neuen Seminar Gebäudes, 1914, von P. F. Junker. Bremen.

Festschrift zur Jubiläumsfeier, 1925, von A. Rücker. Bremen.

Das hundertjährige Jubiläum unserer Missions Gesellsschaft, von A. Marquardt. Zürich.

Festschrift zum 25jährigen Jubiläum des Martha-Maria Vereins, 1914. Nürnberg.

Festschrift zur 25jährigen Jubelfeier des Sonntagsschulbundes des Kantons Zürich, 1896, von L. Peter. Zürich.

Zum 50jährigen Jubiläum der Methodistenkirche in der Schweiz, von J. C. Homberg.

Ein Andenken an die dreifache Jubelfeier in Basil, 1885, von A. Bruns. Basil.

Festschrift zur 50sten Jubelfeier der Methodisten Gemeinden in Pforz-heim und Umgebung, 1912, von K. Ulrich. Bremen.

Fünfzig Jahre Diakonissenarbeit, von Theophil Mann. Bremen.

KLEINE BÜCHERREIHE

In addition to the volumes cited above, The Methodist Book Concern published a series of short reading books averaging about fifty pages and edited chiefly by Heinrich Liebhart. Their content was mostly biographies, stories, and discourses told in such a simple and interesting style that the volumes were read by whole families, and by children in particular. The series, unparalleled in the publishing experience of the Methodist Episcopal Church, was an educational program of prime importance in the development of the immigrant mind in habits of constructive reading. The number of little volumes was about 400.

PERIODICALS

Der Christliche Apologete, Cincinnati 1839-
Der Evangelist, Bremen 1850-
Haus und Herd, Cincinnati 1873-1918
Schweizer Evangelist, Zürich 1894-
Der Christliche Abstinent, Bremen 1884-
Der Leitstern, Bremen 1908-
Evangelist für die Donauländer, Wien 1912-
Der Blaue Stern, Zürich 1920-
Bannerträger, Zürich 1929-

INDEX OF NAMES

INDEX OF SUBJECTS